p.115 Kant
syn forms
cate of understandy

NY Herenberg

52
Jews must
attend to
christianity

p.131 note
rels as problem

209 Renton
+ Christ clears wody

THE LITTMAN LIBRARY OF JEWISH CIVILIZATION

The Littman Library of Jewish Civilization is a registered UK charity
Registered charity no. 1000784

JEWISH THEOLOGY
AND
WORLD RELIGIONS

◆

Edited by
ALON GOSHEN-GOTTSTEIN
and
EUGENE KORN

[handwritten notes:]
149
christn
+
muslems
—

meiri
196
Avodal Zara
cult w/o ethics
+ not idolatry

198 "For you"

211 Heschel No rely or
islam

Oxford · Portland, Oregon
The Littman Library of Jewish Civilization

The Littman Library of Jewish Civilization

Chief Executive Officer: Ludo Craddock
Managing editor: Connie Webber

PO Box 645, Oxford OX2 OUJ, UK
www.littman.co.uk

_____

Published in the United States and Canada by
The Littman Library of Jewish Civilization
c/o ISBS, 920 NE 58th Avenue, Suite 300
Portland, Oregon 97213-3786

First published in hardback 2012
First published in paperback 2016

A catalogue record for this book is available from the British Library

The Library of Congress catalogued the hardback edition as follows:
Jewish theology and world religions / edited by Alon Goshen-Gottstein and Eugene Korn.
p. cm. – (The Littman library of Jewish civilization)
Includes bibliographical references and index.
ISBN 978-1-906764-09-8
1. Judaism–Relations. 2. Religions. 3. Theology. 4. Judaism—Doctrines.
I. Goshen-Gottstein, Alon. II. Korn, Eugene, 1947–
BM534.J49 2012   296.3'9–dc23   2011031222
ISBN 978-1-906764-92-0

Publishing co-ordinator: Janet Moth
Copy-editing: Mark Newby
Index: Christine Headley
Design and production: Pete Russell, Faringdon, Oxon.
Typesetting: John Saunders Design & Production, Eastbourne
Printed in Great Britain on acid-free paper by
TJ International Ltd, Padstow, Cornwall

FROM ALON GOSHEN-GOTTSTEIN

To my mother

ESTHER

*whose breadth of thinking, curiosity, and openness
resonate in me and continue to inspire my work*

◆

FROM EUGENE KORN

In memory of my parents

YA'AKOV BEN SHMUEL V'NETA

and

HINDA BAT YOSEF V'YETTA

May their memory be a blessing

Preface

EUGENE KORN

THE genesis of this book took place when twenty-five scholars of Jewish philosophy, history, education, and halakhah (Jewish law) met at the University of Scranton in Scranton, Pennsylvania in June 2005. They came from the United States, Israel, Canada, and Europe to discuss the theological challenges that inform Jewish attitudes to other religions and how Jewish thought and experience could serve as guides to contemporary life in which Jews interact with non-Jews. The conference was an initiative of the Elijah Interfaith Institute, headed by Alon Goshen-Gottstein, and grew out of the recognition that recent advances in interfaith work required serious progress in Jewish theology if it was to have contemporary credibility. A preliminary conference at Boston College in Brighton, Massachusetts was hosted by Ruth Langer, one of the contributors to this volume. The vision and commitment developed from that meeting found expression in the Scranton conference, hosted by Marc Shapiro, Professor of Jewish Studies at Scranton. The conference proved an occasion for rich and variegated reflection on Jewish relations with non-Jews, Judaism's norms regarding other religions, and the nature of Jewish uniqueness and identity. Because of the remarkable quality of the conference discourse, Alon Goshen-Gottstein and I realized that many of its fruits should be shared on a broader level to stimulate continuing reflection of the issues. We hope this volume achieves this objective.

The conference title, 'Towards a Contemporary Jewish Theology of World Religions', set the agenda for the project. Because of traditional Judaism's focus on halakhah and modern Jewish scholarship's emphasis on historical analysis, Jews have not yet turned their attention to a systematic—or even a non-systematic, but sufficiently nuanced—body of thought regarding contemporary religious 'Otherness' and how Jews can appropriately understand and recognize other religions. Today's world differs radically from the biblical, talmudic, and medieval eras. Traditional precedents for this enquiry need to be supplemented and sometimes even supplanted. The Emancipation brought Jews into the mainstream of non-Jewish and secular societies, so that Jews today live, work, and interact with non-Jews—particularly Christians and Muslims—on a level fundamentally different from that of previous periods. Christianity and Christians no longer pose the threats to Judaism and the Jewish people that they once did, while some interpretations of Islam and many Muslims today see

Judaism, Jews, and Israel as enemies. Jews travel frequently to Asia where they encounter Hindus and Buddhists and their religious systems. In addition, the democratic State of Israel has a large number of non-Jewish citizens and visitors, and it assumes responsibility for their welfare. How are Jews to relate theologically, morally, and existentially to the omnipresent 'Other', his theology, and his religious institutions?

Our interdependent world is significantly more complex than that of past eras, and it demands that Jews construct new paradigms if they are to live successfully and coherently. Many essays in this volume articulate critical questions that cry out for answers in contemporary Jewish reality: 'To what extent is the traditional dichotomy between the exclusive religious truth of Judaism and the assumed religious falsehood of other religions still operative?' 'Is the halakhic category of *avodah zarah*—often understood as "idolatry"—with its manifold restrictions on Jewish–non-Jewish interaction still relevant today, and, if it is, what practical and conceptual meanings can we ascribe to it?' 'How can we understand Asian religions, some of which seem "godless" and animated by religious categories wholly different from those of Judaism?' 'Does interreligious competition make any sense today?' 'How can Jews be a part of future healing rather than contributors to interreligious strife?' Although the contributors to this volume cannot provide comprehensive answers to these questions, they provide sensitive articulations that constitute important cognitive and theological gestures. Ultimately the answers to these questions will have momentous ramifications for the relevance of Judaism and the continuity of the Jewish people in the open, interlocking cultures of the twenty-first century.

The Scranton conference was but the beginning of the process. Goshen-Gottstein and I recognized the need to supplement the conference papers with additional material to provide a comprehensive treatment of the issues. We added the philosophical discussions of Avi Sagi, Raphael Jospe, and Jolene Kellner and Menachem Kellner, which explore the tenability of religious pluralism, since questions of the intelligibility and legitimacy of religious pluralism are never far from the surface of interfaith theology. We also added Paul Fenton's treatment of Islam, Jerome Gellman's consideration of Buddhism, and Goshen-Gottstein's chapter on Hinduism, which were not offered at Scranton.

There are two points of departure, two strategic orientations, from which the essays in this volume proceed. The first is doctrine, philosophy, halakhah, and kabbalah. Some of the contributors to this volume adopt these theoretical/doctrinal positions as starting points and attempt to apply them to today's reality to determine limits and forge new possibilities for a forward-looking Jewish theology of world religions and the religious Other. The second is not normative or theoretical, but personal and empirical. It flows directly from human relations as experienced in the historical relationships of Jews with

Christians and Muslims (so often hostile and polemical) and to a lesser degree with Hindus and Buddhists, as well as the contemporary experience of meeting the Other in interfaith dialogue. Some of the contributors use these experiences as the primary data from which productive Jewish theology towards the religious Other should be constructed.

Ultimately, any successful Jewish theology of world religions must strike a dialectical balance, since authentic Jewish theology takes into account both the normative doctrinal thought of our texts and thinkers as well as the continuing living experience of the Jewish people. Jewish theology is thus dynamic. This must be so if the Jewish people is to fulfil its traditional function as the carrier of a sacred covenant lived out in history and if Jews are to be witnesses to religious truth that resonates throughout human experience. Indeed, while each of the essays may stress one of these points of departure over the other, all of them achieve some degree of integration between the two. Goshen-Gottstein's essay on Hinduism is an exceptional model of this fine dialectical balance: true to both Jewish tradition and experience.

We have organized this volume into logically distinct sections, moving from the more general to the more specific. Goshen-Gottstein frames the issues at the outset to establish the framework for the later material. The essays in Part I analyse philosophically the concept of pluralism and its implications for religious truth. Alan Brill and Rori Picker Neiss lay out four models (exclusivist, pluralist, inclusivist, and universalist) that past and present Jewish thinkers have adopted in understanding other religions and urge Jews to hold on to multiple models in tension with each other. Avi Sagi explores the philosophical justification for religious pluralism and offers a critique of religious exclusivism. He argues that Jews need to adopt a tolerant, pluralistic stance towards others if they are to live coherently in modern democratic society. Raphael Jospe argues passionately for the legitimacy of Jewish religious pluralism, citing precedents and conceptions that arise indigenously 'out of the sources of Judaism'. Following the philosophical approach of Maimonides, Jolene Kellner and Menachem Kellner focus on the rational and universalistic notion of metaphysical truth, which according to their understandings of Maimonides and Jewish theology precludes accepting religious pluralism.

Part II explores aspects of Otherness and the Jewish relationship to the Other, be it the non-Jewish believer or another religious system or doctrine. Stanisław Krajewski asks a question that logically precedes interfaith discourse—one that is devilishly simple but critical for theological integrity—that highlights the distinction: is it possible to relate to another religious system as a true Other, or can we do so only to a person who subscribes to a different religion? The move is more fundamental than the mere grammatical transition from the plural 'you' to the singular 'thou'. Krajewski argues that there is theological value in Jews knowing other religions, but such knowledge has intrinsic limits that carry ethical implications for the knower on the outside. Because other religions always retain this ultimate dimension of unknowability, approaching them demands an attitude of respect and epistemological humility, avoiding the temptation to reduce them to our own through a power-laden programme of knowledge. Meir Sendor analyses the common and unfortunate trend in interfaith dialogue of 'neutralizing' the Other. In an attempt to find commonality, neutralization willy-nilly introduces syncretism and relativism into interfaith discourse. Worse still, it does violence to the unique character of each religion and its practitioners who participate in the dialogue. Examining this through the theories of Levinas, Derrida, and Ricoeur, Sendor shows how authenticity and respect for the Other can only be achieved by highlighting difference and otherness.

Ruth Langer analyses the power and construction of Jewish memory as well as the image of the religious Other in Jewish liturgy, which has been so heavily conditioned by adversarial biblical narratives and the experience of historical persecution. In the memory shaped by Jewish liturgy—be it the daily Amidah, the High Holiday prayers, Passover and Purim texts, or the Ninth of Av *piyutim* (liturgical poems) memorializing the destruction of the Temple, the tragedies of the Middle Ages, and the Holocaust—the religious or political Other is portrayed as almost universally negative. The non-Jew—usually considered in the impersonal abstract, rather than the particular other—is a threat to Jewish uniqueness, disrupting God's covenantal plan for Israel. She also points to the ongoing tension between making historical memory part of our identity and an openness to allowing history to unfold into a future that may move beyond tragedy.

Part III contains essays analysing how Jews and Jewish thought can assess specific world religions today. After mapping four distinct categories of rabbinic attitudes to Christianity, I argue that a historical evolution of halakhic positions towards Christianity is evident. The late rabbinic authorities developed the possibility of Jewish appreciation of Christianity for non-Jews and saw it as a moral and theological advance over other non-Jewish religions. When conjoined with Christianity's rediscovery of the enduring validity of Judaism and the Jewish covenant, new possibilities open up for Jews to develop sympathetic theological understandings of Christians and Christianity. David Novak argues for a nuanced understanding of Maimonides' view of Christianity. Maimonides permitted Jews to study Torah with Christians and added new meaning to the category of *ger toshav* (resident alien), which allow Novak to infer normative behavioural conclusions from Maimonides' thinking. He concludes that Maimonides may have revised his earlier harsh opinion that Christianity constituted *avodah zarah* halakhically no different from ancient paganism.

Paul Fenton examines the cultural encounter between Israel and Ishmael, how it has played a powerful role in shaping Judaism, and how it led the medieval rabbis and Jewish thinkers to oscillate between rejection and reception of Islam. Much of this dialectical attitude is played out through the ambivalent interpretations of the biblical Ishmael and in the polemical histories of Jews and Muslims. Fenton shows the Islamic impact on Judaism in halakhic, kabbalistic, messianic, and even hasidic texts. In contrast to my own optimistic presentation of a contemporary Jewish assessment of Christianity, Fenton's chapter is pessimistic about the enduring value of the Jewish–Muslim heritage, in view of how contemporary political circumstances have redefined Jewish–Muslim relations. Nevertheless, theological advances by Jews and Muslims are both necessary and possible. Through a process of inversion (*teshuvah*) of previous interpretative models regarding each other, Jews and Muslims can pave the way to mutual recognition and acceptance on theological and political levels.

Alon Goshen-Gottstein breaks new ground in considering Hinduism from a Jewish perspective, as Jewish thinkers have paid scant attention to this topic to date. He is best at raising questions about the nature of Hinduism(s), exposing its complexity, and moving beyond the simplistic understanding to a more accurate—even if more confusing—picture of Hindu theology and reality. He notes that Jews in Indian societies have lived with an attitude of acceptance towards their Hindu neighbours. An honest reappraisal of *avodah zarah* applied to contemporary Hinduism is warranted, and he finds support for new theological understanding of Hinduism in the rabbinic wisdom of the medieval sage Menahem Me'iri and the contemporary thinker Adin Steinsaltz. The religious conversation with Hindus is important because of the spiritual opportunities it presents. Thus, Goshen-Gottstein considers the Hindu quest for God and the model of Hindu saints as significant topics for a Jewish–Hindu conversation. Nuancing our understanding of *avodah zarah* and of Hinduism must continue, and the dialogue on spirituality and the benefits of spiritual exchange must advance.

Jerome (Yehuda) Gellman wrestles with the 'godlessness' of Buddhism, striving to understand Buddhism's benefits for Jews and their spiritual consciousness. As a traditionalist proceeding from a position of 'religious exclusivist receptivity' (that is, his belief that Judaism possesses religious truth conjoined with an openness to the possibility that other religions can enrich his spiritual life), Gellman has learned about holiness from Buddhist spirituality in ways he, as a Jew, could not have imagined. Buddhism's aversion to metaphysical ontologizing and its non-theism have helped him shed the agonies of 'the egocentric predicament', functioning similarly to the hasidic concept of *bitul hayesh* (nullification of being). Paradoxically, this godless religion has taught him to focus his attention more successfully on the Jewish God—the permanent, infinite reality that transcends the human ego. It also helps him to understand the Jewish people's chosenness correctly, purged from nation-centrism and national self-absorption. The experiential and spiritual are primary here, while the formal theological issues of 'alien worship' that Buddhism may entail are secondary concerns. The book concludes with Goshen-Gottstein's attempt to draw some synthetic and comparative conclusions from the project as a whole.

Developing a coherent Jewish theology of world religions and contemporary non-Jews is compelling today for many reasons. It enlarges the arena of spiritual experience for Jews, enabling them to find God not only within the Jewish people but also among all of God's children and their diverse religious expressions. It gives Jews and their theological tradition the tools to talk to the outside world. It expands a sensitive Jewish understanding of the world and humanity, and this cognitive appreciation fosters greater tolerance and co-operation on practical and moral planes. The latter is imperative in our day, since religion has burst forth as a powerful and even lethal force in human culture and politics. Whether or not we achieve greater interfaith understanding may well spell the difference between a century of unending religious strife leading to unprecedented global violence or a future of healing and moral progress that promote a degree of human flourishing never before experienced. In the balance hangs not only the fate of Judaism and the Jewish people, but the entire human family and God's universe.

Alon and I would like to express our appreciation to the authors who contributed to this volume. We are honoured to have this work published by the Littman Library of Jewish Civilization, and are particularly indebted to Ludo Craddock, chief executive officer of the Littman Library, and to Connie Webber, Littman's managing editor. They believed in the project from its inception and encouraged us to publish its fruits. Their understanding throughout the process has been a model for co-operative partnership. We also wish to thank Mark Newby and Janet Moth at Littman, who so ably assisted us in editing the text of this volume.

Contents

Note on Transliteration

THE transliteration of Hebrew in this book reflects consideration of the type of book it is, in terms of its content, purpose, and readership. The system adopted therefore reflects a broad approach to transcription, rather than the narrower approaches found in the *Encyclopaedia Judaica* or other systems developed for text-based or linguistic studies. The aim has been to reflect the pronunciation prescribed for modern Hebrew, rather than the spelling or Hebrew word structure, and to do so using conventions that are generally familiar to the English-speaking reader.

In accordance with this approach, no attempt is made to indicate the distinctions between *alef* and *ayin*, *tet* and *taf*, *kaf* and *kuf*, *sin* and *samekh*, since these are not relevant to pronunciation; likewise, the *dagesh* is not indicated except where it affects pronunciation. Following the principle of using conventions familiar to the majority of readers, however, transcriptions that are well established have been retained even when they are not fully consistent with the transliteration system adopted. On similar grounds, the *tsadi* is rendered by 'tz' in such familiar words as barmitzvah. Likewise, the distinction between *ḥet* and *khaf* has been retained, using *ḥ* for the former and *kh* for the latter; the associated forms are generally familiar to readers, even if the distinction is not actually borne out in pronunciation, and for the same reason the final *heh* is indicated too. As in Hebrew, no capital letters are used, except that an initial capital has been retained in transliterating titles of published works (for example, *Shulḥan arukh*).

Since no distinction is made between *alef* and *ayin*, they are indicated by an apostrophe only in intervocalic positions where a failure to do so could lead an English-speaking reader to pronounce the vowel-cluster as a diphthong—as, for example, in *ha'ir*—or otherwise mispronounce the word.

The *sheva na* is indicated by an *e*—*perikat ol*, *reshut*—except, again, when established convention dictates otherwise.

The *yod* is represented by *i* when it occurs as a vowel (*bereshit*), by *y* when it occurs as a consonant (*yesodot*), and by *yi* when it occurs as both (*yisra'el*).

Names have generally been left in their familiar forms, even when this is inconsistent with the overall system.

Towards a Jewish Theology of World Religions
Framing the Issues

ALON GOSHEN-GOTTSTEIN

INTRODUCTION

THEOLOGY of religions is an area of reflection that has grown in prominence in recent years. Social and political changes, dating from before the Second World War, have given new urgency to relations between faiths and their practitioners. The marked increase in interfaith activity makes reflection on the status of other religions a pressing concern. The great increase in such activity has led to the identification and blossoming of this area as a distinct sub-field of theology. Regardless of the religion from whose perspective such reflection is undertaken, any contemporary theology of religions draws from perspectives articulated throughout that religion's history. Yet the field of theology of religions offers perspectives on other religions that are appropriate to contemporary social realities often radically different from those prevailing in earlier periods. This does not automatically mean that a pluralistic perspective that recognizes the other's religion is taken or that a relativistic perspective of one's own religion need be adopted, but it does mean that the challenges of religious pluralism loom large on the theological horizon. Even if the theologian rejects a pluralistic position, he or she is forced to state a position in dialogue with pluralistic theologians. Theology of religions has grown in the shadow of religious pluralism and the increase in interfaith dialogue, and hence it provides the framework for thinking through one's views of other religions with an emphasis on the challenges of religious pluralism. These include the full or partial validation of other religions and a reframing of the unique position, role, and mission of one's own religion.

The discipline of theology of religions grew initially on Christian soil. More than any other thinkers, Christians of all denominations have engaged with the issues and developed the discipline. This is as true of the work of individual theologians as it is of church documents, among which the Second Vatican

Council's *Nostra aetate* takes pride of place. Jewish theologians and others have
entered the discussion following the lead, and in many cases also the language
and categories, of Christian scholars and thinkers.

There are several distinct factors that make a contemporary Jewish assessment
of world religions urgent and timely, both in terms of the broader social currents
that have had an influence upon the emergence of the field of theology of religions and in terms of Judaism's particular history, mission, and self-identity.
Fundamental changes have occurred both in Jewish history and in Judaism's relations with other religions, including changes in the theology of other religions,
advances in interreligious relations, and the new historical situation represented
by the creation of the State of Israel. Each of these alone might have necessitated
a re-examination of Jewish attitudes to other religions, but the creation of the
State of Israel is particularly significant. Changes in power relations between
religions and the task of articulating a spiritual vision for humanity related to the
mission of the Jewish state could drive a sustained programme of theological
reflection. Regrettably, however, little thought has been given to these issues
from the Israeli perspective. Most Israeli and Jewish energies have been focused
on ensuring Jewish survival and continuity. Jewish creative energies have been
turned mainly inwards, and almost no serious thought has been devoted to the
theological challenges to Judaism posed in our contemporary context.

Theology of religions as a discipline has a quest common to all religions:
defining a given religion's views of other religions. However, each religion must
undertake this task in a way that is suitable to its own history and theology, as
well as other significant factors, such as law or precedent. A contemporary Jewish
theology of religions must draw on previous articulations of Jewish views of
other religions. Each period of Jewish thought has bequeathed distinct positions
and resources to this enterprise. The work of the contemporary Jewish theologian thus involves drawing from previous periods, assessing earlier views, examining changing historical circumstances, and articulating a vision for the future.
But perhaps the most important characteristic of the theology of religions is its
attempt to grasp the issues in their entirety and offer an overview of a religion's
views of other religions. New context and comprehensive vision single out a contemporary theology of religions from the cumulative perspectives of generations
that provide the basis for the contemporary theologian's reflections. This is certainly true for a contemporary Jewish theology of religions.

In this chapter, I shall present an overview of the broad range of issues that
must be re-examined in order to construct a contemporary Jewish theology of
world religions.[1] I hope the presentation is sufficiently comprehensive to offer

---

[1] These ideas have been expressed in two earlier Hebrew articles. An overview of the issues, with
an emphasis on how these relate to contemporary practices of interfaith dialogue, was offered in
Alon Goshen-Gottstein, 'Theology of Interreligious Dialogue: A Preliminary Mapping' (Heb.),

a map of the field and a plan for future work. Even if much of what follows is drawn from classical sources, as indeed any theology of religions must be, drawing the resources together, choosing among them, and framing the issues for the future are all done with an awareness of the contemporary context. The essay is my attempt to specify what is involved in articulating a contemporary Jewish theology of religions. In addition to mapping the field, I will also suggest specific positions within it that seem most appropriate to the needs of a contemporary Jewish theology of world religions.

JUDAISM AND WORLD RELIGIONS: THE CHALLENGE OF PARTICULARITY

Any religion's attempt to develop a theology of other religions must grow out of concepts particular to that religion. Consequently, each religion must tackle questions particular to the history of its view of other religions and its internal concerns. In the case of Judaism, we recognize two core questions, and addressing these two questions is the key to developing a contemporary Jewish theology of world religions. Both questions touch upon religious particularity, and their conjunction is crucial to recognizing the challenges facing a contemporary Jewish theology. Two interrelated conceptual foci underlie Jewish particularity: faith in revelation and faith in the election of the Jewish people. It is not simply the faith in one God that distinguishes Judaism from other world religions, for some of those others share that faith. Rather, differences arise with regard to how God reveals himself and which community receives his word and carries it through history to eschatological fulfilment.[2] Judaism's particular spiritual profile is derived from the faith that a particular revelation took place at Sinai, was given to a particular nation chosen for this task, and it is that nation that traverses history to offer testimony to the God who chose his people and gave them his Torah.

The theological challenge that any Jewish theology of world religions must meet is how to uphold faith in the Jewish particularity arising from these two core beliefs, with an openness that makes space for the spiritual and religious existence of others.[3] This is not simply a conceptual or theological challenge,

Akdamot, 18 (2007), 6–40. A focus on the issues from the perspective of religious pluralism was offered in Alon Goshen-Gottstein, 'Interreligious Pluralism: Challenges and Parameters Towards Articulating a Jewish Theology of World Religions' (Heb.), in S. Fischer and A. Seligman (eds.), *The Burden of Tolerance: Religious Traditions and the Challenge of Pluralism* [Ol hasolvanut: mesorot datiyot ve'etgar hapeluralizm] (Jerusalem, 2007), 330–54.

[2] See Martin Jaffee, 'One God, One Revelation, One People: On the Symbolic Structure of Elective Monotheism', *Journal of the American Academy of Religion*, 69 (2001), 753–75.

[3] Due to the centrality of chosenness and particularity to a Jewish theology of world religions, they have been the first subjects to be tackled as part of a theological research and education project supported by the Henry Luce Foundation under the auspices of Yeshivat Chovevei Torah

but also a cognitive and psychological one. These two doctrines shape not only Jewish faith but also a Jewish mentality that is often characterized by withdrawal and separation. Social insularity is often accompanied by attitudinal insularity. Thus in many believing circles the opinion reigns that there is little of value to draw on and learn from others. The elect community, the carrier of the chosen Torah, can teach others, even if it may not be actively engaged in such activity. However, this community has nothing to receive from others. Such insularity is the psychological opposite to the attitudes of listening and openness that underlie true dialogue. Such dialogue provides to a significant extent the impetus for the development of a contemporary Jewish theology of other religions.[4]

There are historical precedents for understanding election in a way that does not preclude openness and receptivity to others. The Maimonidean understanding, according to which election does not mean superiority but commitment to a spiritual way of life involving the acceptance of a proper religious and spiritual understanding, remains a compelling understanding of election for many thinkers,[5] as do understandings of election in terms of mission and responsibility towards humanity. Such understandings could leave room for Israel's mission to be complemented by those of other collectives and religions. Of course, even stronger understandings that view election as creating or founded upon a unique metaphysical reality and a particular essence could also support meaningful relations with and openness to others. However, the psychological orientation born of such understandings tends to shy away from authentic contact with the religious Other.

Judaism is not only a sum of beliefs and religious practices. It is fundamentally related to Israel's particular story. This has consequences for how one conceives of Judaism's relations to other world religions. Judaism has always recognized a balance between the spiritual teaching that it offers and the fact that it is a way of life, intended for a particular people. That Judaism is a nation's way of living enabled Judaism to refrain from active attempts to convert others to its own faith. The fine balance between the national/ethnic and the 'religious' dimensions of Judaism is of great value in developing a contemporary theology of other religions. This balance is vital to pluralistic concerns. Identifying the narrative component of Judaism, which, unlike the conceptual, philosophical, and theological dimensions, is unique to the Jewish people, allows us to focus

rabbinical seminary, in which a series of curricula presenting a variety of traditional sources with an eye to their application in contemporary theological situations has been developed for use in seminary and other educational settings.

[4] The theological imperative draws from various factors, both historical and theological. Advances in interreligious dialogue constitute one important factor. Others are discussed in Goshen-Gottstein, 'Theology of Interreligious Dialogue' (Heb.), 13–15.

[5] See Menachem Kellner, *Maimonides on Judaism and the Jewish People* (Albany, NY, 1991).

upon the particularity of the Jewish narrative, without the necessary negation of other narratives. The story of God making a covenant with his people is the story of a particular nation. It need not be told at the expense of other stories. Thus, the very fact that Judaism is so closely associated with the identity of Israel as a people has great potential for its view of other religions. If other religions, like Christianity and Islam, must approach the challenges of a theology of other religions from a history of active competition, vying for the souls of humanity, Judaism approaches this challenge from a more modest starting point regarding its aspirations for the active implementation of its vision in the world.

The narrative perspective reveals another significant way in which we can open up to the Other and develop a pluralistic view of other religions. The insular world-view translates faith in election into a psychological stance, according to which Jews are better than others, without fully accounting for the chosen nation's story. Israel's story is not a success story; on the contrary, to a large extent, it is a story of failure. This recognition underlies Christian supersessionist claims, and these may account, in part, for the difficulties in internalizing failure and imperfection as part of our own self-understanding. Still, failure is also recognized on internal Jewish grounds. Israel's exile, the kabbalistic notion of the exile of the Divine Presence itself, the destruction of the Temple, and the loss of prophecy are all consequences of sin and failure. Any assessment of Judaism in relation to other religions assumes some spiritual assessment of Judaism and its own spiritual well-being and proper functioning. An honest assessment cannot disregard the gap between Judaism in its ideal form and present-day Judaism. While Jews have come to love this form, to offer themselves in service to God through it, and even to offer their lives for it, one cannot ignore the fact that in many ways this form is flawed in comparison with the spiritual ideals that Scripture articulates. Does the recognition of our own imperfection produce a humbler attitude? Does such an attitude open the door to different relations with other religions? Of course, one can claim that our spiritual ailments preclude genuine openness and necessitate insularity as a form of survival. Moreover, one may argue that whatever imperfection is inherent in present-day Judaism, openness to other religions is not the way to address it, as those religions do not point the way to perfection. These claims cannot be dismissed out of hand, but they are not the only possible response to the acknowledgement of imperfection, and we have at least one important precedent for openness to other religious traditions being justified precisely by appeal to the ailments of the Jewish tradition. Rabbi Abraham Maimonides, son of Moses Maimonides, provides this precedent. He consciously absorbed strong Sufi influences into his religious world-view and his own ritual practice. He justified this through the claim that the Sufis possess a teaching that is properly Jewish, but that had been lost to us due to the circumstances of history and exile.[6] The truth of this historical reconstruction is not our present concern. What is important is the recognition that Judaism may be lacking and that other spiritual traditions may be in a healthier condition. They may be able to sustain and inspire it, even as they help it regain its own former teaching and glory. Thus awareness of our own imperfection can open the door to a genuine openness to the other.

The question of religious particularity is relevant to all aspects of a Jewish consideration of other religions and raises some fundamental issues. I will list four that all touch upon the meaning of particularity, on the one hand, and the potential for pluralistic views, on the other.

1. Can a religious or spiritual path outside Judaism be considered legitimate and valid? As strange as this question seems at first blush, especially in the contexts of interreligious dialogue and of a pluralistic world-view, it is an essential part of the Jewish agenda for contemporary reflection. The legitimacy of other forms of religious life is far from self-evident. The issue touches on the question of the spiritual vision offered by Judaism to the non-Jew and calls for an assessment of other religions within a broader historical perspective. This question touches the core of the pluralistic potential within Judaism.

2. Defining idolatry. The notion of idolatry—or more correctly the notion of foreign worship (*avodah zarah*), worship by methods or of objects foreign to prescribed Jewish worship—orients most Jewish legal and theological discussions of other religions. Despite the centrality of the concept, we are a long way from accounting for its meaning even today. Conflicting positions are articulated in Jewish sources regarding fundamental questions concerning *avodah zarah*. Moreover, we are far from having a considered systematic discussion of the fundamental question: what is *avodah zarah*? As simple as this question 'What is *avodah zarah*?' seems at first sight, further reflection reveals that we do not have a sufficient definition or grasp of such a fundamental concept. This question is vital, not only for our view of other traditions, but also for Judaism's self-understanding. We often encounter the claim that the battle against *avodah zarah* is fundamental to Judaism's very identity as a religious tradition. But then, what is *avodah zarah* today? Answering this question contains the key, at least in part, to Judaism's identity and mission, and hence to the enduring significance of Judaism on the global stage.

3. Revelation and Truth. The attitude to other religions is often seen as a competition between conflicting truths or between different conceptions of truths. The notion of truth introduces into the religious conversation a philo-

---

[6] See Paul Fenton, 'Abraham Maimonides (1187–1237): Founding a Mystical Dynasty', in Moshe Idel and Mortimer Ostow (eds.), *Jewish Mystical Leaders and Leadership in the 13th Century* (Northvale, NJ, 1998), 127–54.

sophical or conceptual notion through which religion is defined. However, religious truth does not see itself primarily as the outcome of philosophical speculation but more properly as the fruit of revelation. Grounding truth in divine revelation affords it absolute validity, thereby making relations between religions more complicated, to the degree that different religions appeal to mutually conflicting or competing truth or revelational claims. How might a Jew preserve the significance of Sinaitic revelation, while neutralizing its 'truth' element? Alternatively, how can one uphold a notion of religious truth that is open to a pluralistic understanding of other religions?

4. **Concern for Jewish continuity and identity.** This is not a philosophical concern, yet it touches the heart of Jewish religious thought, inasmuch as it affirms particularity as a core concern. The underlying assumption of all Jewish reflection on other religions is that they are competitive, and therefore constitute a threat to Judaism in terms of loyalty, membership, and affiliation. An 'us versus them' mentality is deeply ingrained in Jewish approaches to other religions. Even if other religions are not deemed idolatrous and are recognized as legitimate for their believers, there always remain concerns about losing members to other religions. This concern may in fact drive issues 1, 2, and 3. The positions we take in relation to other religions may serve this particular agenda, even when this is not made explicit.

THE LEGITIMACY OF OTHER RELIGIOUS TRADITIONS

In considering the legitimacy of other religious traditions, one must first distinguish between the legitimacy of religions that turn to other gods and those whose adherents understand themselves to be addressing the same God that Jews turn to: Christianity and Islam.[7] This distinction leads us to the biblical heritage of battles against contemporary idolatrous beliefs. Reconciling the biblical anti-idolatry stance and contemporary pluralistic sensibilities is a tall order. To the extent that biblical views continue to inform Jewish attitudes to other religions throughout the generations, one must recognize that a strong anti-pluralist tendency shapes Jewish attitudes to other religions.

Although prima facie there is no room for recognizing religions that turn to other gods as legitimate and acceptable, there may be alternative approaches

[7] The roundabout wording that emphasizes self-understanding stems from the fact that a Jewish view of the Christian God is not as unequivocal in the recognition that it is the same God that is being worshipped as many Christians assume. This issue was recently highlighted through the discussion engendered by the Jewish statement on Christianity *Dabru emet*. The opening clause of the statement affirmed the common belief in the same God. Objections were raised to this claim, in the light of Trinitarian belief. See Jon Levenson, 'How Not to Conduct Jewish–Christian Dialogue', *Commentary*, 112/5 (2001), 36–7.

with regard to such faiths. Rabbi Menahem Me'iri, a fourteenth-century Provencal rabbinic authority, articulated such a position in relation to Christianity and Islam.[8] According to Me'iri, Christianity and Islam should not be considered *avodah zarah*, as many rabbinic authorities then and now maintained. The common understanding of Me'iri explains his views as a consequence of the fact that both religions have an ethical code that enforces morality, law, and order. Me'iri posits a moral criterion, in light of which these religions are viewed. Such a criterion would also be valid in relation to religions of the East and other religions that do not know Israel's God. Me'iri's understanding provides a basis for interreligious pluralism that shifts the discussion from theological to moral considerations. Accordingly, there is a fundamental basis for pluralism that is grounded in human perfection, as expressed in the moral and social order. The type of pluralism of this approach is limited since it does not apply to the conceptual and theological realm. It does, nevertheless, provide a basis for tolerance on a practical level and for mutual acceptance and respect between members of different religions that share the same moral foundation.

A closer look at Me'iri reveals that underlying his recognition of other religions is more than simply recognition of their moral value. As Moshe Halbertal has shown, Me'iri has a highly developed sense of what constitutes a religion.[9] Rather than simply present Christianity and Islam as non-idolatrous, Me'iri describes them as 'religions'. His appeal to the category of 'religion' assumes certain parameters by which a religion is recognized as valid. These parameters include the moral dimension, but the argument from morality does not simply point to God directly. It appeals to the notion of 'religion' as common and recognized ground between religions. Recognizing the centrality of the category 'religion' and 'the ways of religion' in Me'iri's thought allows us to extend his views of other religions and their legitimacy to religions that had not previously been considered in his discussion.[10] More significantly in the present context, it tackles the very issue of the legitimacy of other religions. The appeal to 'religion' as a means of legitimating other religions assumes that other religions, when recognized and classified as such, have validity. Fundamental to Me'iri's understanding therefore is the recognition that true or valid 'religion' is not limited to Judaism.

---

[8] See Jacob Katz, *Exclusiveness and Tolerance: Studies in Jewish–Gentile Relations in Medieval and Modern Times* (London, 1961).

[9] Moshe Halbertal, 'Ones Possessed of Religion: Religious Tolerance in the Teachings of the Me'iri', *Edah Journal*, 1/1 (2000), <http://www.edah.org>.

[10] In my forthcoming *Beyond Idolatry: The Jewish Encounter with Hinduism*, I spend much time exploring the implications of Me'iri's views for a possible Jewish appreciation of Hinduism, both according to the more common 'moral' understanding of Me'iri and according to the understanding that reads Me'iri as developing the category of 'religion' as the validating principle of other religions. See also the discussion in Chapter 11 below.

The desire to protect Judaism's uniqueness and particularity and to justify its continued sense of chosenness and mission has led over the course of generations to a shift from combat against religions that call upon other gods to religions that offer an alternative path to the same God. The deep tension between the two constitutive features of Judaism—a religious way of life for a specific people and a universal spiritual vision—affects the varying positions in relation to these religions. When the national/ethnic component of Judaism is emphasized, it is easier to allow other religions to fill a vacuum that Judaism never sought to fill. Emphasizing the national element in Judaism's self-understanding enables us to adopt in principle a perspective on world religions from the viewpoint of the divine economy that justifies their existence and purpose, while it continues to uphold the meaning of Judaism and its particularity. By contrast, emphasizing the universal 'objective' religious truth of Judaism's teachings makes such acknowledgement more challenging.

Emphasis on the national pole of religious identity not only facilitates adoption of a pluralistic perspective, it also allows us to develop a position that accounts for other religions from the perspective of Israel's particular story. In relation to both Christianity and Islam we find, alongside extensive polemical literature, positions that recognize their legitimacy. There are various strategies for affording such legitimacy. These religions can be considered in the light of the notion of the seven Noahide commandments, the basic moral commandments seen as the minimal behavioural requirement for non-Jews, who did not receive the revelation at Sinai.[11] The revelation of these commandments to Adam and Noah provides an alternative matrix by means of which non-Jews too can have a valid revelation. According to such an understanding, Christianity and Islam are legitimate, as their religious teachings include the Noahide commandments.[12] These religions are thus interpreted in the light of a certain concept that is deemed by the Jewish interpreter to be crucial, regardless of the theological emphasis by which these traditions define and understand themselves.

A different strategy for affording legitimacy is the incorporation of these traditions into Israel's story or the divine plan for humanity. Rabbi Jacob Emden (eighteenth century) presented Christianity as seeking to disseminate the Noahide commandments to non-Jews in an attempt to confer legitimacy upon Christianity as a religious phenomenon that has a different intended audience than the community of Israel.[13] Not only is the practice of Christianity

[11] They are the prohibitions on killing, adultery, idolatry, blasphemy, theft, and the eating of the limbs of a living animal, as well as the obligation to institute a legal system to address civil concerns.

[12] See David Novak, *The Image of the Non-Jew in Judaism: The Idea of Noahide Law*, 2nd edn. (Oxford, 2011); see also Eugene Korn in Chapter 8, below.

[13] See Harvey Falk, 'Rabbi Jacob Emden's Views on Christianity', *Journal of Ecumenical Studies*,

justified, but its story is retold and incorporated into Israel's story. Jesus and Paul become, according to Emden, missionaries for a cause that is properly speaking Jewish, inasmuch as they disseminate and propagate an ideal and a teaching of Judaism in relation to humanity. If Judaism is not only a philosophical world-view, but is related to the particular story of its carrier, the Jewish people, one of the ways of dealing with alternative religious traditions is to incorporate them within the particular Jewish story. The pluralism incorporated in such views is not a principled and a priori pluralism. The acceptance of the Other and the recognition of his legitimacy take place in a limited way, based upon internal Jewish criteria. This is inclusivist pluralism, according to which the degree of pluralism that is possible is a function of the degree to which the other can be interpreted and incorporated within the Jewish world-view, considered on its own terms.[14]

Consideration of the legitimacy of alternative religious systems is inextricably linked to two issues. The first is eschatological expectation. What is the future of other peoples and religions in our view of the eschaton? Does Judaism's eschatological world-view assume that only one religion will reign in the future? To recognize the legitimacy of other religions we must determine who Judaism was intended for. In other words, are Jewish practice and ideals a way of life designed for the Jewish people only or are they a vision for all of humanity in the eschaton? Jewish aspirations for the future make it easier or harder to develop pluralist positions to the degree to which these visions cast the future of humanity in the same light as Israel's present-day reality.[15] An exclusivist eschatological view can be influenced by two factors: the tension between Jews and non-Jews carried over into the religious sphere and the understanding of religion in terms of truth and hence the necessity of truth's ultimate victory.[16]

19 (1982), 105–11; Blu Greenberg, 'Rabbi Jacob Emden: The Views of an Enlightened Traditionalist on Christianity', *Judaism*, 27 (1978), 351–68.

[14] The categories of exclusivism, inclusivism, and pluralism, initially developed by Alan Race as part of his own thinking within a Christian theology of religions, have been examined extensively by Alan Brill and applied to Jewish sources in his recent *Judaism and Other Religions: Models of Understanding* (New York, 2010); see also Alan Brill in Chapter 1, below.

[15] On this issue, see Chaim Rapoport, *'Dat ha-emet* in Maimonides' Mishneh Torah', *Meorot*, 7/1 (2008); Menachem Kellner, 'Maimonides' "True Religion": For Jews or All Humanity? A Response to Chaim Rapoport', *Meorot*, 7/1 (2008). Both available from <www.yctorah.org/content/view/436/10/>.

[16] For extreme forms of exclusivist eschatological expectations, see Israel Jacob Yuval, 'Revenge and Curse, Blood and Libel' (Heb.), *Zion*, 58 (1983), 37–44. An English version appears in id., *Two Nations in Your Womb: Perceptions of Jews and Christians in Late Antiquity and the Middle Ages* (Berkeley, Calif., 2006). The matter is discussed in David Berger, 'On the Image and Destiny of Gentiles in Ashkenazi Polemical Literature', in id., *Persecution, Polemic, and Dialogue: Essays in Jewish–Christian Relations* (Boston, 2010), 109–38.

It is difficult to provide an unequivocal position concerning Judaism's eschatological world-view. Eschatology lies beyond the realm of normativity and common agreement. Different images of the eschaton developed over millennia, reflecting the physical and psychological conditions as well as the spiritual aspirations of the different visionaries. These visions often contradict each other, and the cardinal question of the status of non-Jews in the eschaton has conflicting answers. A contemporary Jewish theology of world religions must therefore study and reflect upon the different Jewish eschatological views concerning other religions, considering the social and historical conditions under which they were shaped, their theological import, and their normative weight. All these are part of the theological challenge of this contemporary enterprise.

A second question regarding the legitimacy of other religions is what Judaism has to offer to non-Jews in today's world rather than in the eschaton. To the extent that this is deemed insufficient or does not satisfy the spiritual needs of non-Jews, space is created for other religions to fulfil these needs. As mentioned, the national element in Judaism restrains it from actively spreading its message to other peoples. Consequently, Judaism's primary teachings for the non-Jew are the Noahide commandments. These commandments are not simply good counsel, but constitute Judaism's spiritual vision for humanity. A non-Jew may either follow full revelation, the Torah received at Sinai, or settle for a limited revelation, the moral code of the Noahide commandments. The Noahide commandments are thus part of a comprehensive view that attempts to offer a way of life considered adequate for the non-Jew.

This view has serious consequences for the meaning of religion outside of Judaism. As Maimonides states:

One does not permit [non-Jews] to invent a new religion and to perform commandments that they make up. One must either be a convert [to Judaism] and accept all commandments, or let one remain bound by the teaching relevant to him [the Noahide commandments], without adding or detracting.[17]

Forbidding other forms of religion is a consequence of the exclusivist view, according to which Judaism also provides the religious vision and practical instruction needed for non-Jews. If a religious programme for humanity exists in the form of the Noahide commandments, the prohibition of developing alternative novel religions constitutes its correlate.

Other understandings of the seven Noahide commandments blunt this exclusivist understanding to some degree. Some Jewish thinkers have identified the Noahide commandments with natural law, thus justifying them and making them easier to accept on rational, non-revelational grounds. Natural law offers an inclusivist perspective into which the Noahide commandments

---

[17] Maimonides, *Mishneh torah*, 'Laws of Kings', 10: 9.

are assumed. Seeing them in terms of creation, rather than of revelation, neutralizes the exclusiveness of the revelation-based perspective. At the same time, it emphasizes the moral dimension, which is available to all.

Yet this understanding also highlights the difficulty in presenting the Noahide commandments as a religious path for humanity. They provide a sound moral foundation, thereby fulfilling one of religion's important tasks. However, they lack a fundamental dimension of the religious life: the development of a relationship with God. Everything related to worship, to a personal relationship with God, to emotional and religious intimacy, and to the fulfilment of emotional and religious needs is beyond the scope of the Noahide commandments. It is difficult to limit the import of religion to the moral life only. A full religious life implies much more than upright ethical living. If all Judaism has to offer to those who do not enter its covenantal framework is a moral way of life, one must consider whether Judaism has a spiritual message to offer the world, short of conversion to Judaism itself.

While the seven Noahide commandments are fundamentally a moral code, they have in fact been broadened and made to serve as a basic form of religious life. Some of the stipulations and reflections concerning their observance have tackled the fundamental limitations built into the concept. Maimonides played a key role in the development of the notion of the Noahide commandments as possessors of broader religious significance. According to him, the Noahide commandments have salvific value, if observed as a form of revelation given to Moses.[18] This stipulation introduces cognitive and salvific dimensions into what might otherwise have been conceived primarily as a moral category. This makes it possible for later authorities to expand the dimension of faith implied in the observance of the Noahide commandments beyond the authoritarian foundations demanded by Maimonides. Thus, they come to include faith in God and the possibility of a life of prayer.[19]

Despite the appeal to the Noahide commandments for developing a broader religious framework, use of this category stops short of developing a fully fledged concept of non-Jewish religion. Maimonides provided a good illustration of the dynamics of the category and how far it can go. Injecting the category with religious and salvific meaning should be considered in the light of his refusal to recognize other forms of religious life as legitimate and hence the prohibition placed upon the birth of other religions. Minimal and maximal

---

[18] See Maimonides, *Mishneh torah*, 'Laws of Kings', 8: 11. One notes, however, that the salvific value of the commandments is dependent on their performance as commandments given to Moses. Hardly anyone who practises these commandments in the framework of another religion does so because of the Mosaic revelation.

[19] See R. Moshe Feinstein, *Igerot mosheh*, 'Oraḥ ḥayim', 2: 25. A discussion of the Noahide commandments and how the category has been broadened can be found in my forthcoming *Israel in God's Presence*.

revelations are all that Judaism has to offer and all that it recognizes. In this context it is worth returning to Me'iri and his use of the category 'religion' as a means of assessing and legitimating other religions. As indicated, his appeal to this category assumes, unlike Maimonides', that other religions have legitimacy. In conformity with this understanding, we note the absence in Me'iri of the prohibition of inventing ritual for religions other than Judaism. Me'iri's broader recognition and acceptance of other religions is thus not limited to their moral dimension, but also includes ritual life, which he recognizes as legitimate as well.[20]

A discussion of the legitimacy of other religions must examine not only the traditional literary and historical sources that formulated attitudes to other religions, but also the phenomenological dimension of other religions, the actual spiritual reality associated with them and their practitioners. An unbiased examination of the spiritual life of other religions will teach us that they have the potential to produce the same fruits of spiritual excellence in their believers to which Judaism also aspires. In addition to moral excellence, these include the development of a religious life and spiritual sensitivity, the formation of a religious personality in the light of the ideals of holiness and accomplishment and fulfilment of a life of prayer as a constitutive element of the religious life. In this context, one should note, in particular, phenomena associated with answering prayers and performing miracles, as these find expression in stories of the lives of saints of other traditions. In the context of interreligious polemic, my 'true' religion is expressed in miracles, and the 'false' miracles of the other's religion are nothing but magic. A perspective that does not negate a priori the spiritual validity of the other's religious life could discover important parallels between the spiritual lives of believers of different religions. If indeed a phenomenological examination of other traditions leads to the discovery of authentic religious life, what are the implications of this recognition for the development of a contemporary theology of world religions? The discovery of significant parallels with the spiritual lives of adherents of other religions shifts our attention from theological considerations to the phenomenological common ground of different religions. The recognition that religious life is much more than the articulation of a belief system and the appropriate actions that accompany it can lead us to the recognition that in certain contexts there is a de facto equivalence between how different religions operate. Does this have any theological or theoretical consequences?

Me'iri opened the door to the acceptance of the Other on the basis of empirical behaviour. His empirical criteria appealed to the moral domain, and more

---

[20] See Gerald Blidstein, 'Maimonides and Me'iri on the Legitimacy of Non-Judaic Religion', in Leo Landman (ed.), *Scholars and Scholarship: The Interaction between Judaism and Other Cultures* (New York, 1990), 27–37.

broadly to an implicit phenomenology of religion, in view of which a religion is considered among the religions and therefore legitimate. The application of Me'iri's approach to other areas of the spiritual life and the examination of other religions from a phenomenological perspective of religious excellence, spirituality, and so on, might allow us to identify additional foci through which we can express an appreciation of other religions. To the extent that these dimensions are considered fundamental and critical to the ultimate purpose of religion, an appreciation based upon recognition of these dimensions would itself be more principled and fundamental.

WORLD RELIGIONS AND THE PROBLEM OF *AVODAH ZARAH*

Let us begin by posing a question of principle, regarding how the category of *avodah zarah* is applied in the framework of theology of religions. Is *avodah zarah* an internal Jewish category, relevant for Jews and the limits of our own religious practices, or is it a category by means of which we should assess the inherent value of alternative systems of belief? Does the halakhic ruling that the practices of a given religion are considered *avodah zarah* mean that the religion is invalid and valueless also for its adherents? When Isaiah mocks idol worshippers,[21] he seems to be making a statement that is relevant not only for believers in the God of Israel but also for the idol worshippers themselves. This may not necessarily be the case for the later halakhic application of the category of *avodah zarah*. I am not certain that the halakhic application of *avodah zarah* must be construed as the total negation and invalidation of the spiritual value and potential benefit to the believers of religious systems to which the category is applied. Halakhic attention is usually paid to the ways in which other religious systems affect Jewish believers and to the consequences of their practices on Jewish practice and belief. The halakhah, as a legal system, may not have intended to make metaphysical assertions and claims regarding alternative spiritual systems, their validity and value.[22]

The question hinges on whether the prohibition of and the criteria for *avodah zarah* are identical for a Jew and a non-Jew. This is itself a matter of debate between different halakhic authorities, and, as I shall presently show, the source of varying opinions concerning Christianity and its status as *avodah zarah*. For Maimonides, *avodah zarah* applies in the same way to Jews and non-Jews.[23] Nahmanides, by contrast, assumes different expectations of Jews and non-Jews in terms of the life of worship. While Jews must worship God alone,

---

[21] See e.g. Isa. 44: 9–20.
[22] The point and its philosophical implications are analysed by Eugene Korn in Chapter 8, below.   [23] See Maimonides, *Mishneh torah*, 'Laws of Kings', 9: 2.

non-Jews may worship the heavenly ministers, appointed to look after them, provided they remain mindful of the ultimate presence of God.[24] Thus, *avodah zarah* could mean one thing when applied to Jews, and another when applied to non-Jews. This difference of opinion, often overlooked in discussions of religions as *avodah zarah*, is significant for any consideration of world religions. While Nahmanides' views are articulated in a commentarial, rather than a halakhic, framework, the distinction itself, and the difference of opinion that legal authorities have in relation to Maimonides' views, is quite explicit also in halakhic discussions. Rabbenu Tam (twelfth century) claims that Christianity should not be considered *avodah zarah*, because Christians, as part of humanity coming under the obligations of the Noahide commandments, are not prohibited from worshipping another being alongside God.[25] This position assumes one should consider Christianity from a dual perspective. For us as Jews it is *avodah zarah*. For Christian believers it is not. This stance is of huge potential significance. *Avodah zarah* is not necessarily a category that establishes metaphysical truths or that determines the legitimacy of belief systems for their believers. Rather, it is a category that regulates the relations of the Jewish faithful to their God and the boundaries of those relations, as they encounter alternative faith systems. If we adopt such a distinction, the way is opened for interesting consideration of the significance, or lack thereof, of *avodah zarah* as a category that shapes a Jewish theology of world religions.[26]

The recognition that *avodah zarah* plays a constitutive role in the shaping of Jewish identity, theology, and world-view pushes us to reflect further upon its meaning, beyond the framework of the halakhic discussion whose interest is to determine whether particular forms of worship of different religious systems should be considered *avodah zarah*. Like other core religious concepts, expressed in normative and legal terms, there is always the danger that a controlling principle, one of the overarching spiritual concerns of the religious system, might get translated into a series of dos and don'ts. Through such a translation, it may be reduced to these practical applications and identified with them, causing us to lose sight of the ultimate spiritual concerns underlying the particular instructions. Does the spiritual concern that leads to the prominence of *avodah zarah* in Jewish discourse find sufficient expression in the practical

---

[24] See Nahmanides, *Perush al hatorah* on Exod. 20: 2; Alon Goshen-Gottstein, 'Other Gods in the Teaching of Nahmanides: Theoretical Constructions and their Implications for a Possible View of Other Religions' (Heb.), in U. Ehrlich et al. (eds.), *By the Well: Studies in Jewish Philosophy and Halakhic Thought Presented to Gerald J. Blidstein* [Al pi habe'er: meḥkarim behagut yehudit uvemaḥashevet hahalakhah mugashim leya'akov blidshtein] (Be'er Sheva, 2008), 25–82.

[25] The technical term for such belief is *shituf*, worship through association of another being alongside God. For a discussion of Rabbenu Tam's position, see Katz, *Exclusiveness and Tolerance*, 34–6; David Berger, *The Rebbe, the Messiah, and the Scandal of Orthodox Indifference* (Oxford, 2001), 157–77.   [26] The point is developed further by Eugene Korn in Chapter 8, below.

halakhic considerations of *avodah zarah*? Conceptually, *avodah zarah* is the negative expression of our very own identity. It represents the very thing to which we are opposed, and in relation to which we establish our own identity. To define *avodah zarah* is, in a significant way, to define ourselves. It is therefore difficult to assume that Judaism's fundamental battle, for the sake of which the Creator of heaven and earth revealed himself to his people, should be limited to opposition to forms of worship of God that rely on graven images or even to refined theological formulations that are found lacking in comparison with alternative notions of the understanding of divine unity. If not, what is *avodah zarah* and what is its contemporary expression? It seems that identifying and combating *avodah zarah* is to a large extent a test, an indication, of our own identity. To the extent that Jews face some kind of spiritual identity crisis, this crisis is also indirectly expressed in what seems to me our inability to meaningfully apply the category of *avodah zarah* in anything but a technical way.

Most of the sources in which *avodah zarah* is addressed seek to deal with some concrete problem. The problem is usually associated with the common life of Jews and members of other religions. Historically, most of our references to issues of *avodah zarah* come from dealings with Christianity. The focus upon the practical concerns of daily coexistence can divert attention from the broader theoretical and metaphysical questions that ought to guide our discussion of world religions. Theologically, we ought to engage in thoughtful and systematic consideration of what *avodah zarah* really is. What is the moral component in *avodah zarah* that might make it as repulsive as it is represented in our sources? To what degree is the issue one of proper faith, of correct practice, or of the totality of life as it is shaped by religion? To what extent does the fundamental distinction and tension between Jews and non-Jews also shape how the religious difference between Judaism and other religions is constructed? And to what extent does the view of other religions as *avodah zarah* express concrete historical pressures of a given period? The discussion of each of these questions has far-reaching consequences for a theology of world religions, and a serious discussion of these questions has barely begun.

Over the past thousand years, concerns about *avodah zarah* have been the subject of discussion primarily in relation to Christianity. The discussions of halakhic authorities with regard to Christianity establish the governing paradigms of attitudes to other world religions. A presentation of core rabbinic attitudes to Christianity thus has significant consequences for any discussion of the implications of *avodah zarah* for a view of world religions. In this context, I would like to present three positions that emerged in medieval halakhic discussions of Christianity.

The most extreme position is often identified with Maimonides, even though many other scholars, in various diasporas, took it for granted.

According to this position, Christianity is *avodah zarah*, for all intents and purposes. Belief in the Trinity and the Incarnation, along with the worship of statues, leads almost by default to the view that Christianity is idolatry.[27] Obviously, this view disregards Christianity's own self-understanding as worshipping the one God, the God of Israel, and does not leave much room for interreligious pluralism. *Avodah zarah* as a category points away from pluralism and tolerance, by passing a harsh judgement and rejecting particular religious systems. Unconditional application of the notion of *avodah zarah* to any religion will lead to viewpoints that do not enable true acceptance of it. At best, they can sustain a de facto tolerance, based on keeping one's distance and upholding that distance as legitimate and expressive of as much respect as can be mustered for the sake of a 'live and let live' ideology. Genuine acceptance and legitimization of the other is not possible when *avodah zarah* is fully evoked.

At the other end of the spectrum one finds the position of Me'iri, whom we have already discussed. According to his view, Christianity should not be considered *avodah zarah*. Christianity has a moral code and grounds an ordered way of life in the recognition of God. It is, for Me'iri, a 'religion', in other words a valid form of the religious life. This raises it above the rank of other religions of old, which lacked such an ordered moral life and in relation to which the status of *avodah zarah* applied. Differences in theological world-view are not, in and of themselves, sufficient grounds for declaring another religion *avodah zarah*. Famous in this respect is the following quote: 'Nations that are bound by the ways of religion and believe in His (blessed be He) existence, His Unity and His power, even though they are in error concerning some matters, according to our faith, the rules discussed above do not apply to them.'[28] Ultimately, for Me'iri, Jews and Christians believe in the same God, even if there are theological variations in how he is understood. Believing in the same God is the other side of the coin of not considering a religion as *avodah zarah*. Having identified criteria in light of which Christianity is understood as believing in the same God, the laws applying to *avodah zarah* are considered as not applicable to Christianity.

[27] It should be noted that in actual fact Maimonides does not make it clear why he sees Christianity as *avodah zarah*. Nowhere does he state explicitly that the problem is theological (i.e. the Trinity), rather than practical (i.e. worship of icons or Jesus). Scholars can only speculate as to why he held these views and how they cohere with his broader world-view. In terms of my own reading of Maimonides, the most likely reason for considering Christianity as *avodah zarah* is that another being other than God is worshipped. For Maimonides (*Mishneh torah*, 'Laws of Idolatry', 2: 1), this is the core definition of *avodah zarah*. This understanding may be alluded to in 'Laws of Kings', 11: 4. On Maimonides and Christianity, see Howard Kreisel, 'Maimonides on Christianity and Islam', in Ronald Brauner (ed.), *Jewish Civilization: Essays and Studies* (Philadelphia, 1985), iii. 156. See also David Novak in Chapter 9, below.

[28] Me'iri, *Beit habeḥirah* on *Git*. 62a. In other words, the laws relating to idol worshippers do not apply to them and these nations are considered to be beyond *avodah zarah*.

A median position is that of Rabbenu Tam, to whom we have also already had recourse.[29] His position was initially articulated in the framework of challenges arising from day-to-day coexistence and the need to maintain ongoing commercial ties with neighbouring Christians. It permitted commercial relations, even though they entailed taking oaths, thereby causing Christians to take an oath in their God's name. As stated, Rabbenu Tam's reasoning was that Noahides, that is, non-Israelites, were not prohibited from worshipping another being alongside God, and hence could, in this instance, take an oath in Jesus' name. Accordingly, worship through association of another being with God is fundamentally different to *avodah zarah*. *Avodah zarah* constitutes a denial and rejection of God. Worship by association, *shituf*, impairs the exclusiveness of worship due to God alone, but does not violate the recognition of the true God. Finding the point of contact and association with the God known to Israel enables acceptance and validation of a worship that would be deemed wrong for Israel itself. Thus, we find here a mechanism by means of which another religion is validated for its practitioners. Full rejection is replaced by de facto acceptance in the context of everyday life. This is accomplished by interpreting the meaning of Christian worship through categories particular to Jewish discourse,[30] rather than in terms of the Christian faith itself.[31] While Rabbenu Tam's position started out as a practical solution for issues of day-to-day coexistence, its later reworkings amount to a principled

---

[29] Rabbenu Tam's views and their halakhic consequences are covered in detail by Eugene Korn in Chapter 8, below.

[30] Insufficient attention has been given to whether the category of *shituf*, central to so much Jewish reflection on Christianity, is really appropriate for describing Christian faith (see Rabbi Jacob Emden, *She'ilat ya'avets*, 1: 41, and my discussion in *Beyond Idolatry*).

[31] Such an interpretation would, of course, have actually increased the acceptability of Christian worship, inasmuch as it would have integrated the Christian effort to uphold belief in the one God, despite a Trinitarian understanding of that God. Jewish thinkers, however, could not affirm Christian monotheism by accepting the Christian understanding of the triune divinity. Historical tensions precluded the integration of these understandings as indications of Christianity's intention to uphold monotheism. In the context of monotheism and the problem of *avodah zarah*, future Jewish reflection on Christianity might consider whether recognizing this intention, as expressed in the history of articulating the nature of the Trinitarian understanding of God, can be divorced from accepting the theological claims and understanding proper to Christian faith. This might be one theological, and even halakhic, move that is enabled by the new situation created by changes in Jewish–Christian relations. One precedent for openness to accepting Christian self-understanding on its own terms is provided by Yehudah Aryeh Leib de Modena (see Daniel Lasker, *Jewish Philosophical Polemics Against Christianity in the Middle Ages*, 2nd edn. (Oxford, 2007), 81–2). His willingness to recognize the legitimacy of Trinitarian belief, understood in a particular way, is complemented by a rejection of the doctrine of the Incarnation, hence of Christian faith. Even more important in procedural terms is the investigation of Christianity by Rabbi Yosef Mesas, *Shut mayim ḥayim*, pt. 2, 'Yoreh de'ah', 108. This discussion, completely tangential in terms of halakhic precedent and marginal in terms of its impact on halakhic discourse, is a model for learning, dialogue, and openness as the foundations for any Jewish consideration of another religion.

acceptance of Christianity as a religion, valid for its believers.[32] Thus Rabbenu Tam's halakhic solution ends up providing the basis for a broader theory of tolerance and of what might, in present-day terms, be considered interreligious pluralism.[33] One extreme expression of such legitimacy is found in an early twentieth-century rabbinic ruling that allows Jews to contribute financially towards the construction of a church, based on Christianity's halakhic status as permitted *shituf*.[34] What might have been initially thought of as a permissible form of *avodah zarah*[35] has become in its later reworkings a principle of almost full acceptance of the legitimacy of the religion of the Other.[36]

The Middle Ages have left us with a heritage of varying positions on Christianity. The fact is we have advanced remarkably little beyond these fundamental discussions and their reiterations. Present-day halakhic Judaism continues to speak in a multiplicity of voices, echoing the earlier halakhic–theological polyphony. Maintaining a plurality of positions, rather than narrowing down the range of legitimate options, is in and of itself laudable. However, in terms of theoretical reflection on Christianity's status as *avodah zarah* (as opposed to reflection on its mission within the divine economy or on its relationship to Judaism) we have moved little beyond where we were several hundred years ago. On the one hand we must revisit the heritage of the Middle Ages and consider the criteria in the light of which we adopt one position or another. This includes revisiting the history of reception of the three positions, their internal evolution, the criteria by which we determine *avodah zarah*, and the possibility of reaching consensus. But even more significantly, this must include a re-engagement with the religions under discussion, starting with Christianity, in an attempt to consider whether earlier positions offered an

[32] See Jacob Katz, 'The Vicissitude of Three Apologetic Passages' (Heb.), *Zion*, 23–4 (1958–9), 181–6.

[33] For a contemporary articulation of this view, in relation to world religions, see my lengthy discussion of Adin Steinsaltz in Chapter 11, below.

[34] See David Ellenson, 'Jewish Covenant and Christian Trinitarianism: An Analysis of a Responsum on Jewish–Christian Relations in the Modern World', *Jewish Civilization*, 3 (1985), 85–100; see also Rabbi Herzl Henkin, *Shut benei banim*, iii, §36 (Jerusalem, 1998); for further analysis, see Eugene Korn in Chapter 8, below.

[35] If Berger is correct (*The Rebbe, the Messiah, and the Scandal of Orthodox Indifference*, 176).

[36] Little attention has been paid to the extension of validation through *shituf* to religions other than Christianity. An important step in this direction, in relation to Eastern religions, is made by Isaac Herzog, 'Minority Rights According to the Halakhah' (Heb.), *Tehumin*, 2 (1981), 178–9. Without claiming that the category extends to them, he entertains the possibility and assumes that only proper study of those religions can determine the issue. It is regrettable that contemporary halakhic decisors fail to study Eastern religions properly prior to issuing halakhic rulings concerning them, a move taken for granted by Herzog. Another important discussion is Adin Steinsaltz, 'Peace without Conciliation: The Irrelevance of "Toleration" in Judaism', *Common Knowledge*, 11/1 (2005), 41–7. I discuss Steinsaltz's presentation in great detail in *Beyond Idolatry* and in Chapter 11 below.

appropriate portrayal and whether the multiple theological understandings within Christianity, especially those that may have emerged since the fundamental positions were first articulated, might necessitate revisiting our view of the religion. For 600 years we have been engaging with halakhic texts and their internal discourse in relation to Christianity. But we have failed to seriously engage with Christian theology itself, and we continue to do so. The twenty-first century began with a similar dynamic in relation to Hinduism, when halakhic decisors engaged with it in a global way. Again, the discussion was internal halakhic discourse, failing completely to engage with Hindu theology or religion in and of itself.[37] If there is anything that should characterize the desired perspective of a contemporary theology of world religions it is that we ought to engage the religions on their own terms, theologically, as a precondition for making pronouncements on those religions. Even if we end up reaffirming old positions, the times and the challenges at hand demand, at the very least, that the procedures by which we evaluate another religion conform to the standards of knowledge and listening that the present day makes possible and even mandates.

REVELATION, TRUTH, AND WORLD RELIGIONS

Judaism is grounded in revelation. This could theoretically lead to a denial of any legitimacy to other religions that would be perceived as competing with Judaism's truth or distorting it. As suggested above, when faith in revelation is coupled with the notion of election this might suggest that Judaism has nothing to learn from others and that truth and falsehood are the best way of describing the relations between Judaism and other religions.

Understanding revelation in terms of truth leads to some reflections on the contribution of philosophical understandings to our discussion. Consideration of Judaism's attitudes to other religions, particularly Christianity and Islam, must take into account the conceptual framework within which these attitudes took shape and the centrality of philosophical discourse to shaping Judaism's wrestling with these religions. The philosophical heritage plays a dual role. On the one hand, it provides important precedents and opens before us interesting possibilities, in the light of which we might reflect upon these issues. The philosophical tradition is an important resource for contemporary reflection, having produced significant positions both for and against and recognizing varying degrees of validity in other religions. On the other hand, the articulation of religious questions in philosophical language could further empower

[37] A critique of the halakhic proceedings in this light was offered by Daniel Sperber, 'How Not to Make Halakhic Rulings', *Conversations: The Journal of the Institute for Jewish Ideas and Ideals*, 5 (Sept. 2009), 1–11, available at <http://www.jewishideas.org/articles/how-not-make-halakhic-rulings>. I deal with this issue at greater length in Chapter 11, below.

exclusivistic religious understandings. A contemporary theology of world religions could thus be built upon philosophical precedents, while being hampered by those very same precedents. The point is particularly relevant when the philosophical heritage is considered historically, in relation to earlier stages of Jewish reflection captured in biblical and rabbinic literature. One of the great conceptual changes heralded by the philosophical tradition is the way that the language of truth and falsehood is used.[38] This conceptual emphasis confronts the attempt to create a contemporary theology of world religions with particular challenges.

The precedent provided by medieval Jewish philosophy was based upon a common philosophical language and understanding. The philosophers of Judaism, Christianity, and Islam all related to this common philosophical infrastructure, which allows us to identify commonalities and mutual appreciation. Alas, today we do not possess a common philosophical language or tradition that shapes our religions. Today it is universal moral challenges that religions struggle with. The common denominators driving interreligious dialogue are the needs of the human person and of humanity, not metaphysical concerns. This emphasis upon the human person and humanity diverts attention from classical religious issues, thereby making the philosophical heritage less relevant as a meeting ground. Moreover, whereas philosophical discourse was limited to Judaism, Christianity, and Islam, contemporary emphasis upon the human (and ecological) condition broadens the frame of reference and areas of concern beyond the boundaries of the philosophical–religious encounter between the religions.

Understanding religious concepts in terms of truth introduces into religious discourse an exclusiveness that is grounded in the philosophical understanding of truth and falsehood. Relating to other religions in these terms constitutes a change from the thought of earlier periods. Understanding religious issues in philosophical terms will lead to understanding philosophical truth as the substance of revelation. According to this understanding, truth is the highest value of the religious world-view. That is, religion and all of its details are understood as truth. One additional consequence of this identification, though belied by some historical precedents, is the exclusive identification of truth with 'our' religion. Truth is 'our' lot, while others are mired in falsehood.

The prominence of this religious understanding is such that it is often assumed to be the natural religious world-view, without seriously questioning its historical and conceptual roots. Contemporary reflection upon world

---

[38] The language itself is used already in the Bible, e.g. Jer. 10: 14; 16: 9. However, the meaning of truth in pre-philosophical usage is very different from its philosophical meaning. As the context of these typical examples suggests, truth is relational and touches upon the authenticity of religious relationships and the efficacy of worship and the spiritual path. Such application of 'truth' must be approached differently than the later philosophical application of the term.

religions must therefore articulate a position on the application of truth as the yardstick by which one's own religion is compared to others. There are, in principle, three possible positions in relation to this issue:

1. Upholding, in principle, the understanding of religion as theological truth, while ignoring, de facto, issues of truth and falsehood in the context of interreligious relations.

2. Maintaining the notion of truth, while refining it in ways appropriate to contemporary challenges and needs.

3. Abandoning truth as a primary means of presenting religion, and preferring alternative religious views and languages.

Let us briefly consider each of these three strategies.

The first possibility serves many of the people engaged in interreligious dialogue and collaboration. The need for concrete collaboration leads them to ignore issues of truth and falsehood, even though they are theologically central to the religions. Truths are seen as the private affair of the believers and their religions, but beyond the pale of practical interreligious collaboration. The decision to ignore the great metaphysical questions that distinguish one religion from one another is a paradigm shift when compared to centuries of theological concerns. Thus a de facto pluralism emerges, while upholding absolutist theological positions. The practical meaning of such a paradigm change is that truth is no longer the supreme value: it has been replaced by other values, such as peace, the human person, and care for the creation. While officially there is no relinquishing of the truth claims of a given religion, this strategy entails a practical willingness to attribute less importance to religious truth than was common in earlier centuries. This willingness and the concomitant preference of other moral and existential values are themselves a quiet religious revolution.

Yet a theology of world religions needs more than practical positions in response to reality. It must be articulated on the basis of reflection and principle. The practical attitude might accordingly be formulated as follows: unlike past understandings of religion as privileging metaphysical truths, a new understanding must be articulated that privileges other elements of the religious life. The contribution of religion to the formation of the individual person and to society is religion's ultimate test. Therefore, one should attach less weight to the conflicting truth claims of religions and consider essential those elements by means of which every religion makes a positive contribution to the shaping of people and society. This formulation does not renounce the truth claims underlying disagreements between religions. It does, however, neutralize them. The degree of conscious change and theological sacrifice that it calls for is minimal. From an epistemological perspective, one might see such a position as an extension of Me'iri's. As indicated earlier, Me'iri was willing to overlook theological differences in favour of the big picture; that is, the recognition of a religion as valid because it accomplishes moral purposes and points to the same God. The specific theological truth claims of each religion are secondary.[39]

The axiological weakening of truth as the supreme value in shaping relations between religions does not of necessity lead to a relativistic view of truth. However, it is likely that psychologically and sociologically affording a less prominent place to truth in the scale of religious values might contribute to the adoption of a relativistic view of truth. This brings us to the second possibility, which touches upon issues of relativism, on the one hand, and the meaning of religious truth, on the other. The classical threat in the light of which other religions have been viewed is the threat to Judaism's continued existence. As we shall see, interreligious dialogue raises serious concerns among faithful Jews regarding conversion and the loss of religious identity that might ensue from dialogue. In addition, one may recognize another concern more intense in the contemporary era than in the era of religious competition. The modern and postmodern eras are characterized by the weakening of belief in absolute truth and the rise of the notion of relative truth.

Religious traditions have several possible responses to the threat of relativism. The first is a reaffirmation of the validity of truth, as understood throughout the generations. However, it seems that a certain devaluation of truth, classically understood, is inevitable in the new context. Catholic efforts to affirm classical truth-based and exclusivistic understandings, in the face of repeated devaluation, are a hallmark of Pope Benedict XVI's theology and they received a famous articulation in the 2000 document *Dominus Iesus*. These efforts are testimony both to the attempt to uphold classical understandings and to the erosion such understandings inevitably undergo. The relativistic understanding that, the authors of *Dominus Iesus* assume, some Catholic theologians had reached and against whom the document is composed, taken together with the difficult reception of the document in various Catholic theological circles, indicate how central the problem of relativism is to those engaged in a theology of other religions.

I want to suggest an alternative to the position that struggles to uphold classical understandings of absolute truth. The following move seeks to preserve the notion of truth, while refining it from within the conceptual world and terminology provided by the religion itself, in our case, Judaism. Unlike the

---

[39] This does not mean that 'truth' loses all religious significance. It is either accorded second place, following moral and spiritual criteria, or it is understood in other terms. One could point to a continuity between a biblical appeal to truth and an understanding of truth such as that which emerges from Me'iri's position.

challenge to absolute truth from outside religion, one may think of an internal relativization of truth. Most discussions of truth and falsehood assume a simple dichotomy between true and false. Consequently, religions may be classified as one or the other. Classically, 'we' have truth, or at least 'we' possess it fully, while 'they' have falsehood. A richer understanding of 'truth' suggests more nuanced ways of describing relations, while preserving the notion of truth. To do so, one must identify expressions of the internal relativization of the contents of religion. There are Jewish mechanisms and concepts that suggest that even core values should be understood as relative. For example, one midrashic tradition teaches that the Torah we possess is only the incomplete form of supernal wisdom.[40] According to this *midrash*, the Torah—probably Judaism's most central value—pales in comparison with the spiritual reality of wisdom that it seeks to represent. Rather than being fully identified with this wisdom, Torah remains a reflection of it, a lower level of what is in and of itself the absolute. Such relativization of wisdom allows us to see in the Torah something less than the theoretical alternative view that fully identifies the Torah we possess with supernal divine wisdom. The notion of truth is similarly relativized in various texts. Hierarchy is a way of relativizing, and a hierarchy of truths allows us to relativize the lowest level, identified with the truth as we understand and practise it. One teaching juxtaposes truth, language of truth, and ultimate truth, as three degrees or ways of conceptualizing truth.[41] Thus, truth and relative understandings of truth may be part of internal religious discourse, not only pressures brought to bear from the outside.

The question for consideration is to what extent one may adapt such internal applications of relativizing truth to the challenges coming from without, in particular to the challenges posed by the competing truth claims of different religions. Can we broaden the use of such internal relativizing language to include alternative religious systems? If so, we may construct what might be termed a hierarchical pluralism. Rather than identifying 'our' form of religion with absolute truth, we might ask where, within the hierarchy of truth, we might position our own religious system. Some might identify their religion with a higher rung on the ladder of truth, while conceding some dimension of truth, albeit on a lower rung, to another religion. Alternatively, all forms of religious expression might be considered on a lower rung, compared to a higher spiritual reality that transcends religious forms or their common perception and practice. Such an understanding has great potential in an interreligious context. Our religion may simultaneously possess a share of the absolute, as well as the relative, truth. Truth would not be seen as a point that one reaches,

---

[40] *Genesis Rabbah* 17: 5.
[41] See Yosef Yitzhak Schneerson, 'Simhat torah: 1929' (Heb.), in id., *Likkutei Dibburim: An Anthology of Talks* (New York, 1992), i. 192. The original terms are *emet, sefat emet, emet la'amitah*.

but as a scale that one ascends and within which we recognize a hierarchy. All religions can share in the different positions within this hierarchy.

One cannot assume that internal mechanisms for reflecting upon truth can always be exported to a religion's views of other religions. Certain perspectives and certain flexibilities may be the prerogative of the internal spiritual discourse. Yet to the extent that spiritual literature conditions our view of religion, we can require it to extend beyond the boundaries of its normal application. If our theological challenge is how to deal with the consequences of applying the language of truth to our religious discourse, then identifying ways in which this very language has already been transmuted within tradition provides an important resource. Broadening the range of spiritual uses of religious terms allows us to approach other religions with a more spiritual vocabulary and world-view, thereby mitigating the competitive effects of the simple binary application of the language of truth in the religious sphere.

A third way of addressing the question of truth and falsehood is the most radical. It is the relinquishing of truth as an appropriate concept in religious discourse. This may be part of a broader relinquishing of philosophical language as suitable for describing religious life. At the very least, religious life is something else, something more than the correct philosophical–religious formulation of reality. Perhaps the very presentation of religion in terms of truth distorts something fundamental about religion. Such relinquishing may be motivated by additional considerations. In a Jewish context, we often encounter the claim that Judaism has neither theology nor dogma.[42] (Solomon Schechter is said to have quipped that Judaism's only dogma is that it lacks any.[43]) This means that Judaism does not place the same emphasis upon proper articulation of belief and sets of beliefs as other religions, particularly Christianity, do. In this sense, Judaism is much more concerned with orthopraxy than with orthodoxy. When we couple the ethnic component of the religion with the orthoprax guidance it offers its believers, Judaism's spiritual profile emerges as different from those religions that make correct formulation of belief the pillar of their faith. This emphasis on orthopraxy allows Jews to raise the question of the very relevance of truth to a definition of Judaism. While important forms of historical Judaism, particularly the philosophical,[44] relied heavily upon truth and creed, there are other earlier and, for some, more authentic forms of Judaism that did not. Therefore one of the issues facing a

[42] See e.g. Abraham Geiger, cited in translation in Alfred Jospe (ed.), *Studies in Jewish Thought: An Anthology of German Jewish Scholarship* (Detroit, 1981), 44.

[43] Despite the reputable scholarly standing of the authority from whom I have heard this *bon mot*, it is clearly belied by Schechter's essay 'The Dogmas of Judaism', in Solomon Schechter, *Studies in Judaism: First Series* (Philadelphia, 1915), 147–81.

[44] See Menachem Kellner, *Dogma in Medieval Jewish Thought: From Maimonides to Abravanel* (Oxford, 1986).

Jewish theology of world religions is to what degree one should continue using religious–philosophical language rather than other languages. A return to a pre-philosophical religious language, as found in our pre-philosophical sources, is one option.

The difficulties posed by the philosophical casting of revelation as the revelation of truth may not be posed by earlier understandings of the moment of revelation, the Sinai event. The biblical understanding of Sinai is devoid of any relation to the concept of truth. Sinai is the moment of covenant making. The covenant is the religious framework that structures Israel's religious identity. Rather than being a category of abstract truth, covenant is a historical and relational category that provides meaning to Israel's particular story. Much like the covenant between the king and his people or between husband and wife, God makes a covenant with his people. At the heart of the covenant is the ordering of relations within the relational framework that the covenant provides. Understanding Judaism generally, and the Sinai revelation in particular, in terms of covenant places a specific relationship within a particular story at the heart of a religious world-view and at the heart of a specific revelation. All this is very different from viewing Sinai in abstract truth terms.

A return to a relational understanding as constitutive of religious identity may have far-reaching ramifications for Judaism's relationship with other religions. A relational understanding does not assume the same exclusiveness that a philosophical view of truth and falsehood does. Just as a covenant within human relations does not assume that other parallel covenants and relationships cannot exist (for example, between other couples), so the religious covenant does not, in principle, rule out the possibility of the existence of other covenants.[45]

Describing the religious life in relational terms has much to commend it from another perspective. Our understanding of religious life draws analogies and finds similarities with other areas of life. If we see the religious life in

---

[45] This is a point repeatedly made by David Hartman in his own theology of other religions. While I consider this an important strategy, we ought to also be aware of how dicey the analogy is. Human covenants recognize many partners all fulfilling the same role in their own marriages. Applying the analogy to the human–divine relationship would assume multiple gods fulfilling the same covenantal role in relation to others as the God of Israel does in relation to his people. Such an understanding may indeed be found in several biblical passages (e.g. Gen. 31: 53; Judg. 11: 24). This raises the challenging question of whether covenantal theology must be non-monotheistic. The possibility of multiple relations with the same God already assumes a notion of one true God to whom all turn. It is thus already a philosophical, or conceptual, view that transforms the simple understanding of covenant. The biblical metaphors also break down at this point, as they can no longer describe such a reality, which may have been outside the purview of the religious imagination that initially expressed itself through the notion of covenant. It does remain, however, a serious theological option, even if it has in some ways gone beyond the original biblical framework.

cognitive and philosophical terms, highlighting notions of truth and falsehood, our encounter with the religious Other will be governed by the penetrating gaze that seeks to discern truth from falsehood. Our entire attitude to the religious field will be derived from this abstract view. The same is true for the proposal to understand the religious life in terms analogous to human relationships. Once we describe Israel's relationship with God in terms of human relationships, the fundamental question becomes, 'To what extent might one describe relationships between religions in terms that are taken from interpersonal relationships?' Drawing this analogy has more far-reaching consequences than our ability to justify other religions as valid alternative relationships.

There are moral consequences to presenting relationships between religions in analogy to human relationships. There is often a serious gap between the teachings of religions regarding the path of moral perfection in interpersonal relationships and their teachings regarding relationships between religions. All religions have developed moral teachings that emphasize the spiritual and moral perfection of the individual in relation to other individuals. To the extent that we are prepared to take seriously the analogy between religious and human relationships, there follows a series of consequences that touches upon how believers of different religions will be asked to treat each other. Humility, readiness to learn from the other, openness, love of the other—spiritual conclusions that grow out of a principled pluralistic understanding—are some possible applications of seeing relations between religions as similar to ordinary human relations. One wonders: 'Could it be that in the same way that no single person can bring to perfection all the talents and human potentialities, so it is with the world's religions?' 'Does the multiplicity of religious forms reflect an inherent spiritual need, much as does the multiplicity of human beings?' Much thought still awaits us along these lines. That Judaism's theological roots are in the covenant and therefore in the framework of personal relationships with God allows us naturally to develop such a Jewish religious view.

Let us put the matter differently: Judaism is a religion and a way of life for a particular people. This may create certain difficulties for dialogue, but it also opens up possibilities for creativity and flexibility in the Jewish theology of other religions. A practical consequence of whether the national or the religious pole of Jewish identity is emphasized is the question of universal conversion to Judaism. Emphasizing the religious component alone leads to highlighting Judaism's message to the world in terms of truth, a truth that should speak to all. Cast in these terms the conclusion is inevitable: Judaism's superiority as a system of truth mandates spreading its message to humanity and, at the very least, a generous opening of the doors to converts. Conversely, emphasizing the national component highlights the interest in a people's specific story and its particular relationship with God. As suggested, this emphasis neutralizes the missionary drive that is derived from the principle of truth. Whoever defines Judaism in terms of truth must account for why he refrains from acting in kindness towards the rest of humanity and sharing with them the finest that can be shared—the ultimate truth. Is it not inconceivable that the Creator of all would limit perfect truth to a narrow group and not seek to share his good truth with the entirety of humanity? The complexity of Jewish attitudes over the generations towards the spreading of Judaism to others is a window onto the complexity of Jewish self-understanding. Emphasizing the national pole in Jewish identity provides profound justification for neutralizing the missionary drive. Thus, conceptualizing religion in relational terms brings forth a less exclusivist understanding of religion that can better contain the Other within its world-view.

The emphasis upon relationship does not detract from the meaning of revelation. On the contrary, were it not for revelation, one could not describe the special relationship between God and his people. It is precisely the making of the covenant at Sinai that is inseparable from revelation and that creates the special relationship between God and Israel. Understanding revelation as constituting a people rather than as revealing a truth enables openness to the Other, as long as such openness does not affect the faithfulness mandated by the covenant. It is precisely the understanding of revelation in terms of such a creation that enables mutual openness and recognition. If there is something exclusivist in revelation that creates a boundary between those who received the revelation and those who did not, creation is always the pole of religious thought that emphasizes that which unites, because we are all creatures. The unifying potential of creation is relevant not only in relation to the universal creation from which all the variety of humanity later evolved, but also in relation to understanding Israel's status in terms of creation. To think of creation is to think of what it means to be created and to recall the Creator. In the final analysis, we are all created in some way or another, constituted by God in accordance with his will. If the moment of revelation casts Jews as being created for a unique role, we do not thereby lose relation with other creatures. On the contrary, we share with them the fundamental fact that all that we are is itself a creation of God. The different expressions of creation may thus engage each other, even as creatures interact with each other. To be created is to be in dialogue with other parts of creation. Revelation thus establishes the framework from which we engage others in a dialogue of being, rather than limiting our interest in others as sole possessors of truth.

Emphasizing relationship rather than truth as the focus of religious life leads us to place faithfulness as the supreme value. Our religious duty is not to deny the value and validity of other religions. Rather, it is to be faithful to the covenantal relationship to which we belong, much as a spouse's responsibility is to be faithful to his or her partner, rather than to deny the fundamental legitimacy of all other couples. The development of such a religious world-view leads us back to the biblical roots of our faith. These include prophecies concerning the relation between world religions. It is worth considering the following prophecy of Micah in the present context:

In days to come the mountain of the Lord's house shall be established as the highest of the mountains, and shall be raised up above the hills. Peoples shall stream to it, and many nations shall come and say: 'Come, let us go up to the mountain of the Lord, to the house of the God of Jacob; that he may teach us his ways and that we may walk in his paths.' . . . For all the peoples walk, each in the name of its god, but we will walk in the name of the Lord our God forever and ever.[46]

Two seemingly contradictory ideals are articulated here. On the one hand we find the nations coming to the mountain of the Lord's house, to learn God's ways. On the other we find the affirmation that ideally all nations are to follow their own gods, while Israel follows God. How, then, can one reconcile the pluralistic view of multiple relations coexisting with the prophecy that acknowledges something unique that Israel has to share with the rest of humanity? Instead of resolving this paradox, I would like to present it as a hermeneutical and theological challenge that captures the complex situation that a Jewish theology of world religions now faces. The challenge of the passage is still greater when we consider the eschatological perspective that it offers and pose the question of whether both perspectives in this text can be carried through from present time to the ideal future time.

I would like now to draw together the insights already mentioned with some new ones in order to revisit an issue fundamental to the relevance and meaning of other religions. I have argued for an understanding of revelation in relational terms. This understanding allows us to downplay truth claims as fundamental to an understanding of religion, while at the same time permitting learning and receiving inspiration from other religions, in much the same way as these are considered normal and constitutive features of human relationships. Nevertheless, extending the paradigm of human relationships to relationships between religions requires more than simply modelling the one on the other. For such a move to make sense in a Jewish theological framework, it must be supported by additional arguments. Belief in revelation must be shown to be compatible with openness to other religions. There are several strategies by means of which belief in revelation can be reconciled with the openness that permits genuine exchange, sharing, and learning from others.

[46] Mic. 4: 1–5.

The possibility of multiple revelations. The most far-reaching theoretical possibility is that revelation is not exclusive. In principle, multiple revelations could take place alongside one another. This possibility is particularly relevant if we emphasize the relational element in the construction of identity, since one relationship does not exclude another. Yet even if truth and falsehood continue to occupy prominent places in our religious self-understanding, the recognition that we were given a revelation does not in and of itself preclude the possibility that other revelations may have been shared with other groups or religious communities. Rabbi Nethanael ibn al-Fayyumi, a twelfth-century Yemenite Jewish mystic who may have influenced Maimonides,[47] entertained this idea in the context of Jewish thought. Despite this particular precedent, the idea was not raised often. The primary reason for this is that the contents of other revelations seemed false to Jews throughout history, and thus they did not attempt to harmonize them. Accepting this position must be accompanied by acknowledging how little it has served in the past and by defining the boundaries within which it could be applied.

Revelation and its existential impact. We have already mentioned that the philosophers of the Middle Ages understood particular religious revelations against the background of a broader philosophical understanding. This background could theoretically lend itself to multiple revelations, all of which would be understood in light of the common philosophical world-view. Given that today's science and philosophy lack such a common world-view, this specific strategy cannot be implemented. We may, nevertheless, still be able to consider revelation in the light of a universal criterion that can serve as a testing ground for revelation and its consequences. As noted, modern understandings of religion place more emphasis on the contribution of religion to the life of the individual and of society and less on the meaning of truths in and of themselves. How religions work and the influence they have are thus significant criteria for their evaluation. These criteria are relevant to teaching and preaching. How religions 'sell' themselves is largely based on their contribution to the lives of their believers. These criteria take us from the realm of the philosophical and into the fields of behavioural and social sciences. Can they provide a common testing ground in reality for the spiritual life of religions in their diversity? If so, one could consider the influence of religions on the lives of their believers. Their moral, spiritual, psychological, educational, and mystical lives are areas worthy of examination when studying the effects and value of diverse religious traditions. If different religions end up doing the same thing for their believers, we have here an opening for dialogue and

---

[47] Nethanael ibn al-Fayyumi, *Bustan al-Ukul*, Judaeo-Arabic text and English translation, ed. D. Levine (New York, 1908), 108; see also Paul Fenton in Chapter 10, below.

mutual understanding.[48] Such a common basis could neutralize the engagement in the speculative and metaphysical dimensions that tend to distinguish religions and highlight the similarity of their contribution to believers' lives. According to this suggestion, revelation has less to do with the abstract truths revealed than with how it manifests itself in the lives of believers. Multiple revelations can thus be recognized according to the fruits they bear in the lives of their believers.

Revelation and creation. Placing an emphasis upon creation allows for greater commonality and openness between creatures. Creation is one whole. In highlighting difference we ignore the common foundation of creation and prefer alternative conceptual foundations, such as election or the exclusivist understanding of revelation. The conceptual foundation of creation allows us, in principle, greater openness and receptivity to others and even to what they may have to teach us. The notion of the image of God may be central in this context. If humans are made in the image of God, there is a spiritual basis for integrating and providing religious meaning to a wide range of human thought and creativity. This could also include religious speculation and the discovery of ways by which humans have come close to God. Jewish thought has, on the whole, made little use of this concept compared to the emphasis upon Israel's particularity.[49] One of the reasons for the qualified use of the concept is precisely the tension between its universal potential and the national emphasis prominent in many Jewish theological world-views throughout the centuries. A rediscovery of the conceptual potential of the image of God and creation might provide a fruitful direction for Jewish reflection upon world religions. Accordingly, other religions may be viewed as expressions of the fulfilment of human potential. Recognizing the full potential of humans made in the image of God can provide a counterpoint to the emphasis commonly placed upon revelation and allow us to recognize the traces of the divine within human reality, including and maybe especially its religious and spiritual expressions.

It is interesting in this context to consider the position of the holy person, the saint, in world religions. The holy person constitutes a test for the effectiveness of the religious system as well as a symbol of the perfection to which it can lead. The ability of religions to produce holy men and women should be a fundamental criterion in the light of which we consider those religions. Such

---

[48] This was powerfully argued in Dalai Lama, *Toward a True Kinship of Faiths: How the World's Religions Can Come Together* (New York, 2010).

[49] See Alon Goshen-Gottstein, 'The Body as Image of God in Rabbinic Literature', *Harvard Theological Review*, 87 (1994), 171–95. This overall assessment contrasts with that of Yair Lorberbaum, *The Image of God: Halakhah and Aggadah* [Tselem elohim: halakhah ve'agadah] (Jerusalem, 2004).

holiness includes moral perfection as well as a broad range of supernatural phenomena associated with saints, particularly the depth, power, and efficacy of their prayers. The kind of insularity characterizing Jewish attitudes to other religions is accompanied by ignoring or interpreting away expressions of spiritual excellence in those traditions. When we examine the criteria by which a saint is recognized in different religions, we see that those criteria are strikingly similar, even as differences typical of the religions are also expressed in their respective ideals. Should not some degree of legitimacy and recognition be conferred upon a religion that produces saintly expressions of human spiritual excellence, even if thereby we do not validate the entire religious system? The phenomenon of saints presents a serious challenge to a theology of religions. In some way the saint is himself or herself a revelation, a channel for revealing the divine in the world. This channel of revelation is an alternative to the classical channels of revelation upon which the great traditions are founded, and as such it must lead to some recognition of the other tradition.

Torah and wisdom. One of the ways in which Jewish tradition has justified learning from the world outside revelation is through the distinction between Torah and wisdom. As the Midrash states, 'if one tells you there is wisdom among the gentiles—believe him'.[50] According to this distinction, it is permissible to learn wisdom from outside, but not Torah. Of course, this distinction describes what learning means to us, rather than the self-understanding of the one from whom we learn. It may be that one man's Torah (or revelation) is another man's wisdom. Thus we can consider multiple levels of significance in relation to the teachings of a given religion. Accepting the legitimacy of multiple perspectives may facilitate interreligious conversation.

One possible understanding of 'wisdom' is moral wisdom, in contradistinction to divine revelation. According to this understanding, one can distinguish between the religious field, which touches upon the divine and our relation to it, and the moral field, which is particular to wisdom. Moral wisdom is the arena most appropriate for the encounter between different religions and the field that provides legitimacy for other religions.[51]

Considering the categories of wisdom and Torah in and of themselves makes us realize that the distinction between Torah and wisdom is not as clear-cut as it appears. In the case of Jewish Scripture, the wisdom in the third part of the tripartite Hebrew Bible is considered to be part of revelation, even if the mechanism through which this revelation came about is of a lower order.[52]

---

[50] *Lamentations Rabbah* 2: 13.

[51] This understanding could find support in the reading of Me'iri that highlights morality as the criterion for legitimacy of religions.

[52] See Sid Z. Leiman, *The Canonization of Hebrew Scripture: The Talmudic and Midrashic Evidence* (Hamden, Conn., 1976), 169–70 nn. 293–4.

Moreover, the words of wisdom of the sages of the Oral Torah are simultaneously recognized as wisdom and as an expression of revelation. The sages did not simply pass on the Oral Torah handed down at Sinai. They actually created it through their interpretative efforts and their own wisdom. Therefore, the boundary between wisdom and revelation is not as sharp as we may have thought. Accordingly, the precedent of sages who provide through their own minds and consciousnesses an expression for continuing revelation may even provide a precedent for the appreciation of sages from other religious traditions. Can they too not reveal the divine through their own expressions of wisdom, even without the express and visible revelation of God in ways as dramatic as the revelation of the Torah at Sinai?

Restoring lost revelation. A unique strategy for addressing the issue of revelation in relation to other religions was mentioned above in relation to Abraham Maimonides. One cannot dissociate the historical revelation particular to Israel from the particular history that ensues from that revelation. Receiving revelation and remaining faithful to it are not one and the same. In principle, it is possible that revelation was received but lost or became otherwise impaired, and the gap created thereby may be filled by other religions. Other religions may have received their own autonomous revelations or may have drawn from our own original revelation. One way or another, encounter with other religions can appeal to the image of an ideal revelation, as distinct from the concrete historical expression of Judaism as we know it. Thus, Abraham Maimonides considers all perfection to have been contained in our ideal revelation, even while its actual contents may need to be recovered from those who learned from us what we over time forgot. This strategy permits us to relate to a concrete historical religious Other, including its positive and edifying expressions, without detracting from revelation remembered in its ideal perfection. The attitude expressed here is one of profound humility. Willingness to learn from another religious tradition not only expresses the fundamental humility that is part and parcel of true religious life, but more particularly it humbly acknowledges the historical circumstances particular to the Jewish people, including their sin and its consequences. Abraham Maimonides developed a spiritual attitude that contains a kind of pluralistic depth—one that may be termed historical pluralism and that is distinct from the more common metaphysical pluralism.

SAFEGUARDING JEWISH IDENTITY AND CONTINUITY IN THE FACE OF WORLD RELIGIONS

Concern for Jewish continuity and identity is not a philosophical problem. It is a religious problem, inasmuch as Israel's identity, nationhood, and continuity are all seen as part of the covenant and, hence, as primary components of Judaism and Jewish life. Dealing with this concern is therefore less a matter of philosophical speculation and more a matter of psychological and educational sensitivity. The experience of thousands of years of competition with other religions, including religious persecution and the threat of conversion by force or social circumstances, has created in Jews a great suspicion of other religions. This attitude is responsible for the erection of barriers to protect Judaism from the harmful influences that contact with other religions might have. Many Jews feel that such barriers help maintain Jewish identity, preserving its integrity and the continuity of Jewish life. Concern for Jewish continuity has only intensified in the modern and postmodern periods. To a large extent, it defines the agenda of public Jewish life. Yet it is precisely the changed circumstances in which Jews tackle the problem that raise the question of whether upholding attitudinal barriers to other religions is today part of the problem or part of the solution. Do the attitudinal barriers provide walls of protection, or have the sheep already leaped over the fence, leaving only the shepherds of old within its confines?

I would like to explore the possibility that controlled openness to other religions, when practised by mature and well-informed members of the Jewish community, may not only not weaken Jewish identity, but might actually enhance it. I make the argument in three ways.

The first has to do with the community one serves and how to reach it. The protective tendency is characteristic of certain communities within the Jewish world, particularly the Orthodox and ultra-Orthodox. Other Jews already have various encounters with other religions and their members. Increasingly, members of the Orthodox world, especially young Israelis, have gone beyond the boundaries of their tradition's previous encounters with other traditions. This is true of the broad turning to the East, but not exclusive to it. Sizeable sectors of the Jewish community are seeking an authentic Jewish life that is not defined by the walls erected to keep out other groups. A Jewish theology of world religions that does not enshrine boundaries as the hallmark of a Jewish approach to other religions will attract large sectors of Jewish society. One who reflects positively and constructively on other religions will gain access to the hearts and minds of Jews who have been fascinated by or drawn to them.

There is a more principled way of arguing the case. Strengthening identity by maintaining boundaries is to resort to an extreme form of negative identity formation. In other words, I am myself because I am different from you. Upholding that difference reinforces identity. In this instance, the difference is upheld by maintaining boundaries that preclude any sharing of common religious ground, thereby reinforcing the sense of otherness. I have seen time and again how other religions have become straw men in the religious imagination of educators. They imagine other religions as certain stereotypes, against which Judaism is judged superior. The argument for Judaism's superiority, hence for the loyalty of the student, is made by characterizing the other religion—most often Christianity—facilely and ignoring nuance, development, and the real spiritual lives of that religion's believers.

Engagement with other religions serves as an antidote to such conventional practices in one of two ways. First, the imagined differences give way to real differences, thereby bringing into relief who the two partners in the dialogue really are and what might justify their continuing differences. Living with an imaginary Other can be the source of a future crisis, when we discover the Other in his or her reality. Recognizing real differences is more respectful to one's own self and to the actual Other. But there is a far more significant consequence of encounter with the real, rather than the imaginary, Other. It forces us to articulate positively why we are what we are, rather than as just different from the imaginary Other. In terms of identity formation, it is far superior to base one's Jewish identity on positive grounds than to justify one's Jewish existence as being unlike others. Of course, positive identity formation does not require the presence of an Other. However, the encounter with the Other does force us to deepen our own understanding of Jewish religious identity, thereby shifting it from negative to positive grounds. According to this line of reasoning, openness to the Other can point the way to healthier and more meaningful identity building.

The third argument is based on experience and reinforces the previous suggestions. I offer it as a testimony that has grown out of over a decade of organizing interreligious educational programmes, geared towards religious leaders, future religious leaders, and other educated representatives of religions. I discovered early on that the effect of encountering a religious Other is not the weakening of one's identity, but the contrary, its strengthening. Time and again I have found that students did not feel threatened by an encounter with members of other religions but rather felt called upon to deepen their own religious lives and discover depths in them that were previously unknown to them. While the opposite effect obviously remains a theoretical possibility, the reality has consistently not been that feared for generations. To a large extent, this seems built into the dynamics of contemporary interreligious encounter, which are fundamentally different from those that governed the encounter in earlier periods. Thus on the theoretical level and the experiential level as well, we find interreligious encounter inspiring and strengthening identity, not weakening it.

This testimony brings us back to the question of religious truth and its centrality, or otherwise, to religious identity. I am sure that someone who is reinforced in his or her religious belief through relationship with a member of another religion has not, through that encounter, discovered that his or her religion is truer than previously thought. Encounter exposes one to deeper existential and experiential dimensions of what it means to be religious. Experience and encounter enliven our faith, rather than reinforcing our truth claims. An exchange of faith is not a debate about what is true. It is carried out in a different relational framework and with different aims. The fruit of the encounter is appreciating faith in the life of the believer, rather than faith as a set of religious affirmations and beliefs demanding recognition as being more true than those of the other. Ultimately, truth and falsehood are not where the most important spiritual movements take place. The realm of faith, while related to the cognitive dimension of truth, draws on deeper and more complex dimensions in the human person. These are awakened in the interreligious encounter at its best. Interreligious dialogue thus understood is more a dialogue of the faithful than a dialogue about faith and its veracity. This is why, in my view, the benefits to religious identity emerging from it far outweigh the potential harm to identity that it might bring about.

Encounter with another faith is just that, encounter. It is not a competition of ideas or a philosophical debate. Because it is an encounter, it involves those dimensions of the person that are affected through encounter. It touches emotions as much as ideas. Indeed, opposition to it often draws on emotional patterns that have long informed Jewish attitudes to other religions. These emotional patterns cannot be parried effectively by arguments or testimonies about the positive benefits of encounter and why it does not constitute a threat to identity. Dealing with these emotional charges is a work unto itself. It involves studying and understanding the changes that have occurred and continue to occur in other religions, primarily Christianity, in relation to Judaism. Like any human relationship it requires healing, understanding, and forgiveness. Religious identity built over and against the identity of the Other is an identity built on pain and its enduring memory. Negativity and pain are often building blocks of Jewish identity, while healing of memory is one possible outcome of true encounter. This healing paves the way to the construction of Jewish identity on firmer, more spiritual grounds than those of painful memory and the walls of separation they have built. Instead I argue that if we are to be successful in our attempt to construct Jewish identity in a way that will ensure Jewish continuity, we need to discover identity grounded in the spiritual uniqueness of Israel's vocation. The way to such discovery includes dealing with and going beyond those forms of identity construction that have made suffering, difference, and competition the cornerstones of Jewish identity.

CONCLUSION: TOWARDS A JEWISH THEOLOGY OF WORLD RELIGIONS AND DISCOVERING OUR OWN IDENTITY

This chapter has examined the development of a contemporary Jewish theology of world religions in broad strokes, raising core issues and suggesting basic strategies. Implicit throughout is the idea that both historically and theoretically there is a wealth of precedents, options, and possibilities from which Jews can choose and in light of which a Jewish theology of religions—ultimately Judaism's own theology—must be carried out. This multiplicity of options exists diachronically, throughout Jewish history, and synchronically, in the many positions that exist in our times, as in others. We are thus called to choose.

Our choice is not simply one of how to act on a day-to-day basis. Properly speaking, day-to-day questions belong to the realm of tolerance, to the social and political realm of coexistence. A theology of religions makes us think what deeper acceptance and recognition of the Other might mean. One consequence of genuine acceptance is the willingness to learn from the Other and recognize expressions of spiritual reality in one's life that can provide inspiration also to those beyond the Other's religion. Our choice thus touches upon fundamental theological and spiritual matters. Its implications are broader than the development of an appropriate attitude to other religions.

The key questions of our discussion touch upon the most fundamental ways that we understand Judaism. The tension between the national and the religious dimensions of Judaism comes up repeatedly as a defining issue in a theology of world religions. There are different emphases on how inward Judaism is, a path guiding a particular people along its historical journey, or how broad it is in its vision, providing meaning for humanity, setting its proper sights, and establishing its eschatological hopes. Our own view of other religions is a function of how we view Judaism and how we view our place in history. We are thus challenged to an authentic and unbiased assessment of our own spiritual standing. The challenge of a Jewish theology of world religions is thus an internal theological challenge, no less than a challenge presented by contemporary history and circumstances. Because it is, above all, an internal spiritual challenge, we must undertake the task with utmost seriousness. Seen this way, the theological challenge at hand is a key to the theological and spiritual regeneration that we so badly need.

PART I

PHILOSOPHICAL PERSPECTIVES ON JEWISH PLURALISM

ONE

Jewish Views of World Religions
Four Models

ALAN BRILL
with Rori Picker Neiss

THEOLOGY of religions is a growing discipline within the broader context of Christian theology, and Jews sometimes wonder whether Judaism has a theology, let alone a theology of religions. Judaism possesses both, and when viewed historically, Jews have rich resources that they can use to reflect on other religions and to construct contemporary theologies of other religions. The goal of this chapter is to introduce a range of traditional sources bearing on the question of the theological relationship between Judaism and other religions.

While the discussion of other religions has characterized Judaism in some way since its very formation, this discussion has particular value in the present circumstances, both practically and theoretically. In practical terms, it serves the growing field of interfaith relations by providing a framework for understanding relations between religions. In theoretical terms, it enables Jews to benefit from recent insights and approaches developed by the discipline of theology of religions. This chapter seeks to examine a wide variety of Jewish texts in the light of categories originally developed in the framework of a Christian theology of religions. I will focus on four categories (inclusivist, universalist, pluralist, and exclusivist,) and will analyse traditional Jewish sources within their framework.

Alan Race first suggested the above categories in 1982. Their popularization in the writings of the British philosopher of religion John Hick (b. 1922) led to their wide use in the field of theology over the past twenty-five years.[1] This is their first extended application to a wide variety of Jewish opinions, and even as I apply them first to Judaism, they have begun to reach their limits of usefulness and have already attracted criticism. Some critics have noted that, in

---

[1] Alan Race, *Christians and Religious Pluralism: Patterns in the Christian Theology of Religions* (Maryknoll, NY, 1983); John Hick, *God Has Many Names* (London, 1980). Readable summaries are provided by Paul F. Knitter, *Introducing Theologies of Religions* (Maryknoll, NY, 2002); Veli-Matti Kärkkäinen, *An Introduction to the Theology of Religion: Biblical, Historical, and Contemporary Perspectives* (Downers Grove, Ill., 2004).

practice, theologians rarely fit neatly into one of the categories. Only philosophers who construct their theories a priori can fit totally into a single category. Theologians, who work with the complexity of textual traditions and social circumstances, cannot be thus restricted, and lived communities of faith can never operate in a single mode. Some thinkers will be included in one, two, three, or all four categories.

1. **Inclusivism: one religion is best but weaker forms of religious truth can exist in other religions.** Inclusivism acknowledges that many communities possess their own traditions and truths, but maintains the importance of one's comprehension as culminating, subsuming, or perfecting all other truths. One's own group possesses the truth, but inclusivists believe that truth, wisdom, and even revelation can be found in other religions.

2. **Universalism: the truth is one.** Universalism is the midpoint between inclusivism and pluralism, where one acknowledges that the universal truths of God, soul, intellect, and ethics have been made available by God to all people. This is usually a God-centred approach, in which the theism transcends the other elements of religion.

3. **Pluralism: all major world religions have truth.** Religious pluralism accepts that no one tradition can claim to possess the singular truth. All groups' beliefs and practices are equally valid, when interpreted within their own culture. Thus, no one religion is inherently better than or superior to any other major world religion. For pluralists, there may be differences in rituals and beliefs among these groups, but on the most important issues, there is great similarity. Most religions, pluralists claim, stress love for God and have a form of the Golden Rule.

4. **Exclusivism: there is only one true religion.** Exclusivism claims that one's own community, tradition, and encounter with God comprise the one and only exclusive truth; all other claims about encountering God are false a priori. There is *only* one way to God and salvation. Thus one religion is uniquely and supremely true and all other religions are false. Those who accept exclusivism usually affirm that other religions possess some elements of wisdom, but these religions do not teach 'the truth' of salvation, and revelation.

These four models will serve as a matrix within which to view positions that Jews articulated throughout Jewish history. I will present each of these in turn, mentioning some figures associated with each model and concentrating in each case on one specific figure who illustrates the thinking typical of that model.[2]

---

[2] These issues are treated in greater detail in Alan Brill, *Judaism and Other Religions: Models of Understanding* (New York, 2010). Discussion of individual figures and their thoughts can be found there.

THE INCLUSIVIST MODEL

Inclusivism sees other faiths as included within Jewish concepts, especially the philosophical-monotheistic concept of God. This theological monotheism allowed Jews to treat the philosophical first cause, the god of Plato and Aristotle, Christian Trinitarians, and all other people of faith, as one essential, unique God, even though these non-Jewish believers may have had an incorrect view of his attributes. This inclusivism works because medieval Jewish thinkers understood the Bible as teaching a doctrine of philosophical monotheism (for example, they understood Isaiah's vision of God's providence as a cosmological argument). In addition, inclusivism can view other religions as derived from Jewish concepts of revelation, ethics, or messianism. For inclusivists, knowledge of these ideas was spread by Judaism's daughter religions, Christianity and Islam.

From an inclusivist perspective, other religions are explained by one's own religion: one may acknowledge a world beyond one's own, but must rely on one's own world-view to make it comprehensible and give it meaning. An inclusivist speaks the language of his or her own theology and uses its vocabulary to describe outsiders. Sometimes, the inclusivist finds language in the other religion to help explain it and make it understood by a wider audience. An inclusivist allows any real adherent of any of the great religions to be already informed of the word of God by finding a common denominator such as monotheism or a moral code.

A number of post-Vatican II Catholic theologians have tended to follow this approach, accepting that God is God for all people, and other religions can give witness or fulfil aspects of one's own religion. There is one basis for religious fulfilment but several means of access. For the inclusivist, God is concerned not just with one faith but also with members of other religions. The other religions have a real encounter with the divine and have some connection to monotheism, revelation, and redemption.

Jewish inclusivism affirms the uniqueness of Judaism, like Jewish exclusivism, but rejects the idea that non-Jews lack religion. One can, however, still acknowledge that there are differences from Judaism in some essential theological points and even consider their views mistaken. Yet one can attribute these mistakes to social, cultural, and historical circumstances or think that non-Jews have distorted the truth but nevertheless they have some of it.

Inclusivists are able to appreciate the general aspects of ethics, mission, the search for God, and revelation in other faiths, but they bracket out the other religion's views of ritual, festivals, and theology. For some, inclusivism is seen as colonial and liberal in that it forces the other religion into the cultural and linguistic norms of one's own. One only sees the good from one's own perspective and not from that of the other religion. A philosophical problem for the inclusivist position is its creation of a wedge between the ontological and the epistemological, between seeing the world as a multiplicity of religions and explaining them according to one's particular perspective.

The inclusivist position can be subdivided into four categories. The first uses a lens of historical mission in which knowledge of God and his will plays itself out in the wider world of other religions. Judah Halevi, Maimonides, Nahmanides, Jacob Emden, Samson Raphael Hirsch, and Abraham Isaac Kook all look to biblical history where other nations play a role in the unfolding of God's plan.[3] In the second variation, non-Jewish religion finds its place in the metaphysical realm, where all references to God must point to the one true God. Other religions are seen as binding themselves to metaphysical realms, though on a lower level than the relationship found in Judaism. David Kimhi, Joseph Gikitilla, and the Zohar take this metaphysical approach.[4] The third view makes the acceptance of Mosaic revelation the dividing line between faiths. It assumes that all knowledge, morals, and law come solely from Sinai (broadly defined) and that other religions are derived from them. Solomon ben Aderet and Isaac Arama speak of revelation in these terms.[5] Finally, the fourth category

---

[3] On Halevi, see below. For Maimonides, see *Guide of the Perplexed*; id., *Teshuvot harambam*, ed. Joshua Blau (Jerusalem, 1960); additionally, there is a large literature on Maimonides' attitude towards other religions, including David Novak, *Maimonides on Judaism and Other Religions* (Cincinnati, 1997); Gerald Blidstein, 'The Status of Islam in Maimonidean Halakhah', in *Studies in Halakhic and Aggadic Thought* (Be'er Sheva, 2004), 237–47; Yosef Kapah, 'Islam and the Relation to Muslims in Maimonides' Teachings' (Heb.), *Mahanayim*, 1 (1992), 16–23; A. Hacohen, 'Islam and its Believers' (Heb.), *Mahanayim*, 1 (1992), 41–5; A. Sloshberg, 'The Relationship of Maimonides to Islam' (Heb.), *Pa'amim*, 42 (1990), 42–5; Howard Kreisel, 'Maimonides on Christianity and Islam', in Ronald A. Brauner (ed.), *Jewish Civilization: Essays and Studies* (Philadelphia, 1985), iii. 153–62. See Nahmanides, *Writings and Discourses*, ed. Charles Chavel (New York, 1978); Jacob Emden, *Seder olam rabah vezuta* (for the full Hebrew text of Emden's treatise on Christianity with the eighteenth-century discussions, see the superb new critical edition by Lior Gottlieb, 'The Breaking of Those who Lead Astray by Rabbi Jacob Emden, First and Second Editions, with Introduction, Textual Comparisons, and Explanatory Notes' (Heb.), in Binyamin Ish-Shalom and Amihai Berholts (eds.), *On the Paths of Peace: Studies in Jewish Thought, Presented to Shalom Rosenberg* [Bedarkhei shalom: iyunim behagut yehudit, mugashim leshalom rosenberg] (Jerusalem, 2007), 295–321; see also Moshe Miller, 'Rabbi Jacob Emden's Attitude Toward Christianity', in Michael A. Shmidman (ed.), *Turim: Studies in Jewish History and Literature: Presented to Dr. Bernard Lander* (New York, 2007), 105–36); Samson Raphael Hirsch, *The Pentateuch*, trans. Isaac Levy (Gateshead, 1989), on Num. 29: 13; id., 'Talmudic Judaism and Society', in *Principles of Education* (New York, 1991); Abraham Isaac Kook, *Letters of the Ra'ayah* [Igerot hara'ayah] (Jerusalem, 1985); id., *Clouds of Purity* [Arpelei tohar] (Jerusalem, 1993).

[4] See David Kimhi, *Commentary on Isaiah*, 159: 7; Joseph Gikitilla, *Gates of Light*, trans. Avi Weinstein (San Francisco, 1994); Zohar i. 13*a*, ii. 84*a*, iii. 161*b*, iii. 215*a*.

[5] Solomon ben Aderet, *Teshuvot harashba*, ed. Haim Z. Dimitrovsky (Jerusalem, 1990), 162–4; see also Harvey J. Hames, *The Art of Conversion: Christianity and Kabbalah in the Thirteenth Century* (Leiden, 2000). Isaac Arama, *Akedat yitshak* (Tel Aviv, 1960), gates 60 and 70; see also his com-

of inclusivism is humanistic and theocentric, in which there is a divine concern for humanity as the image of God. Obadiah Seforno looks to the image of God possessed by all members of humanity.[6] Below is a more extensive look at the historical mission viewpoint of Judah Halevi.

Judah Halevi

Judah Halevi (*c.*1075–1141), the twelfth-century heir to Spanish philosophical and poetic traditions, wrote a defence of Judaism called *A Treatise in Defence of a Despised Tradition*, popularly known as the *Kuzari*. The opening of Halevi's book takes the form of a fictitious dialogue between a Jew, a Muslim, and a Christian, each of whom attempts to convince a pagan king of the truth of his own religion. Halevi used a discussion of other religions as a means of formulating his own Jewish theology.

In defending the Jewish tradition, Halevi emphasizes that God relates to all people, yet he singled out Judaism as central. Halevi likens this centrality to the heart in a body or to the trunk of a tree.

Israel among the nations is like a heart among the organs of the body. It is the healthiest, as well as the one most prone to disease. As the verse states, 'Only you have I known from all of the families of the earth; therefore shall I punish you for your iniquities' [Amos 3: 2].[7]

God has a secret and wise design concerning the Jewish people. This may be compared to a seed that falls to the ground, where it undergoes external transformation through its contact with earth, water, and dung, until it is virtually unrecognizable. However, it is the seed itself that transforms earth and water to its own substance, carrying them from one level to another until it refines these elements and transmutes them to its own form. The [plant] casts off its husks and leaves to reveal a heart that has been purified and refined and is fit to bear fruit like itself.

Similarly, all religions that came after the Torah of Moses are part of the process of bringing humanity closer to the essence of Judaism, even though they appear its opposite. The nations serve to introduce and pave the way for the long-awaited messiah. He is the fruit and they, in turn, will all become his fruit when they acknowledge Him. Then all nations will become one tree, recognizing the common root they had previously scorned.[8]

For Halevi, Israel is a chosen people who transform the world. Employing a

ments on Exod. 12: 1; Deut. 4: 35, 26: 1, where it might be implied that 'Israel' means any *tsadik* whether of Jewish or gentile origin. See also Charles Touati, 'Le Christianisme dans la théologie juive', *Revue des Études Juives*, 160 (2001), 495–7; Leopold Zunz, *Das gedachtniss der Gerechten in Geschichte und Literatur* (Berlin, 1919), 371–89.

[6] See Obadiah ben Jacob Seforno, *Commentary on the Bible* (Jerusalem, 1980), esp. Exod. 19: 5–6; Deut. 33: 3.

[7] Judah Halevi, *Kuzari*, 2: 36 (trans. Hartwig Hirschfeld (New York, 1905)).

[8] Ibid. 4: 23.

metaphor from nature, he claims that other religions share a common root of Judaism; all religions are of the same tree with Judaism as the trunk. These other religions are not needed for Jews to understand their obligations from Mosaic prophecy, but not to recognize the nature of branch religions is to fail to properly understand the world and, in effect, God's providential plan.

Many misread Halevi's position as arguing for the exclusive uniqueness of Judaism and the corollary falseness of other religions, implying that Jews have the truth and others are completely wrong. As the passage given earlier shows, however, Halevi does not deny the importance of other religions; he merely notes that the other religions are mere limbs on the trunk of Judaism. Eventually, all will bear fruit on a single tree. His example demonstrates that openness to other religions does not preclude finding a place for them within one's system even if it includes rejecting part of non-Jewish theologies, nor does it prevent understanding non-Jews in one's own inclusivist terms.

It is important to note that, for Halevi, the base of the trunk, and the fountain of all true revelation, is Mosaic faith, not Abrahamic faith. The nations of the world are all part of the divine plan and not bereft of historical providence. Other religions will be reintegrated into the biblical vision at the end of days.

Halevi limits prophecy to Judaism, but that does not preclude the availability of some form of natural revelation to all. His book *Kuzari* opens with a story of a non-Jewish king getting inspiration from God through a dream and thereby, through his search, coming to learn of the higher Mosaic revelation.[9] True dreams and divine inspiration are available to all faiths as general revelations, while the special revelation of Sinai, prophecy, was only available to Jews.

Although Halevi recognizes the quest for God in other religions and their purpose in the divine scheme, he still rejects ideas in other religions that he deems incorrect. Halevi rejects the Christian doctrines of the Virgin Birth, the Incarnation, and the Trinity as not based on logic, without rejecting the common core that Judaism and Christianity share in their belief in the God of the Bible.[10] This understanding of other faiths using the categories of one's own and the acceptance and rejection of parts of other religions illustrates the entire inclusivist position.

Inclusivism allows a commitment to one's own texts and theology, but still acknowledges other faiths. Inclusivism as a natural theology can point to the

[9] On the ability of non-Jews to receive revelation provided a distinction is made between prophetic and ordinary revelation, see Robert Eisen, 'The Problem of the King's Dream and Non-Jewish Prophecy in Judah Halevi's "Kuzari" ', *Journal of Jewish Thought and Philosophy*, 3/2 (1994), 231–47; see also Charles Manekin, 'Hierarchy and Race in the Thought of Judah Ha-Levy', in B. C. Bazán, E. Andújar, and L. G. Sbrocchi (eds.), *Les Philosophies morales et politiques au Moyen Âge / Moral and Political Philosophies in the Middle Ages*, Proceedings of the Ninth International Congress of Medieval Philosophy, Ottawa, 17–22 August 1992 (Ottawa, 1995).

[10] Halevi, *Kuzari*, 1: 5.

commonalities between religions in belief in one God and prophetic know-ledge. As historical theology it can fit Christianity and Islam into a Noahide, Abrahamic, or Mosaic context; as an approach to seeking the mystical light of the divine, it allows an understanding of the common quest while preserving a sense of uniqueness. Some may find the inclusivist approach too paternalistic and others may find it too universal, but its importance lies in its overcoming the simple dichotomy between exclusiveness and pluralism, thereby forcing Jewish thinkers to formulate a subtle middle position.

THE UNIVERSALIST MODEL

Over the centuries, many Jewish thinkers have embraced an approach in which the universalism of the prophets is joined with the philosophical monotheism of the Middle Ages. They accept a universal truth available to all humanity, beyond revelation but not against it. In universalism there is no need to refer to Judaism as the single truth; rather, all knowledge is grounded in a higher divine knowledge, or in a unified sense of rationality, or in the natural abilities of the mind and soul. At times, this approach blurs the line between religion and philosophy or between religion and ethics. However, religious universal-ists remain close to the inclusivists in that everything is grounded in the teach-ings of Judaism.

This category does not exist in the standard Christian typology since histor-ically Christian theology required salvation only through Christ. By contrast, medieval Jewish philosophers could freely accept a God greater than any one religion, especially since some Islamic philosophers held a similar position.

This universal monotheism is found in Sa'adiah Gaon, Solomon ibn Gabirol, Abraham ibn Ezra, some Maimonideans, and the poets Immanuel of Rome and Judah Abarbanel.[11] Even more universal, Nethanael ibn al-Fayyumi offers a unique position that allows for a universal potential of revelation.[12] The beginning of the modern era witnessed a shift to a rationalist universalism by Moses Mendelssohn[13] and a moral universalism from thinkers such as Israel

[11] See Raymond P. Scheindlin, *The Gazelle: Medieval Hebrew Poems on God, Israel, and the Soul* (Philadelphia, 1991); Aaron Hughes, *The Texture of the Divine: Imagination in Medieval Islamic and Jewish Thought* (Bloomington, 2004); Maimonides, *Guide of the Perplexed*, i. 36; Fabian Alfie, 'Immanuel of Rome, alias Manoello Giudeo: The Poetics of Jewish Identity in Fourteenth-Century Italy', *Italica*, 75/3 (Fall 1998), 307–29; Aaron W. Hughes, 'Transforming the Maimonidean Imagination: Aesthetics in the Renaissance Thought of Judah Abravanel', *Harvard Theological Review*, 97/4 (2004), 461–84; Judah Abarbanel, *The Philosophy of Love (Dialoghi d'Amore)*, trans. F. Friedeberg-Seeley and Jean H. Barnes (London, 1937).

[12] See D. Levene, *The Garden of Wisdom* (New York, 1907), ch. 6.

[13] See Moses Mendelssohn, *Selections from his Writings*, ed. and trans. Eva Jospe (New York, 1975); id., *Jerusalem and Other Jewish Writings*, ed. and trans. Alfred Jospe (New York, 1969); Zvi Jonathan Kaplan, 'Mendelssohn's Religious Perspective of Non-Jews', *Journal of Ecumenical Studies*, 41/3 (2004), 355–66.

Lipschutz, Samuel David Luzzatto, and Mendel Hirsch.[14] Other thinkers in the age of discovery, such as Menasseh ben Israel, Elijah Benamozegh, Henry Pereira-Mendes, and Joseph Hertz, presented a historical universalism of a lost truth from Adam that makes itself manifest in cultural diversity.[15] Below is an in-depth look at a universal monotheism developed in the Middle Ages by Sa'adiah Gaon.

Sa'adiah Gaon

Sa'adiah Gaon (882–942) was a leading rabbi and early medieval Jewish philosopher whose *Book of Beliefs and Opinions* (*Sefer emunot vede'ot*) set the parameters for the Jewish philosophical tradition by employing the Islamic strategy of freely using Platonic, Aristotelian, and Stoic texts to produce a rational Jewish theology. As befits a classical philosopher, Sa'adiah presents religion as a universal phenomenon and accepts a type of religious truth transcending Judaism.

In the introduction to his book, after discussing empirical, rational, and deductive sources of knowledge, which are all clearly universal, he states:

As for ourselves, the community of monotheists, we hold these three sources of knowledge to be genuine. To them, however, we add a fourth source . . . the validity of authentic tradition . . . This type of knowledge . . . corroborates for us the validity of the first three sources of knowledge.[16]

In other words, people can rationally attain a universal knowledge of the monotheistic God. Revelation and tradition serve to corroborate this rational

[14] See Israel Lipschutz, *Tiferet yisra'el* to *Avot*; Marc Gopin, 'An Orthodox Embrace of Gentiles? Interfaith Tolerance in the Thought of S. D. Luzzatto and E. Benamozegh', *Modern Judaism*, 18 (1998), 176; Noah H. Rosenbloom, *Luzzatto's Ethico-Psychological Interpretation of Judaism: A Study in the Religious Philosophy of Samuel David Luzzatto* (New York, 1965); Samson Raphael Hirsch, *The Nineteen Letters*, trans. Bernard Drachman (New York, 1942), letter 15; Mendel Hirsch, *Judaism and Humanism* (London, 1928), repr. in Jacob Breuer, *Fundamentals of Judaism: Selections from the Works of Rabbi Samson Raphael Hirsch and Outstanding Torah-True Thinkers* (New York, 1949), 167–79.

[15] See Menasseh ben Israel, *The Conciliator* (London, 1842); Aimé Pallière, *The Unknown Sanctuary* (New York, 1928); Elijah Benamozegh, *Israel and Humanity*, trans. Maxwell Luria (Mahwah, NJ, 1995); Henry Pereira-Mendes, 'Orthodox or Historical Judaism', in Walter R. Houghton (ed.), *Neely's History of the Parliament of Religions* (Chicago, 1894), 217–18, repr. in Richard Hughes Seager (ed.), *The Dawn of Religious Pluralism: Voices from the World's Parliament of Religions* (La Salle, Ill., 1993), 328–30. One should also note Henry Pereira-Mendes's *The Jewish Religion Ethically Presented* (New York, 1905), in which he presents twenty-one objections to contemporary Christian practice followed by a statement wishing that Christians would return to the religion of Jesus himself. He was also against the ecumenical trends in Reform Judaism that blurred their distinction from Unitarians. See also Joseph H. Hertz, *Pentateuch and Haftorahs* (London, 1963), 103, 759.

[16] Sa'adiah Gaon, *The Book of Beliefs and Opinions*, Introduction, §5 (trans. Samuel Rosenblatt (New Haven, 1948), 16).

knowledge of God.[17] Following the Kalam, the Islamic theological arguments for creation and the unity of God that apply to Islam and Christianity as well as Judaism, Sa'adiah could not have denied the monotheistic nature of Islam nor that of Christianity, since they accept the God of creation with the attributes of life, power, and knowledge.[18] According to Raphael Jospe, Sa'adiah's argument with the Christian doctrine of the Trinity follows his discussion of essential attributes, not his refutation of dualism and polytheism, and therefore implies contextually that Christianity is not polytheistic, but an incorrect form of monotheism. Moreover, when discussing believers in the Trinity, Sa'adiah refers to 'the communities of the monotheists'.[19]

Sa'adiah's 'community of monotheists' is also used by later Jewish philosophers. For example, in his pietistic work *Duties of the Heart*, Bahya ibn Pakuda (eleventh century, Spain) refers to 'the people of monotheism', where the distinction is not between Jew and non-Jew, but between varying degrees of comprehension among people who affirm God's unity.[20] Halevi also refers to 'monotheists' in a non-Jewish context, when the Christian says to the Khazar king: 'For we are truly monotheists, although the Trinity appears on our tongues.'[21] In Maimonides' *Guide of the Perplexed*, 'we, the community of true monotheists' refers to those who have a correct philosophical understanding of the divine attributes.[22]

The universal positions within Judaism have been considered marginal in most narratives of Jewish identity. As a whole, these religious universalists, with their gaze on the oneness of God, differ sharply from pluralists, who consider all religions as diverse human constructs. Most Jewish universalists affirm that theism, ethics, and revelation can be known naturally. The important point to note is that there are medieval universalists. Indeed, this position did not have to wait until modernity. The Enlightenment position of Mendelssohn has common roots with prior universal thinkers like Sa'adiah Gaon. These positions can serve as an opening to discussions of the role of the universal in Judaism and how it differs from the pluralists discussed below.

---

[17] Raphael Jospe, 'The "Authentic Tradition" of Rabbi Sa'adiah Gaon: Who Are "The Community of the Monotheists"?' (Heb.), *Da'at*, 41 (Summer 1998), 5–17; Raphael Jospe, 'Additional Note', *Da'at*, 42 (Winter 1999), p. ix. He disagrees with Pines, who interprets 'the community of monotheists' exclusively as the Jews (Shlomo Pines, 'A Study of the Impact of Indian, Mainly Buddhist, Thought on Some Aspects of Kalam Doctrines', *Jerusalem Studies in Arabic and Islam*, 17 (1994), 182–203).

[18] Sa'adiah Gaon, *Book of Beliefs and Opinions*, 2: 5.

[19] Ibid., Introduction, §5 (trans. Rosenblatt, p. 16); see also Raphael Jospe in Chapter 3, below.

[20] Bahya ibn Pakuda, *Duties of the Heart* [Ḥovot halevavot], 1: 1–2.

[21] Halevi, *Kuzari*, 1: 4.

[22] Maimonides, *Guide of the Perplexed*, i. 53 (trans. Pines (Chicago, 1963), 122).

THE PLURALIST MODEL

Religious pluralism is a modern philosophical approach that accepts that one's religion is not the sole and exclusive source of truth. On the social level, this approach cherishes difference and diversity. Unlike universalists, who see the possibility for all to come to the same truth, pluralists stress the inadequate nature of any truth. Pluralism sees a universal truth available to all people as an impossibility, suggesting instead that each religion has limited access to truth.

Many people popularly use the term pluralist or the phrase 'religious pluralism' as synonyms for any encounter or openness to other faiths. In this definition of pluralism is a mistaken notion that approaching other religions is an either/or dichotomy of exclusivism or pluralism. If one rejects exclusivism then one must be a pluralist, and universal and inclusivist thinkers are considered to have set precedents for pluralism. Pluralists acknowledge that both moral and intellectual truths exist, but they cannot be accessed due to the limitations of the human mind. Pluralists actively distinguish themselves from relativists who deny any moral or intellectual truth. The pluralist recognizes that the great world religions have equally valid religious claims, and addresses others in their own language. There is no universal world court or absolute philosophy in which the rival truth claims could be adjudicated.

John Hick, who originally popularized the categories of exclusivist, inclusivist, and pluralist, accepts a philosophical pluralism that functions as a kind of a priori commitment to the *philosophia perennialis*, which claims that all religions are fundamentally the same, similar to the neo-Hindu model that there is a single Absolute behind the many religions. Hick rejects or radically revises divine revelation, creation, and miracles and considers most religious statements as myths or poetic expressions. For example, Sinai should be understood metaphorically. For his critics, Hick's insistence that all religions eventually abandon their claims to uniqueness and universality results not in interfaith dialogue, but rather in a roundtable of liberals where no actual religious card is ever laid on the table. Some judge this kind of tolerance as both patronizing and inauthentic.

Pluralism became more popular than universalism after 1987 when Hick and Paul Knitter gathered together in a single volume essays by many scholars who espoused the pluralist position.[23] There are three main types of pluralism: ethical, mystical, and epistemological. There are also two terms that are often used by twenty-first-century pluralists—difference and diversity. Epistemological pluralism states that there are limits to human knowledge and therefore we have to accept the truth of all religions. Ethical pluralism argues that all

[23] John Hick and Paul F. Knitter (eds.), *The Myth of Christian Uniqueness: Toward a Pluralistic Theology of Religions* (Maryknoll, NY, 1987).

ethical people are on the right path, and mystical pluralism contends that the encounter with God transcends any human categories. Moreover, difference is the acknowledgement that there are many approaches to religion, each to be tolerated and accepted without discrimination, while diversity is the acknowledgement that the each approach is valuable and desirable for the diversity of human life.

Many Jewish pluralist thinkers did not start out as pluralists. David Hartman began as a universalist and developed different forms of pluralism.[24] Raphael Jospe offers an ethical pluralist viewpoint.[25] Zalman Schachter-Shalomi represents the mystical pluralist approach.[26] Seeking an acceptance of diversity, Irving Greenberg shows how all faiths may each contribute to human dignity.[27] Elliot Dorff is a philosophical pluralist who denies the viability of metaphysical truth claims[28] and Jonathan Sacks seeks to defend difference and decries absolutes in an age of globalization with nods to moral and epistemological pluralism.[29] Michael Kogan's position, analysed in detail below, offers a Jewish version of the general philosophical pluralist position.

Michael Kogan

The pluralist position of many academic Christians starts with a universal quest for transcendence or the universal phenomena of religion, not the

[24] See David Hartman, 'On the Possibility of Religious Pluralism from a Jewish Viewpoint', *Immanuel*, 16 (1983), 101–13; id., *Conflicting Visions: Spiritual Possibilities of Modern Israel* (New York, 1990); id., *A Heart of Many Rooms* (Woodstock, Vt., 1999); id., 'Jewish and Christian in a World of Tomorrow', *Immanuel*, 6 (1976), 70–81; id., 'Judaism Encounters Christianity Anew', in Eugene Fisher (ed.), *Visions of the Other: Jewish and Christian Theologians Assess the Dialogue* (New York, 1994), 67–80.

[25] See Raphael Jospe, 'Pluralism Out of the Sources of Judaism: Religious Pluralism Without Relativism', *Studies in Christian–Jewish Relations*, 2 (2007), 92–113 (a revised version of this article is published as Chapter 3, below).

[26] See Zalman Schachter-Shalomi, 'Bases and Boundaries of Jewish, Christian, and Moslem Dialogue', <http://www.havurahshirhadash.org/rebzalmanarticle7.html>; id., 'Jesus in Jewish–Christian–Moslem Dialogue', <http://www.havurahshirhadash.org/rebzalmanarticle8.html>; Zalman Schachter-Shalomi and Netanel Miles-Yepez, *A Heart Afire: Stories and Teachings of the Early Hasidic Masters* (Philadelphia, 2009).

[27] See Irving Greenberg, *For the Sake of Heaven and Earth: The New Encounter between Judaism and Christianity* (Philadelphia, 2004); id., 'Theology after the Shoah: The Transformation of the Core Paradigm', *Modern Judaism*, 26 (2006), 213–39; id., 'Judaism and Christianity, Covenants of Redemption', in Tikva Frymer-Kensky, David Novak, Peter Ochs, David Fox Sandmel, and Michael A. Signer (eds.), *Christianity in Jewish Terms* (Boulder, Colo., 2000), 141–58.

[28] See Elliot N. Dorff, 'This Is My God: One Jew's Faith', in John Hick (ed.), *Three Faiths One God: A Jewish, Christian, Muslim Encounter* (Albany, NY, 1989), 7–29; id., *To Do the Right and the Good: A Jewish Approach to Modern Social Ethics* (Philadelphia, 2002).

[29] See Jonathan Sacks, *The Dignity of Difference: How to Avoid the Clash of Civilizations* (London, 2002); id., 'Exposition of the Hebrew Scriptures: The Relationship Between the People and God—the Covenant', <http://www.chiefrabbi.org/UploadedFiles/Articals/lambethconference28july08.pdf>; id., *To Heal a Fractured the World* (New York, 2005).

doctrine or experience of a given religion. Then and only then, after accepting
a plurality of positions, do they argue that since we have so much in common,
every religion—not only one's own religion—is just one of the many paths to
God.

Michael Kogan, a contemporary American academic, gives the Jewish reader
a version of this approach. Kogan's version has two parts: (1) that Judaism and
Christianity are similar and related in their teachings, and (2) that pluralism is
the approach Jews should take to all religions.

For Kogan, the stories of Judaism and Christianity 'are so closely related
that they represent two ways of expressing parallel redemptive concerns'.
The two faiths share the Bible, liturgy, ethics, and rhythms of daily life. Christianity as a continuity of the biblical message is but 'one form of Jewish outreach into the world'. Through Jesus' 'outreach, the gentiles come to share in
the covenant, and in the messianic, redemptive life of the people of God'.
Christianity is also the fruit of new divine initiative and revelation to open the
covenant to the world. Jews need therefore to accept Christianity as part of the
Jewish tradition and that Christians share in the promises of the Hebrew
Bible.[30]

Given that the two faiths are so closely related, Kogan asks the logical
question:

> How far can Jews and Christians go in affirming the faith of the other? . . . What we
> must be willing to do is to reevaluate our negative convictions. In altering our views
> of the other we recognize that both Judaism and Christianity have crucial roles to
> play in sacred history . . . Several church statements have affirmed that while
> Christianity needs Judaism for its self-understanding, Judaism can fully define itself
> without reference to Christianity. Not true! Since Christianity has been a conveyer
> of the word of Israel's God to the nations, it is impossible for Jews to understand
> their role as inheritors of the commission to Abraham while blinding themselves to
> the work among the nations of the church that shares that commission and that
> inheritance.[31]

Boldly, Kogan thinks that Judaism cannot be fully understood without taking
Christianity into account.

Kogan correctly notes how far he has come by stating that: 'for Jews, a new
understanding of Christians and Christianity will take them entirely beyond
the parameters of their rabbinic faith and biblical sources out of which it grew.
Jews never encounter the term "Christianity" in their biblical or rabbinic
studies', and these texts cannot be used to understand the present. Yet they can
help if we are willing to interpret classic texts anew in the light of the contem-

---

[30] Michael Kogan, *Opening the Covenant: A Jewish Theology of Christianity* (New York, 2008), 68.
[31] Ibid. 118.

porary situation. Modern Jews should develop a living and dynamic approach
to interfaith theology and start by asking questions afresh. Kogan credits the
great strides made in the past by Menahem Me'iri, Moses Mendelssohn,
Eliyahu Benamozegh, Martin Buber, Franz Rosenzweig, and the work of
Vatican II. He believes that they bequeath to us the continuing mandate to
make great strides in the future towards dialogue and acceptance.[32]

Kogan's second point is that human reality is greater than any of our religions or interpretations; therefore 'we cannot assume that we posses all truth'.
He rejects the claim that all religion is just human symbols, without a call from
God. Rather he follows Paul Knitter, the pluralistic theologian, who thinks
that 'religions are not human paths to God, but divine revelations to human
beings . . . God sends different revelations to different people at different
points in history.' Kogan seeks to follow the fragile religion of the poet Alfred
Tennyson, declaring that 'revelation is the breaking of the infinite into the
finite'. Hence, we need to grasp the echo of the infinite voice within our finite
religions; the divine initiative, not systems or dogma.[33]

Kogan concludes from his study that religious pluralism requires not only
mutual respect but ongoing mutual influence. A pluralistic theory of multiple
revelations means we need to learn from one another and share our limited
insights to gain a fuller understanding of the infinite God: 'If we Jews, with at
most 15 million people, insist that we are the only bearers of truth, not only
are we narrow and egocentric, we are indulging in a kind of theological
madness.' Hence Kogan advocates 'a plurality of pluralities' from within one's
own Jewish tradition. 'Each group's theology must recognize and make room
for the theologies of others.'[34] In order to make this mutual influence work,
Kogan believes there must be a universal ethic to judge the good from the bad
within religion and to avoid religion's ability to unleash the demonic.

Attempts to outline universal ideas of God, even those of medieval universalists, scare pluralists with the spectre of exclusivism. Those attempts create
a false dichotomy between sectarian withdrawal from society and engagement
through pluralism. In the end, pluralist approaches claim we all have our own
paths. This generous appreciation for diversity creates several problems for a
theology that seeks to encounter the other: (1) it leaves the other religion as a
personal decision, another path, unknown and unknowable; (2) it does not
define theologically what I see when I see the other; and (3) it does not delineate specific Jewish ideas from general religious ideas.

Jewish pluralists write that God has chosen Jews to walk the way of the
Torah, Christians to follow Christ, Hindus to be guided by the Vedas, and
Muslims to follow the way shown by the Quran. Does this statement express
a universal truth, obligatory to all, that should be accepted by non-Jews as well?

[32] Ibid. 168.　　　[33] Ibid. 176.　　　[34] Ibid. 183.

If so, then Jewish pluralism is a camouflaged universalism. It takes for granted that there is a God who chooses people to follow a path. This belief makes sense only on the grounds of biblical religions. Buddhists and Hindus would not recognize themselves in the statement. Maybe, as S. M. Heim claims, there are many different ultimate goals to which different religions guide people. The other religions may not be answering the same questions as Judaism.[35]

THE EXCLUSIVIST MODEL

Jewish exclusivism assumes that the sole domain of truth is the Torah and that Judaism is the only revealed religion. This differs from the traditional Christian use of the word exclusivism because it does not usually deny salvation to non-Jews. Instead, Jewish exclusivists limit discussion to acknowledging the merit of individual righteous non-Jews, but do not acknowledge the collective virtues in other religious groups.

For Jewish exclusivists, Judaism is the sole path to God; those who are not Jews follow a mistaken path and are at best bystanders in the divine scheme. At worst, they are antagonists. Exclusivist positions tend to be less philosophical than those of the inclusivists and are therefore by nature less universal. The texts recount various typological, and sometimes apocalyptic, struggles between Judaism and Rome. They rely on midrashic texts forged in historical experience, yet raise the ideas expressed therein to metaphysical abstraction.

For the exclusivist, other religions are simply false. There is no broader, outside world whose claims need to be harmonized and addressed; instead, there is only the realm of the 'other side'. Those who accept this position deny salvation to believers in other faiths and value to their religion. The exclusivist position has a broad spectrum of formulations, from emphasis on actually belonging ethnically or tribally to a given religion to giving special status to one's own beliefs.

The exclusivist position generally retains a high degree of urgency about reaching out to others. It is ontologically dependent on the unique elements of that religion, for example Christ in Christianity or halakhah in contemporary Orthodox Judaism. Truth and salvation are available solely through these unique elements. Exclusivism also has a strong sense of the reality of evil and a need to overcome it through the discipline of a specific religion.

The more extreme form of exclusivism is restrictivism, where salvation can only come from the explicit teaching and acceptance of the details of one religion. The restrictive perspective views religion as a small lifeboat, which can

---

[35] Piotr Sikora, 'Judaism Open to the Religions of the Nations: A Polish Catholic Theologian Reads an American Jewish Pluralist', <http://www.jcrelations.net/en/?item=2804>; S. Mark Heim, *The Depth of the Riches: A Trinitarian Theology of Religious Ends* (Grand Rapids, 2001).

only carry a few people, and God as only concerned with that small number of people. Even among exclusivists there is a tendency to recoil from these extremes. What of God's concern for humanity? Do we think that God limits his concern to a small percentage of the earth's people?

For the Jewish exclusivist, the universe is Judaeo-centric and other religions are irrelevant; at best we can speak of individual non-Jews as righteous and understand there is knowledge among the nations. Jews can judge doctrines based on Jewish criteria and even see an overlap with some ideas like monotheism or ethics, but the overlap remains the coincidental adaptation of acceptable Jewish ideas. We find the restrictive position among some halakhic approaches that require the non-Jew to submit formally and publicly to Judaism and enter into a semi-conversion to a separate religion of the seven Noahide laws as defined by the rabbis.

Jewish exclusivism splits the world around us into two groups: Jews and all others. Most of the time such a viewpoint remains a form of myopia, assuming that Jews are the only protagonists in the march of history.

Some early Jewish writers, such as Elazar Kalir and Rabbi Shelomoh Yitshaki (Rashi), include the debate about *verus Israel* (the true Israel) and their texts contain mockeries of Christianity.[36] Others, such as Rabbi Yehudah Loew (Maharal) and many hasidic texts, continue the rabbinic approach of viewing the non-Jew as the opposite of the Jew.[37] Some, such as Bar Hiya and Tsemah Duran, continue the apocalyptic eschatological visions found in the book of Ezekiel and suggest that non-Jews will be eradicated at the end of days.[38]

---

[36] See Morris Goldstein, *Jesus in the Jewish Tradition* (New York: Macmillian, 1950), 148–54; Leon J. Weinberger, *Jewish Hymnography: A Literary History* (London, 1998), 38; Gustaf Dalman, *Jesus Christ in the Talmud, Midrash, Zohar, and the Liturgy of the Synagogue* (Cambridge, 1893; repr. New York, 1973); Israel Jacob Yuval, *Two Nations in Your Womb: Perceptions of Jews and Christians in Late Antiquity and the Middle Ages* (Berkeley, Calif., 2006); S. J. D. Cohen, 'Does Rashi's Torah Commentary Respond to Christianity? A Comparison of Rashi with Rashbam and Bekhor Shor', in H. Najman and J. H. Newman (eds.), *The Idea of Biblical Interpretation: Essays in Honor of James L. Kugel* (Boston, 2004), 449–72; Elazar Touitou, 'Rashi's Commentary on Genesis 16 in the Context of Judeo–Christian Controversy', *Hebrew Union College Annual*, 61 (1990), 159–83; id., 'Rashi and his School: The Exegesis on the Halachic Part of the Pentateuch in the Context of the Judaeo-Christian Controversy', in Shimon Schwarzfuchs, Yvonne Friedman, and Bat-Sheva Albert (eds.), *Medieval Studies in Honor of Avrom Saltman*, Bar Ilan Studies in History 4 (Ramat Gan, 1995), 231–51; Menachem Klein, 'Rethinking Jew–Gentile Relations', <http://www.netivot-shalom.org.il/parshaeng/toledot5763.php>; Avraham Grossman, *Rashi* (Heb.) (Jerusalem, 2006).

[37] See Maharal on BT *San.* 21b; id., *Gevurat hashem*, 23; id., *Netsah yisra'el*, 25; id., *Be'er hagolah*, 7; id., *Kedushat levi vayehi*, cited in Or Rose, 'The Non-Jew in Hasidism: The Case of Levi Yitzhak of Berditchev' (unpublished manuscript); Zadok Hakohen, *Sefer mahshevot haruts*; id., *Poked akarim*, 19; on Rabbi Zadok, see Alan Brill, *Thinking God* (New York, 2002).

[38] See Abraham bar Hiyya Savasorda, *The Meditation of the Sad Soul*, ed. Geoffrey Wigoder (New York, 1968); Shimon ben Zemah Duran, 'Keshet U-Magen: A Critical Edition', Ph.D. thesis, trans. Prosper Murciano (New York University, 1975).

Some, like Naftali Zvi Yehudah Berlin (Netsiv), focus on the chosenness of the Jewish people, minimizing the righteous from among the nations.[39] And finally there are contemporary thinkers who reject non-Jews in order to maintain political and social isolationism. Rabbi Zvi Yehudah Kook, who is discussed below, is an example of a modern Jewish thinker who denied any truth to Christianity and whose views influenced those advocating political and social isolationism for the State of Israel.

Zvi Yehudah Kook

Rabbi Zvi Yehudah Kook (1891–1982), the son of Rabbi Abraham Isaac Kook, was blessed with a long life, many students, and a highly influential messianic theology. Kook claimed that the current era was a fulfilment of the biblical messianic prophecies of the return of the Jews to the Land of Israel. His theology served as part of a religious ideology for a greater Israel attained through battle, as in the time of the biblical King David. He was the ideological father of the settler movement and therefore influential in late twentieth-century Israeli political life.

The ideology itself is noteworthy for a staunch anti-Christianity that culls two millennia of sources without acknowledging any of the countervailing traditions. Kook renews many classic anti-Christian polemics with a vigour not seen for a millennium. Among these polemics are the ideas that Christianity should be dismissed as an internal Jewish heresy and that the Jewish God is alive whereas the Christian God is dead. He claims that all references to sectarian heretics (*min, minim*) in later rabbinic literature refer to Christianity. According to Kook, Christianity is the refuse of Israel, an image in line with the ancient talmudic portrayals of Jesus punished through boiling in excrement.[40] The stories of *Toledot yeshu* are considered to be a valid part of the Jewish tradition. Kook originally formulated these ideas soon after the founding of the State of Israel, in a 1952 essay that attacked any Jewish attempts to reclaim Jesus.

For Kook, the battle of the second to fourth centuries for the true Israel is continued in the theological battle for the establishment of the State of Israel, presented as a war against Western Christendom. Christian theology is considered 'the war against the eternality of Israel',[41] as well as a battle against the very foundation of the Oral Law as the correct interpretation of the Bible.[42] For Kook, Jewish exclusivism manifests itself in the meaning of contemporary Israel. Since he considers the current modern state to be the fulfilment of the

---

[39] Naftali Zvi Berlin, *Ha'emek davar*, on Gen. 15: 5; Deut. 33: 2, 8: 3.

[40] Zvi Yehudah Kook, *Judaism and Christianity* [Yahadut venatsrut] (Beit El, 2001). One of his students considers Islam as idolatrous, because of its alleged pagan folk customs (see Israel Ariel, 'Israel One Nation in the Land' (Heb.), *Zefiah*, 3 (1989), 115–222).

[41] Zvi Yehudah Kook, *Ways of Israel: Collected Essays* [Linetivot yisra'el: kevutsat ma'amarim] (Jerusalem: Menorah, 1966), 23.   [42] Ibid. 36, 58, 62.

biblical prophecy of the messianic age, he deems all deviations from his political vision as the very opposite of Judaism and of redemption.[43]

Why was Kook's exclusionist position formulated at the end of the twentieth century? His theology shows the change that comes about from living in a non-diaspora context, which enabled a rejection of Western culture. The State of Israel can lead some to a secure acceptance of the Other, especially the religious Other, or conversely, it can engender xenophobic rejection. Even though the overwhelming majority of Jews do not personally entertain these ideas, this position is often passively tolerated.

Jewish chosenness and uniqueness are two of the foundations of rabbinic thought, and positions that emphasize and highlight the special relationship of Jews and God. They create a stabilizing oppositional identity in a world of infinite choices and a strong dedicated community with a sense of mission and uniqueness. Theologically, evaluating these positions needs to be part of a bigger project examining Jewish chosenness and formulating a contemporary theology of the chosen status of Israel. However, some forms of Jewish exclusivism are not merely chosenness, but a categorical rejection of other religions combined with a dualistic sense of separatism. Chosenness, and the special status of Israel itself, is not the problem.

Kook's writings are usually only cited today by those with a special need for isolation, such as those within the settlers' movement or seeking the isolationism of a life of Torah study in purity. At the other extreme, they are also cited by antisemites and anti-religious writers (who are themselves sometimes previously religious) wanting to show the narrowness of traditional Jewish texts. Most responsible Jews today use these texts in conjunction with the inclusivist and universal texts to create a viable normative position. When teaching, these texts are often just politely skipped or explained away as historical relics.

We are part of a living tradition which values classic texts and applies them to the current situation. All religions have terrible texts that are not usually acknowledged or confronted. As the Lutheran Church has acted to undo the harmfulness of some of Luther's statements and the Catholic Church has worked since Vatican II to address the teaching of contempt, Judaism needs to address its hateful texts. We cannot ignore problematic texts or flaccidly respond that mid-twentieth-century rabbinic authorities did not teach them. We have to admit that these texts exist, roll up our sleeves, and deal with them.

CONCLUSION: LIVING WITH MULTIPLE MODELS

The discussion of a theology of other religions cannot go forward without a sound grounding in the classic texts of Judaism as well as an engagement with

---

[43] Ibid. 62–3.

past theological thinking. Analysing earlier texts can show us useful perspectives which might easily be overlooked, although we must also be aware of the difficulties of some of these texts. Inclusivism teaches us to see the universal call of God in ethics, metaphysics, and revelation, the basis of theological study. Particularism teaches us the need to preserve and take pride in that which is unique to Judaism, such as the holiness of Israel and its basis in textual study. Universalism opens us up to the natural human elements in coming towards God and the brotherhood of man, the basis of religious humanism. Pluralism lends dignity to human difference and diversity.

For an example of how each of these positions can play out theologically, we can examine how the Shema can be imagined differently for each of the positions. For the exclusivist, the Shema's significance lies in its historical use as a particularistic call for martyrdom, a reminder of the position of a besieged minority consisting of the sole bearers of the truth of God's unity. An inclusivist may hear the Shema as a vision of all faiths acknowledging God's kingship, either now or at the eschaton. For the universalist, it speaks of a unity of God so profound that all are included. And for the pluralist, it proclaims a Jewish version of a common religious truth.

I do not think that one needs to choose between the models; we accept different approaches in different situations. As dutiful Jews, we need not always choose one position over the others; each can play a role in our religious lives. There will be days when our recitation of the Shema will carry universal intentions, and days when we will close our eyes and think exclusively. Among the components from which we build our religious lives and identities are the exclusive martyrdoms of the Maccabees and the Jewish victims of the crusades, the inclusivism of the psalms and of modern thinkers of the last 200 years, and the universalism of Isaiah, Ibn Gabirol, and Abraham Isaac Kook.

We live by narratives that allow or even encourage us to shift our stories between inclusivist, exclusivist, and pluralist positions in accordance with our own inner dialogues, external contexts, and existential situations. On a practical level, people employ all three positions, shifting stances with their changing circumstances. We should learn to pay attention to how we use different texts to guide us in different aspects of our lives. Different contexts call for appropriate responses in the situations they present. For example, sociologists note that in civic situations such as health care as well as in most pragmatic scenarios the majority of Americans are pluralists, while they may have a different default position of exclusivist faith at their own place of worship. Many Orthodox Jews who are full participants in American civil society are outraged when it is insinuated that they would withhold health care from a non-Jew in the name of religion; yet they are comfortable with an exclusivist theology in the synagogue.

We need to appreciate what the broad palette of traditional texts says about other religions. Often that palette is wider than we imagine. The range of opinions, of which only a small segment has been examined in this essay, is far larger than most people think. Jews travel heavy and do not throw texts away. Taken together, all these positions can create a fuller theological narrative for self-understanding. In the new realm of encountering other religions in an age of post-secular globalization, Jews have a need to learn when and in what contexts to apply a given text and how to put the texts together into a broader theory.

In our era we do not need an either/or choice of exclusivism or tolerance, but a both/and relationship. Any opinion we formulate should be based on knowing that many positions—inclusivist, exclusivist, universalist, pluralist, and empiricist—exist. The positions are mutually correcting and they presuppose one another, thereby limiting, protecting, and offering reciprocal adjustment to the other opinions. The combination of these opinions is thus greater than the sum of its parts.

TWO

Justifying Interreligious Pluralism

AVI SAGI

RELIGIOUS EXCLUSIVISM: A CRITICAL ANALYSIS

HISTORICAL religions cover a broad spectrum of beliefs about the world and about God that are represented in symbols, myths, and practices. In this spectrum, each religion presents a unique world picture, incompatible with the others. Every religion, at least in its traditional garb, is exclusive—it claims to be the only true religion, presenting the most accurate picture of God and of reality. My main thesis is that religious exclusivism is a hard position to defend philosophically and that a pluralistic thesis that advocates the inner value of different religions is logically preferable. With respect to Judaism, however, pluralism entails a conceptual revolution within the tradition.

The motivation for religious exclusivism is clear. First, through this approach, believers convey their absolute commitment to their religion and their faith. For many, exclusivism conveys acceptance of their religion's sole and absolute authority, interpreted to mean that all other religions have no share in the truth. Exclusivism, then, reflects the believers' religious pathos.

Second, exclusivism appears as 'coherent and rational', and believers who fail to endorse it appear to express doubts about the validity of their faith.[1] This claim relies on two assumptions: (1) my faith is valid and (2) my faith is incompatible with all others. Hence other faiths are invalid.[2] The second assumption is the crucial one for this argument, for without it the conclusion would be redundant, and believers could sustain the validity of their own faith without necessarily negating the validity of others. The incompatibility of various religions relates to two constitutive aspects: their factual and metaphysical beliefs about the world and about God and their system of practical obligations. This crucial assumption, then, compels the conclusion that not all religions can be true, implying the dismissal of interreligious pluralism as a valid possibility.

Third, every religion offers a way to salvation attainable only through God's

Thank you to Batya Stein, who translated this essay from the Hebrew.

[1] Raimundo Panikkar, 'Religious Pluralism: The Metaphysical Challenge', in Leroy S. Rouner (ed.), *Religious Pluralism* (Notre Dame, Ind., 1984), 102. [2] Ibid.

true revelation. Salvation as the purpose of religion, then, compels religious exclusivism.[3] These justifications of religious exclusivism suggest that it conveys the beliefs of the faithful more successfully, in addition to possessing a sound theoretical foundation.

An exclusivist approach might seem unappealing because it ostensibly denies the supporters of 'untrue' religions the right to their faith, but this is not necessarily so. People may believe their religion is true and valid without denying others the right to uphold mistaken beliefs. A person can be both exclusivist and tolerant. Indeed, tolerance first emerged within an exclusivist world-view, and John Locke's *Four Letters of Toleration* clearly illustrates a combination of exclusivism and toleration of other religions. Sociologically, exclusivism has often led to coercion, but we should not draw conclusions about exclusivist versions of religion from history and sociology. If exclusivism is to be rejected, the argument affirming the right of others to sustain their faith cannot be the decisive consideration.

Opponents of religious exclusivism raise a series of objections. The first is a theological one: the loving God cares for the salvation of all human beings. The exclusivist conclusion, arguing that only followers of the true religion will be redeemed, is incompatible with God's universal goodness.[4] The second is a moral argument: people leading worthy lives can hardly be doomed simply because they belong to another religion.[5] The geographical–historical argument is a third objection: membership in a particular religion is usually a matter of random historical and geographical circumstances rather than choice, the product of birthplace, education, environment. To assume that something as crucial as human redemption might possibly depend on such fortuitous events is highly disconcerting.

Even if these objections are valid, however, they do not necessarily substantiate interreligious pluralism, and two other conclusions are possible. The first is the endorsement of religious inclusivism, an approach claiming that one religion is indeed the true one, but God's mercy extends to members of other religions as well. This, for instance is the approach of the theologian Karl Rahner, who claims that Jesus' expiation of sin is an objective fact applicable to all human beings.[6] A second and perhaps more plausible conclusion is

[3] See Michael Peterson et al., *Reason and Religious Belief: An Introduction to the Philosophy of Religion* (New York, 1991), 222; Avishai Margalit, 'The Ring: On Religious Pluralism', in David Heyd (ed.), *Toleration: An Elusive Virtue* (Princeton, NJ, 1996), 147–57.

[4] See Joseph Runzo, 'God, Commitment, and Other Faiths: Pluralism vs. Relativism', *Faith and Philosophy*, 4 (1988), 347; John Hick, *God Has Many Names* (Philadelphia, 1982), 17; Keith Ward, 'Truth and the Diversity of Religions', *Religious Studies*, 26 (1990), 1.

[5] Peterson et al., *Reason and Religious Belief*, 223; Ward, 'Truth and the Diversity of Religions', 1.

[6] For a detailed analysis of religious inclusivism, see Peterson et al., *Reason and Religious Belief*, 228–30. For the terminological distinction between exclusivism and inclusivism, see John Hick, *Problems of Religious Pluralism* (London, 1985), ch. 3. For a discussion of inclusivism, see ibid.

that human redemption is not at all contingent on religion. If God cares about human redemption, how can people be doomed because they were born in the wrong place? Human redemption, then, cannot depend on religion but on leading a worthy life. Furthermore, exclusivists could endorse these arguments without implying that redemption is attainable outside the true religion and claim that 'the righteous among peoples of the world have a portion in the world to come'.[7]

A more persuasive argument against religious exclusivism is one that makes the validation of religion contingent on a special type of experience—'religious experience'.[8] Relying on this argument, John Hick argues we should ascribe equal value to the religious experience of others: 'In acknowledging this we are obeying the intellectual Golden Rule of granting to others a premise on which we rely ourselves.'[9] In a later paper, Hick formulates this conclusion even more emphatically: 'This basic principle [assuming the primal character of religious experience] has to be applied not only to Christian but also to other forms of theistic experience, and indeed not only to theistic but also to non-theistic forms of religious experience.'[10] On these grounds, Hick seeks to reject exclusivism and validate interreligious pluralism.

The argument from religious experience could be formulated as follows. (1) Every religion is based on a particular religious experience. (2) The religious experience of a believer in one religion differs from the religious experience of a believer in another religion. (3) Believers are justified in relying on their religious experience. All believers, therefore, can justifiably view their own faith as valid. But rejecting exclusivism and justifying interreligious pluralism on these grounds is questionable, since the only conclusion of this argument is that believers in various religions have an epistemic justification for continuing to uphold their beliefs, without any conclusions necessarily following concerning the truth of their religions.[11]

32–4. Hick had engaged in a preliminary discussion of this issue, without resorting to this terminology, as early as 1982 (see Hick, *God Has Many Names*, 33–6).

[7] Maimonides, *Mishneh torah*, 'Laws of Repentance', 3: 13 (trans. Moses Hyamson (Jerusalem, 1981)); see also 'Laws of Kings', 8: 11.

[8] See e.g. John Hick, *An Interpretation of Religion: Human Responses to the Transcendent* (New Haven, 1989), ch. 13; id., 'Religious Pluralism and the Rationality of Religious Belief', *Faith and Philosophy*, 10 (1993), 242–9; William Alston, *Perceiving God: The Epistemology of Religious Experience* (Ithaca, NY, 1991); Alvin Plantinga, 'The Foundation of Theism: A Reply', *Faith and Philosophy*, 3 (1986), 298–313; id., 'Justification and Theism', *Faith and Philosophy*, 4 (1987), 403–26; id., 'Is Belief in God Properly Basic?', in R. Douglas Geivett and Brendan Sweetman (eds.), *Contemporary Perspectives on Religious Epistemology* (New York, 1992), 133–41.

[9] Hick, *An Interpretation of Religion*, 235.

[10] Hick, 'Religious Pluralism and the Rationality of Religious Belief', 245.

[11] Cf. S. Mark Heim, 'The Pluralistic Hypothesis, Realism, and Post-Eschatology', *Religious Studies*, 28 (1992), 209.

Another widespread objection to the argument from religious experience challenges the third assumption: are believers indeed justified in relying on their religious experience? The justification usually assumes that religious experience is a particular instance of standard empirical experience, but these experiences are distinctly different. Whereas standard empirical experiences are more or less uniform (almost everyone facing a tree experiences a tree), religious experiences are different and even incompatible.[12]

The argument from religious experience may, at most, justify a claim that a different religious experience might be certain, but this does not imply it has been positively validated. Religious exclusivism, then, cannot be dismissed on the grounds of a claim based on religious experience.

Attempts to reject religious exclusivism have frequently resorted to the phenomenological argument, which relies on the actual historical existence of many and different religions. Notwithstanding its appeal, however, we can draw no conclusions from it. Exclusivists do not deny historical experience but claim that, in and by itself, it is insufficient to refute their approach. The attitude to the phenomenological datum cannot be derived from the datum itself. For supporters of pluralism, interreligious pluralism will be an additional confirmation of their outlook. Normative monists or religious exclusivists, however, will go on claiming that the phenomenological datum proves nothing, that all other religions are mistakes, and only their religion is true. Exclusivists will not, on these grounds, scorn other religions. They may even view them as sublime human creations and may even be touched by the intensity and sincerity of their believers, but without concluding that they must therefore reject exclusivism. Interreligious pluralism will only impress someone who is already a pluralist.

Notwithstanding other arguments against religious exclusivism, most of them do not threaten it. The crucial challenge to religious exclusivism is what I call 'Hume's dilemma'.

HUME'S DILEMMA

Hume formulates the dilemma as follows: 'In matters of religion, whatever is different is contrary; and it is impossible that the religions of ancient Rome, of Turkey, of Siam, and of China should, all of them, be established on any solid foundation.'[13]

Hume advances this formulation as an argument for religious scepticism. My discussion focuses on this argument and on its implications for religious

[12] David Basinger, 'Plantinga, Pluralism and Justified Religious Belief', *Faith and Philosophy*, 8 (1991), 70–1.

[13] David Hume, *Enquiries Concerning the Human Understanding and Concerning the Principles of Morals*, ed. L. A. Selby-Bigge (Oxford, 1975), 121.

exclusivism, and considers several versions of the dilemma. The first one follows.

For any particular religion (X), two options are possible:

(*a*) Religion X is true.
(*b*) Religion X is false.

If (*a*) is correct, and on the assumption that 'whatever is different is contrary', every other religion is false. If (*b*) is correct, however, it does not necessarily follow that every other religion is true, since many other false religions may exist. At best, we may conclude from (*b*) that other existent religions could be true, and the question then is: how do we distinguish a true religion from a false one? Both options show that justifying the falsity of religions is easier than justifying their truth. How, then, do exclusivists validate their position?

Whether this version of the dilemma validates interreligious pluralism depends on what we mean by 'interreligious pluralism', an issue I discuss below. At this stage of the discussion, we may formulate the following argument: at least according to versions stating that pluralism does not endorse Hume's assumption that 'whatever is different is contrary', then, even if Religion X is true, we need not conclude that all other religions are false. A pluralist who rejects this assumption could argue that exclusivism is best avoided because it is self-defeating, and will eventually undermine its own religious *Weltanschauung*.[14]

Another formulation of Hume's dilemma follows William Alston and Mark McLeod.[15] In this version, the datum is the existence of incompatible religions. To decide which one is true we cannot rely on the inner criterion of any one religion, and we require an overarching standard allowing us to compare them. Since no such standard is available, however, I cannot claim that my religious beliefs are more credible or correct than others. This version challenges religious exclusivism by pointing to the lack of an epistemological criterion that might serve to determine the preferable religion.

According to this formulation, however, Hume's dilemma cannot serve to validate interreligious pluralism. An approach supporting interreligious pluralism should not be equated with scepticism about religions in general. In this regard, the interreligious pluralist and the exclusivist find themselves in a similar quandary. As I show below, however, 'interreligious pluralism' is a rubric that groups together several approaches that cannot be discussed as one, and the dilemma does not apply to versions claiming that various religions

[14] Hick, who rejects Hume's assumption, quotes him repeatedly in an attempt to challenge religious exclusivism (see e.g. Hick, *Problems of Religious Pluralism*, 38; id., *An Interpretation of Religion*, 228–9).

[15] Alston, *Perceiving God*, 268–9; Mark S. McLeod, 'The Limits of Theistic Experience: An Epistemic Basis of Theistic Pluralism', *Philosophy of Religion*, 34 (1993), 80.

are not incompatible or that religions do not suggest truth claims about the world.

Another version of Hume's dilemma claims that incompatibility between religions leads to another problem. If the various religions are incompatible, and if the faithful in each religion have justifications for believing in it, we arrive at the following conclusion: 'If I am rationally justified in believing x, and you are rationally justified in believing not-x, then we are both justified in believing the other to be deluded, or in some other way mistaken.'[16] Consequently, neither believer enjoys an advantage, and both religions are equally uncertain. No religion, then, has any basis for certainty, and exclusivism faces a problem. This argument, however, could also pose a threat to certain versions of interreligious pluralism, as it challenges the very justification of religious faith per se.

Another version deals with the meaning of the belief that x is true. According to Keith Ward, believing that x is true means believing that not-x is false: 'To believe a proposition is to think that it is true. To think that it is true is to affirm that reality is as it is described by that proposition . . . Thus an affirmation by its nature excludes some possible state of affairs; namely, one which would render the proposition false.'[17] This argument shows that, logically, different truth claims cannot possibly be compatible. Ward advances this argument against the very possibility of interreligious pluralism, since the conclusion that follows from this argument—'it is a necessary truth that not all possible religious traditions can be equally true'[18]—is plainly opposed to a pluralistic stance.

The various versions of Hume's dilemma, then, challenge the possibility of religious exclusivism. Yet in certain versions they also challenge interreligious pluralism, as they cast doubt on its assumption that truth claims, even though mutually incompatible regarding the world, could still be true. Because Hume's dilemma challenges religious validation from both perspectives, we can refer to it as a 'paradox'. What defence can we adduce for an exclusivist or a pluralistic position facing the challenge of Hume's dilemma?

The source of Hume's dilemma is the existence of mutually incompatible religions. The dilemma conveys the problem evoked by interreligious pluralism, and the discussion below offers two central strategies for dealing with it. The first offers a modified version of validation in general and of religious justification in particular. The second offers a modified version of the concept of truth. Ultimately, these strategies make pluralism a position more defensible than exclusivism.

---

[16] Ward, 'Truth and the Diversity of Religions', 13.   [17] Ibid. 2.   [18] Ibid.

MODIFYING THE CONCEPT OF JUSTIFICATION

The Radical Approach

Alvin Plantinga is the main proponent of the thesis that religion is a 'basic belief', which he defines as a faith that is not justified in terms of another.[19] This concept covers the whole range of our cognitions. Thus, for instance, the equation $1 + 2 = 3$ does not rest on any other. Similarly, the belief that I saw a tree does not rest on other propositions. Plantinga stresses that the absence of a justification that relies on other propositions should not be interpreted as an absence of justification altogether; my specific experience with the tree, as well as other circumstances, justify my faith.[20] According to Plantinga, we have 'cognitive faculties designed to enable us to achieve true beliefs with respect to a wide variety of propositions—propositions about our immediate environment, about our interior lives . . . about our universe at large . . . These faculties work in such a way that under the appropriate circumstances we form the appropriate belief.'[21]

Plantinga claims that religious faith is a kind of basic faith requiring no justification in other terms, anchored in a tendency or a disposition to perceive experience as religious:

God has so created us that we have a tendency or disposition to see his hand in the world about us. More precisely, there is in us a disposition to believe propositions of the sort 'this flower was created by God' or 'this vast and intricate universe was created by God' when we contemplate the flower or behold the starry heavens and think about the vast reaches of the universe.[22]

In terminology suggested elsewhere, Plantinga argues that God created us with specific aptitudes such that 'when they are working in the way they were designed to work by the being who designed and created us and them' we arrive at theist beliefs.[23]

In this view of religious faith, believers do not have to be concerned with the positive justification and validation of their beliefs and only need to deal with 'negative apologetics', that is, they only need to reject the counterclaims of faith's opponents.[24] According to Plantinga, the approach supporting rational justifications of faith is part of the Enlightenment legacy, which claimed that when we say rational we mean based on incontestable propositions.[25]

---

[19] See Plantinga, 'The Foundation of Theism'; id., 'Justification and Theism'; id., 'Is Belief in God Properly Basic?'   [20] Plantinga, 'Is Belief in God Properly Basic?', 136.

[21] Plantinga, 'Justification and Theism', 405.

[22] Plantinga, 'Is Belief in God Properly Basic?', 137.

[23] Plantinga, 'Justification and Theism', 411.

[24] See Plantinga, 'The Foundation of Theism', 313 n. 11.   [25] Ibid. 307.

This solution to Hume's dilemma, then, is to negate any need for positive validation in the religious domain. I will not enter here into a detailed critique of Plantinga's position,[26] but, assuming for the sake of the discussion that Plantinga is right, the question still remains open: what is the relationship between the various religious faiths? Religious aptitude is not responsible for shaping a particular faith, so can theists be satisfied merely with warding off attacks? Does not the pluralist datum reopen the issue of the epistemic status of religious faith as a basic belief? Does it not challenge the statement that religious faith, which from now on is always a particular faith—Christian, Jewish, and so forth—does not require validation? If believers do not offer positive validation, is the inevitable conclusion a total negation of their faith or merely a challenge to its certainty? These questions have no answer within the framework of Plantinga's thesis and, in this sense, Plantinga leaves Hume's dilemma unresolved.

In many ways, Plantinga's approach is close to that of neo-Wittgensteinian thinkers such as D. Z. Philips. Both Philips and Plantinga reject foundationalism. According to Philips, the choice of foundationalism as the preferred perspective in the analysis of religion is 'one of the scandals of the philosophy of religion'.[27] Relying on Wittgenstein, Philips claims that religious faith is the believer's 'absolute disposition' towards the world. Believers do not argue about the certainty of religious beliefs in the same terms they use to argue about the truth of statements about the world, because their commitment to religious truths is absolute and unconditional, unlike their commitment to statements about the world.[28] According to this approach, the religious realm leaves no room for justifications—not because religion is a product of the religious aptitude but because religion is the absolute starting point from which believers grasp the world. The basic structure of justification, which rests on other claims, undermines the primary quality of religious faith as an absolute disposition.

This approach makes the religious realm one of inner meanings, expressing the believer's inner world. But the key question touches on the meaning of this disposition. Does it make claims about the world, or does it only express the believer's feelings and values? Is religious faith only expressive of the believer's inner world, or is it cognitive and realistic and making claims about the world and God?

---

[26] For a detailed critique, see e.g. Basinger, 'Plantinga, Pluralism, and Justified Religious Belief'.

[27] D. Z. Philips, *Faith after Foundationalism* (London, 1988), 3.

[28] For a summary of Philips's position, see Alan Keightly, *Wittgenstein, Grammar, and God* (London, 1976), 73–4; see also Ludwig Wittgenstein, *Lectures and Conversations on Aesthetics, Psychology and Religious Belief*, ed. C. Barrett (Oxford, 1970), 56–8.

To assume that it makes claims about the world is the more plausible interpretation of 'absolute disposition',[29] but it exacts an onerous religious price since it fails to match the practical experience. For most believers, religion is an intentional activity directed towards a real God who created the world and guides it with infinite mercy and grace. Therefore, if Hume's dilemma is the justification of such an approach, this solution seems too costly.

If making claims about the world and about God is the more plausible interpretation of this concept,[30] believers who start out from an absolute disposition adopt their specific religious statements in preference to others, even to atheistic ones. But preference is not justification. One cannot engage in rational metaphysical discourse while totally negating the possibility of criticism; religious language is not in a separate and autonomous realm divorced from standard discourse.[31] Thus the idea that criteria of truth regarding religious language will not be open to criticism in the name of 'the absolute disposition' is unacceptable.

Another option is that the absolute disposition is synonymous with personal choice and preference.[32] According to this approach, justifications are out of place here, since we are explicitly dealing with choice. The problem with this position is its complete renunciation of a rational critique of choice, which it equates with an arbitrary act or a casual whim.[33] This is not the perception of most believers, who view their religious faith as justified and not merely an arbitrary act. Most believers are born into a religion, just as they are born into a specific society and culture. They do not reach faith through a process of critical consideration or because of an arbitrary choice, leaping, as it were, into a religion. Yet we cannot therefore conclude that believers will not invest effort in justifying their beliefs. The attempt to turn religious discourse into one that reports choice and preference a posteriori leads many believers to view this discourse as devoid of meaning.

The radical approach, as I have presented it here, claims that the religious domain leaves no room for justification, and Hume's dilemma is therefore not

[29] Some scholars place Philips in this category, although I am not convinced this is the case (see Hick, *An Interpretation of Religion*, 198).

[30] Peter Winch takes this position. He stresses that religion is not merely expressive but makes claims about an entity and about the world, although this entity exists only within the religious context. Winch has stated this position repeatedly (see Peter Winch, 'Understanding a Primitive Society', in Bryan R. Wilson (ed.), *Rationality* (Oxford, 1985), 82; id., *Trying to Make Sense* (Oxford, 1987), ch. 8).

[31] Compare Kai Nielsen, 'Wittgensteinian Fideism', in Steven M. Cahn and David Schatz (eds.), *Contemporary Philosophy of Religion* (New York, 1982), 247.

[32] This is the approach suggested by Basinger, who speaks of solving the pluralist challenge 'in a personal, private fashion' ('Plantinga, Pluralism and Justified Religious Belief', 77).

[33] See Hick's similar critique of Basinger ('Religious Pluralism and the Rationality of Religious Belief', 247).

a challenge to believers. But even if we ignore all the objections to the various versions of this approach and consider it a successful strategy, it will be of no use to exclusivists. Supporters of the radical approach, in all its versions, cannot claim that they are the only ones in possession of the truth, and that their faith is justified and absolutely preferable to all others. Advocates of this strategy cannot, by the very nature of their claim, negate pluralism.

The Limited Approach

Whereas the radical approach alleges that religious faith is not within the realm of propositions requiring justification, it is possible to make a more limited claim, arguing that the justification of faith is not necessarily universal. Different people professing different and incompatible beliefs can all be justified, without one faith's justification negating the other. William Alston suggests such an approach, when he claims that incompatible religious plural-ism raises a problem regarding the justification of my own faith.[34] Exclusivists contend with this datum by dismissing the truth value of other faiths. Alston, however, argues that preference for a particular religion cannot be justified in terms of the religion itself. To determine which religion is preferable, we must rely on a criterion that all competing religions will find acceptable. This cri-terion must be external and cannot be grounded on one specific religious tradition, because all religious traditions claim to be preferable to all others. Since in his view no such external criterion is available, we have no way of comparing different religions and determining which one is preferable.[35] In sum, 'we have no idea what a non-circular proof [which assumes the truth of religion a priori] of the reliability of CMP would look like'.[36]

Why is an external criterion for examining religions impossible? Alston claims that the incommensurability of religions follows from their incompat-ibility.[37] But this justification of incommensurability is problematic. The incompatibility of religions shows they do not have shared *internal* criteria, but not that no *external* criterion may be found.[38] A better defence of Alston's position would dismiss as implausible the assumption that a shared external criterion may give one religion a prominent advantage over others.

This approach appears to lead to the conclusion that no position enjoys any advantage over others and that upholding a particular faith is pointless. Alston's innovation is that he rejects this conclusion and claims that upholding

[34] William Alston, 'Religious Diversity and Perceptual Knowledge of God', *Faith and Philosophy*, 8 (1991), 433–48; id., *Perceiving God*.   [35] Alston, *Perceiving God*, 268–80.
[36] Ibid. 272. CMP is an acronym for Christian Mystical Perceptual Doxastic Practice. This argument is pertinent to all religions and not necessarily to Christianity as interpreted by Alston.
[37] Ibid. 268.
[38] This thesis is well demonstrated in Daniel Statman, *Moral Dilemmas* (Amsterdam, 1995), esp. ch. 3.

a particular religious view based on religious experience is both meaningful and justified, even if unjustifiable in universal terms. The lack of universal justification for my faith does not imply it lacks justification altogether. The religious domain, according to Alston, is a particular case where incompatible propositions are justified to different people.[39] Individuals can continue to rely on their religious experience without committing themselves to the claim that this experience is of universal value.[40] Alston, therefore, circumscribes the meaning usually ascribed to justifications and argues that universality is not a necessary condition of them.[41]

Thus far the discussion indicates that modifications in the concept of justification are incompatible with religious exclusivism and that preserving the traditional concept of justification leads to Hume's dilemma. A pluralistic stance, therefore, emerges as epistemically preferable to exclusivism.

MODIFYING THE CONCEPT OF RELIGIOUS TRUTH

Modifying the concept of religious truth implies adopting one or another version of the pluralistic position. In this section, I examine several versions of this modification and, accordingly, several types of religious pluralism.

Moderate Pluralism

A standard pluralistic position makes at least two assumptions. (1) Competing systems are incompatible. (2) No shared criterion is available for choosing between systems.[42] Moderate pluralism may restrict the connotations of both these assumptions. Two types of moderate pluralism will be succinctly outlined in this section: one claims that an exhaustive description of a pluralistic religious reality is not a description of incompatible systems, and the other that we do not need to choose between different systems.

The first type, sometimes called 'universal pluralism',[43] claims that God, the Entity, and the Absolute are all one, and that every particularistic religion reflects its specific experience of God or the Absolute Entity. The variance reflects the range of cultures represented in different images of God.[44] Hick develops this approach at length, but a detailed analysis exceeds the scope of this paper so I will confine myself to a concise summary.[45]

[39] Alston, *Perceiving God*, 275.
[40] Alston, 'Religious Diversity and the Perceptual Knowledge of God', 440.
[41] Advocates of interreligious pluralism tend to support the argument of limited justification (see John Kekes, *The Morality of Pluralism* (Princeton, NJ, 1993), 95). [42] Ibid. 53–9.
[43] Yong Huang, 'Religious Pluralism and Interfaith Dialogue: Beyond Universalism and Particularism', *Philosophy of Religion*, 37 (1995), 127–8. [44] Hick, *God Has Many Names*, 105.
[45] Note that Jewish theologians have suggested a similar approach (see e.g. Daniel Polish, 'Understanding Religious Pluralism', *Religion and Intellectual Life*, 4 (1987), 50–63).

Hick, was influenced by Kant's distinction between the phenomenon and the noumenon,[46] and he draws a distinction between the Entity as such (God) and the modes of experiencing it. The Entity is one, while the modes of experiencing it are many, but all are different modes of experiencing the very same thing. To illustrate his approach, Hick returns to the Greek parable about blind men laying their hands on various parts of an elephant: each one perceives the object differently, but all still perceive the same thing.[47] As the Entity or the Absolute are infinite, beyond speech and thought, the object of worship in the various religions is not the Absolute itself, but the Absolute as perceived within the religious experience.[48] Consequently, Hick argues that different religious experiences may seem incompatible but are actually complementary, and that this claim also applies to religious truths, all of which relate to various aspects of the same Entity.

Why does Hick persist in retaining the assumption of one Entity, rather than confine himself to pointing out the different religious experiences? Hick describes his approach as 'inductivist', a perspective that takes the human religious experience regarding the transcendent seriously. On this basis, he postulates the existence of a single Entity.[49] According to this approach, Hume's dilemma should not lead to religious scepticism; in fact, as noted, Hick views the dilemma itself as evidence of the shared grounds underlying the various religions.[50]

Hick's approach has evoked widespread controversy. He argues that the believer's intentional activity is ultimately directed towards God as experienced by members of a particular religious community rather than towards the real God as such. According to Hick, relating to the real God is impossible. This approach, however, contradicts the basic faith of believers, who do direct their activity towards a real God.[51] Furthermore, is Hick suggesting a new perception of religion, an alternative to the existing religions, or a second-order analysis or meta-religion about religions as they actually are? From Hick's writings, and from his deep commitment to believers' religious experience as they themselves describe it, he appears to be advancing a second-order analysis of religions.

The test of a second-order analysis is twofold: first, the consistency and the coherence of the analysis itself; second, the extent to which the analysis is congruent with the datum to which it relates. Hick fails not only according to the first criterion but also, and particularly, according to the second. He does not

---

[46] See e.g. Hick, *God Has Many Names*, 104–5; John Hick, *Philosophy of Religion* (Englewood Cliffs, NJ, 1983), 119–20. [47] Hick, *Problems of Religious Pluralism*, 37.
[48] Hick, *Philosophy of Religion*, 111. [49] Ibid.
[50] Hick, 'Religious Pluralism and the Rationality of Religious Belief', 248.
[51] See Peterson et al., *Reason and Religious Belief*, 227; Robert McKim, 'Could God Have More Than One Nature?', *Faith and Philosophy*, 5 (1988), 383.

take into account believers' own religious experience in the various faiths. Every religion considers itself entirely different from all others, and every religion perceives itself as relating to the real God. The value of a second-order analysis that fails to interpret these data is at best dubious.[52] Hick argues that the source of the differences between the various religions relates to sociological and historical differences between believers. Most probably, Hick does not mean to confine religion to historical–sociological data. He does not intend to claim that religion is the product of a given society and culture, and consistently emphasizes that the Entity is absolute and does, indeed, exist 'there'. What, then, is the relationship between this Entity and the religious experience? If the religious experience is decisive, how can we use it to spring the reductionist trap?[53] Hick's assumption, that religious experiences share a common ground, fails the phenomenological test. Indeed, a comparison of different religious traditions reveals that the differences between them far exceed the similarities, as Ninian Smart notes: 'There is no common core, but rather . . . there are different sorts of religious experience, which recur in different traditions, though not universally. From a phenomenological point of view it is not possible to base the judgement that all religions point to the same truth upon religious experience.'[54]

Finally, consider the elephant parable: who has the external perspective enabling the conclusion that the blind are indeed experiencing the elephant rather than something else? Certainly not the blind themselves. According to Hick, however, the religious experience resembles that of 'the blind'. Hick assumes we do not experience the Entity or the Absolute, so who does have the external perspective from which we might determine that the religious experience is indeed the experience of this Absolute? Why not assume that the religious experience is not intentional, has no realistic meaning, and is by nature expressive? In brief: if God can be described, we are not blind; and if nothing can be said about God, religion is either an illusion or, at most, an expression of human perceptions and judgements.[55]

Aware of this difficulty, Hick tries to contend with it. In his view, individuals have no external perspective allowing them to know that their experience is actually realistic. Good reasons do exist, however, for relying on the religious experience, which is unquestionably directed towards the actual Entity.[56] Yet this move takes us no further, since the key question still is: 'What is there in the religious experience?' If this experience conveys a relationship with a real

---

[52] See Harold A. Netland, 'Professor Hick on Religious Pluralism', *Religious Studies*, 22 (1986), 254–5. [53] Ibid. 253.
[54] Ninian Smart, 'Truth and Religion', in Steven M. Cahn and David Schatz (eds.), *Contemporary Philosophy of Religion* (New York, 1982), 299.
[55] See Netland, 'Professor Hick on Religious Pluralism', 259–61.
[56] Hick, *Problems of Religious Pluralism*, 37.

Avi Sagi

God, Hick's thesis collapses since he assumes that no relationship with this Entity is possible. Alternatively, we might endorse the claim that the religious experience is unreliable and merely an illusion. But if the religious experience relates only to the image of God, why not assume it has no real object whatsoever? Even assuming epistemic justification for relying on the experience, no ontological conclusions can be drawn from it. The moderate pluralistic model of the Hick variety therefore fails to overcome the basic problem raised by Hume's dilemma.

Another model of moderate pluralism assumes that all religions have something in common (that is, they all reflect the divine revelation), thus making choice unnecessary. David Hartman offers an interesting development of this approach. In his view, God's revelation expresses God's will 'to meet human beings in their finitude, in their particular historical and social situation, and to speak to them in their own language'.[57] Instead of a theory postulating one divine revelation, then, Hartman suggests a theory of multiple revelations. This multiplicity relies on two interrelated assumptions, one theological and one anthropological. The specific revelation is always fragmented because God's infinite abundance cannot be exhausted by 'divine–human encounters'.[58] First, revelation is an encounter between God and concrete human beings, implying that God turns to human beings out of consideration for their concreteness. Revelation, therefore, is not the 'source of absolute, eternal, and transcendent truth'.[59] In principle, then, revelation cannot be universal and is always particular, with various religions as different expressions of divine infinity. According to Hartman, awareness of the plurality of faiths 'is spiritually redemptive'.[60]

In this approach, a given obligation (O) can be a religious obligation within one faith, whereas another faith may define its negation (not-O) as an obligation. The fact that religions are incompatible is a consummate expression of the nature of divine revelation. Hence we do not need a criterion that determines truth in each religion. All are true in the sense that they convey an encounter between human beings and God.

The advantage of this approach over the previous one is clear: Hartman does not assume a distinction between the real God and the image of God and claims that each religion worships the real God in its own unique fashion. This approach, however, is also fraught with problems. First, what does this formulation represent—a new perception of religion or a second-order analysis of religions? If Hartman is seeking to offer a second-order analysis, his claim is antithetical to that of the religions. For instance, Christianity believes that Jesus is the redeemer and the messiah, and this is precisely the creed that Jewish believ-

---

[57] David Hartman, *Conflicting Visions: Spiritual Possibilities of Modern Israel* (New York, 1990), 247.
[58] Ibid. [59] Ibid. 248. [60] Ibid.

ers negate. The beliefs of different religions are mutually contradictory. Hartman claims that every religion offers a fragmented, intrinsically correct truth that does not negate another, but this is not the view that religions endorse.

Second, how does this theory of revelation explain the religious value of the various religions? Hartman makes two assumptions, one theological and one anthropological, but neither of them compels the conclusion he wishes to infer. Even if God is an infinite abundance that cannot be exhausted through any particular revelation, in no way does it follow that there will be other revelations in the future. All we may infer from God's infinite abundance is that no revelation can exhaust God, but not that revelation will recur. Furthermore, only in Christianity does revelation relate to God as such; in Judaism and Islam what is revealed is not God but the obligations incumbent on humanity, or the book that is the bedrock of these obligations. In these religions, God's infinite abundance is irrelevant to the nature of the revelation.

Third, are the historical religions a product of culture and other concrete facts or do they embody the divine norms and true beliefs? If they represent a cultural product, religion is reduced to history; if they embody truth, what exactly is the role of concrete history in the shaping of religion?

Finally, this approach assumes a relationship between the concrete history of a society and a culture on the one hand and religious expression on the other. But what is the relationship between Christian society and culture and the specific manifestations of Christian religion or Christian religions? Also, why is the wearing of phylacteries, for instance, appropriate to Jewish rather than to Islamic history? Why is eating the host appropriate to Christianity rather than to Judaism? Every religion may have an ethos, normative expressions, myths, or symbols linked to the concrete history and language of members of a particular religious community, but why should we assume that this is true of all expressions? This question is particularly relevant given the many religious expressions lacking all signs of concrete historicity.

Similarly to the problems I pointed out concerning the first approach, these problems also indicate that the attempt to allow pluralistic openness through a strategy involving a softening of pluralist assumptions (for example, claiming that all religions address the absolute or create an encounter between God and human beings) is highly problematic. In this light, the option that has been called 'radical pluralism',[61] seems more appealing to the pluralistic believer.

Radical Pluralism

Radical interreligious pluralism rests on the two pluralistic assumptions and dismisses any denominator common to all religions. According to this

---

[61] See McKim, 'Could God Have More Than One Nature?', 380.

approach, each religion offers a closed and sealed world of beliefs and values, detached from all others. The truth or falsity of a religion is not decided through a comparison with other religions, but tested within the intra-religious context.[62] A survey of the literature suggests two views of radical pluralism, which I refer to as 'realistic' and 'expressionist'.[63]

The realistic approach is antithetical to the one Hick proposes, and Mark Heim, one of its chief proponents, indeed formulates his thesis in direct confrontation with Hick.[64] From a pluralistic perspective, the realistic approach detects a fundamental problem in Hick's approach. Hick's pluralism emerges as ultimately artificial because it appears only at the level of the phenomenon, in God's various images, while the noumenon (the Entity, the Absolute, or God) is one and identical in all religions. This pluralism, then, relies on a universalistic assumption, which the realistic approach rejects. Realists claim that every religion offers its own perception of the transcendent Entity rather than presenting an image of God. Even if the deity is transcendent, this need not imply that the believer cannot experience God, since experiencing an attachment to God does not mean experiencing all the divine attributes to the full.[65] Heim therefore argues that we cannot rule out the option that religions do grasp the divine Entity.[66] He then moves one step further and claims that every religion perceives the divine Entity differently: 'The God in whom we [Christians] believe is not quite the same as that of the Jew or Muslim, since our God's character is fundamentally defined by different standards.'[67] This approach, therefore, argues that religions suggest different concepts of God, concepts that reflect the actual divine Entity and not only our perceptions of it. Radical pluralism is therefore realistic, because it claims that God exists beyond our perceptions and is not contingent on us. It is also radical, because it assumes that every religion offers a different Entity as the divine.

Peter Winch has suggested something close to this approach. For Winch, what is real and unreal is within and not beyond the religious language, and 'the conception of God's reality' is only meaningful within a specific religious language.[68] He does not mean that religious language is only expressive and lacks realistic cognitive content, but that the concept of 'God' assumes

---

[62] See Purusottama Bilimoria, 'A Problem for Radical (Onto-Theos) Pluralism', *Sophia*, 30 (1991), 23. Runzo argues that pluralistic positions endorse a theory of idealistic truth ('God, Commitment, and Other Faiths', 350). This formulation, however, is misleading. Although pluralistic theories do renounce the comparative test as a way of testing the truth of religions, they do not thereby endorse idealistic theories of truth.

[63] Both approaches are a possible development of Wittgensteinian thought models, since both view the various religions as different 'language games'. Several neo-Wittgensteinian thinkers support one of these two approaches, as shown below.

[64] See Heim, 'The Pluralistic Hypothesis, Realism, and Post-Eschatology'.

[65] Ibid. 213.   [66] S. Mark Heim, *Is Christ the Only Way?* (Valley Forge, Pa., 1985), 25.

[67] Ibid. 143.   [68] Winch, 'Understanding a Primitive Society', 82.

meaning only within a specific religious context. This context does not negate God's existence; rather, God's existence and meaning are determined by the specific religious context.[69]

The advantage of radical pluralism over the previous version is clear. Rather than blurring the differences between religions, radical pluralism chooses to highlight them dramatically, since these differences exist not only at the level of the phenomenon but also at the level of the noumenon.[70] Radical pluralism also negates any room for comparison between religions, which could lead to a decision about the one true religion. All religions can be true, in the sense that they describe the divine Entity accurately, even though the divine Entity is different.[71] Finally, radical pluralism successfully conveys the phenomenological fact that religions, in their full garb, are ultimately different from one another.

However, this approach encounters many problems. First, its metaphysical world picture remains blurred. Prima facie, radical pluralism claims that the various divine entities—the Christian God, the Jewish God—exist independently of the respective religions. The world is thus full of divine entities, as many as there are religions. Postulating a multiplicity of divine entities, however, fails the test of Ockham's razor. The only reason for assuming this multiplicity is that the various religions relate to such entities, but is this a sufficient reason to substantiate this assumption? To assume that religious discourse is beyond the critique of standard ontological discourse is groundless.

Second, what are the attributes of these divine entities and what is the relationship between them? Whereas some of the attributes ascribed to these entities are common to all, some are exclusive. Thus, for instance, monotheistic religions claim that God is good, infinite, and so on and ascribing identical attributes to different entities implies no contradiction. Yet, some of these attributes are exclusive, ascribed to one particular deity. For instance, Judaism claims that the redeemer of humanity is the God of Israel and not Christianity's God, whereas Christianity claims that redemption is precisely an attribute of the Christian rather than the Jewish God. Some of the attributes that believers ascribe to one particular deity are negated by the other religion. Judaism negates the incarnation of the Christian God. Divine entities, according to radical pluralism, are both identical and contradictory. The metaphysical world of this pluralism is full of entities and non-entities, and we have no way of discerning between what is and what is not.

Finally, in what sense is any religion true? If truth implies an accurate description of the divine Entity, the assumption underlying this statement is that, in some religions, an unconditioned Entity exists that this particular reli-

---

[69] Winch, *Trying to Make Sense*, ch. 7.
[70] See Huang, 'Religious Pluralism and Interfaith Dialogue', 131.   [71] Ibid.

gion describes successfully. The basic flaw of radical pluralism stems from its desire to uphold the two contradictory trends that guide it. On the one hand, it seeks to uphold a realistic position claiming that the God of religions is a real and unconditioned Entity and, on the other, it claims that every religion has a different perception of this Entity, implying that this Entity is defined and confined by religion.[72]

The problems facing radical pluralism were not the only forces driving the development of expressive pluralism as a credible alternative, but they did help to make the latter a meaningful and appealing option. Expressive pluralism, as I show below, is linked to postmodern trends in theology.

Expressive pluralism differs from realistic pluralism in its dismissal of any claims regarding God as an entity, or any ascription of religion to God. God is not an unconditioned entity sustaining a relationship with human beings, or an intentional object of religious activity. God is a concept that only becomes intelligible and meaningful within religious language and praxis. This approach changes not only the standard meaning ascribed to the concept of 'God', but also the meaning of religion. Religion is not a type of relationship between the individual and God but a life pattern, whose source and meaning lie within human activity. As postmodernist thought flourished, more and more thinkers adopted this model of pluralism.[73]

Expressive pluralism stresses that individuals do not become attached to a particular religion after critical evaluation. People are born into a community where a particular religious tradition usually prevails.[74] Their readiness to adopt religious beliefs and values is motivated by many factors—social relationships, a commitment to an active tradition, or the religion's ability to organize the individual's experiences within a meaningful framework.[75] The motivation for choosing a religion is not the measure of its truth. Believers do not view the philosophical and theological justifications of the various religions as a condition of their own religiosity, nor do they find philosophical and theological critiques necessarily impressive.[76] If the believer's attachment to reli-

---

[72] For further criticism, see McKim, 'Could God Have More Than One Nature?', 383.

[73] On the link between postmodernism and expressive pluralism in modern theology and thought, see the summary of Nancy Murphy and James W. McClendon, 'Distinguishing Modern and Postmodern Theologies', *Modern Theology*, 5 (1989), 191–214; see also John Milbank, '"Postmodern Critical Augustinianism": A Short Summa in Forty-Two Responses to Unasked Questions', *Modern Theology*, 7 (1991), 225–37.

[74] See John Hick, 'Religious Pluralism and Absolute Claims', in Leroy S. Rouner (ed.), *Religious Pluralism* (Notre Dame, Ind., 1984), 194.

[75] See Ward, 'Truth and the Diversity of Religions', 3; Huang, 'Religious Pluralism and Interfaith Dialogue', 133.

[76] Neo-Wittgensteinian thinkers emphasize this point (see e.g. Norman Malcolm, 'The Groundlessness of Religious Belief', in Stuart C. Brown (ed.), *Reason and Religion* (Ithaca, NY, 1977), 143–57; Philips, *Faith after Foundationalism*).

gion is not based on its being true, however, this means that religion has another role.

Supporters of expressive pluralism stress that in organizing human experience, religion and faith in God play a key role by giving existence meaning. Gordon Kaufman sharpens this formulation, stating that the analysis of religion must rest on the awareness that discourse about God is only meaningful within a symbolic framework, which develops in a particular historical context. The symbol of 'God' emerges when a picture of the world gradually unfolds within a specific set of historical circumstances and allows people to cope, more or less successfully, with their needs for survival. Like other symbols, this one too must be understood as a product of human imagination.[77]

In the expressive approach, 'God' plays a practical role rather than being the name of a concrete Entity found in the world. The claim that 'God exists' implies that this concept plays a role in the organization of our concrete life experiences.[78]

Expressive pluralism does not necessarily rule out the use of the term 'truth' in regard to religion, but it invests the term with a different meaning. In this language, the concept of truth has a double meaning: consistency and congruency. A true religion is one where the theoretical and practical realms are consistent or one whose believers consider that it organizes their experience fully and comprehensively.[79]

In postmodern terms, every religion offers a different narrative. Hence, the questions of the justification and truth of a religion in the usual sense of these terms is irrelevant. No meta-narrative exists that might determine which narrative is in fact preferable.[80] From this perspective, the classic discussion between exclusivism and pluralism becomes illegitimate. Not only are exclusivists mistaken but so are pluralists, if they assume that pluralism describes reality more accurately. Religious pluralism is merely a description of human reality—as reality is manifold and diverse, so is religion, which is one of its products.[81]

Expressive pluralism has a prominent advantage over realistic pluralism: it is not committed to a problematic metaphysical *Weltanschauung*. Its main drawback is that it belies the world of the believers themselves, who do not view God as a product of their imagination. God is for them a concrete Entity to whom they address their religious action. Expressive pluralism offers a second-order analysis that fails to take into account the datum to which it

---

[77] Gordon Kaufman, *In Face of Mystery: A Constructive Theology* (Cambridge, Mass., 1993), 39–40.   [78] Hick, *An Interpretation of Religion*, 199.
[79] Compare Murphy and McClendon, 'Distinguishing Modern and Postmodern Theologies', 206.
[80] Peter Donovan, 'The Intolerance of Religious Pluralism', *Religious Studies*, 29 (1993), 223–7.
[81] Cantwell Wilfred Smith, *Questions of Religious Truth* (London, 1967), 73.

relates. Indeed, it offers a transformation of religion itself. Although expressive pluralism is possible, the question is whether it is useful: it seems in no way helpful to believers and is superfluous to non-believers.

The conclusion of this analysis is that all pluralistic approaches confront difficulties when attempting to offer a coherent picture of religion. My claim is that these difficulties do not threaten the pluralistic approach, nor do they compel us to relinquish it. They merely point out the task confronting the supporters of interreligious pluralism—to build a theory of interreligious pluralism. When doing so, they must take heed of the participants in the pluralistic game, which include not only the various religious partners but also the deniers of religion. To claim that all or most religions have internal value, whereas approaches that negate religion must be rejected a priori is unacceptable. The analysis has shown that religious justification is fundamentally limited. This limitation, however, applies not only to the relationship between religions, but also to the relationship of the various religions with non-religious or anti-religious approaches. Differences between religions are as wide as the differences between various religions and non-religious or anti-religious conceptions. An epistemic umbrella covering all the various religions would, in principle, be pertinent to other approaches as well. Does interreligious pluralism detract from people's loyalty to their religious faith?

RELIGIOUS LOYALTY

Does loyalty to one religion logically entail the negation of all others? Moreover, does not interreligious pluralism imply an acknowledgement of the relativism of a religion's truth?

These questions necessitate a reanalysis of what we mean by loyalty to values. Underlying all of them is a concept that I call 'the stringent view of loyalty'. This concept claims that denying other options as false is a necessary condition of normative loyalty and thereby assumes a necessary link between loyalty and a cognitive position. The usual justification for this assumption is the suspicion that people who fail to negate other values may eventually deviate from their particular normative system and be ready to replace it with another. This assumption appears questionable, however. Precluding any option of normative change requires a radical step involving the dismissal of rational criticism and foreclosing the possibility that, on further thought, something considered right might emerge as wrong. I doubt that most supporters of the stringent view of loyalty would be willing to go that far. Insofar as rational-critical discussion remains legitimate, therefore, the option that a given normative system might be replaced cannot be precluded by negating the value of other systems. Excluding all other options cannot be a necessary condition of loyalty.

Many individuals loyal to their moral and religious values are incapable of offering epistemic justifications for them. They express their loyalty by organizing their lives in the light of these values and through their willingness to pay a high price for their adherence to them. But people unable to justify their values could still assume that such justifications do exist, even if they do not know them. This line of argument is already a retreat from the stringent view, since it attests to the lack of a necessary link between loyalty and actual epistemic justification. Even if loyal individuals do keep this assumption within their consciousness, however, their actual loyalty can hardly rest on the belief that someone else knows their values to be true.

Exclusivists could claim that the negation of other options, while not a necessary condition of every normative system, is still pertinent in the religious realm because we thereby acknowledge the absolute sovereignty of the God of religion. The recognition of possible truth in other religions appears to erode this absolute sovereignty. Yet this line of defence is redundant because, as long as rational-critical discourse remains available, this sovereignty remains vulnerable to potential challenges. Religion's absolute sovereignty is embodied in the usual ways of representing sovereignty—the readiness to obey God's commands. This readiness need not be incompatible with a cognitive acknowledgement of the value of other options for other people. Believers go on obeying their God although others do not do so, and this understanding brings us closer to a different interpretation of the concept of loyalty.

A plausible interpretation of normative loyalty views it as a kind of inner relationship between loyal persons and their values. People loyal to their values are ready to live by them, although they could choose otherwise. Despite the availability of other, not necessarily negative, options, people demonstrate their loyalty to their own values by favouring them over others. The test of loyalty is internal: rather than the cognitive acknowledgement of the truth of a normative system, loyalty conveys a form of integrity.[82] Isaiah Berlin concluded 'Two Concepts of Liberty' as follows:

Principles are not less sacred because their duration cannot be guaranteed. Indeed, the very desire for guarantees that our values are eternal and secure in some objective heaven is perhaps only a craving for the certainties of childhood or the absolute values of our primitive past. 'To realize the relative validity of our convictions,' said an admirable writer of our time, 'and yet stand for them unflinchingly, is what distinguishes a civilized man from a barbarian.' To demand more than this is perhaps a deep and incurable metaphysical need; but to allow it to determine one's practice is a symptom of an equally deep, and more dangerous, moral and political immaturity.[83]

[82] For further discussion of this issue, see Peter Winch, *Ethics and Action* (London, 1972), 193–209.
[83] Isaiah Berlin, 'Two Concepts of Liberty', in id., *Four Essays on Liberty* (Oxford, 1969), 172.

Supporting interreligious pluralism, then, seems preferable to exclusivism. This conclusion accords with the prevalent trends of our culture, which tends to reject normative monism, and is also that of many believers. My claim is that interreligious pluralism is preferable not only because it is consistent with the prevalent trends, but because Hume's dilemma provides solid epistemic grounds for its adoption.

PLURALISM AND JEWISH TRADITION

Does the endorsement of pluralism imply the breakdown of religious traditions in general and of Jewish tradition in particular? The answer is 'No'. Even if pluralism reformulates accepted religious truths, its innovations are hardly more significant than the ones that Jewish thinkers have offered since the dawn of their tradition. Is the price of a pluralistic stance higher than that of a typical medieval philosophical position that turned God into a transcendent Entity of the Maimonidean variety? The ability of a tradition to absorb change is tied to many elements and is never contingent on solely one element, such as adherence to metaphysical truths.

Some turning points in a tradition sharpen the split between past and present. The present gradually erases all remnants from the past, even when ensuring them a decent burial. But when the dialogue with the past acknowledges its intrinsic value and consistently seeks to bring it into the present, the past comes back to life in the present, even if in other garb. At times, the return to the past through the patterns of the present guarantees its continuity, since the reinterpretation process implies a renewed commitment to the tradition.

A dialogue with the past from the perspective of the present necessarily assumes change, but not every change implies the dismissal of tradition. Ultimately, two main elements determine continuity: the similarity of practices and the disposition towards aspects of the tradition.

Paradoxically, interreligious pluralism emerges as a stable anchor in the shaping of a new disposition towards the tradition. In the past, the power of tradition rested on truth claims. However, truth claims are by nature contingent, and pluralism can elude contingency because in a pluralistic setting the validity of a value system no longer rests on being the exclusive 'truth' for all humanity. It rests, rather, on its internal recognition. The passion of commitment to these values is not contingent. Pluralism, including interreligious pluralism, is a liberating power that allows us to express commitment without fearing that we might be wrong. Indeed, it enables us to return to the tradition without reservations. Pluralism is not free of problems, but the return to tradition is not one of them. Given the challenges that exclusivism faces, it is pluralism that emerges as the main road for a return to tradition.

Even if pluralism is possible and worthwhile, when we apply it to Judaism we create a conceptual revolution that is not easily compatible with the apparent rigidity of halakhic language and action. Indeed, halakhah may find it easier to support a pluralistic approach in its attitude to other religions than in its attitude to non-halakhic Jews. A Jew who does not observe the Torah and the commandments is described in halakhic language as a transgressor, ignorant of the law, and acting under duress. Moreover, transgressing some commandments is considered equivalent to violating the entire Torah. Public desecration of the sabbath is of special importance in this context.

As Rashi noted, the unique status of the sabbath is related to its theological meaning: 'The sabbath transgressor denies his acts, and falsely attests that the Holy One, Blessed Be He, did not rest on the sabbath.'[84] The conceptual revolution faces a hard challenge here, because the sabbath's unique status denotes the presence of a deep metaphysical foundation in the halakhic realm. No less important, however, is the ensuing halakhic implication. A mainstream halakhic tradition that stretches from *Halakhot gedolot*[85] through the literature of the early authorities[86] and up to modern halakhic literature[87] speaks of public sabbath violators as complete idolaters who are no longer included in the Jewish collective.

However, various rabbinic authorities developed a more tolerant attitude to sabbath violators for other reasons. Some relied on considerations of result, claiming that viewing public sabbath desecrators as non-Jews would lead them to abandon the Jewish people. Others relied on sociological considerations, arguing that the precondition for breaking the sabbath in public is the existence of a society that observes the sabbath. However:

In our times, they are not called public sabbath desecrators because this is what most people do. When most Jews are guiltless, the few who dare to transgress are denying the Torah, committing an abomination, and excluding themselves from the Jewish people. Unfortunately, however, when most Jews are transgressors, the individual believes this is not such a serious offense and one need not hide.[88]

The transgressor's intention is thus a necessary condition for determining the seriousness of the offence. In light of secularization, the sabbath desecrator has no consciousness of being a sinner and therefore is not in the classic halakhic category of a public sabbath violator.

[84] Rashi on BT *Ḥul.* 5a, *ileima mumar*.

[85] Azriel Hildesheimer (ed.), *Sefer halakhot gedolot* (Berlin, 1888), 516.

[86] See e.g. Abraham ben Yitshak of Narbonne, *Sefer ha'eshkol*, ed. Shalom and Hanokh Albeck (Jerusalem, 1984), pt. 2, 105; Yitshak bar Sheshet (Ribash), *Responsa*, no. 4; *Beit yosef*, 'Yoreh de'ah', no. 119; and others.

[87] See e.g. Moses Sofer (Hatam Sofer), *Responsa*, pt. 3, 'Deletions', no. 195; Moses Schick (Maharam Schick), *Responsa*, 'Ḥoshen hamishpat', no. 61; Hayim Elazar Shapira, *Minḥat eli'ezer*, pt. 1, no. 74.

[88] David Zvi Hoffman, *Melamed leho'il* [responsa] (Frankfurt: Hermon, 1926–32), vol. i, no. 29.

At best, these considerations can substantiate toleration, but under no circumstances can they justify pluralism.[89] Pluralism contradicts halakhah's basic assumption, which is that all Jews are compelled to observe the Torah and the commandments by virtue of the Sinai covenant, making pluralism an extremely difficult position to sustain in religious terms. First, pluralism is committed to a conceptual religious revolution. Second, this revolution is not sufficient either, since halakhah might be compatible with toleration but not with pluralism. In other words, the maximum possible is a pluralistic consciousness and halakhic toleration.

Is pluralism then entirely incompatible with traditional Judaism? Halakhah is indeed hard to integrate with a pluralistic stance, but a conceptual religious revolution is not a negligible feat even if it cannot be directly translated into practice. It creates a new consciousness that could be significant and, indirectly, could also contribute to practical trends. Even if unable to foster a pluralistic halakhah, it might promote tolerant trends that will somehow progress towards pluralism. The religious pluralist may be doomed to live in permanent tension, fluctuating between a religious and pluralist pole, on the one hand, and, on the other, a halakhic pole that, at best, will be tolerant. This tension is a good illustration of the pluralist's participation in two communities—a Western community that endorses pluralism and a halakhic Jewish community unreservedly committed to its own directives. Membership in these two communities at times leads to a deep value conflict. Yet, as I have shown elsewhere,[90] affirming a conflict between two different value systems is, in logical terms, a measure of the deep commitment felt towards both. The conflict, then, is the quintessential affirmation of membership in both communities.

Finally, do religious believers have any reason for embracing religious pluralism despite the heavy religious price it exacts? The answer is highly complex. Good religious reasons can be adduced for doing nothing at all, from the religious concessions that pluralism would demand of tradition to the ultimately deleterious effects of any action and its future implications for political and social life in general and religious truths in particular. A believer wishing to remain in a traditional framework could hardly accept arguments that lead to its erosion and would have no reason to adopt a pluralistic outlook. The question is only relevant to a believer leaning towards pluralism, and, for that believer, are there any rational justifications for this inclination? The reasons justifying the preferences of pluralist believers will not make traditional believers change their minds, yet they are most valuable to the pluralist. These

---

[89] On the distinction between pluralism and toleration, see Avi Sagi, *Jewish Religion after Theology*, trans. Batya Stein (Boston: Academic Studies Press, 2009), 3–42.

[90] See Avi Sagi, 'The Suspension of the Ethical and the Religious Meaning of Ethics in Kierkegaard's Thought', *International Journal for Philosophy and Religion*, 32 (1992), 83–103.

reasons are a conscious reconstruction of the pluralist believer's world and an explication of the first datum in the pluralist's consciousness. In other words, these reasons provide pluralist believers with a theoretical foundation for the religious world they have already been inhabiting for a long time.

A serious attempt to contend with the questions raised by pluralism is desirable on two counts. First, pluralism challenges traditional believers who see themselves as members of Western liberal societies, compelling them to examine to what extent they can negate the intrinsic value of the other's world without hindering this membership. Second, concerning many public and value-based questions, believers who have opened up to the world endorse a pluralistic outlook. If they translate this outlook into actual behaviour, they must meet the theoretical challenge of formulating a pluralistic religious world-view.

My conclusion to this analysis of the possibility of toleration and pluralism within Judaism is that, conceptually, toleration is an easier position for a traditional Jewish believer to accept and it may be compatible with a traditional Jewish world-view. Endorsing pluralism, however, requires a religious revolution and while it exacts a heavy religious price, it is pluralism more than toleration that is compelling to contemporary Jews living in a modern democratic world.

THREE

Pluralism out of the Sources of Judaism
The Quest for Religious Pluralism without Relativism

RAPHAEL JOSPE

THE CHALLENGE OF TOLERATION VERSUS PLURALISM: ALEXANDER ALTMANN AND AVI SAGI

IN HIS 1957 lecture before the Council of Christians and Jews in London, my teacher Alexander Altmann discussed tolerance and the Jewish tradition.[1] In Altmann's analysis, Jews in the biblical and rabbinic periods found ways to tolerate non-Jews while rejecting internal toleration of Jewish dissent. Altmann then argued that Jews and Christians today meet on secular ground, while their theologies remain mutually exclusive. Therefore, he concluded, although theologically Jews and Christians cannot 'tolerate' each other's religions, they need each other for a common stand in the face of contemporary 'virulent paganism'. Thus, while theology divides; religion, which is broader than theology, can bring the two groups together by emulating God's love.[2]

Altmann's lecture, of course, was given prior to the radical changes in Christian–Jewish relationships since Vatican II, and could not take into account later developments. He questioned the possibility of theological toleration; half a century later, we face the question of whether we can move from mere toleration to a pluralistic acceptance of each other. Nevertheless, Altmann's perceptive distinction of internal or intra-Jewish toleration of dissent from external, interreligious toleration continues to challenge Jews involved in interreligious dialogue and promoting pluralism today,[3] and

---

[1] Alexander Altmann, *Tolerance and the Jewish Tradition*, Robert Waley Cohen Memorial Lecture (London, 1957); Heb. trans.: David Singer, in A. Altmann, *Faces of Judaism* [Panim shel yahadut] (Tel Aviv, 1983), 217–32.   [2] Altmann, *Tolerance and the Jewish Tradition*, 19.
[3] See Avi Sagi in Chapter 2, above. An earlier Hebrew version appeared in *Iyyun*, 45 (Fall 1996), 419–42, repr. in Avi Sagi, *A Challenge: Returning to Tradition* [Etgar hashivah el hamasoret] (Jerusalem, 2006), 302–23.

was a problem explicitly addressed some two centuries previously by Moses Mendelssohn, on whose thought Altmann was the leading authority.[4]

John Locke had argued that if the state cannot religiously coerce the Jew, it certainly cannot coerce dissenting Christians:

Now if we acknowledge that such an injury may not be done unto a Jew, as to compel him against his own opinion, to practice in his religion a thing that is in its nature indifferent; how can we maintain that anything of this kind may be done to a Christian?[5]

Mendelssohn inverted Locke's argument when he opposed the rabbinic ban of excommunication (*ḥerem*): if the Jews now enjoy external toleration by the Christians among whom they live, how can they not practise internal toleration of dissenting opinion within their own community?

I have that confidence in the more enlightened of the Rabbis, the elders of my nation, that they will be glad to relinquish so pernicious a prerogative, that they will cheerfully do away with all church and synagogue discipline, and let their flock enjoy, at their hands, even that kindness and forbearance, which they themselves have been so long panting for. Ah, my brethren, you have hitherto felt too hard the yoke of intolerance, and perhaps thought it a sort of satisfaction, if the power of bending those under you to such another yoke were allowed to you ... You, perhaps, let yourselves be seduced to adopt the very same system; and the power of persecuting was to you the most important prerogative which your own persecutors could bestow upon you. Thank the God of your forefathers, thank the God who is all love and mercy, that that error appears to be gradually vanishing. The nations are now tolerating and bearing with one another, while to you also they are shewing kindness and forbearance ... If you would be protected, tolerated and indulged, protect, tolerate and indulge one another. Love, and ye will be loved.[6]

Mendelssohn's innocent confidence regarding external toleration—that the nations 'are now tolerating' each other—and even more, regarding internal toleration—that the rabbis would willingly and even 'cheerfully' give up whatever coercive power they are granted by the state (including in our day by the

---

[4] See Alexander Altmann, *Moses Mendelssohn: A Biographical Study* (London, 1973).

[5] John Locke, 'A Letter Concerning Toleration', in *Locke on Politics, Religion and Education*, ed. Maurice Cranston (New York, 1965), 126.

[6] Moses Mendelssohn, preface to the German translation of Menasseh ben Israel, *Vindiciae Judaeorum*; Eng. trans.: M. Samuels, in Mendelssohn, *Jerusalem: A Treatise on Ecclesiastical Authority and Judaism* (London, 1838), i. 115–16. Selections may be found in Moses Mendelssohn, *Selections from his Writings*, ed. and trans. Eva Jospe (New York, 1975), 89–92. See my discussion of Mendelssohn's political philosophy as a critique of Locke and Lessing and as moving from toleration to pluralism while maintaining, in matters of core theology, a traditionalist stance, in Raphael Jospe, 'Moses Mendelssohn: A Medieval Modernist', in R. Fontaine, A. Schatz, and I. Zwiep (eds.), *Sepharad in Ashkenaz: Medieval Knowledge and 18th Century Jewish Enlightened Discourse* (Amsterdam, 2007), 107–40.

State of Israel)—has, unfortunately, proven to be exaggerated. The challenge of toleration and pluralism, both external and internal, remains acute.

In recent years, Avi Sagi has characterized different grades of toleration and pluralism.[7] We tolerate what we reject and view the tolerated position as error. In short, we tolerate the person, not the idea. By contrast, in pluralism we see the other position as valid and possessing value. A 'weak pluralism' is based on the sceptical view that there is one truth, but that, because of our fallibility, we have no way to discover it except through the confrontation of opposing ideas. The weak pluralist is thus not sure that he has the truth, as opposed to the person who tolerates dissent, because he is certain of his truth.[8] 'Strong pluralism', on the other hand, does not affirm only a temporary value of opposing views leading to ultimate truth, but regards different views as having inherent value of their own. Such pluralism thus adopts a measure of relativism.[9] In Sagi's analysis, weak pluralism can coexist with religious authority, because it adopts only a hypothetical epistemological relativism, but strong pluralism has generally been understood as presenting an impossible challenge to religion, by requiring that it give up its claims to religious truth, which it cannot do.[10] Sagi concludes, nevertheless, by calling for a revolution of attitudes, if not of halakhic practice. There is a need for pluralism in Western society; in practical terms, most of Western society is already pluralistic; and pluralism follows from the subjectivity of the religious experience. Sagi therefore calls for an 'intellectual golden rule': let others have their own experience and recognize its value.[11]

In Chapter 2 above, Sagi takes on the task of analysing critically the epistemic claims of exclusivism, inclusivism, and pluralism, with the explicit agenda of advocating interreligious pluralism as epistemically preferable and more logically justifiable than exclusivism and as the way to resolve David Hume's dilemma that differing religious claims are necessarily contrary, so that if one religion's claims are true, the claims of others must be false. At the same time, when Sagi's masterful presentation of various theoretical grounds for interreligious pluralism shifts to the question of internal Jewish pluralism, he concludes that traditional Jewish commitment to halakhah may be compatible at most with toleration, not pluralism: 'At best, these considerations can substantiate toleration, but under no circumstances can they justify pluralism . . . conceptually, toleration is an easier position for a traditional Jewish believer to accept and it may be compatible with a traditional Jewish world-view.'[12]

[7] Avi Sagi, 'The Jewish Religion: Tolerance and the Possibility of Pluralism' (Heb.), *Iyyun*, 43 (1994), 175–200.

[8] Ibid. 184.   [9] Ibid. 185–6.   [10] Ibid. 194–5.   [11] Ibid. 198–200.

[12] Above, pp. 84–5. Regarding the greater problem of internal rather than external pluralism or toleration, Avishai Margalit similarly observes: 'Religious expectations from people perceived as belonging to one's own religion are liable to be much more demanding than those relating to

In traditional terms, Sagi is undoubtedly correct, as he is in pointing out that we live with a fundamental tension between the two worlds in which we are citizens, traditional Judaism (which can at best foster internal toleration) and modern, liberal society (which promotes, and in a sense demands, pluralism).

I do not claim to have necessarily succeeded in moving beyond the point at which Sagi stops, but I fully concur with his analysis that we need a conceptual religious revolution,[13] for which undoubtedly most traditionally religious Jews are as yet unprepared, and which they will reject out of hand, especially given the increasing rigidity, entrenchment, and outright hostility to modern liberal culture in much of the Orthodox Jewish community. My own chapter can, accordingly, be construed as an attempt to apply in a Jewish context what Sagi is outlining in general theoretical terms, and thereby to show that Jewish sources do in fact provide, or can be understood as providing, a theoretical basis and paradigm for pluralism.

My sources are, however, not halakhic literature (as some of Sagi's are), but rabbinic, medieval, and modern Jewish thought, especially on the divine revelation which is, after all, the purported authority of the halakhah to begin with. A new look at how revelation has been or can be understood Jewishly, may therefore enable us at least to begin the conceptual religious revolution that Sagi recognizes is needed to break out of the halakhic impasse precluding internal Jewish pluralism, and to encourage a radical shift in attitude and in behaviour, directed both internally and externally, from mere toleration to genuine pluralism.

In the course of this chapter, I will have occasion to relate to specific arguments that Sagi makes. However, since Sagi appropriately devotes a fair section of his analysis to a presentation and critique of John Hick's pluralism, and since at about the same time that Sagi wrote his original paper Hick was subjected to an interesting critique by Gavin D'Costa, it may be useful to supplement Sagi's analysis with D'Costa's critique and Hick's important response to it. A brief summary of both is therefore relevant to Sagi's analysis and to my own thought, which reflects from a Jewish perspective some of the same

people on the outside' ('The Ring: On Religious Pluralism', in David Heyd (ed.), *Toleration: An Elusive Virtue* (Princeton, NJ, 1996), 147).

[13] For example, Sagi suggests that Jewish continuity would no longer be based on traditional truth claims, which are contingent, but on (1) similarity of practices and (2) disposition to aspects of tradition; the 'pathos of commitment is not contingent'. There are points of striking similarity, beyond the scope of this chapter, between Sagi's approach at this point and the reconstructionist thought of Mordecai Kaplan (1881–1983), especially Kaplan's theory of *sancta* and his statement (in personal correspondence with me when I was a student) that 'in Judaism as a civilization "belonging" is prior to "believing", although meaningless without "believing" '. Sagi's description of expressive pluralism (especially that of Gordon Kaufman) also parallels in many respects Kaplan's approach to God as a 'functional noun', in which the focus is not on God as a being but how the concept of God functions in our lives.

or parallel considerations that Hick previously discussed from a Christian perspective.

D'Costa argues that pluralism is logically a form of exclusivism; that pluralism and exclusivism share the same logic and that nothing called pluralism really exists.[14] As D'Costa presents it, exclusivism is the claim that only one religion is true, and that others are, therefore, false. Pluralism is faced with two choices. The first option is to deny that there are any criteria external to the religious traditions by which to evaluate their truth claims. In that case, we have no basis for denying the truth claims of Nazism or other pernicious ideologies. The second option is to deny the validity those pernicious truth claims—but in that case, the pluralist uses the same logic as the exclusivist, namely that his truth claims are correct and provide the basis for determining that others are false. D'Costa concludes that the pluralist and the exclusivist thus differ only regarding the criteria they employ for determining the truth, but that there is no difference in the logic of their claims.[15]

D'Costa calls Hick's Kantian distinction (to which we will return later) of what we know—the phenomenon—from the unknowable absolute reality— the noumenon—'transcendental agnosticism' and asks how, then, can Hick actually know that the Real transcends language and is indescribable? Transcendental agnosticism thus also makes specific truth claims. And if those claims are true, that the Real cannot be known, then religious claims to revelation are false, in which case, again, D'Costa concludes that Hick's ostensible pluralism ultimately is exclusivist, because it claims for itself the truth (that the Real is unknowable), and denies the truth of other religious claims (that we know God through revelation).

Hick responded directly and forcefully to D'Costa's critique.[16] The fact that there may be more than one true religion does not mean that *all* religions are true paths to the Real, nor does pluralism mean relativism, namely, that there are no criteria whatsoever for judging truth, and that all claims (including those of Nazis) are equally valid. The criterion for differentiating true from false religion, however, is moral.

This criterion is a basic moral insight . . . Within the terms of the pluralistic hypothesis this criterion represents the moral consensus of all the great world faiths. The Golden Rule, in which this basic consensus is encapsulated, is common to them all.[17]

---

[14] Gavin D'Costa, 'The Impossibility of a Pluralist View of Religions', *Religious Studies*, 32 (1996), 223–32. [15] Ibid. 226.

[16] John Hick, 'The Possibility of Religious Pluralism: A Reply to Gavin D'Costa', *Religious Studies*, 33 (1997), 161–6. Hick also succinctly summarized the pluralistic theories he developed in a series of books in John Hick, 'Religious Pluralism', in Mircea Eliade (ed.), *Encyclopedia of Religion* (New York, 1987), xii. 331–2.

[17] Hick, 'The Possibility of Religious Pluralism', 164.

Exclusivism, Hick maintains, is a self-committing affirmation of faith, whereas pluralism is a philosophical hypothesis to explain the data of different religions, a 'meta-theory' (what Sagi refers to as Hick's 'meta-religion' or 'second-order analysis') about the relationship between historical religions. Hick rejects D'Costa's description of his theory as 'transcendental agnosticism' and insists that he does not claim to 'know' that the Real is beyond language. The 'ineffability', as Hick calls it, of the Real is a 'hypothesis' explaining how diverse religions are equally effective (or ineffective) contexts for salvific transformation of human life despite their diverse conceptions.[18]

Rejecting a purely expressive interpretation of religion as a function only of the human imagination and not as relating to some reality,[19] Hick affirms that the pluralistic hypothesis:

starts from the basic faith that religious experience is not purely imaginative projection, but is also (whilst including such projection), a cognitive response to a transcendent reality. The hypothesis is thus explicitly a religious interpretation of religion.[20]

[18] Hick, 'The Possibility of Religious Pluralism', 163. Although also beyond the scope of this essay, it seems to me that Hick's approach here bears a strong resemblance to Mordecai Kaplan's analysis of the function of religion in a civilization and his 'functional definition' of God as the power that makes for salvation, that is, experiencing life as meaningful and worthwhile.

[19] Jon Levenson reflects a similar concern for the truth and a rejection of the understanding of religion merely as 'self-expression' when he warns of 'the danger of relativism, which prompts one to say that each vision is true for the person who has it, indeed that every vision is true for whoever experiences it, and specifically that all religions are equally valid and all putative witness to the truth of one's own religious tradition is but self-expression in support of private opinion . . . I question, though, whether it is wise for a religious minority to dismiss the question of truth so readily' (Jon Levenson, 'Can Roman Catholicism Validate Jewish Biblical Interpretation?', *Studies in Christian–Jewish Relations*, 1 (2005–6), 173). Levenson also cites Pope John Paul II's encyclical letter *Fides et ratio* (1998): 'A legitimate plurality of positions has yielded to an undifferentiated pluralism, based upon the assumption that all positions are equally valid, which is one of today's most widespread symptoms of the lack of confidence in truth' ('Can Roman Catholicism Validate Jewish Biblical Interpretation?', 174). Rather than such 'undifferentiated pluralism', Levenson proposes 'autonomous pluralism', namely that Religion A should not discuss Religion B in its own terms and norms but only in Religion B's or neutral terms. For example, Judaism refers to the Tanakh, which Christianity refers to as the 'Old Testament', while 'Hebrew Bible' is the 'neutral' term used in historical-critical study. On the uniqueness and incommensurability of individuals and religious communities, and the insistence that each be understood in its own terms, see Joseph B. Soloveitchk, 'Confrontation', *Tradition*, 6/2 (1964), 5–29.

[20] Hick, 'The Possibility of Religious Pluralism', 164. In his study of the doctrine that *extra ecclesiam nulla salus*, Jesuit scholar and theologian Francis A. Sullivan has criticized Hick's pluralism: 'Hick's theory is incompatible with Christian belief that Jesus Christ is the incarnate word of God' (*Salvation Outside the Church? Tracing the History of the Catholic Response* (Mahwah, NJ, 1992), 170). Nevertheless, Sullivan's study documents how, throughout Christian history, the exclusivist doctrine was frequently mitigated by the inclusivist concern that those who are not culpable in rejecting (or being ignorant of) the Christian message can, nevertheless, attain salvation outside the Church. As Sullivan concludes, salvation is possible outside the Church, but the Church still plays an essential and necessary role in 'the divine economy of salvation' (ibid. 204). In other words, in Sullivan's view, on the individual level, salvation is indeed possible *outside* the

Claiming that one's own religious experience is not purely subjective, but is in some sense at least partially an experience of reality, need not preclude recognizing that the different religious experience of others is also a cognitive response to a transcendent reality.

However, claiming that religious experience is not entirely subjective or expressive is not to deny that there is a significant subjective component to the religious experience. Both Sagi and Hick point out that opponents of pluralism often fail to take into account the subjective nature of faith and religious experience. The difference between faith and knowledge is that we *know* something that we can demonstrate and for which we have evidence, whereas we *believe* something to be true when we lack demonstration and evidence and yet affirm it to be true.[21] Since faith deals with unproven and unprovable affirmations, it is inherently subjective and culturally relative. At least a weak form of pluralism seems to follow inevitably from such subjectivity and cultural relativity.

CHRISTIAN CHALLENGES

Religious pluralism has intrigued me for years, and led me to write several articles dealing with the concept of chosenness, exclusivity versus inclusivity, and chosenness's compatibility with pluralism.[22] My thesis has been that, correctly

Church, but on the universal level, there is no salvation *without* the Church, because of its unique role in 'the divine economy'.

[21] Menachem Kellner's approach to faith is that it involves trust, which should find expression in behaviour, whereas knowledge involves acquiescence in the truth of certain claims, which do not necessitate any specific behaviour. Kellner identifies his approach with that of Maimonides. Regardless of whether Kellner is correct that this is Maimonides' understanding of the nature of faith (and Kellner's reading is not necessarily supported by Maimonides' insistence that the common people should accept on authority certain basic beliefs (*Guide of the Perplexed*, i. 35)), his approach reflects that of Martin Buber, who contrasted two types of faith: Jewish faith, 'the fact that I trust someone, without being able to offer sufficient reasons for my trust in him'; and Christian faith, 'likewise, without being able to give a sufficient reason, I acknowledge a thing to be true' (Martin Buber, *Two Types of Faith*, trans. N. Goldhawk (New York, 1961), 7). Moses Mendelssohn makes a similar point, that *emunah* means 'trust' (*Jerusalem and Other Jewish Writings*, ed. and trans. Alfred Jospe (New York, 1969), 71; cf. the translation by Allan Arkush, with introduction and commentary by A. Altmann (Hanover, 1983), 100). In any event, as Buber admits more candidly than Kellner does, even a behavioural, rather than cognitive, understanding of *emunah* still involves an attitude 'without being able to offer sufficient reasons for my trust', that is, there is no demonstrative evidence to justify the trust.

[22] See Raphael Jospe, 'The Concept of the Chosen People: An Interpretation', *Judaism: A Quarterly Journal*, 43/2 (Spring 1994), 127–48; id., 'Educating for Interreligious Responsibility: Ritual Exclusivity vs. Spiritual Inclusivity', in Emmanuel Agius and Lionel Chircop (eds.), *Caring for Future Generations: Jewish, Christian and Islamic Perspectives* (Twickenham, 1998), 20–41; id., 'Chosenness in Judaism: Exclusivity vs. Inclusivity', in Raphael Jospe, Truman Madsen, and Seth Ward (eds.), *Covenant and Chosenness in Judaism and Mormonism* (Madison, NJ, 2001), 173–94. An earlier version of the current chapter appeared in *Studies in Christian–Jewish Relations*, 2 (2007), 92–113.

understood, the Jewish concept of the chosen people is not externally directed, implying that Jews in fact are better than other people; rather, chosenness is internally directed, challenging Jews to become better people. This concept, I maintain, is compatible with religious pluralism, based on the paradigm of the Jewish obligation to live in accordance with the commandments of the Torah while accepting the legitimacy of other ways of life in accordance with the paradigm of the universal 'seven commandments of the children of Noah'.[23] I propose a reversal of traditional claims: instead of spiritual exclusivity—the notions that there is only one truth, that one group has exclusive possession of that truth and thus of the keys to salvation—which logically leads to ritual inclusivity (the impulse to proselytize and include others in one's own religious community), we should work for spiritual inclusivity; that is, the recognition that different groups can understand the truth, albeit frequently in diverse ways. This logically leads to ritual exclusivity, or pluralism; that is, the legitimacy and desirability of different religious approaches and ritual practices, and there is no reason to seek to proselytize others.

My thoughts on these questions were prompted and enriched by two Catholic thinkers. The radical theologian Hans Küng has said that without peace among the world's religions, there will be no peace among the nations[24]—a proposition that strikes me as self-evidently true in this era of the 'global village' and growing world-wide religious fanaticism, strife, and terror.[25] In our world, unfortunately, religion is rarely a force for peace and is

[23] In a panel discussion of my thesis in Jerusalem some years ago, and borrowing from current diet-drink terminology, Krister Stendahl criticized this structure as relegating non-Jews to a kind of second-class 'Torah-lite' status.

[24] Hans Küng, 'World Peace—World Religions—World Ethic', in Agius and Chircop (eds.), *Caring for Future Generations*, 69–81, esp. 74. Küng previously edited a volume advocating a world ethic from diverse religious perspectives (*Yes to a Global Ethic* (London, 1996); orig.: *Ja zum Weltethos, Perspektiven für die Suche nach Orientierung* (Munich, 1995)) based on a 'Parliament of the World's Religions' convened in Chicago in 1993. In his preface, 'Will a Global Ethic Prevail?', Küng states: 'All over the world, religious convictions are often the cause, not of peace, understanding and reconciliation, but of war, intolerance and fanaticism. There are fundamentalist tendencies in all religions, but at present they are making themselves felt in a particularly cruel way in Muslim countries . . . But before we point at fundamentalism in other religions, it is better to fight its causes where we are.' It is in this spirit of 'where we are' that I am attempting here to formulate a Jewish paradigm for pluralism (in response to Menachem Kellner), as my earlier papers did for inclusivism, which I suggest is compatible with the traditional concept of chosenness.

[25] Some fifty years ago, in the aftermath of the Second World War and the Holocaust and at the height of the Cold War, Isaiah Berlin wrote: 'One belief, more than any other, is responsible for the slaughter of individuals on the altars of great historical ideals . . . This is the belief that somewhere, in the past or in the future, in divine revelation or in the mind of an individual thinker, in the pronouncements of history or science . . . there is a final solution. This ancient faith rests on the conviction that all positive values in which men have believed must, in the end, be compatible' (Isaiah Berlin, 'Two Concepts of Liberty', in id., *Liberty*, ed. Henry Hardy

often used (or abused) to exacerbate conflicts that are by nature national and political, not theological.

Conversely, in 1994, at an interreligious conference in Jerusalem, Cardinal Joseph Ratzinger (now Pope Benedict XVI), who is generally known for his conservative approach, asked whether we can move from mere toleration to mutual acceptance.[26] This question had a profound influence on the development of my own thought, as I have attempted to develop a Jewish paradigm for pluralism.[27]

As is often the case with thinkers, posing a conceptual challenge is more important than the specific answer proposed by the thinker himself. For as became clear in his subsequent official declaration *Dominus Iesus*, Ratzinger's call for mutual acceptance meant only respect for the personal equality of the other, not acceptance or recognition of the validity of the other's doctrinal

(Oxford, 2002), 212). While modern weapons of mass destruction obviously render the problem more urgent, the concern that religions not create or exacerbate deadly conflict is not new. Hans Küng's call for peace among the religions is reminiscent, for example, of 'On the Peace of Faith' (*De pace fidei*) of Nicolaus of Cusa (1401–64), which opens with the prayer that God 'might moderate the persecution, which raged more than usual on account of diverse religious rites' (Nicolaus of Cusa, 'On the Peace of Faith', in *Toward a New Council of Florence: 'On the Peace of Faith' and Other Works*, trans. William Wertz, Jr. (Washington, DC, 1993), 231). 'Many turn their weapons against each other for the sake of religion and in their power compel men to renounce long observed doctrines or kill them . . . It is a condition of earthly human nature to defend as truth lengthy custom, which is regarded as part of nature. And thus no small dissensions arise, when any community prefers its beliefs over another's' (ibid. 232–3). In turn, we find remarkable similarity between some of the arguments in 'On the Peace of Faith' and positions expressed in the 'Letters of the Brethren of Purity' (*Rasa'il Ikhwan al-Safa*), a collection of fifty-one or fifty-two letters (depending on the numbering) of a tenth-century group of Ismaili Muslim intellectuals in Basra (see I. R. Netton, *Muslim Neoplatonists: An Introduction to the Thought of the Brethren of Purity* (London, 1982); *The Case of the Animals versus Man before the King of the Jinn*, trans Lenn Evan Goodman (Boston, 1978)). For example, in the letter 'On the Generation of Animals and their Kinds' the king of the Jinn asks the Persian spokesman why people 'slay one another if all their faiths have the same goal of encounter with God'. The Persian replies: 'This does not arise from faith, for "there is no compulsion in faith," rather, it comes from the institution of faith, that is from the state . . . Religion cannot do without a ruler to command the people to uphold his institutions out of allegiance or by force. This is the cause of the adherents' of different religions slaying one another—the quest for primacy and power in the state. Each desires that all people should follow his own faith or sect and the laws of his own religion' (*The Case of the Animals versus Man*, trans. Goodman, p. 194). The quote: 'There is no compulsion in faith' (or 'Let there be no compulsion in religion') is from Quran 2: 256, *la ikraha fi'l din*.

[26] Ratzinger posed this challenge in the International Jewish–Christian Conference on Religious Leadership in a Secular Society in Jerusalem (Feb. 1994).

[27] In this age of widespread, murderous religious fanaticism and terror, mere toleration would frequently be a great improvement. This chapter attempts to develop, in response to Ratzinger's challenge, a Jewish paradigm for moving beyond toleration to pluralism. Irving Greenberg argues for going beyond pluralism to Jewish–Christian partnership (*For the Sake of Heaven and Earth: The New Encounter Between Judaism and Christianity* (Philadelphia, 2004), 42). Later in the book, however, he refers to 'the possibility of true pluralism, i.e., a love pluralism of passionate people, not the tolerance of apathy' (ibid. 119).

position. Such acceptance is at best only *de facto* and not *de jure*, according to Ratzinger, 'the Church's constant missionary proclamation is endangered today by relativistic theories which seek to justify religious pluralism, not only *de facto* but also *de iure*.'[28]

A JEWISH CHALLENGE: MENACHEM KELLNER

Shifting from Roman Catholic influences to the context of contemporary constructive Jewish philosophy, my position on pluralism stands in theoretical contrast to the thought of my friend and colleague, Menachem Kellner. Although in practical terms of traditional religious lifestyle, Zionist commitment, and moral and political values Kellner and I are not far apart, in theory we differ sharply. Our two papers in *Covenant and Chosenness in Judaism and Mormonism* represent clearly contrasting views.[29] I have called Kellner's approach 'an enlightened and sophisticated form of traditional triumphalism',[30] because in Kellner's view, 'in the messianic future' the dichotomy between Jews and non-Jews 'will be overcome, and all human beings will share the same relationship with God. In the messianic world, there will be no Jews and gentiles, only worshippers of the one true God.'[31] The distinction between Jews and non-Jews will be 'overcome', not because all non-Jews will convert to Judaism in its current, particularistic form, but because in Kellner's reading of Maimonides, Judaism is a matter of affirming the truth and not merely an ethnic identity. Therefore, by accepting the truth non-Jews, in effect, will become Jewish in a universal sense: 'The messianic age will witness not so much a triumph of Judaism so much as the triumph of truth.'[32]

Kellner concludes:

I must express my sympathy for Maimonides. To my mind the 'postmodern'

[28] 'Declaration "Dominus Iesus" on the Unicity and Salvific Universality of Jesus Christ and the Church' (6 Aug. 2000). This Roman Catholic concern about relativism and the equation of religious pluralism with relativism were reflected several years later, when I was sent by the Israeli Ministry of Foreign Affairs to lecture at the Vatican (Sept. 2001) and presented my pluralistic thesis at the Urbaniana Pontifical University in Rome. The Rettore Magnifico Abrogio Spreafico asked me whether the pluralism I propose is not, in fact, tantamount to relativism. I replied that I did not equate pluralism with relativism, and then said that even if my epistemology was wrong, I was morally certain that relativism has not killed people the way absolutism has. My reply received terrible confirmation exactly twenty-four hours later. Unknown to me, while I was flying back to Israel from Rome, the murderous 9/11 attacks of al-Qaeda in America were taking place.

[29] Raphael Jospe, Truman G. Madsen, and Seth Ward (eds.), *Covenant and Chosenness in Judaism and Mormonism* (Madison, NJ, 2001). Kellner's paper, 'Overcoming Chosenness' (pp. 147–72), maintains a universalistic understanding of the truth, and proposes a Maimonidean universal 'religion of truth' for the future.

[30] Jospe, 'Chosenness in Judaism', 193 n. 28. Irving Greenberg writes: 'Surrendering religious exclusivism or triumphalism is a crucial moral step' (*For the Sake of Heaven and Earth*, 134).

[31] Kellner, 'Overcoming Chosenness', 152.   [32] Ibid. 160.

approach takes an unfortunate reality—that we cannot agree on what is true, or even on what truth is—and turns it into an ideal. This position is, I think, self-refuting to the extent that it makes real communication among human beings impossible. It is also based upon a rejection of the idea of revelation, at least as it has been historically understood in Judaism, according to which the Torah is truth. This truth may be misunderstood, it may be viewed differently in different times, it may be better or worse understood as we get further from Sinai and closer to the Messiah, it may exist only in Heaven, here being approximated, but truth there is. In short, Maimonides' vision of a universalist, not pluralist, messianic future was unusual in his day, consistent with his basic beliefs, necessitated by the understanding that revelation teaches truth, and thoroughly admirable.[33]

Kellner's position is clear: pluralism is at best an 'unfortunate reality' in our current condition and is 'self-refuting'. We must strive for the ultimate triumph in messianic times of universal truth, a truth that Kellner believes is taught in historic Jewish revelation.

This view is reiterated and reinforced in his book *Must a Jew Believe Anything?* 'Judaism teaches truth, and . . . Orthodoxy understands that truth more completely than competing versions of Judaism. These competing versions are wrong and mistaken.'[34] Nevertheless, on several theoretical and pragmatic grounds Kellner argues that calling these versions 'heretical is simply not helpful'.[35] Although he rejects 'Maimonides' dogmatic version of Judaism', he does not 'wish at the same time to reject the . . . claims that Judaism teaches truth and that there is one absolute truth—for these are claims that I am in no way willing to give up'.[36]

In his new Afterword to the second edition, Kellner adds that:

[There is a problem] inherent in the concept of religious pluralism itself: why not extend the bounds of pluralism beyond the bounds of Judaism? If one relativizes truth within Judaism, on what grounds can one refuse to relativize it outside Judaism?[37]

Kellner's argument here—that internal Jewish pluralism is unacceptable because one could then no longer oppose external interreligious pluralism—strikes me as a peculiar adoption of the logic employed by Peter Stuyvesant, the governor of the Dutch colony of New Amsterdam who in 1654 attempted unsuccessfully to keep Jews out of the colony, arguing that 'giving them liberty, we cannot refuse the Lutherans and Papists'.[38] Kellner's objection to recognition of Jewish

---

[33] Ibid.
[34] Menachem Kellner, *Must a Jew Believe Anything?* (London, 1999); 2nd edn. with new Afterword (Oxford, 2006), 125.   [35] Ibid. 125.   [36] Ibid. 113.   [37] Ibid. 140.
[38] Cited in Jonathan Sarna, *American Judaism: A History* (New Haven, 2004), 2; Henry Feingold, *Zion in America: The Jewish Experience from Colonial Times to the Present* (New York, 1974), 23.

dissenting opinion is thus justified on the grounds that it might lead, God forbid, to recognition of Christian dissenting opinion.

Kellner's logic is the opposite of that employed by Moses Mendelssohn. In his preface of March 1782 to the German translation of Manasseh ben Israel's *Vindiciae Judaeorum*,[39] Mendelssohn argued that the Jews could scarcely expect to be tolerated by Christians, from whom they differ so fundamentally, so long as they are themselves intolerant of much less significant internal, Jewish dissent: 'If you wish to be shown concern, tolerance and forbearance by others, show concern, tolerance and forbearance to each other.'[40] Mendelssohn's argument, that external, interreligious toleration should lead to internal, intra-religious toleration, strikes me as far more persuasive than Kellner's argument against internal Jewish pluralism on the grounds that it might lead to external religious pluralism.

Kellner's argument also fails to deal with what I regard as empirically true of many Jews and Christians and probably of many Muslims also: it is often easier to attain external, interreligious toleration or pluralism than to attain internal toleration or pluralism within the religious community, precisely the point that Sagi makes in halakhic terms in Chapter 2 above.

Most of my thesis here relates to pluralism in general, without specific regard for important questions pertaining to possible differences between internal and external forms of pluralism. At this point, on the level of internal pluralism (or at least toleration), I note that Kellner's statement, 'Judaism teaches truth, and . . . Orthodoxy understands that truth more completely than competing versions of Judaism', strikes me as counterfactual or at best as wishful thinking. Jewish Orthodoxy in its modern, enlightened, and moderate form—typified by people like Kellner—is today an endangered species and has been outflanked and overwhelmed by sectarian ultra-Orthodoxy, which is largely fundamentalist, literalist in its traditional, rabbinic reading of the Bible and the Talmud, suspicious of science, and opposed to much of modern culture.[41] Such Orthodoxy, as Kellner well knows, affirms as absolute truths many traditional assumptions that are patently false when taken literally. To cite a few: some of the astronomical assumptions on which Jewish calendrical

---

[39] Menasseh ben Israel wrote *Vindiciae Judaeorum* to Oliver Cromwell, arguing for the readmission of the Jews to England.

[40] Mendelssohn, *Selections from his Writings*, 99–100. A complete translation by M. Samuels was published in Mendelssohn, *Jerusalem: A Treatise on Ecclesiastical Authority and Judaism*, i. 77–116.

[41] By 'literalist' I do not mean corporealist, that is, that they take biblical anthropomorphisms literally, but rather that their reading of the Bible is shaped by an exclusive reliance on rabbinic tradition (or on certain aspects of that tradition), and in turn that their reading of the rabbis is lit-eralist and uncritical, even when the rabbis' own non-literal and midrashic readings of Scripture or other views are implausible. Such literalist reading of the rabbis is strongly criticized by Maimonides on Mishnah *San.* 10, Introduction.

calculations are based; biblical and rabbinic statements about the age of the universe or regarding medicine or that preclude the evidence of evolution, archaeology, and biblical criticism. Had Kellner expressed admiration for the disciplined traditional Jewish way of life and appreciation of observant Jews' dedication and commitment to the Torah and to study, often entailing personal hardship and demanding sacrifice, he would have been on far safer ground than his attribution of absolute truth to Orthodoxy in a book devoted largely to an admirable attack on historically false and ideologically dubious contemporary Orthodox dogmatics.

Finally, at the 2005 World Congress of Jewish Studies organized by the Elijah Interfaith Institute as a follow-up to the Scranton conference, Kellner devoted much of his lecture to a critique of my thesis of pluralism, on two grounds: first, he regards pluralism as inherently absurd, theoretically self-refuting, and essentially relativistic; second, he maintains that there are no precedents for such pluralism in traditional Jewish thought.

What follows is my response to these critiques. It is first important to note, however, that pluralism is frequently equated with relativism,[42] as in Ratzinger's *Dominus Iesus*, in Gavin D'Costa's critique of John Hick, and in statements by Kellner. Yet pluralism cannot be correctly equated with relativism. Plural understandings of the truth, or even plural truths, are not the same as no truth at all, and they are certainly not the same as no moral standards. As Maimonides pointed out,[43] moral judgements do not deal with what is theoretically true and false (intelligible: Arabic: *ma'qulat*; Hebrew: *muskalot*), but with practical determinations ('generally accepted' propositions: Arabic: *mashhurat*; Hebrew: *mefursamot*) of what is good and proper or evil and improper. To confuse theoretical pluralism with moral (and other) relativism blurs this important distinction.[44]

Irving Greenberg also argues admirably for maintaining this distinction:

Pluralism means more than accepting or even affirming the other. It entails recognizing the blessings in the other's existence, because it balances one's own position and brings all of us closer to the ultimate goal. Even when we are right in our own

---

[42] See n. 28, above.

[43] Maimonides, *Guide of the Perplexed*, i. 2; id., *Treatise on Logic*, ch. 8. There is serious question as to whether the *Treatise on Logic* was written by Maimonides.

[44] This is, as we have seen, a point underlying John Hick's response to Gavin D'Costa, that the criterion for differentiating true from false religion is a moral one. On the confusion of pluralism with relativism, Irving Greenberg has written: 'To my great frustration, the Orthodox failed to distinguish between pluralism and relativism; to my failure, I could not persuade them of the essential difference between these positions—in other words, that one could uphold the authority of tradition while making room for other religious systems' (*For the Sake of Heaven and Earth*, 11). I share Greenberg's frustration, but not only Orthodox Jews fail to make this important distinction.

position, the other who contradicts our position may be our corrective or our check against going to excess . . . Pluralism is not relativism, for we hold on to our absolutes; however, we make room for others' as well.[45]

Relativism . . . is the loss of capacity to affirm any standards. But the deepest religious response is pluralism—the recognition that there are plural absolute standards that can live and function together, even when they conflict. The deepest insight of pluralism is that dignity, truth and power function best when they are pluralized, e.g., divided and distributed, rather than centralized or absolutized . . . The essential difference between pluralism and relativism is that pluralism is based on the principle that there still is an absolute truth . . . Pluralism is an absolutism that has come to recognize its limitations.[46]

Unfortunately, after stating that 'we hold on to our absolutes', Greenberg does not explain how to reconcile claims to absolute truth with pluralism. If one's position is held to be absolutely true, it may need a moral 'check' against practical excess, but why should absolute truth require theoretical correction? Greenberg and I agree that pluralism is not relativism, but how can it be compatible with absolutist claims? Does not Greenberg's vision of 'divided and distributed, rather than centralized or absolutized' truth contradict the 'absolute truth' that he affirms? How are we to understand Greenberg's assertion that 'pluralism is an absolutism that recognizes that an absolute truth/value need not be absolutely right to be absolute'?[47]

More than two centuries ago Moses Mendelssohn advocated a clearer and more consistent form of pluralism that avoided such problematical claims to absolute truth, or that Judaism is 'absolutely the best' religion.[48] Along these lines, I shall argue that claims to absolute truth are not merely morally dangerous,[49] but theoretically meaningless.

---

[45] Greenberg, *For the Sake of Heaven and Earth*, 196. Gordon Grayham argues that there is no necessary connection between pluralism (or toleration) and relativism. Relativism does not necessarily lead to toleration; one can regard all religions as false, and yet regard some as admirable and others as contemptible. Conversely, objectivism need not lead to intolerance, if disagreement and argument are seen as part of the process of arriving at the truth. See Gordon Grayham, 'Tolerance, Pluralism and Relativism', in David Heyd (ed.), *Toleration: An Elusive Virtue* (Princeton, NJ, 1996), 50.   [46] Greenberg, *For the Sake of Heaven and Earth*, 201–3.

[47] Ibid. 205. The tension (which I regard as unresolved) in Greenberg's thought between pluralism and absolutism, which may prove inevitable in much progressive yet faithful religious thought, also characterizes much of Nicolaus of Cusa's 'On the Peace of Faith', a consistent theme of which is the need to avoid conflict and to respect religious diversity, which 'may bring an increase in devotion', and to tolerate different rites (Nicolaus of Cusa, 'On the Peace of Faith', 233, 268). At the same time, since all the diverse religions 'presuppose' a common, single religion and wisdom (ibid. 236–7, 272), ultimately 'all diversity of religion ought to be brought into one orthodox faith . . . The Lord has taken pity on His people and agreed to the plan to lead all diversity of religions through mutual agreement of all men harmoniously back to a single, henceforth inviolable religion' (ibid. 235).   [48] See the discussion below and n. 95.

[49] Isaiah Berlin concludes his 'Two Concepts of Liberty' with the warning that to see guaran-

Returning to relativism, the truly meaningful question is not whether pluralism necessarily entails some degree of relativism in general, but *what kind of relativism*. I cannot imagine that anyone is bothered by a pluralism of flavours of ice cream, if it should prove to be the case that one's favourite taste is both subjective and relative. As a Jew, what concerns me most is moral relativism, which implies that there are no meaningfully binding standards (however derived) on all people. The experience of twentieth-century totalitarianism generally, and the Holocaust in particular, should teach us the obvious dangers of such a position, and the Nuremberg Trials correctly, from my perspective as the child of a German Jewish family many of whose members were murdered by the Nazis, established international recognition that there are certain norms to which all people can and should be held, regardless of whether they were following what their country posited to be legal orders.

Isaiah Berlin, who was a clear and consistent advocate of pluralism (in a broader political context), found no inconsistency between affirming pluralism and the belief in universal moral values.

There are universal values. This is an empirical fact about mankind . . . The idea of human rights rests on the true belief that there are certain goods—freedom, justice, pursuit of happiness, honesty, love—that are in the interest of all human beings as such, not as members of this or that nationality, religion, professional, character . . . There are certain things which human beings require as such . . . because they lead human lives as men and women.[50]

Yet, Berlin insists, emphasizing only universal moral ideals, as many liberals and revolutionaries do, when they speak on behalf of people's 'real selves', that is, their supposedly true human interests, often reflects a failure to understand people as they are (rather than as the liberals or revolutionaries think they should be), and can lead to a loss of liberty:

They do not allow for the variety of basic human needs. Nor yet for the ingenuity with which men can prove to their own satisfaction that the road to one ideal also leads to its contrary . . . The belief that some single formula can in principle be found whereby all the diverse ends of men can be harmoniously realized is demonstrably false.[51]

Pluralism, Berlin concludes, entails negative liberty (freedom from interference) and is thus more humane and a truer ideal than monistic, authoritarian positive ideals.

tees of the eternal and objective validity of our values reflects a deep childhood craving for certainty, but to allow that need for certainty to affect our behaviour 'is a symptom of an equally deep and more dangerous, moral and political immaturity'. Berlin argues that 'principles are not less sacred because their duration cannot be guaranteed' ('Two Concepts of Liberty', 217).

[50] Ramin Johanbegloo, *Conversations with Isaiah Berlin* (London, 1992), 37–9.
[51] Berlin, 'Two Concepts of Liberty', 208–14.

Similarly, John Kekes, who openly acknowledges his indebtedness to Berlin, argues that pluralism is not equivalent to relativism but is an alternative to both monism (the position that there is only one reasonable set of values, always and everywhere) and relativism (the notion that all values are merely conventional and lack objective validation). In Kekes's view, pluralism is both a first-order ethical theory, concerned with values, and a second-order meta-ethical theory, analysing moral judgements.[52]

The first of Kekes's 'six theses of pluralism' is the plurality and conditionality of values. Pluralists deny the monistic belief in one absolute and overriding value, transcending all other values, because all values are conditional in the sense that they may be superseded by other conflicting values. For example, the value of human life, which a monist might regard as absolute, is conditional, because it may be superseded by another value, namely the need to fight tyranny or injustice, even if life is lost in the process.[53] However, this pluralist opposition to monism cannot be reduced to relativism, because at least some values are still affirmed as universally valid.

Kekes differentiates between 'primary values', which concern benefits and harms that are universal and transcend cultural differences, and 'secondary values', which reflect diverse cultures, traditions, individuals, and periods. Although people agree on the universal primary values, they may legitimately differ on secondary values. Pluralism thus shares with relativism a rejection of monist absolutism—that one absolute value always overrides others—but it shares with monism a rejection of the relativist denial that values can be justified independently of context. Kekes similarly maintains that 'deep conventions' protecting the minimal requirements for all good lives, however conceived, derive from universal human nature, unlike 'variable conventions', which differ by traditions and contextual conceptions of the good life. Like Berlin, Kekes concludes, therefore, that pluralism affirms universal 'primary values' and 'deep conventions' (and, therefore, cannot be equated with relativism):

This pluralist argument is intended to apply only to secondary values that do indeed give appropriate forms to primary values . . . The pluralist view is that in a morally acceptable tradition there must be some deep conventions. What makes them deep is that they protect the minimum required of all good lives.[54]

Despite these arguments, it seems to me that if it should still be the case that pluralism entails some degree of relativism, we would then be obliged to differentiate between moral relativism, which may entail clear and immediate practical dangers, and various epistemic relativisms that may have theoretical errors but do not present existential danger. Moral relativism affects interpersonal

[52] John Kekes, *The Morality of Pluralism* (Princeton, NJ, 1993), 12–13.
[53] Ibid. 17–20.   [54] Ibid. 34.

matters (*bein adam leḥavero*), whereas epistemic relativism (if it be relativism at all, rather than pluralism) regarding diverse understandings of God refers to highly speculative areas of personal and subjective questions between the individual and God (*bein adam lamakom*).

As a Jew, I am far less troubled by at least some degree of epistemic relativism, since even people who claim revelation can readily admit that their human understanding of divine truth is limited and reflects cultural and other influences, thus acknowledging a limited epistemic relativism. Nevertheless, my position may be easier for a Jew to affirm than for a Christian, given the greater emphasis in Judaism on deed, which does not necessarily entail abstract truth claims, and the greater emphasis in Christianity on creed, which forces one to deal with truth claims. Whatever 'salvation' or 'justification' mean, the traditional Jewish notions that Israel must live according to the 613 commandments of the Torah and that righteous non-Jews who also, like Israel, have 'a portion in the world to come' are those who observe the universal 'seven commandments of the children of Noah',[55] clearly emphasize behaviour, with truth claims playing at most a minor role in the scheme of Jewish attitudes towards non-Jews. Conversely, the Pauline notion of justification by faith places truth claims at the focal point of Christian theological concern and together with belief in 'one way' may make it far more difficult for Christians to relegate epistemic relativism to the back row of the debate on pluralism.

Even if Kellner's claim that there are no precedents for pluralism in Jewish thought were correct, the lack of precedent would not invalidate pluralism in principle. Kellner surely would not reject democracy on the grounds that it is derived from Athenian and not from biblical or later Jewish thought. I shall show, however, that in fact there are ample Jewish precedents for pluralism.

As I attempt to respond to Kellner's two challenges (that pluralism makes no inherent sense and is self-refuting and that there are no precedents in traditional Jewish thought for my position) I am guided by a twofold belief: on a theoretical level, claims to 'one absolute truth' are inherently meaningless; and on a practical level, such spiritual exclusivity constitutes an existential danger to world peace, especially in the era of the 'global village' and increasingly widespread weapons of mass destruction. As long as religions continue to compete with each other with their exclusivistic claims, they will not be able serve as an effective force for peace and co-operation. Rather, they will perpetuate their all too frequent desecration of God's name and affront human dignity.

---

[55] See the discussion of these points in Jospe, 'Chosenness in Judaism', 178–180 nn. 15–19; id., 'The Concept of the Chosen People', 130–1 nn. 15–20.

SUBJECTIVITY AND CULTURAL RELATIVITY
IN REVELATION

Prima facie, revelation appears to preclude pluralism. The rabbis, however, understood the revelation at Sinai to be adjusted to the subjective capacity of each person, and to the relative cultures of the seventy nations of the world. Commenting on the peculiar phrase, 'all the people saw the voices' of the revelation at Sinai (Exod. 20: 15), the Midrash picks up on the plural *kolot* ('voices' or 'sounds'):

It says 'All the people saw the voices'. It does not say 'voice' here but 'voices.' Rabbi Yohanan said, The [divine] voice went out and was divided into seventy voices, into seventy languages, so that all the nations could hear, each nation hearing it in its own national language . . . Come and see how the voice would go out to each Israelite according to his capacity [*ko'aḥ*, lit. 'power'], the elders according to their capacity, the youth according to their capacity, the children according to their capacity, infants according to their capacity, and the women according to their capacity, and even Moses according to his capacity . . . Therefore it says, 'The voice of the Lord is in power [*ko'aḥ*]. It does not say 'in his power' but 'in power', in the power [i.e. capacity] of each individual.[56]

In short, revelation according to this rabbinic view was not absolute or monolithic; it had to be adjusted to the subjective capacity of each individual to understand, and to the relative cultures of the various nations.[57]

---

[56] *Exodus Rabbah* 5: 9. Discussing contradictory truths, Avishai Margalit interprets this passage not as meaning that the same revelation was understood in seventy different ways, but that there were different revelations to the seventy nations (see Margalit, 'The Ring: On Religious Pluralism', 153). Margalit, it should be noted, argues that Giovanni Boccaccio's parable of the three rings, famously adopted by Gotthold Ephraim Lessing in his *Nathan the Wise*, contains much descriptive truth, and not merely framework sentences (with which one can disagree without contradiction). Therefore, Margalit concludes, the burden of proof remains on advocates of pluralism to rebut the idea that revealed religion cannot ascribe value to contradictory claims. On Lessing and his use of Boccaccio's parable, see the discussion in Altmann, *Moses Mendelssohn: A Biographical Study*, 569–76.

[57] Kellner argues that I am reading into the text views its authors would have rejected, because all they meant was that the same text can be understood on different levels, just as the same geometry can be taught to graduate students or to school children on different levels. But is graduate-level, advanced non-Euclidean geometry really the same geometry as that taught in elementary or middle schools? At what point is a critical understanding of Scripture or other religious sources merely quantitatively more advanced than what children are taught, as opposed to qualitatively different?

ABRAHAM IBN EZRA AND
THE LIMITATIONS OF REVELATION

Abraham ibn Ezra (1089–1164), a prominent biblical exegete, grammarian, poet, and philosopher, argued[58] against the traditional rabbinic view that both versions of the Decalogue (Exod. 20 and Deut. 5) were revealed simultaneously.[59] After listing in detail all the differences between the two versions, Ibn Ezra explained that many of these differences (especially in the commandment regarding the sabbath) are substantive, not merely stylistic. No person is capable of understanding two different notions spoken simultaneously and in such a case would understand neither of them. A simultaneous revelation of both versions would thus have been incomprehensible and meaningless.[60]

It is impossible that 'remember' and 'observe' [the sabbath] were spoken simultaneously, even by a miracle . . . How could many verses be miraculously spoken simultaneously, when they do not have the same meaning? . . . Reason cannot tolerate [*ein hada'at sovelet*] these notions . . . And if we were to say that God's speech is not like human speech, how could Israel have understood what God said? For if a person would hear 'remember' and 'observe' simultaneously, he would not understand either one.

For Ibn Ezra, the limitations on revelation are thus imposed not from above, on God as the speaker, but from below, by the limited capacity of the people hearing it. In other words, it is meaningless to discuss the absolute nature of revealed truth because of its divine origin. Successful communication—whether divine revelation or a radio broadcast—must be effectively received as well as broadcast, and the limited capacity of the human receiver is what necessarily subjectivizes and relativizes revelation. Thus the problem of revelation is not what is spoken, but what is heard.

AL-FARABI AND MAIMONIDES: RELIGIOUS VERSUS
PHILOSOPHICAL LANGUAGE

Abu Naṣr Muḥammad al-Farabi (870–950), one of the greatest early Islamic philosophers, who had an immense influence on Maimonides,[61] applied Platonic

[58] Ibn Ezra, long commentary on Exod. 20: 1. For a recent survey and updated bibliography on Ibn Ezra, see Uriel Simon and Raphael Jospe, 'Ibn Ezra, Abraham', in *Encyclopaedia Judaica*, 2nd rev. edn. (Detroit, 2007), ix. 665–72.

[59] BT *RH* 27a (*inter alia*): *zakhor veshamor bedibur eḥad ne'emru* ('remember' and 'observe' [the sabbath] were said as one statement).

[60] Ibn Ezra concludes that the version in Exodus, where it says that 'God spoke all of these things' (Exod. 20: 1) is the actual record of the revelation, whereas the version in Deuteronomy, where Moses says: 'I stood between God and you at that time, to tell you the word of the Lord' (Deut. 5: 5) is the paraphrase by Moses, forty years later.

[61] For a discussion of Al-Farabi's influence on Maimonides, see Shlomo Pines, 'Translator's

political philosophy to revealed religion, and identified the philosopher-king with the prophet. In his *Political Regime*, Al-Farabi argued that there is one reality, but that there are many images or reflections of reality. Therefore, there can be many religions, because each nation has its own ways to represent these images of reality, although not all the ways are equally excellent.[62]

Because it is difficult for the multitude to comprehend these things themselves as they are, the attempt was made to teach them these things in other ways, which are the ways of imitation. Hence these things are imitated for each group or nation through the matters that are best known to them; and it may very well be that what is best known to the one may not be the best known to the other.[63]

Similarly, in his *Attainment of Happiness*, Al-Farabi suggested that philosophy deals with demonstrative knowledge of beings, whereas religion entails assent, secured through persuasion, to images of things.

If he perceives their ideas themselves with his intellect, and his assent to them is by means of certain demonstration, then the science that comprises their cognitions is philosophy. But if they are known through similitudes that imitate them, and assent to what is imagined of them is caused by persuasive methods, then the ancients call what comprises those cognitions religion . . . Therefore, according to the ancients, religion is an imitation of philosophy . . . In everything of which philosophy gives an account based on intellectual perception or conception, religion gives an account based on imagination.[64]

To translate Al-Farabi's theory into contemporary terminology, the language of science is discursive, whereas the language of religion is mythological. In such language, which is a function of imagination, not of reason, we have the possibility of multiple images, reflections or imitations of reality, once again raising the possibility of religious pluralism.[65]

Introduction: The Philosophical Sources of the *Guide of the Perplexed*', in Pines' English translation of Maimonides, *Guide of the Perplexed* (Chicago, 1963), pp. lvii–cxxxiv.

[62] Al-Farabi, *The Political Regime*; Eng. trans.: F. M. Najjar, in Ralph Lerner and Muhsin Mahdi (eds.), *Medieval Political Philosophy* (Ithaca, NY, 1978), 31–57.

[63] Al-Farabi, *The Political Regime* (ed. Lerner and Mahdi, pp. 40–1).

[64] Al-Farabi, *The Attainment of Happiness*, §55; Eng. trans.: Muhsin Mahdi, in Lerner and Mahdi (eds.), *Medieval Political Philosophy*, 76–7; also in *Alfarabi's Philosophy of Plato and Aristotle*, trans. Muhsin Mahdi (Ithaca, NY, 1962), 44–5.

[65] This does not mean that Al-Farabi was positing a 'double truth' theory, in the sense of thirteenth-century Latin Averroists at the University of Paris, namely that reason and revelation are two separate and autonomous realms of truth. Al-Farabi is suggesting that the truth can be expressed scientifically, in discursive, rational terms for intellectuals. This is the realm of philosophy. The same truths need to be expressed, for the common people, in terms they are capable of understanding, namely by 'similitudes' derived from the imagination, which 'imitate' those truths; this is the realm of religion. On the 'double truth' theory, see the discussion and references in Raphael Jospe, 'Faith and Reason: The Controversy Over Philosophy in Jewish History', in Irene Kajon (ed.), *La storia della filosofia Ebraica* (Milan, 1993), 99–135, rev. in Raphael Jospe,

Moses Maimonides (1135–1204) was profoundly indebted to Al-Farabi, especially his identification of the prophet of revealed religion with the Platonic philosopher-king. Whereas the philosopher has a perfected intellect, and the politician has a perfected imagination (which enables him to lead effectively, by appealing to popular emotion), the prophet is perfect in both respects.[66] Although Maimonides emphasized the unique rank of the prophecy of Moses, which did not entail imagination,[67] he also insisted that 'the Torah speaks according to human language' (*dibrah torah kilshon benei adam*).[68] In other words, the Torah had to employ anthropomorphic and anthropopathic language to accommodate the primitive understanding of the ancient Israelites. These two positions, that the prophecy of Moses did not entail imagination, but that the Torah had to use primitive language and mythological imagery, are not necessarily contradictory. In the first case, Maimonides was referring to Moses' own experience of revelation, in which there was no involvement of imagination, whereas in the second case he was referring to how Moses subsequently conveyed those abstract truths to the people in imaginative terms they could understand.

Thus Maimonides' political theory again forces us to separate historical revelation from claims of absolute truth, since even the Torah had to adapt its method of expression to limited and primitive human understanding. The Torah's corporealist method of expression is not only frequently misleading—thus the 'perplexed' student for whom Maimonides' wrote his *Guide of the Perplexed*—but actually dangerous, when people take literally corporeal attributes that are themselves false. In Maimonides' view, a person who believes in a corporeal God is worse than an idolater.[69]

THE POSSIBILITY OF MULTIPLE REVELATIONS: NETHANAEL IBN AL-FAYYUMI[70]

In several places, most notably in the ninth of his Thirteen Principles, Maimonides, rejected the possibility that any subsequent revelation could

Jewish Philosophy: Foundations and Extensions, vol. i: *General Questions and Considerations* (Lanham, Md., 2008), 55–90.

[66] See Maimonides, *Guide of the Perplexed*, ii. 37.   [67] Ibid. 36, 45.

[68] Ibid. 26. The phrase occurs, *inter alia*, in BT *Ber.* 31b. Whereas Rabbi Akiva would interpret (*darash*) every word, and even the letters, of Torah as significant, Rabbi Yishma'el's hermeneutic was based on the principle that the Torah speaks according to human language. Maimonides was not the first medieval philosopher to apply this hermeneutic principle philosophically, in the sense that the Torah had to adapt itself to the primitive understanding of the masses (cf. Bahya ibn Pakuda, *Duties of the Heart* [Hovot halevavot], 1: 10).

[69] Maimonides, *Guide of the Perplexed*, i. 36.

[70] See other references to Ibn al-Fayyumi in this volume by Alon Goshen-Gottstein (Introduction) Alan Brill with Rori Picker Neiss (Chapter 1), and Paul Fenton (Chapter 10).

abrogate the Torah.[71] But what of revelations to other nations that would not abrogate the Torah? Joseph Albo's *Book of Principles* (*Sefer ha'ikarim*) (*c*.1425) discusses 'divine laws' besides the Torah that were revealed to prophets, reflecting changing human needs (like a patient whose changing condition requires revised prescriptions), but these revelations were all to pre-Sinaitic prophets, such as Adam, Noah, and Abraham, and Albo did not regard Christianity and Islam to be divinely revealed religions.[72]

Conversely, the *Bustan al-Ukul* (*Garden of the Intellects*) of Nethanael ibn al-Fayyumi (*c*.1165, Yemen)[73] explicitly discusses multiple revelations both before and after the revelation of the Torah. These post-Sinaitic revelations, however, do not abrogate the Torah, which will not be abrogated even in the messianic era:

Nothing prevents God from sending unto His world whomsoever He wishes, whenever He wishes, since the world of holiness sends forth emanations unceasingly from the light world to the coarse world, to liberate the souls from the sea of matter—in the world of nature—and from destruction in the fires of Hell. Even before the revelation of the Law He sent prophets to the nations, as our sages of blessed memory explain, 'Seven prophets prophesied to the nations of the world before the giving of the Torah: Laban, Jethro, Balaam, Job, Eliphaz, Bildad, and Zophar.'[74] And even after its revelation nothing prevented Him from sending to them whom He wished, that the world might not remain without religion. The prophets declared that the other nations would serve Him from the rising of the sun to the setting thereof: 'For from the rising of the sun to the setting thereof great is my name among the nations' [Mal. 1: 11].[75]

This leads Ibn al-Fayyumi to explicit religious pluralism:

Know that God commanded that all the people should serve according to the Law; and He permitted to every people something which he forbade to others, and He forbade to them something which He permitted to others, for He knoweth what is

---

[71] The Arabic term Maimonides uses, *naskh* (abrogation), is a technical term in Islam. Since the Quran was given over a period of years, a later revelation to Muhammad could abrogate an earlier revelation (see Quran 2: 106), just as in general, Muhammad, as the last and greatest prophets and as the 'seal of the prophets' (Quran 33: 40), could abrogate prior revelations to earlier prophets. Maimonides' use of the Islamic term in a polemic against Islam is thus not accidental.

[72] Irving Greenberg refers to what he understands to be divine revelations and other nations' access to God in Gen. 14: 18–20; Num. 22–24; Amos 9: 7; Mic. 4: 5 (*For the Sake of Heaven and Earth*, 57).

[73] Nethanael ibn al-Fayyumi, *Bustan al-Ukul*, Judaeo-Arabic text and English translation, ed. D. Levine (New York, 1908); Judaeo-Arabic text with Hebrew translation, ed. Yosef Kafih (Jerusalem, 1954).

[74] The reference is to BT *BB* 15*a*, where, however, the list differs slightly: Balaam, his father, Job, Eliphaz, Bildad, Zophar, and Elihu.

[75] Ibn al-Fayyumi, *Bustan al-Ukul*, ch. 6 (ed. Levine, 103–4; ed. Kafih, 114–15).

best for His creatures and what is adapted to them, as the skilled physician understands his patients.[76]

Ibn al-Fayyumi then cites the Quran (14: 4): 'He sends a prophet to every people according to their language.'[77] We thus have in *Bustan al-Ukul* what is probably the clearest statement of religious pluralism in medieval Jewish thought, reflecting pluralistic trends in the Ismaili thought of the 'Brethren of Purity' (*Ikhwan al-Safa*).[78]

SA'ADIAH GAON AND 'THE COMMUNITY OF MONOTHEISTS'

One might, of course, dismiss Nethanael ibn al-Fayyumi as a relatively insignificant and exceptional figure in medieval Jewish thought. But one cannot dismiss Sa'adiah Gaon (882–942), the first medieval Jewish philosopher, whose *Book of Beliefs and Opinions* (Arabic: *Kitab al-Amanat w'al-I'tiqadatt*, Hebrew: *Sefer emunot vede'ot*) established a whole tradition of Jewish philosophizing. Sa'adiah does not discuss multiple revelations, but he does discuss a type of religious truth transcending Judaism.

In the introduction to his book, after discussing empirical, rational, and deductive sources of knowledge, which are all clearly universal, he states:

[76] Ibid. (ed. Levine, 107; ed. Kafih, 118–19). Ibn al-Fayyumi's arguments have sometimes been called relativistic, for example, by Y. Tzvi Langermann and others (see below), although Langermann clearly refers to it as 'religious relativism' and not as moral relativism. It seems to me that what our text is referring to is not relativism in the moral sense, that is, that there are no moral standards however derived, but pluralism in the religious sense, that different groups have diverse ritual requirements that only apply within that group, because of their particular conditions. It is only in the sense that the rituals differ according to particular conditions that one can suggest some kind of 'relativism' in the ritual practices, just as the physician's prescriptions are 'relative' to patients' conditions and needs, but we do not usually regard a diabetic's need for insulin, which would endanger a non-diabetic, as constituting 'relativism'. Similarly, the ritual dietary restrictions of *kashrut* in the Torah apply only to Jews, and those of the Book of Mormon apply only to Latter Day Saints, just as in a civil context citizens of one country salute only the flag of their country and not of other countries. I understand Ibn al-Fayyumi's text as referring to such pluralism and not to relativism.

[77] Ibn al-Fayyumi, *Bustan al-Ukul*, ch. 6 (ed. Levine, 109; ed. Kafih, 121).

[78] See S. M. Stern, 'Fatimid Propaganda Among the Jews', 85–6, in id., *Studies in Early Ismai'ilism* (Jerusalem, 1983), cited in Y. Tzvi Langermann, 'Some Astrological Themes in the Thought of Abraham ibn Ezra', in I. Twersky and J. Harris (eds.), *Rabbi Abraham ibn Ezra: Studies in the Writings of a Twelfth-Century Jewish Polymath* (Cambridge, Mass., 1993), 72 n. 118. Langermann refers here to Ibn al-Fayyumi's 'religious relativism'. For an example of religious pluralism in the Brethren of Purity, see *The Case of the Animals versus Man*, trans. Goodman, p. 194: in response to the king's question, 'Why do you disagree in your notions, sects and creeds if your Lord is one?' the Persian spokesman says: 'Because religions, doctrines, sects are only different paths of approach, different means and avenues, but the Goal we seek is one. From whatever quarter we seek to encounter Him, God is there.'

As for ourselves, the community of monotheists [*jama'at al-muwaḥḥadin*], we hold these three sources of knowledge to be genuine. To them, however, we add a fourth source . . . the validity of authentic tradition [*al-khabar al-ṣadiq*] . . . This type of knowledge . . . corroborates for us the validity of the first three sources of knowledge.[79]

This type of knowledge (which can also be translated as 'reliable report' or 'reliable tradition') has generally been understood by scholars such as Shlomo Pines as 'drawn only from the Jewish prophetic books' and as 'intended solely for the benefit of the Jewish community'. Pines also interprets 'the community of monotheists' exclusively as the Jews.[80]

However, this view requires modification. Sa'adiah cannot have denied the monotheistic nature at least of Islam (if not of Christianity), since he follows the Mu'tazilah Kalam arguments for creation and the existence and unity of God. His argument with Christian Trinitarianism follows his discussion of essential attributes[81] and not his refutation of dualism and polytheism and therefore contextually implies that Christianity is an erroneous form of monotheism not polytheism. Moreover, Sa'adiah later refers in the plural to 'the communities of the monotheists' (*ma'ashir al-muwaḥḥadin*)[82] when discussing Christian Trinitarianism. So Sa'adiah's understanding of 'the community of monotheists' cannot be limited to the Jewish people. The fourth type of knowledge, authentic tradition, which is possessed by the 'community of monotheists', must, therefore, also be shared by non-Jews (as becomes even more obvious by his example, that without such knowledge a person would not even be able to know who his father is). In Sa'adiah's usage, authentic tradition is by no means identical with revelation, although at least in the case of the Jews it is based on and related to revelation. Nevertheless, we have here at least an implicit, if not explicit, pluralistic conception of religious truth in the thought of one of the most influential of the Jewish philosophers of the Middle Ages.

This universalistic reading of Sa'adiah's 'community of monotheists' is further reinforced by later Jewish philosophers. Bahya ibn Pakuda refers to 'the people of monotheism', where the distinction is not between Jew and non-Jew but between varying degrees of comprehension of people who affirm God's

---

[79] Sa'adiah Gaon, *Book of Beliefs and Opinions*, Introduction, §5 (trans. Samuel Rosenblatt (New Haven, 1948), 16; Arabic text with Hebrew translation, ed. Yosef Kafih (Jerusalem, 1970), 14). For a complete discussion of this issue, see Raphael Jospe, 'Sa'adiah Gaon and Moses Mendelssohn: Pioneers of Jewish Philosophy', in id. (ed.), *Paradigms in Jewish Philosophy* (Madison, NJ, 1997), 37–59, rev. in id., *Jewish Philosophy*, 91–111; id., 'The "Authentic Tradition" of Rabbi Sa'adiah Gaon: Who Are "The Community of the Monotheists"?' (Heb.), *Da'at*, 41 (Summer 1998), 5–17; id., 'Additional Note', *Da'at*, 42 (Winter 1999), p. ix; id., 'Another Note', *Da'at*, 63 (Summer 2008), 169–70.

[80] S. Pines, 'A Study of the Impact of Indian, Mainly Buddhist, Thought on Some Aspects of Kalam Doctrines', *Jerusalem Studies in Arabic and Islam*, 17 (1994), 182–203.

[81] Sa'adiah Gaon, *Book of Beliefs and Opinions*, 2: 4.

[82] Ibid. 2: 5 (trans. Rosenblatt, p. 104; ed. Kafih, p. 91).

unity.[83] Judah Halevi also refers to 'monotheists' in a non-Jewish context, when the Christian spokesman says to the Khazar king: 'for we are truly monotheists, although the Trinity appears on our tongues'.[84] Maimonides writes: 'We, the community of true monotheists', where the category is philosophical, not parochial, and refers to those who have a correct philosophical understanding of the divine attributes.[85]

If my universalistic understanding of 'the community of monotheists' in Sa'adiah Gaon, Bahya ibn Pakuda, Judah Halevi, and Maimonides is correct, the universal nature of this type of truth implies at least a degree of pluralism, for the simple reason that the truth takes different forms in diverse cultures, all of which are, nevertheless, acknowledged to be true monotheisms.

All of these cases support my claim, contra Kellner, that there are precedents in Jewish thought, both rabbinic and philosophic, for pluralistic and inclusive understanding of religious truth. The concept of revelation need not, and indeed cannot, be understood to mean exclusive possession of absolute truth, since even the revelation of the Torah at Sinai had to be adjusted to subjective human understanding and to diverse national cultures.

ON CULTURAL RELATIVISM IN CONCEIVING OF GOD

The insight that our very conceptions of God and the universe are culturally relativistic is not new. The pre-Socratic philosopher Xenophanes (570–475 BCE) had already made the point:

But mortals consider that the gods are born, and that they have clothes and speech and bodies like their own.

The Ethiopians say that their gods are snub-nosed and black; the Thracians that theirs have light blue eyes and red hair.

But if cattle and horses or lions had hands, or were able to draw with their hands and do the work that men do, horses would draw the forms [Greek: ideas] of the gods like horses, and cattle like cattle, and they would make their bodies such as they each had themselves.[86]

In the seventeenth century Baruch Spinoza continued in the same humorous vein:

---

[83] Bahya ibn Pakuda, *Duties of the Heart*, 1: 1–2.

[84] Halevi, *Kuzari*, 1: 4 (trans. Hartwig Hirschfeld (New York, 1905)).

[85] Maimonides, *Guide of the Perplexed*, i. 53 (trans. Pines, p. 122); a similar usage is found in i. 75.

[86] G. S. Kirk and J. E. Raven, *The Presocratic Philosophers* (Cambridge, 1964), nos. 170–2, pp. 168–9. Franz Rosenzweig refered to Xenophanes and Spinoza in his article 'Anthropomorphism' for the original German *Encyclopaedia Judaica* (1928–9). The Hebrew translation by Yehosua Amir may be found in Franz Rosenzweig, *Naharayim* (Jerusalem, 1960), 31–40.

Let us imagine . . . a little worm, living in the blood . . . This little worm would live in the blood, in the same way as we live in a part of the universe, and would consider each part of blood, not as a part, but as a whole.[87]

Some years later, he went even further:

I believe that, if a triangle could speak, it would say, in like manner, that God is eminently triangular, while a circle would say that the divine nature is eminently circular. Thus each would ascribe to God its own attributes, would assume itself to be like God, and look on everything else as ill-shaped.[88]

MOSES MENDELSSOHN AND RELIGIOUS PLURALISM

Moses Mendelssohn (1729–86) was the first Jewish philosopher to address the question of the compatibility of a traditional loyalty to the Torah with a modern, pluralistic vision of religious co-operation in the liberal state.[89] Mendelssohn objected to classical Christian exclusivity of salvation and to Locke's theory of toleration on both philosophical and Jewish grounds and proposed, rather, religious pluralism.

On the first issue, Christian claims of exclusivity of salvation, Mendelssohn wrote in favour of greater respect for dissenting opinion:

It is my good fortune to count among my friends many an excellent man who is not of my faith . . . I enjoy the pleasure of his company and feel enriched by it. But at no time has my heart whispered to me, 'What a pity that this beautiful soul should be lost' . . . Only that man will be troubled by such regrets who believes that there is no salvation outside his church . . . Some of my countrymen hold views and convictions which, although I consider them wrong, do belong to a higher order of theoretical principles. They are not harmful, because they have little or no relationship to the practical concerns of daily life. Yet they frequently constitute the foundation on which people have erected their systems of morality and social order and are of great importance to them. To question such notions publicly merely because we consider them biased or erroneous would be like removing the foundation stones of a building in order to examine the soundness of its structure.[90]

In Mendelssohn's view, such religious exclusivism is thus both theoretically wrong and practically dangerous.

---

[87] Baruch Spinoza, Letter 15, to Oldenburg (1665?), in *The Chief Works of Benedict de Spinoza*, trans. R. H. M. Elwes (New York: Dover, 1955), ii. 291.

[88] Baruch Spinoza, Letter 60, to Hugo Boxel (1674), in *The Chief Works of Benedict de Spinoza*, ii. 386.

[89] For a detailed discussion of Mendelssohn's theories, see Jospe, 'Moses Mendelssohn: A Medieval Modernist'.

[90] Moses Mendelssohn, Open Letter to Lavater (12 Dec. 1769), in id., *Jerusalem and Other Jewish Writings*, 118–19.

Locke's theory of toleration differentiates between the respective realms of state (which is interested in the temporal affairs of this world) and religion (which is interested in the eternal affairs of the world to come). Such a differentiation between the temporal and the eternal, Mendelssohn argues, simply does not hold up either theoretically or practically. It fails theoretically because the temporal is part of the eternal and the eternal is an extension of the temporal. It fails practically, because people's behaviour in this world is predicated, at least to some extent, on their beliefs regarding the world to come. Instead, Mendelssohn applies the traditional rabbinic differentiation between those matters between a person and another person (*bein adam leḥavero*), which he assigns to the state, and those matters purely between a person and God (*bein adam lamakom*) and which do not involve other people, which he assigns to religion. Furthermore, Locke had argued pragmatically that the state is incapable of determining which religion is true, and must, therefore, tolerate dissent and variety.

Mendelssohn goes beyond such a pragmatic view of toleration and affirms the inherent value and desirability of religious pluralism. Diversity is part of the divine plan for humanity. Addressing Christian rulers, he concludes his *Jerusalem or on Religious Power and Judaism*:

Dear Brothers, you are well-meaning. But do not let yourselves be deceived. To belong to this omnipresent shepherd, it is not necessary for the entire flock to graze on one pasture or to enter and leave the master's house through just one door. It would be neither in accord with the shepherd's wishes nor conducive to the growth of his flock.[91] ...

A union of faiths, if it were ever to come about, could have only the most disastrous consequences for reason and freedom of conscience ... If the goal of this universal delusion were to be realized, I am afraid man's barely liberated mind would once again be confined behind bars ... Brothers, if you care for true godliness, let us not pretend that conformity exists where diversity is obviously the plan and goal of Providence.[92] Not one among us thinks and feels exactly like his fellowman. Why, then, should we deceive each other with lies? It is sad enough that we are doing this

[91] Although Jesus' claim to be Israel's shepherd can be seen as referring to Ezek. 37: 24, it seems to me that Mendelssohn here deliberately employs the image of multiple doors for the sheep, to counter the exclusivism of Jesus' statements: 'I am the door of the sheep ... I am the door, if anyone enters by me, he will be saved' (John 10: 7–9). Mendelssohn thus anticipates by more than two centuries John Hick's argument that different religions, despite their diverse beliefs, are equally effective contexts for salvific human transformation (Hick, 'The Possibility of Religious Pluralism', 163).

[92] Whereas Mendelssohn speaks here of pluralistic diversity as the plan of providence, John Kekes speaks of the 'evolutionary value' of pluralism: 'The more various our lives are, the better are our chances of being able to cope with a variety of circumstances ... From the point of view of both the species and individual members of it, the plurality of conceptions of the good life is a benefit rather than an obstacle' (*The Morality of Pluralism*, 30).

in our daily relations, in conversations that are of no particular importance. But why also in matters which concern our temporal and eternal welfare, our very destiny? Why should we use masks to make ourselves unrecognizable to each other in the most important concerns of life, when God has given each of us his own distinctive face for some good reason? . . . A union of faiths is not tolerance. It is the very opposite.[93]

Mendelssohn had long and consistently held to such pluralistic views, rejecting the exclusivistic claims made by any religion. Early in 1770 he wrote to Prince Karl-Wilhelm about liberal Christian reformers:

They must not base their system . . . on the hypothesis that Judaism and, even more so, natural religion, are inadequate means to ensure man's salvation. Since all men must have been destined by the Creator to attain eternal bliss, no particular religion can have an exclusive claim to truth. This thesis, I dare to submit, might serve as a criterion of truth in all religious matters. A revelation claiming to show man the only way to salvation cannot be true, for it is not in harmony with the intent of the all-merciful Creator.[94]

Mendelssohn's consistency in this regard is evident in his explicit application of his pluralistic principles to Judaism, not only to Christianity and to other religions. In another letter written in 1770 he differentiated internal, natural religion, which is universal, and involves basic, demonstrable truths all people should accept on a rational basis, from a pluralistic variety of external positive religions:

Worship, however, as everyone knows, can be private as well as public, internal as well as external, and one does well to differentiate between the two. The internal worship of the Jew is not based on any principles except those of natural religion. To spread these is, indeed, incumbent upon us . . . Our external worship, however, is in no way meant to address itself to others, since it consists of rules and prescriptions that are related to specific persons, times and circumstances. I grant that we believe that our religion is the best, because we believe it to be divinely inspired. Nevertheless, it does not follow from this premise that it is absolutely the best. It is the best religion for ourselves and our descendants, the best for certain times, circumstances and conditions.[95]

---

[93] Mendelssohn, *Jerusalem and Other Jewish Writings*, 107–10.

[94] Moses Mendelssohn, Letter to Prince Karl-Wilhelm (1770), in id., *Selections from his Writings*, 116–17.

[95] Mendelssohn, *Jerusalem and Other Jewish Writings*, 134. Mendelssohn thus also anticipates by over two centuries what Irving Greenberg says: 'Thus any truth may speak absolutely to me and others, yet it is not intended for others who may be spoken to by other revelations and chosen for another sector of service' (*For the Sake of Heaven and Earth*, 204). Mendelssohn wisely avoids, however, the trap into which Greenberg falls, because Mendelssohn avoids the claim that Judaism 'is absolutely the best', whereas Greenberg still claims absolute truth.

For Mendelssohn, a pluralism of positive religions is thus a theoretical desideratum and a practical necessity.

KANT'S UNKNOWABLE *DING AN SICH* AND HEISENBERG'S 'UNCERTAINTY PRINCIPLE'

Kellner claims that pluralism is inherently meaningless and self-refuting. It seems to me that we are forced to conclude the contrary, that any claims of objective knowledge of absolute truth are inherently meaningless and self-refuting or, to put it simply, absurd. When even divine revelation as the purported basis for claims of objective knowledge of absolute truth is subject to the limits imposed by subjective human understanding and cultural relativism, as freely acknowledged by the talmudic rabbis, pluralistic understandings of the truth become inevitable and inescapable.

An additional nail in the coffin of absolutist epistemology was provided by Immanuel Kant (1724–1804). By definition, whatever we cognize and experience is the phenomenon, the form and order of which depend on the human synthetic forms of sensibility and categories of understanding. These synthetic principles and categories, such as space and time, are prior to and transcend sense data—but they are the necessary and a priori conditions for human experience of the phenomena, by which we synthesize the sense data, or forms, which mind imposes on the sense data—and are not objective properties of things in themselves. The noumenon, the 'real' world, as opposed to the phenomenon, cannot be known, and its existence is postulated by practical reason. The 'thing in itself' (*Ding an sich*) can thus never be known.

As already acknowledged, John Hick before me applied the Kantian insight to argue for religious pluralism. The Real may be understood in monotheistic religions in theistic, personal terms or in non-theistic religions in impersonal terms, but either case is discussed by Hick in explicitly Kantian terminology: 'We may then distinguish the Real *an sich* . . . and the real as humanly experienced and thought . . . To this basic distinction we must add our modern recognition (initially formulated by Immanuel Kant) of the human mind's indispensable contribution to all conscious awareness.'[96] Hick employs Kantian language not only to posit pluralism, but also to reject a purely expressive pluralism: 'To postulate the divine *noumenon*, the Real *an sich*, as the ground of the different experienced divine *personae* and *impersonae*, is to affirm that religion is not *in toto* illusion, but is, however partial and inadequate its manifestations, our human response to the most real of all realities.'[97]

Sagi argues that Hick's analysis ultimately fails because it assumes that religions thus share a common ground (the noumenon, the Real *an sich*), which

[96] John Hick, 'Religious Pluralism', 331–3.   [97] Ibid.

cannot, however, be deduced from the variety of religious experience (the phenomena). But that was a point Hick took into account (discussed above) in
response to Gavin D'Costa's critique, when he acknowledged that he does not
actually know that the Real transcends knowledge and language, but that this
is the best hypothesis to explain the religious data. Nevertheless, Sagi correctly
points to the central epistemic problem of any such Kantian analysis: if human
experience conveys reality (as Hick affirms but admittedly cannot know or
prove), that is, a relationship with a real God, then his thesis collapses because
by definition we cannot relate to the noumenon. If, on the other hand, the religious experience is merely expressive or illusory, why assume that it has any
real object?

Once again, we may find in the medieval sources insights that anticipated
this modern dilemma, even if they cannot necessarily resolve it any more than
we can. If religious pluralism is purely expressive and illusory, then we have the
option of the utilitarian (and somewhat cynical) pluralistic advice of the archetypal Aristotelian philosopher to the king of the Khazars in Judah Halevi's
Kuzari: God transcends knowing or caring about what humans do and does
not hear their prayers, so endeavour to know the truth and choose whichever
religion is most effective in governing your country.[98] Of course, that utilitarian pluralism is based on the notion that all positive religions are equally false,
not equally true, and the mythic claims of religion can be reduced to what Plato
called noble lies,[99] or what Maimonides called 'beliefs necessary for the welfare
of the state' as opposed to 'true opinions'.[100]

Conversely, if religious experience in some way, however partial, points to
some transcendent meaning, however vaguely defined, we may benefit from
Al-Farabi's notion (which also resonates in Maimonides' political theory) of
religious language as mythic (because it is a function of imagination) and as an
'imitation' of the discursive language of science (which is a function of reason),
and that there can, therefore, be multiple 'images' or 'imitations' of reality.
Nevertheless, Al-Farabi cannot resolve our Kantian dilemma, because for Al-
Farabi, the reality can still be described, although in the discursive language of
philosophy and science and not in the mythic language of religion that only
imitates that reality. The Kantian *Ding an sich*, however, cannot be discussed
or even described by any kind of language, discursive or mythic, philosophical
or religious.

Here, then, is where Ibn Ezra's emphasis on what is heard below rather than
on what is spoken above may again prove helpful, if not in resolving the

---

[98] Judah Halevi, *Kuzari*, 1: 1.

[99] Plato, *Republic* 3.414b, 3.389b, 5.459c. In Plato's conception, the ruler may engage in the
noble lie for the sake of society, as a kind of medicine.

[100] Maimonides, *Guide of the Perplexed*, iii. 28 (trans. Pines, p. 517).

Kantian dilemma then at least in helping us refocus the discussion. Our challenge is not to define the indefinable noumenon or 'Real *an sich*' but to formulate a pluralistic paradigm for religion, and religion, after all, is not God or the 'Real *an sich*' but the way people attempt to encounter it, whether in personal theistic or in impersonal terms. Pluralism is not rejected by people who regard the religious claims to be purely expressive. Moreover, they do not need to be persuaded to accept pluralism because for them religion is an entirely subjective experience without objective reference; hence there is no reason for them to maintain exclusivist claims. They can regard religion as an important and valid human exercise, which differs for different people, or dismiss it as pure illusion. Yet in neither case will they insist that the claims of any particular religion are absolutely or objectively true. The people who need to be persuaded of the value of pluralism are those who still make exclusivist claims to objective or absolute truth, based on revelation. For them, Ibn Ezra's insight may be a way to recast their claims to divine revelation with greater intellectual and spiritual modesty, not by ending with Kant, but by taking the next step after Kant.

For Kant, the necessary synthetic principles and categories of understanding are transcendental and a priori. He could, therefore, still affirm universal, objective knowledge, and I do not suggest that Kant should be construed as a cultural relativist or deconstructionist. Nevertheless, since in his view the categories of understanding are not objective properties of things in themselves, but are the forms and order the human mind imposes on the sense data it synthesizes, we can extend Kant's insight and say that it opens up the possibility that human cognition reflects inescapable cultural relativism and individual subjectivism and not just universal human ways of cognizing, whatever the phenomena in question. In the light of Abraham Ibn Ezra's insight, that the problem comes from below, that is, from the human capacity to comprehend, rather than from above, even the phenomenon of what is alleged to be divine revelation would have to reflect these limiting factors. In other words, if Kant is correct regarding the synthetic principles and categories, namely that they are characteristics of the way we cognize and not objective properties of the things in themselves, then he is wrong in ignoring the cultural relativity and individual subjectivity, which also seem to be fundamental components of cognition.

Philosophy has developed considerably since Kant's day, and even if his epistemology is only partially correct in the light of more recent developments, it seems helpful in getting us away from thinking that whatever we cognize is the *Ding an sich* or absolute truth. Whatever we know is as much a reflection of our own processes of cognition, which necessarily introduce at least some elements of individual subjectivity and cultural relativism, as it is a reflection of some kind of external reality. Therefore, Kant's insights, however obsolete, are an important step in freeing us from the error of absolutism, that somehow any and all of us can claim possession of absolute truth.

A final (at least for the moment) nail in the coffin of epistemological absolutism is provided by Werner Heisenberg (1901–76), who argued that the theory of relativity undermines Kant's a priori categories of space and time, as separate and objective categories, because he did not take into account the notion that space (extension) and time (energy) are actually interchangeable. Therefore, 'the common words "space" and "time" refer to a structure of space and time that is actually an idealization and oversimplification of the real structure'.[101] According to Heisenberg, Kant's arguments for the a priori character of causality no longer apply, and synthetic judgements are relative truth:

The *a priori* concepts which Kant considered an undisputable truth are no longer contained in the scientific system of modern physics . . . What Kant had not foreseen was that these *a priori* concepts can be the conditions for science and at the same time can have only a limited range of applicability . . . Classical physics and causality have only a limited range of applicability. It was the fundamental paradox of quantum theory that could not be foreseen by Kant. Modern physics has changed Kant's statement about the possibility of synthetic judgments *a priori* from a metaphysical one into a practical one. The synthetic judgments *a priori* thereby have the character of relative truth . . . Any concepts or words which have been formed in the past through the interplay between the world and ourselves are not really sharply defined . . . we do not know exactly how far they will help us in finding our way in the world . . . We practically never know precisely the limits of their applicability. This is true even of the simplest and most general concepts like 'existence' and 'space and time.' Therefore, it will never be possible by pure reason to arrive at some absolute truth.[102]

According to Heisenberg's 1926 'uncertainty principle' of quantum mechanics, the minimum quantum of light needed to measure the position and velocity of a particle will disturb the particle and change its velocity in unpre-

---

[101] Werner Heisenberg, *Physics and Philosophy: The Revolution in Modern Science* (New York, 1958), 114. Another nail in the coffin of epistemological absolutism, and Kant's notion that the a priori categories of cognition are universal and objective, may be developed in the light of recent research in 'cultural neuroscience'. For example, even in such ostensibly universal and objective areas as mathematics, it turns out that people of diverse cultural backgrounds (in the case of one study, native English and native Chinese speakers), while performing numerical tasks, activate different parts of the brain. Native English speakers use areas associated with language processing, whereas native Chinese speakers use an area associated with visual-spatial processing (see Nalini Ambady and Jamshed Bharucha, 'Culture and the Brain', *Current Directions in Psychological Sciences*, 18/6 (2009), 342–5). Regarding such interaction of biology and culture (or the old 'nature vs. nurture' argument), Sharon Begley writes: 'This raises an obvious chicken-and-egg question, but the smart money is on culture shaping the brain, not vice versa' (Sharon Begley, 'West Brain, East Brain: What a Difference Culture Makes', *Newsweek* (1 Mar. 2010), 20).

[102] Heisenberg, *Physics and Philosophy*, 90–2.

dictable ways; the more accurately one measures the particle's position (requiring a shorter wavelength of light and therefore greater energy), the more one disturbs its velocity, and therefore the less accurately one can measure its velocity; and the more accurately one measures its velocity, the less accurately one can measure its position. In other words, the very act of observing affects the observed phenomena. In Stephen Hawking's words:

> This limit does not depend on the way in which one tries to measure the position or velocity of the particle, or on the type of particle: Heisenberg's uncertainty principle is a fundamental, inescapable property of the world . . . The uncertainty principle signaled an end to Laplace's dream of a theory of science, a model of the universe that would be completely deterministic: one certainly cannot predict future events exactly if one cannot even measure the present state of the universe precisely![103]

So what is the 'absolute' truth? Is light to be understood as particles or as waves, or simply to be treated, depending on the needs of the experiment, as both? There is, at least as yet, no 'unified theory' combining quantum mechanics on the sub-atomic level, and gravity on the astronomic level of general relativity.[104] If, then, we are forced to acknowledge fundamental uncertainty in physics, how can we continue to insist on certainty and absolute truth in metaphysics?

On a different level, the insights of quantum mechanics, in which the primary 'substance' of the world is energy,[105] force us to think in terms of process and relation more than in the classical terms of substance. In this regard, it is interesting to note that the audacious shift proposed by Mordecai Kaplan (1881–1983) away from 'substantive nouns' to 'functional' or 'relational' nouns and therefore to God in terms of process rather than being,[106] not only reflects Maimonides' insistence that the only positive statements of God that we can make are attributes of action and nothing essential (that is, we

---

[103] Stephen Hawking, *A Brief History of Time* (New York, 1988), 55. See also 'The uncertainty principle is a fundamental feature of the universe we live in. A successful unified theory must therefore necessarily incorporate this principle' (ibid. 155–6). Note that Hawking does not deny scientific determinism per se, since any given state of the mechanical system would still determine subsequent states. What he denies is that we can have a 'model' that is 'completely deterministic'. In a sense, Hawking's 'model', or what we can 'measure . . . precisely', is parallel to Kant's knowable 'phenomenon', as opposed to the unknowable determinism of 'the universe' itself, parallel to Kant's 'noumenon'.   [104] Ibid. 133, 155–6.

[105] 'In the philosophy of Democritus all atoms consist of the same substance . . . The elementary particles in modern physics carry a mass in the same limited sense in which they have other properties. Since mass and energy are, according to the theory of relativity, essentially the same concepts, we may say that all elementary particles consist of energy. This could be interpreted as defining energy as the primary substance of the world' (Heisenberg, *Physics and Philosophy*, 70–1).

[106] Mordecai Kaplan, *The Future of the American Jew* (New York, 1948), 183; id., *The Meaning of God in Modern Jewish Religion* (New York, 1962), 325.

can only know what God does, not what God is), but also parallels the shifts taking place in physics at around the same time.

'THE LORD IS CLOSE TO ALL WHO CALL HIM IN TRUTH'

How, then, can one continue today to be certain that any individual or any particular group has attained perfect and objective knowledge of absolute truth? Are not such claims and self-confidence epistemically empty, spiritually smug, and perhaps even morally offensive?

What, furthermore, shall we make of the verse in Psalm 145: 18, 'The Lord is close to all who call him, to all who call him in truth [*be'emet*]'? We often misunderstand the qualifier 'in truth', which was translated literally by the Targum as *bikeshot*, by the Septuagint as *en aleitheia*, and by the Vulgate as *in veritate*. Luther correctly avoided translating the qualifier cognitively and instead rendered it as *die ihn mit Ernst anrufen*, although I do not think the psalmist meant 'earnestly'. Moses Mendelssohn was more on the mark when he translated it as *die aufrichtig ihn anrufen*. This rendition of *be'emet* as 'sincerely' reflects the comment of the medieval rationalist, biblical exegete, grammarian, and philosopher Rabbi David Kimhi (Radak, *c.*1160–1235), with whose commentaries Mendelssohn was familiar. Kimhi, whose exegetical works are replete with anti-Christian polemic, nevertheless interprets 'the Lord is close to all who call him' as meaning 'from whatever nation he may be, so long as he calls him in truth, that his mouth and heart be the same'.[107]

CONCLUSION: PLURALISM AS THE WAY OF TORAH

I believe that I have replied effectively to Kellner's two critiques, that pluralism makes no sense and that there are no precedents for it in Jewish literature and thought. As for the Christian challenge of equating pluralism with relativism, I have constructed a paradigm of religious pluralism that avoids moral relativism, while at the same time avoiding the kind of extreme epistemological relativism of radical deconstructionism. If in the process we have arrived at a degree of moderate epistemological relativism, I happily plead guilty, since if my understanding of the rabbis, Jewish philosophers, Al-Farabi, Kant, and Heisenberg's uncertainty principle is correct, the shoe is on the other foot: the burden of proof shifts to those who still, despite all the evidence, wish to maintain absolutist epistemic claims that are intellectually untenable and even morally dangerous to our religious coexistence.

[107] Irving Greenberg similarly writes on this verse: 'God is close to those who call God's name, whose yearning born out of love and fidelity calls out truthfully and sincerely to the Lord' (*For the Sake of Heaven and Earth*, 66–7).

As for Jewish precedents, there is ample evidence for both internal and external pluralism in the sources, despite the halakhic constraints to which Sagi calls our attention, and for which, as he says, we need a conceptual revolution. For example, we find both internal and external pluralism supported by rabbinic interpretation of Jeremiah 23: 29: 'Is not my word like fire, says the Lord, and like a hammer smashing a rock?' In his comments on Genesis 33: 20 and Exodus 6: 9, Rashi cites this verse to justify diverse, internal pluralistic interpretations, like the sparks set off by the hammer smashing the rock into pieces.

Rabbi Yishma'el interpreted this verse as alluding to both internal and external pluralism. Internally, the Talmud records his statement that 'as this hammer is divided into several sparks, so does a single biblical text contain several meanings'.[108] Elsewhere, the Talmud records Rabbi Yishma'el interpreting our verse in support of external pluralism, that 'as this hammer is divided into sparks, so was every single commandment that God spoke divided into seventy languages'.[109]

Such pluralism, even if it entails a degree of moderate epistemic relativism, does not imply a strong relativistic conception of multiple truths, but of multiple perspectives on the truth, or what the rabbis called the 'seventy facets of the Torah' (*shivim panim latorah*).[110] It is not coincidental that the 'seventy facets' of the Torah's internal pluralism are identical in number to the 'seventy languages' of its external pluralism.

I believe it is this rabbinic commitment to pluralism that underlies their apparently paradoxical statement that an argument which is not for the sake of heaven will not endure, but an argument which is for the sake of heaven will endure (*sofah lehitkayem*).[111] One might think that an argument for the sake of heaven should lead to a peaceful resolution, yet that is not the rabbis' intention. An argument not for the sake of heaven, as when a person sues another person for a debt, has to be resolved by the court; closure must be attained, and justice must be served. But when the argument is for the sake of heaven, there is no winner and there is no loser. The truth can never be closed; it must always continue to be sought through the open exchange of diverse views. Therefore, 'the argument which is for the sake of heaven will endure', will continue without end, because it can be said of both sides: *elu ve'elu divrei elohim hayim*—'These and those are the living words of God.'[112]

---

[108] BT *San.* 34*a*.   [109] BT *Shab.* 88*b*.
[110] *Numbers Rabbah* 13: 15 (*inter alia*).   [111] Mishnah *Avot* 5: 17.
[112] BT *Eruv.* 13*b*; *Git.* 6*b*. The phrase could also be translated: 'These and those are the words of the living God.'

FOUR

Respectful Disagreement
A Response to Raphael Jospe

JOLENE S. KELLNER *and* MENACHEM KELLNER

O UR FRIEND and colleague Raphael Jospe has presented a moving case in support of a non-relativistic religious pluralism. He seeks to ground that admirable stance in the sources of Judaism. We are not convinced by his arguments and we will show why this is the case.

It is important to be clear on matters of terminology. By 'relativism' we understand (following the *American Heritage Dictionary*) the view that holds that 'conceptions of truth and moral values are not absolute but are relative to the persons or groups holding them'. By 'religious pluralism' we understand the normative (as opposed to simply descriptive) claim that different religions make equally correct truth-claims, that they are equally acceptable. Assuming that he accepts these definitions, it is obvious that it would be hard for Jospe to defend religious pluralism without also adopting the relativistic stance that no one religion teaches truth—that in terms of truth and falsity there is no reason to prefer Judaism over Islam or Christianity, or over African, Native American, or South-East Asian religions as well. Jospe's thesis is that 'the Jewish concept of the chosen people is not externally directed, implying that Jews in fact are better than other people; rather, chosenness is internally directed, challenging Jews to become better people'. We agree with this statement, but it also reflects much of what separates us and why we think that his argument either proves nothing that anyone would disagree with or must fail. He bases his discussion on the centrality of the Jewish people, moving from the people to their Torah. In a very real sense this move makes his argument for him. It is no challenge to show that biblical and many rabbinic expositions of the doctrine of election do not imply that Jews are in any inherent fashion superior to non-Jews.[1] After all, God created all humanity in the divine image

---

[1] For the Bible, see Jon D. Levenson, 'The Universal Horizon of Biblical Particularism', in Mark G. Brett (ed.), *Ethnicity and the Bible* (Leiden, 1996), 143–69; Joel S. Kaminsky, *Yet I Loved Jacob: Reclaiming the Biblical Concept of Election* (Nashville, 2007). For rabbinic Judaism, see Menachem Hirshman, 'Rabbinic Universalism in the Second and Third Centuries', *Harvard Theological Review*, 93 (2000), 101–15; id., *Torah for all Beings: The Universal Element in Tannaitic*

and can hardly be uninterested in the fate and spiritual and physical well-being of non-Jews.[2] Since, on many readings (such as those of Isaiah and Maimonides[3]) distinctions between Jew and non-Jew will melt away in the messianic era, the notion of election poses a fairly small challenge to Jospe's pluralism.

If, instead of following Jospe and Solomon Schechter ('Judaism is the religion of the Jewish people'), who move from the Jewish people to Judaism, we follow Sa'adiah Gaon and move from Judaism to the Jewish people ('our nation is a nation only by virtue of its laws [Torah]'[4]), it will be much harder to support the sort of religious pluralism that Jospe seeks to ground in the texts and traditions of Judaism. The reason for this is that the notion of revelation embodied in the claim that the Torah was divinely revealed involves the claim that the Torah teaches truth. Once that claim is made we must ask, what is the status of truth-claims made by competing religions? Either Jesus is the messiah and the son of God or not; either the New Testament supersedes and renders null and void the Hebrew Bible or not; either Muhammad is the seal of all the prophets or not; either the story of Abraham, Isaac, and Ishmael as told in Genesis is true, and the story told in the Koran is false, or vice versa.

Another way of putting this is that Jospe takes Judah Halevi as his starting point, while we take Maimonides as ours. For Halevi, the Jews received the Torah because they were antecedently the chosen people; for Maimonides, it is the receipt of the Torah that made the Jews chosen. One can move beyond Halevi's essentialist particularism, as Jospe does, while still following him in making identification with the Jewish people the core element of Judaism, as Jospe also does. As we said above, this renders relatively simple the task of creating a Jewish theology of the religious Other: the notion that a Jew can keep faith with the Jewish people while affirming the value of a Muslim's keeping faith with the *ummah* of Islam and of a Christian's keeping faith with the Church makes intuitive sense—after all, Red Sox fans do not support the Yankees, but expect fans of the Bronx Bombers to do so.[5]

Jospe proposes to reverse traditional religious claims:

Literature and its Relation to the Wisdom of the Nations [Torah lekhol ba'ei olam: zerem universali besifrut hatana'im veyahaso lehokhmat he'amim] (Tel Aviv, 1999). For medieval views, see Menachem Kellner, *Maimonides' Confrontation with Mysticsm* (Oxford, 2006).

[2] Although many contemporary Orthodox Jews would be surprised by this, the liturgy assumes that God judges all humans on Rosh Hashanah and Yom Kippur, not just Jews. For a clear example of this, see how the *piyut Unetaneh tokef* uses Mishnah *RH* 1: 2 and Ps. 38: 5.

[3] See Menachem Kellner, 'Maimonides' "True Religion": For Jews, or All Humanity? A Response to Chaim Rapoport', *Meorot*, 7/1 (2008), <http://www.yctorah.org/content/view/436/10/>.

[4] Sa'adiah Gaon, *Book of Beliefs and Opinions*, 3: 7 (trans. Samuel Rosenblatt (New Haven, 1948), 158).　　　　　　　　　　[5] It will become clear below why we choose so trivial an example.

instead of spiritual exclusivity—the notions that there is only one truth, that one group has exclusive possession of that truth and thus of the keys to salvation—which logically leads to ritual inclusivity (the impulse to proselytize and include others in one's own religious community), we should work for spiritual inclusivity; that is, the recognition that different groups can understand the truth, albeit frequently in diverse ways. This logically leads to ritual exclusivity, or pluralism; that is, the legitimacy and desirability of different religious approaches and ritual practices, and there is no reason to seek to proselytize others.

Note that Jospe speaks here of 'the truth', a truth which can be understood in diverse ways. He wants to say here that all religions (or all Western monotheistic religions) teach the same truth, but that different religious communities understand that truth in diverse ways. If we restrict our gaze to the most fundamental of basics, this claim is surely true: Judaism, Christianity, and Islam are all monotheistic faiths, and adherents of these faiths are expected to reject polytheism, idolatry, and so on. But each of these faiths makes very important claims which the other denies: does the Torah reflect the will of God now as it did before the advent of Jesus and the revelation of the Koran? Are the Jews, as descendants of Abraham, Isaac, and Jacob, the Israel with which God is covenanted, or is it the *verus Israel* of the Church(es)? Is Moses the greatest of the prophets, or Muhammad? Are human beings born fundamentally flawed and cut off from God in a way that only the sacrifice of Jesus can overcome or not? The list goes on and on. Beyond the very palest and thinnest monotheism, in what serious sense can it be said that Judaism, Christianity, and Islam teach the same truth?

Two further points must be made: why stop with Christianity and Islam? If we are going to adopt a Jospean stance of religious pluralism, why not include Hinduism, with its pantheon of divinities, or Buddhism, which seems not to have any personal divinity? To go even further, once we adopt a pluralist stance, why not extend our refusal to reject as false African animism, contemporary neo-paganism, and so on? In parochial terms, on what basis does Jospe exclude from the pluralist tent Jews for Jesus?

Second, by ignoring this issue and reverting to the ground on which Jospe actually makes his argument (Christianity and Islam), he creates comparisons where none are appropriate. Underlying his discussion and lending it plausibility is the notion that Judaism, Christianity, and Islam are three different but comparable versions of Western monotheism. This we think is a mistake: Judaism is not a religion in the sense that Christianity and Islam are religions. Judaism's emphasis on election, covenant, and *mitsvot* make it something different from Christianity and Islam. By ignoring this crucial point, Jospe levels the playing field in ways that make his argument easier to sustain, but not, ultimately, more convincing. In order to support his quest for religious pluralism,

Jospe has to treat Judaism, Christianity, and Islam as different expressions of the same archetype—but they are not.

The overall point here may be clarified by the following oft-recited story. Representatives of Judaism, Christianity, and Islam come together to unify the world's monotheisms in the hope of bringing about an era of universal peace and justice. Each group is called upon to sacrifice something essential, in order to make the goal of unification possible. The Christian representatives agree to sacrifice belief in the divinity of Jesus; the Muslims agree to renounce the claim that Muhammad is the seal of the prophets; the Jews, after a lot of internal squabbling, and with great pathos and fanfare, announce that in order to further the dream of universal peace and justice that they are willing to give up . . . the recitation of the second paragraph of the Yekum purkan prayer. Here we see traditional Jewish faithfulness to the past, relative disinterest in abstract theology, and emphasis on *mitsvot*. Judaism is not one of three flavours of Western monotheistic ice cream; it is a different snack altogether.

Jospe's position consists of two claims: first, one can be a theological relativist (that is, a religious pluralist) without being an epistemological relativist; second, one can responsibly ground this position in normative Jewish sources. In what follows we dispute these two claims and sketch out an alternative position: while not giving up on the idea that revelation (be it Jewish, Christian, or Muslim) teaches truth in some hard, exclusivist sense, putative addressees of revelation ought to be modest about how much of it they understand, and restrained in the claims they make on and about adherents of other religions. Admittedly, it is easier for a Jew to advance this position than for a Christian or a Muslim. Until the Middle Ages, at least, Jews sought to understand how God instructs them to inject sanctity into their lives and paid very little attention to the question of how God expects them to think. Given the notion that the Torah contains many levels of meaning and the profound differences among Jewish thinkers about the nature and content of those meanings, a stance of theological modesty *ought* to be easy for Jews to maintain. Jews, not thinking that one must be Jewish in order to achieve a share in the world to come, have traditionally paid little attention to the beliefs and practices of others. But that said, we are struggling here towards a *Jewish* theology of the religious other, not a non-specific theology of religious others for all religions.

Before beginning, we take a moment to review Jospe's characterization of Menachem's position. He writes:

Kellner's position is clear: pluralism is at best an 'unfortunate reality' in our current condition and is 'self-refuting'. We must strive for the ultimate triumph in messianic times of universal truth, a truth that Kellner believes is taught in historic Jewish revelation.

The 'unfortunate reality' to which Menachem was referring is that in today's world 'we cannot agree on what is true, or even on what truth is'.[6] The epistemological relativism to which this leads many postmodernists is what Menachem called (and still calls) self-refuting. If the messianic era means anything, it means that at some points humans will agree on what truth is and what is true—it makes sense to call us epistemological messianists. Judaism without such a belief is a strange Judaism. Jewish tradition maintains that that messianic truth is what the Torah teaches; it does not insist that we understand that truth today, thus leaving room for deeper and fuller understanding of the truths taught by the Torah as we come ever closer to the messianic era. There is no inconsistency between the claim that the Torah teaches truth and the demand that we remain modest about our claims to understand that truth.[7]

The key theoretical claim about which we and Jospe differ is the following:

pluralism cannot be correctly equated with relativism. Plural understandings of the truth, or even plural truths, are not the same as no truth at all, and they are certainly not the same as no moral standards.

One could argue with Jospe's definitions here, but we will leave that to others. Rather, we want to focus on what we believe is the core of Jospe's error. At issue here is the question of religious truth. Can a Jew affirm the truth of Judaism while simultaneously affirming the truth of Christianity and Islam? Obviously not, unless one makes what we take to be Jospe's move, and reframe the question as follows: can Jews affirm the truth of Judaism for themselves while simultaneously affirming the truth of Christianity for Christians and of Islam for Muslims? Put this way, the question is no longer about truth, but about lifestyle choices (flavours of ice cream in Jospe's example, baseball teams in ours). Jospe is, in effect, quick to admit this:

it seems to me that if it should still be the case that pluralism entails some degree of relativism, we would then be obliged to differentiate between moral relativism, which may entail clear and immediate practical dangers, and various epistemic relativisms that may have theoretical errors but do not present existential danger. Moral relativism affects interpersonal matters (*bein adam leḥavero*), whereas epistemic relativism (if it be relativism at all, rather than pluralism) regarding diverse understandings of God refers to highly speculative areas of personal and subjective questions between the individual and God (*bein adam lamakom*)

But this is the reddest of red herrings. In terms of moral demands, Judaism,

---

[6] Menachem Kellner, *Must a Jew Believe Anything?* (London, 1999); 2nd edn. with new Afterword (Oxford, 2006), 125.

[7] There are other ways in which we believe that Jospe misunderstands what Menachem tried to convey in his earlier writings, but they are not strictly relevant to the points at issue between us here. We therefore take them up at the end of this essay.

Christianity, and Islam (and to the best of our very limited knowledge, Native American, African, and South-East Asian religions as well) are extraordinarily alike. They all agree that there must be moral standards, and to a very great degree agree on what those standards are.[8] Jospe repeatedly defends himself against the charge of moral relativism, a charge wholly irrelevant to our discussion.

Crucially relevant, on the other hand, is Professor Jospe's claim that 'diverse understandings of God [refer] to extremely personal and subjective questions between the individual and God'. For Judaism, Christianity, and Islam, the faithful person's relationship with God is extremely personal, but not subjective in the sense Jospe needs to support his position. Jospe frames his discussion in terms of individuals and their beliefs, while we continue to insist that the only truly fruitful way of framing the discussion is in terms of Judaism, Christianity, and Islam as bodies of doctrines and practices.

Jospe turns out to be arguing with us at cross-purposes in other ways as well. We ask if an adherent of Judaism can meaningfully affirm the truth of Christianity and Islam *simpliciter*. Jospe responds that Christians and Muslims can be saintly people. He has in no way shown that our negative answer to the first question is incorrect, while we have no problem with enthusiastically recognizing the saintliness of many Christians and Muslims.

Let us summarize the discussion to this point: we have argued that religious pluralism in a strong sense (that adherents of Judaism, Christianity, and Islam can each affirm the truth of the others' revelation) renders the notion of revelation in any classic sense of the term incoherent. There is nothing in Jospe's argument that refutes this claim. Rather he argues (and here we emphatically second him) that Jews, Christians, and Muslims can respect each other on the level of moral behaviour.

There is another aspect of Jospe's approach that troubles us. It seems fundamentally disrespectful of the belief-claims made by non-Jews and, for that matter, Jews. To be a consistent pluralist of the Jospean sort one must tell the religious Other that they do not hold their religious claims as seriously as they think they do, since they must hold them to be true only for themselves (and their co-religionists), but not true in any absolute, exclusivist sense. Jospe may want to make that claim for himself, but is there not an element of *chutzpah* in making it for others? If he does not make the claim for others, his is a one-way-street sort of pluralism: recognizing the truth of other faith-claims, while not insisting on similar treatment of his own.

So far as we can see, then, Jospe has failed to make his theoretical case for religious pluralism. Turning to the second pole of his discussion, do Jewish

[8] For a recent statement of this view, see Francis Collins, *The Language of God: A Scientist Presents Evidence for Belief* (New York, 2006).

texts support Jospe's strong epistemological pluralism? Let us examine his examples.

Exodus Rabbah 5: 9 speaks of God's voice at Sinai as having been heard by all nations and all people. Each of the seventy nations into which the Sages divide humanity heard God's voice in its own language, while the Jews each heard it according to his or her own individual capacity. Jospe wants to see this as a claim that revelation was adjusted to 'relative cultures of the various nations'. To our eyes, this text distinguishes between the seventy nations, each of which heard the divine voice in its own language (so it could not come later with complaints that the Torah had not been offered to it, a common rabbinic motif), from the Israelites at Sinai, each of whom heard it at the level appropriate to her or him.[9] We fear that in his enthusiasm to find rabbinic support for his position, Jospe forces this text in directions it was never meant to go.

Similarly with the interesting citation from Ibn Ezra. Ibn Ezra does not qualify the truth of God's revelation but may, if Jospe is correct in his reading of this notoriously enigmatic exegete, provide an argument for what we have been calling epistemological modesty. The Torah teaches truth; we may not hear that truth in its fullness and ought therefore to be modest in our claims to understand it and certainly ought to be modest in our condemnations of those who hear it differently. Yet that does not mean that there can never be a time when all who have the ability will hear the same voice (that is, the messianic era); at that time 'the knowledge of the Lord will cover the earth as the waters cover the sea' (Isa. 11: 9).

To cite Maimonides in support of a pluralist vision of truth seems almost perverse. If there was ever a Jewish thinker who held truth to be one, objective, and unchanging it was Rabbi Moses ben Maimon. The texts cited by Jospe in no way qualify that claim; they only emphasize Maimonides' intellectualist elitism.

For the sake of argument, we are willing to grant Nethanael ibn al-Fayyumi to Jospe, if only to emphasize that one has to scrape pretty far down the barrel to find an actual religious pluralist in the sense needed for his argument to work. Jospe admits this, recognizing Ibn al-Fayyumi as 'a relatively insignificant and exceptional figure in medieval Jewish thought'. Jospe contrasts Ibn al-Fayyumi with Sa'adiah—no one's idea of an insignificant figure in Jewish thought—and seeks to find in his thought 'a type of religious truth transcending Judaism'. That religious truth is monotheism. It is indeed the case that Sa'adiah and Maimonides recognized Islam as a monotheistic religion. On this basis, Jospe makes the following illegitimate move:

[9] Jospe's note here does not refute the claim that revelation teaches truth, but, rather, supports the claim that we ought to be epistemologically modest when we condemn others for not agreeing with our understanding of that truth.

If my universalistic understanding of 'the community of monotheists' in Sa'adiah Gaon, Bahya ibn Pakuda, Judah Halevi,[10] and Maimonides is correct, the universal nature of this type of truth implies at least a degree of pluralism, for the simple reason that the truth takes different forms in diverse cultures, all of which are, nevertheless, acknowledged to be true monotheisms.

On the contrary, all this proves is that for thinkers like Sa'adiah and Maimonides not everything in Islam is false. Indeed, we would assume that they would maintain that those aspects of Islam that are true are derived from Judaism—hardly a helpful form of 'pluralism'. Again, to try to turn Maimonides, the author of the fiercely polemical and derisive Epistle to Yemen, into a religious pluralist is to prove the truth of Maimonides' claim that the gates of figurative interpretation are never sealed.[11]

Before bringing this part of our argument to a close we briefly point out that the thrust of the Hebrew Bible as we read it works against Jospe's thesis. It seems to us that one meaning of the story of the Tower of Babel is that pluralism is a punishment for overweening pride. Judaism looks forward to a future era when that punishment will end and God will 'turn to the peoples a pure language, that they may all call upon the name of the Lord, to serve him with one consent' (Zeph. 3: 9, one of Maimonides' core messianic verses, not surprisingly).

Furthermore, the Torah offers two fundamental metaphors for the relationship between God and Israel: a king and his people, and a loving couple. Let us focus on the second for a moment. Judaism has a very traditional conception of marriage: one man, one woman, much love. God loves all humanity but is married, so to speak, to Israel. Pushing this metaphor a bit, Jospe's version of religious pluralism seems based upon a more open, contemporary model of marriage, in which the partners are free, so to speak, to play the field.

But for an instant let us grant Jospe his historical claims (but only for an instant). Do they constitute 'precedents in Jewish thought, both rabbinic and philosophic, for pluralistic and inclusive understanding of religious truth', and is it true that 'the concept of revelation need not, and indeed cannot, be understood to mean exclusive possession of absolute truth, since even the revelation of the Torah at Sinai had to be adjusted to subjective human understanding and to diverse national cultures'? Even if Jospe's texts teach what he wants them to teach (and we believe they most certainly do not), when weighed against the huge body of Jewish teachings, they constitute at best minuscule and not 'ample' precedent for his position.

[10] For the sake of simplicity, we ignore Jospe's comments about Halevi and Bahya, and also his argument that for Sa'adiah Gaon, at least, Christianity is also monotheistic; our discussion of Sa'adiah and Maimonides holds for Bahya and Halevi as well.

[11] Maimonides, *Guide of the Perplexed*, ii. 25.

Let us for a further moment grant Jospe his thesis, which, as we understand it, boils down to the claim that it makes both philosophical and Jewish (as well as moral) sense for a Jew to affirm the truth of Judaism for Jews while affirming the truth of Christianity for Christians, of Islam for Muslims, and so on. We find two problems with this, one fairly slight and one deeply significant.[12] We do not see how Jospe can formulate a Jewish argument against assimilation, intermarriage, and religious syncretism. If Judaism, Christianity, and Islam, and so on are different paths to the same truth, or competing but complementary truths, or complicated combinations of truth and falsity each, then why prefer one over the other? For Jospe it would seem to boil down to a matter of choice.[13] If one chooses to abandon Judaism altogether, through assimilation or through outright apostasy, or if one chooses to become a Jew for Jesus, on what grounds can Jospe complain?

This brings us to the more significant point. The late Emil Fackenheim constantly reminded us that remaining Jewish is not a morally neutral act. Literally millions of Jews were killed in the Holocaust because their great-grandparents refused to assimilate. Given the frightening resurgence of worldwide antisemitism to which we are unwilling witnesses,[14] does anyone have the right to raise children as Jews unless they are convinced that Torah has something uniquely beautiful and true to teach to the world, something worth living for and even, God forbid, worth dying for?

APPENDIX: REPLIES TO SPECIFIC POINTS

Jospe accepts as self-evidently true Hans Küng's assessment that 'without peace among the world's religions, there will be no peace among the nations'. On our reading of the history of the last two centuries, it is nationalism, especially when coupled with a secularized messianism, which has been the main obstacle to peace among the nations.[15] One of us recently had the privilege of

[12] We repeat here points made in Menachem Kellner, *Must a Jew Believe Anything*—Jospe's discussion here has not succeeded in showing how these points are wrong.

[13] There may be some influence of the late Yeshayahu Leibowitz on Jospe here.

[14] And here we would like to salute Jospe, one of the few Israelis who recognize the threat for what it is and who in his writings and interfaith activities does something effective about it. Recent studies on the subject which we have found useful include Paul Berman, *Terror and Liberalism* (New York, 2003); Bernard Harrison, *The Resurgence of Anti-Semitism: Jews, Israel, and Liberal Opinion* (Lanham, Md., 2006); Andrei Markovits, *Uncouth Nation: Why Europe Dislikes America* (Princeton, NJ, 2007).

[15] Küng and Jospe may or may not be right—that question is certainly beyond the scope of our comments here. It is certainly the case that the recent deluge of evangelical atheists agrees with them. See e.g. Richard Dawkins, *The God Delusion* (Boston, 2006); Daniel Dennett, *Breaking the Spell: Religion as a Natural Phenomenon* (New York, 2006); Sam Harris, *The End of Faith: Religion, Terror, and the Future of Reason* (New York, 2004); Christopher Hitchens, *God Is Not Great: How Religion Poisons Everything* (New York, 2007). All of these books see religion as 'the main obstacle

attending an interfaith meeting of Jews, Christians, and Iranian Shiite Muslims. The premise of the meeting was that it is easier today to talk about religion than it is about politics, and so it turned out to be. This brings up an important point. Jospe thinks that adopting a stance of religious pluralism will bring about a diminishment of interreligious tension. We have our doubts about that: the people for whom and to whom theologians such as Jospe speak (for example Hans Küng) do not need to adopt a pluralist stance to treat Jews and Muslims (and, we assume Hindus, Buddhists, and so on) with respect and fraternity. But the co-religionists of the theologians—now that's a different story! We self-proclaimed intellectuals easily forget how few people actually listen to us.

Looking at all this from a narrowly Israeli perspective leads us to another observation. Anti-Zionism is by and large not a response to Israeli behaviour; antisemitism is almost never a response to Jewish behaviour. Jospe knows this better than most and has spoken out about it bravely and forthrightly. But implicit in his argument, or so it appears to us, is the assumption or hope that if we Jews are 'nicer' theologically to other religions, their adherents will be nicer to us. We doubt it.

Again, looking at Jospe's argument from an Israeli perspective it in some ways reminds us of the call made by many so-called 'progressives' to turn Israel into a 'state of all its citizens'. In this state citizens would not be Jews or Arabs (or others), just Israelis. The state as such would divest itself of all specifically Jewish characteristics. In many ways it is an attractive prospect, but one that ignores the fact that almost all actual human beings (as opposed to philosophical abstractions) both want and need to mediate their human identity through the prism of some particular national or cultural identity.[16] In seeking to minimize theological differences (and that is surely the upshot of theological pluralism), Jospe seems to want to turn the world of religious believers into a state of all its citizens. It does not work on the political level, and we see no reason why it should work any better on the theological level.

Jospe writes: 'Kellner's objection to recognition of Jewish dissenting opinion is thus justified on the grounds that it might lead, God forbid, to recognition of Christian dissenting opinion.' It is important to remember that Menachem made that objection in the context of calling for unceasing argument with Jewish dissenting opinion coupled with a call for the acceptance of dissenting Jews.

---

to peace among nations'. Given the history of the twentieth century, it seems to us that such claims make sense only if 'religion' is expanded to include Communism and Nazism.

[16] People who propose turning Israel into a state of all its citizens, such as the late Tony Judt of NYU, also ignore the fact that such a move would almost certainly ultimately result in the massacre of the new state's Jewish population. In our eyes, people who hold this view are either knaves or fools or both.

Jospe's discussion of Kellnerian Jewish Orthodoxy makes an illegitimate move from sociology to theology. That many strictly Orthodox (*haredi*) Jews today hold views that Jospe and both of us are convinced are patently false in no way undermines the claim that the Torah teaches truth. It just means that those Jews have more reason than most to be modest about their claims to understand Torah.

Jospe understands epistemological 'relativism' to mean the claim that there is no truth, and cites Irving Greenberg in support:

Pluralism means more than accepting or even affirming the other. It entails recognizing the blessings in the other's existence, because it balances one's own position and brings all of us closer to the ultimate goal. Even when we are right in our own position, the other who contradicts our position may be our corrective or our check against going to excess . . . Pluralism is not relativism, for we hold on to our absolutes; however, we make room for others' as well.[17]

Greenberg, like Jospe, wants to affirm the goodness of the Other (a goal we share) and thinks that in order to do so he must give up on the notion that revelation teaches truth. We have argued here that one does not imply the other. In this passage Greenberg seeks to have his cake and eat it too: if we are right in our position, how can we make room for the other's absolute?

Again, we propose as an alternative the model of epistemological modesty: Sinai teaches truth, a truth all will acknowledge in the end of days, but at this point in history we can hardly be confident that we have plumbed its depths. We hardly think that this position justifies the loaded adjective 'triumphalist' which Jospe attaches to it.

Jospe writes:

Even if Kellner's claim that there are no precedents for pluralism in Jewish thought were correct, the lack of precedent would not invalidate pluralism in principle. Kellner surely would not reject democracy on the grounds that it is derived from Athenian and not from biblical or later Jewish thought. I shall show, however, that in fact there are ample Jewish precedents for pluralism.

Here we have an important point, one which distinguishes our approach from Jospe's. For Jospe the Jewish past has a vote in, but no veto over, the Jewish future. In that sense, he is freer than we are to formulate a Jewish theology of the religious Other only very loosely based upon Jewish precedent. The comment about democracy is a red herring: the texts and traditions of Judaism are agnostic about pre-messianic government. There is no reason why a Jew should not be a democrat (or even a Republican). On the contrary, on the level of values, if not of procedures, it is easy to show a fundamental coherence between Torah and democracy.

[17] In the second paragraph quoted (p. 100 above) Greenberg slides from epistemology to ethics.

PART II

JUDAISM AND THE OTHER

FIVE

Can Another Religion Be Seen as the Other?

STANISŁAW KRAJEWSKI

THE OTHER

WHO IS the Other? A basic understanding of the term 'other' is shared by the man in the street and the philosopher: the other is an individual human being. But the philosopher sometimes uses a capital 'O': the Other. The typographical modification is used to express an important idea: the Other is so fundamentally important, so basic an ingredient of the world, so unique, and so inexhaustibly deep that the Otherness of a human person is of a different quality than the otherness of things, and it opens a specific dimension of being.

While this Otherness is a philosophical notion, it has a theological flavour. Indeed, I think it is equally a theological concept. After all, the idea of the uniqueness of another person is close to the concept of the soul and to the vision of being created in God's image.

With that Otherness in mind, the basic question within the framework of interfaith dialogue is whether the other religion can be perceived as having a similar dimension of otherness, one that deserves the capital 'O'. The experience with the concepts of philosophers of dialogue such as Martin Buber, Franz Rosenzweig, Emmanuel Levinas, and of those in the phenomenological, hermeneutical, existentialist traditions suggests at least this: if the naive view of another person has proved to be an introduction to deeper insights, perhaps the same may be the case with religions. We can ask, therefore: 'Can we reach beyond the naive view of the other religion?' This chapter offers comments on possible attitudes to other religions, suggested by insights derived from both modern philosophy and Jewish tradition.

THE PLURAL 'YOU'

One way of using the philosophy of the Other as an inspiration for the shaping of the vision of other religions is to transfer discoveries from the realm of individual persons to the realm of religions. Whatever religions are—and this is far from clear—it is certain that they entail understanding individuals as belonging to a supra-individual entity. When we direct our attention to another religion we encounter not only individuals but also a group. Facing a religion, we both face a person and relate to a group. Hence the idea of transferring the insights used to describe the other individual, the Thou, to the *plural* other, the You. Yet this attempt can be easily misdirected. Not everything can be transferred from the singular to the plural You, and perhaps the deepest insights are simply irrelevant when applied to anything other than an individual human being. However, one cannot be sure before trying, and, moreover, inspiration is always possible, even when transfer is inaccurate.

Transferring contemporary philosophical approaches from the individual to religion can be seen as a grammatical move, a passage from the singular to the plural. This can be related to the grammatical description of the development of philosophy. Dialogical philosophy discovered the Other by paying attention to the special role of the Thou, irreducible to anything else—neither to the It nor to the I. Taking the Thou seriously suggests that the development of philosophy can be described as going through subsequent phases, each retaining the previous ones as a dimension. Thus the movement is from the It, or 'It is' (Aristotle), to the I, or 'I am' (Descartes), to the Thou, or 'Thou art' (Buber, Levinas, with forerunners such as Feuerbach). The first, ancient, phase stresses the objective and the truth. The second phase stresses the subjective and the subject's freedom. The modern phase stresses the inter-human dimension and the ethical.[1] Of special importance here is the notion of responsibility. Responsibility is always for the Other. Humans are addressed and answer. They are answerable. When the human condition is described in this manner the notions of the Other and the Thou approximate each other.

From a purely grammatical perspective, what remains after taking care of the I, the Thou, and the It? The We, the (plural) You, and the They. Usually philosophers understand the plural cases as derivative.[2] When religions become our main focus, turning to the plural may be seen as the natural step. Much more is involved, however, than just a formal move based on grammatical considerations.

We can attempt various ways of acknowledging the Otherness of another religion, but we should constantly come back to one basic and obvious point: we never encounter 'religions'. We encounter *descriptions* of religions, which

---

[1] The account of the history of philosophy *more grammatico* has been proposed by Jacek Filek (*Filozofia odpowiedzialności XX wieku* (Kraków, 2003), 5–6).

[2] The 'We' is a possible exception. Robert R. Williams claims that Fichte and Hegel began to explore the problem of the Other and Otherness (*Recognition: Fichte and Hegel on the Other* (Albany, NY, 1992)). Hegel's Geist is 'an I that is a We, and a We that is an I' (*Phänomenologie des Geistes*).

are a far cry from the real thing. All genuine manifestations of religion, like texts, rituals, and buildings, are important, but they are nothing without religious people. Above all, we must encounter individual human beings who profess a religion.

When we treat someone not merely as a person but as a religious person we move beyond the purely inter-human nature of the relation with the Other. This suggests going beyond the description made by philosophers of dialogue. According to Levinas, when describing the fundamental level of this relation it is essential to exclude 'specific features of character, social condition and in fact all predicates'.[3] From his perspective Otherness is without characteristics, which excludes accepting someone's religiosity as a constitutive element of a philosophical description of the fundamental level of the situation. However, when an interreligious relationship is described, we would have to acknowledge not just the Thou, but also the plural You. It is not just the singular You that is fundamental, but also the collective You. We need to acknowledge not just some set of predicates, but someone's exceptional and socially rooted aspect—his religiosity. Religiosity is exceptional because unlike other social characteristics, it entails transcendence. Religions are ways of accessing transcendence, which is another fundamental philosophical dimension of our human world.

THE JEWISH PRIESTHOOD

Philosophically defined approaches are, of necessity, general. We must complement them by specific approaches based on a given religion's resources for relating to other religions. Whether they include real respect for others or not, those religious traditions must be taken into account. In considering the case of Judaism, we must remember that it is irreversibly linked to the history of the Jewish people. Therefore we must consider religious concepts and their role in varying historical circumstances. Jewish tradition contains diverse motifs (all of them present in other religions as well, but not occurring in the unique Jewish combination), each of which influences Jewish attitudes to other religions: universalism and particularism; opening and closure; the affirmation of the essential fraternity of all people forming the human community, best illustrated in the biblical vision of Adam, the common ancestor of humankind;[4] and the idea of a singular vocation of the Jews, God's chosen people, that results from Sinaitic revelation and manifested in the Mosaic covenant.

There is one specific Jewish approach that I find particularly important to

---

[3] Emmanuel Levinas, *Of God Who Comes To Mind*, trans. Bettina Bergo (Stanford, Calif.: Stanford University Press, 1998), 80.

[4] See Mishnah *San.* 4: 8, which emphasizes that all humanity stems from Adam.

our discussion: Jews are called to be a *mamlekhet kohanim*—a kingdom of priests. While this phrase is so well known that it seems obvious, the consequences of this vision are rarely pondered. Not only do Jews have priests, *kohanim*, in the strict Aaronic sense, but *all* Jews should be priests. Clearly, the idea of chosenness, the postulate to remember the revelatory events of the Exodus, and large portions of the halakhah can be described using the idea of the totality of Jews as priests. Whatever *mamlekhet kohanim* implies, one thing is obvious: priests never exist just for themselves. It makes no sense to be a priest if everyone is a priest. So the meaning of being a priest is to be a priest for the sake of others, those who are not priests. When Jews are *mamlekhet kohanim*, who are the others? The answer is, of course, everyone who is not Jewish. Jews are to be priests for the rest of humanity.

We can try to see what this means using general knowledge about human cultures and specific Jewish injunctions regarding priests. However, it is clear that whatever the priesthood means vis-à-vis the rest of humanity, it can apply in one of two basic ways: in relation to non-priests, a priest can either turn his back or face them—literally and metaphorically. It is well known that traditional Jews often turn their back on others and ignore the outside world. This can happen for several reasons, among them perceptions of enmity from outside and of Jewish vulnerability. This is historically understandable, but generated from outside and thus not intrinsic to Judaism. Perhaps there is also an internal reason. Jews concentrate so much on internal issues—or if we continue our metaphor of Jews as priests, on the ways of behaving appropriate to their priestly status—that they tend to ignore the rest of the world.

To extend the metaphor, the actual behaviour of the *kohen* during the recitation of the Aaronic blessing (Num. 6: 24–6) to the congregation suggests that there is a middle way between facing and turning one's back. Namely, facing the congregation, but not seeing it. They turn to it, but cover their faces and concentrate inwardly. They can bless everyone and thereby accept everyone's particular religiosity. Everyone? Admittedly, one could dispute this statement. The *kohanim* bless the Jews who take part in prayers, and Jews are supposed to accept, or at least recognize, the special role of the descendants of Aaron. Hence one could say that Jews-as-priests function only with respect to those who accept or recognize the priestly status of Jews. Only they, according to this interpretation, would be counted as those who receive the blessings of Jews. In this view, a special position would be assigned to Christians, who can be seen—under some interpretations—as accepting the priestly role of Jews. Those interpretations are now present in official theologies of most churches, epitomized by the affirmation that the Jewish covenant is eternally valid. Muslims are markedly less accepting of this Jewish self-understanding, but perhaps they can also be seen as somehow recognizing the priestly role of Jews.

This would mean that Christians, and perhaps Muslims, deserve a special place in the Jewish vision of the world. Not only did they bring to every corner of the world the revelation about the God of Israel, but they are also able to recognize the specific mission of the Jewish people.

The fact that Christians, and perhaps Muslims, subscribe to the Jewish understanding of the priestly role of Israel is important. However, its significance should not be exaggerated. The Talmud[5] states that during the festival of Sukkot, Temple sacrifices were offered for the seventy nations that represent the whole of humanity. The message is that the whole world is the arena for Jewish priestly activity, even those who are unaware of it. According to the rabbis, 'if the nations of the world had only known how much they needed the Temple, they would have surrounded it with armed fortresses to protect it'.[6] They did not, and yet Jews continue the Temple *avodah* service in a different way: all Jews participate. The priestly role of all Jews is even more visible in the absence of the Temple cult. Moreover, although an actual or potential recognition of the priestly status of the Jewish people by the others is essential, it should be emphasized that from the Jewish perspective the role itself is not dependent on anyone else's approval. While we believe that the nations need the Jewish people, Jewish faithfulness, and Jewish priesthood, there is no way to convince those who do not see that. The Jewish lifestyle, which should bear witness to God, together with the priestly mission, must be maintained regardless of the others' opinions. This is the message of Judaism for Jews.

THE PRIESTHOOD AND OTHER RELIGIONS

Can this concept of Jews as priests help us be more open to other religions? This may be doubtful for a number of reasons. For example, all priests need a community to minister to. This means that each group of priests is naturally in competition with other groups of priests relating to the same community, the priests of another rite. I have argued that the community Jews serve should rightly be seen as the whole human race, so for Jews the representatives of other religions can be seen as rival priests. If we insist that to approach another religion properly requires acceptance of other persons and their religiosity, we need to find a way of looking at other religions without seeing them as competitors. Yet when we limit our attention to Judaism, are the other religions truly competitors? I think not, and I see two main reasons for this.

Judaism is not a missionary religion, hence competing for converts is not part of the Jewish agenda, and other religions should not feel that Judaism is after their members. The special way in which Jews can be seen as priests is not connected to any specific expectations of non-Jews. The only exception can be

---

[5] BT *Suk.* 55*b*.   [6] *Numbers Rabbah* 1: 3.

seen in those Noahide laws that forbid idolatry and immorality. Yet ultimately Jews are priests with respect to everyone else even if those others are idolaters or practise immorality. The hope is they will improve, as we all should, but we are always to continue in our ways, expecting the day when 'the Lord be one and His Name one'.

Second, other religions would offer no competition to Judaism, if the value of Judaism were genuinely appreciated. We should differentiate between the practical danger for Jews from missionary activities and the fundamental threat to Jews posed by the existence of other religions and their claims. Jewish historical experience is clear: for generations there were Jews who converted to Christianity and other religions, both under duress and voluntarily. The best way to oppose this is to strengthen devotion to Judaism. I believe that when Judaism's vast resources are understood deeply enough, exposure to other religions is not a threat. This strong claim is based on my own experiences in Poland and Europe—growing from no Jewish knowledge and extensive exposure to other religions to deep Jewish involvement—but the point is general. Strong identity implies a lack of fear of other religions. When Jews have a strong sense of self and heritage, their attraction to other religions is of no consequence, no matter how much they are exposed to them. Only weak identity and superficial devotion will dissolve on meeting other religions. While hopes and attempts to convert Jews will probably continue, it is possible in our age to aim at achieving the level of Jewish knowledge and devotion that minimizes the danger of conversion to other religions. Shlomo Carlebach expressed this aim beautifully, if not realistically: the Jewishness of Jews should be so strong that 'nothing in the world can un-Jewish them. Yet on the other hand their Jewishness has to be completely connected to every human being in the world.'[7]

Thus, if we disregard the danger of missions to convert Jews—a step I understand that many Jews are not ready to make—other religions can be seen as non-threatening. To illustrate this point, let us use another standard Jewish motif, *kashrut*. Despite the burden of history, other religions when professed by others are not more dangerous to Jews than non-kosher food, forbidden by the Jewish religious law but not defective as such. Pork is, to be sure, valuable nourishment for those who have no religious reason to avoid it. Ideally, when the heritage of pogroms, the Holocaust, and forced conversions is overcome, Christianity, Islam, and other religions should be acceptable to Jews as valuable spiritual nourishment for other people. We can do this even if we know that non-Jews wish to convince us that their religions constitute the best 'food' in the world.

---

[7] 'Profile: Shlomo Carlebach', *Religion and Ethics Newsweekly* (2 May 2008), <www.pbs.org/wnet/religionandethics/week1135/profile.html>.

ATTITUDE, NOT KNOWLEDGE

The argument of the previous section shows that it is valuable to know other religions. While this is true, the matter is complex, as openness does not necessarily equate to knowledge. The basic lesson we learn from philosophy is that the Thou is not reducible to general categories, schemes, or processes.

To see the other person as the Other, that is, in his or her 'wholeness, uniqueness', is the opposite of the analytical, reductive approach, claims Martin Buber in the 'Elements of the Inter-human'.[8] The modern scientific approach is Cartesian-analytic.[9] It seeks to find constitutive parts and synthesize the whole from them by the application of schematic structures. While this is useful in many ways, we must remember that it destroys the 'mystery of inter-human'. It leaves the other and destroys the Other.

This point was emphasized by Levinas in a different way. He maintains that not only is every reduction destructive, but the very act of knowledge is destructive. Knowledge, comprehension, the fact of making something one's own should not be our aims because they do not respect the otherness of the Other. 'The realm of intelligibility . . . deprives the Other of his alterity by reducing it to the same.'[10] We approach the Other properly if we do it in a way that is different from the act of knowing. To know is to approach someone as an It. To say 'Thou' is to relate to someone in a different manner. The act of knowing as seen from the perspective of dialogical philosophy is sinister. To know is to comprehend, to encompass, to assimilate to my world, thus to myself; knowledge has an imperialist character, a totalizing, even a totalitarian one. In fact, Levinas proposed a vision of the philosophical foundations of totalitarian thought within the European tradition.[11] To comprehend or grasp is to suppress and possess the other. Ontology as first philosophy is a philosophy of power. It is based on the concept of *totum*, the whole, which eliminates unbridgeable differences. In other words, it is the culture of immanence that eliminates transcendence.

Levinas linked the culture of immanence and the philosophy of power to paganism. Conversely, Judaism, he says, is 'anti-paganism *par excellence*'.[12] This implies Judaism's imperative against the use of violence, a view as inspiring as

---

[8] Martin Buber, 'Elements of the Interhuman', in id., *The Knowledge of Man*, trans. Ronald Gregor Smith and Maurice Friedman (New York, 1966), 72–88.

[9] Because of the method, not because of the *cogito*.

[10] Edith Wyschogrod, *Emmanuel Levinas: The Problem of Ethical Metaphysics* (New York, 2000), 103.

[11] Emmanuel Levinas, *Totality and Infinity: An Essay on Exteriority*, trans. Alphonso Lingis (Pittsburgh, 1969).

[12] Emmanuel Levinas, 'A propos de la mort du Pape Pie XI' (1939), repr. in *Sens*, 9/10 (1996), 365.

it is challenging, in view of the fact that to achieve security the State of Israel relies on the use force.

Applying the above insights to our attitudes to religions, we ask again: 'Is it good to know other religions?' While traditionalists, who tend to ignore others, would answer 'No', it would seem that a more liberal attitude implies a positive answer: it is good to have knowledge of other religions and necessary to have sound knowledge if we want to have interfaith dialogue with other religions. To the uninitiated it appears that the more we know the more we can show respect. While this is true on some level, the insights of the philosophers of dialogue suggest something different, indeed the opposite. The issue is not knowledge, but proper attitude.

The centrality of attitudes may be seen as common sense. We all know from experience that our approach to phenomena, including religions, depends not merely on knowledge. To describe the role of attitudes we should consider notions developed in the philosophy of dialogue. For Buber, there are situations that are like mysteries; their meaning is closed to those who are not participants. No narration can grasp that, as the partners do not tell anything *about* the other; rather, they face each other. There is no concept, no knowledge, no image between the I and the Thou. Levinas goes further, providing a deeply ethical reading of the inter-human situation. According to him, 'the inter-human lies in a non-indifference of one to another, in a responsibility of one for another. The inter-human is prior to the reciprocity of this responsibility, which inscribes itself in impersonal laws and becomes superimposed on the pure altruism of this responsibility.'[13]

While it may be difficult to take into account the ethical dimension, the basic insight of the philosophy of dialogue is that other individual persons are unknowable to me. This should apply to their religiousness too. Therefore, I am unable to know the real religiosity of another person and I certainly cannot define it for her. A second insight is that respect for the other precedes our knowledge of him. This move beyond knowledge can be applied to religions. A respectful attitude should be assumed in advance. This may be seen as an imperative of epistemological humility, the awareness that we are not able to know another religion as it really presents itself to its believers.[14] The third insight is that the I–Thou relationship opens a window on the formerly ignored sphere of existence—the between, the realm that is not neutral—but

[13] Emmanuel Levinas, 'Useless Suffering', in Robert Bernasconi and David Wood (eds.), *Provocation of Levinas: Rethinking the Other* (London, 1988), 165.

[14] This theme is developed in Stanisław Krajewski, 'A Meditation on Intellectual Humility, or On a Fusion of Epistemic Ignorance and Covenantal Certainty', in James Heft, Reuven Firestone, and Omid Safi (eds.), *Learned Ignorance: An Investigation into Humility in Interreligious Dialogue among Christians, Muslims and Jews* (New York, 2011), 241–56, and the other papers in the same volume.

is accessible only to the participants in the encounter. This suggests the possibility of acknowledging the presence of the specific interreligious dimension,
accessible only to the participants in an interreligious encounter, which has not
yet been properly described.

Here we can point to a parallel between these philosophical ideas and the
behaviour of the *kohen* during the blessing. The *kohen* covers his eyes when he
intones the blessing. He is not supposed to see the audience, to learn about its
members, but rather only to have them in mind and enter into a relation with
them. Again, what is important is the proper attitude, acknowledging the
others and the special relationship with them.

THE IRREDUCIBILITY OF EVERY RELIGION

When applied to religions, the insight about the need to go beyond knowledge
suggests that there is no common denominator for religions; each religion is
to be faced as a separate entity. Indeed, the very term 'religion' becomes
suspect. The word 'religion' suggests that there is a generic category 'religion',
of which various religions are instances. This can be contested not just because
of philosophical parallels or historical considerations,[15] but also by more direct
experience.

Of course, in some contexts the term 'religion' is not problematic. For
instance describing the structure of a society or the results of an opinion poll,
we do use the term in such a way: Judaism is a religion, Christianity is a religion, Islam and Buddhism are religions, and so on. When faced, however, with
such a list many of us feel uncomfortable. First, because one could continue
with sects, groups, and gurus and arrive at such a multitude that hardly anything meaningful could be done in the realm of interreligious dialogue. So
there is a need to distinguish acceptable religions from the rest. This is not easy
and is always debatable.[16]

Yet the discomfort I feel when I look at a list of religions that includes
Judaism alongside others is due not only to the difficulty of finding the right
criteria or to the prospect that we could include the Reverend Moon's
Unification Church or the half-dozen followers of someone who had an

[15] A classic argument against the existence of well-determined entities called religions was
offered by Wilfred Cantwell Smith (see 'Conferring Names Where They Did Not Exist', in
Wilfred Cantwell Smith: A Reader, ed. Kenneth Cracknell (Oxford, 2001), 160–76).

[16] I have suggested that a religion should be considered acceptable for the purpose of deep inter-
faith dialogue if it can boast at least seven generations of continuous transmission (Stanisław
Krajewski, 'Towards the Philosophy of Inter-Religious Dialogue', in Lucia Faltin and Melanie J.
Wright (eds.), *The Religious Roots of Contemporary European Identity* (London, 2007), 179–91).
Another way is to make a list of acceptable religions, for example, Judaism, Christianity, Islam,
Hinduism, Buddhism, Taoism, and also Jainism, Sikhism, and so on up to Shintoism, Mormonism,
and Bahaism.

illumination last week. This discomfort is more fundamental. I feel strongly that Judaism is distinct from the other items on the list in such a basic way that putting all the religions together in one list is misleading. Despite all their common elements, aspects, and patterns, Judaism—or should I say, Jewishness—is *sui generis*. In fact, even Jews as a social group cannot be fully described using standard sociological categories. If Jews as a group do not belong to any standard category, then a fortiori no category is appropriate for Judaism, which is a multi-dimensional reality, including people, religion, Torah, priesthood, and more.

I am not unique in claiming this uniqueness. Karl Barth said much the same and more strongly about Christianity: because of its revelation (in Christ), Christianity is unique. It is not a religion, and in fact other religions are futile attempts to reach the true revelation. Franz Rosenzweig was more generous: according to him, both Judaism and Christianity were originally not conceived as religions. And this is not the end of the story: certainly Hinduism and others have a similar self-perception. In fact, Alon Goshen-Gottstein maintains that it is the common strategy that most religions use. Each claims it is not a 'religion', only others are.[17] While for Rosenzweig this disclaimer applies only to Judaism and Christianity, he also uttered the inspiring remark that seemingly applies to all of us: 'God did not, after all, create religion; He created the world.'[18]

There may be no 'religions', but there are many religious beliefs and practices. From the Jewish perspective, the problem of idolatry is unavoidable. It is a historical fact—or at least the way Jews understood the past—that from the beginning the main objective of Judaism was to distinguish itself from the other religions by rejecting idol worship. We still do the same. When we consider non-Jewish worshippers, we can ask: are they idolaters or not? Do they worship false gods? Abraham smashed the idols of his father, but are the same sorts of idols still around? Greek gods, Middle Eastern gods are not taken seriously anymore. They belong only to the history of religions. Even Hindu gods are explained by some as manifestations of the one God, much like angels, or, some would say, *sefirot*. Whatever answer we give to the problem of idols, we must notice that the Jewish way of looking at the problem is far from being an exception. Today, the question about idolatry can be posed differently: do they worship idols or, perhaps, do they only worship and address God differently? If the latter is correct, as Rabbi Menahem Me'iri ruled with regard to Christianity, then, even if the other form of worship is unacceptable for Jews, the practice may have a value from the Jewish perspective.[19] This possibility did not exist when Judaism was being formed.

---

[17] Alon Goshen-Gottstein, personal communication.
[18] Franz Rosenzweig, 'The New Thinking', cited in Nahum Glatzer, *Franz Rosenzweig: His Life and Thought* (New York, 1998), 201.　　　　[19] See Eugene Korn in Chapter 8, below.

The question about idolatry may still be valid therefore, but its context is now vastly different. In much of the world, for many generations the problem of idolatry has been commonly perceived precisely from the Jewish perspective. Of course, there are differences, such as Christian icons, which were always offensive to the Jews, but it is no coincidence that the opposition to icons has been present in the Christian tradition as well. Regardless of the differences, the situation that has emerged in the Western world as a result of the dominance of Bible-based monotheisms demands that Jews develop an appropriate understanding of idolatry.

To a certain extent, facing idolatry is a common challenge. It is not only in Judaism that an exaggerated trust in one's own estate displays features characteristic of idolatry. (The Jewish commandment to spend some time in huts every year during the festival of Sukkot, that is, in primitive conditions, serves supposedly as a counter-measure.) Indeed, in our era, in Europe, the Middle East, America, and Australia, idolatrous religiosity appears when a religion teaches its adherents only a negative identity based on the rejection of or contempt for other religions and their worshippers. One can make an idol of one's own religion, even of Judaism, which so strongly rejects idolatry. Abraham Heschel asserted this when he said that religion 'becomes idolatrous when regarded as an end in itself . . . To equate religion and God is idolatry.'[20] This is a striking teaching of modesty. We can respect other religions without compromising our principles. In fact the opposite may be the truth: the respectful approach to others can be Judaism's way of demonstrating respect for itself.

Let us try, then, to be as generous as possible and treat all religions on their own terms and as worthy of unconditional respect, even if only provisionally. If we accept the possibility of every religion's uniqueness, each is granted a singular status—one that is properly designated as the Other with a capital 'O'.

---

[20] Abraham Heschel, 'No Religion is an Island', in H. Kasimow and B. L. Sherwin (eds.), *No Religion is an Island* (New York, 1991), 13.

SIX

The Violence of the Neutral in Interfaith Relations

MEIR SENDOR

A RECENT article in *The Boston Globe* highlighting the struggle within the Muslim community worldwide to promote tolerance of other religions described Saudi scholar Hasan al-Malki, as 'one of the country's most daring voices for moderation and tolerance'. Al-Malki encouraged Muslim tolerance of other faiths on the basis of precedent: 'The prophet sat with Jews. He treated non-Muslims as though they were Muslims. This is the real Islam.'[1] Jews experienced at interfaith dialogue can appreciate Al-Malki's concern to find precedent within his tradition for tolerant behaviour. We might also smile at his charming expression, that tolerance of others means treating 'non-Muslims as though they were Muslims': a statement for a newspaper, not a technical theological formulation. He is expressing inclusiveness, however overstated, and he conveys a poetically concise and warm-hearted hospitality. We ourselves might be wary, on several counts, of defining tolerance in terms of treating non-Jews as though they were Jews. Even so, we might give thought to the underlying attitudes and perspectives that drive Jewish interfaith initiatives, and ask ourselves whether we, too, ever get free of such parochialism, and whether we should.

A recent scholarly work of significant value to interfaith understanding between Jews and Christians, and to which several participants in this volume contributed, is entitled *Christianity in Jewish Terms*. The title itself is noteworthy for its precision. Co-editor David Novak warns in his introduction that 'participants in Jewish–Christian dialogue must be careful to avoid five negative conditions', among which he includes 'syncretism' and 'relativism'. While many contributors to the volume invest great care in offering comparisons of Jewish and Christian doctrine and practice that avoid these pitfalls, a careful analysis of several otherwise thoughtful articles demonstrates that syncretism and relativism are not at all easy to filter out, and both can operate surreptitiously in even the most vigilant approaches to other religions.[2] The results

[1] C. A. Radin, 'Two Visions of Faith Collide', *The Boston Globe* (8 May 2005), A1, 12–13.

[2] David Novak, Introduction, in T. Frymer-Kensky et al. (eds.), *Christianity in Jewish Terms* (Boulder, Colo., 2000), 2.

can be a subtle example of treating non-Jews as though they were Jews, or treating Jews as though they were non-Jews. What is so dangerous about syncretism and relativism in our relations with those of other religions?

In this regard, the mission statement of the conference that gave rise to the present volume deserves careful consideration. We were told that 'a fresh examination of these issues, from a more neutral historical vantage point, is a deep need of the Jewish religion and of the Jewish community'.[3] This statement was not intended as a formal theological position but rather as a stimulus to discussion. Yet the choice of a 'neutral historical vantage point', a framework for contemporary efforts at interfaith understanding so common that its propriety is often regarded as apodictic, is by no means innocuous. It has been the subject of extensive analysis in the phenomenology of alterity, and its role in interfaith discussions deserves a closer look. Does the adoption of a 'neutral historical vantage point' perhaps prejudge, or surrender, the outcome of this enterprise and endanger its meaningfulness and value from the start? This essay is an attempt to explore a few of the underlying assumptions and attitudes of current interfaith initiatives at a phenomenological level, with reference to studies by Emmanuel Levinas, Jacques Derrida, and Paul Ricoeur, and to contribute to our critical awareness of these initiatives.

THE PROBLEM

Exploring the possibility of promoting honest relations between adherents of differing religious groups is a challenge worthy of informed postmodern sensibilities. Here, the problematic of self and other is susceptible to a peculiar exaggeration and a special urgency. Clifford Geertz has observed that religions, as cultural systems, reinforce and reify group ethos and identity.[4] Group identity is always defined partly by the exclusion of non-members. The identity of a religious group is often protected by erecting theologically justified barriers against non-members. For a committed member of one religious group to authentically encounter a committed member of another religious group can be especially difficult and delicate. The possibility of real, sustained openness to the other, which is never guaranteed even under the most optimal conditions, in marriage, family, or friendships within one's native social group, is here overlaid with complex antipathies and disincentives. Yet for that very reason, interfaith relations offer a unique opportunity to discover true alterity. Religion exacerbates the problem of otherness, yet it is to religion that we often turn to try to solve or resolve this problem. We should ask why.

[3] Alon Goshen-Gottstein, 'Toward a Theology of the Religious Other', Mission Statement for the Inaugural Conference, Elijah Interfaith Institute (Scranton, Pa., 2005). I am assuming the phrase should be understood with a comma: 'a more neutral, historical vantage point'.
[4] Clifford Geertz, *The Interpretation of Cultures* (New York, 1973), 89–90.

Common sense might dictate that, if the problem of interfaith relations is perceived as overcoming estrangement, the solution would be to seek common ground, explore commonalities, identify common cultural and theological themes, develop a common language, and make accommodations in order to help alienated groups become more comfortable with each other. In order to do this, we might adopt a neutral vantage point conditioned by historical relativism to smooth the way to mutual conciliation. This approach seems to have not only political utility, but even some truth to it. The entire thrust of the thought of Emmanuel Levinas argues otherwise, however. According to Levinas, to proceed in this way is to doom the possibility of real relationship from the start and to fall prey to the most insidious and destructive habit of Western thought: the deception of the Neutral that derives from the tyranny of the Same.

EMMANUEL LEVINAS

Levinas's critique of the neutral stance is one of the momentous contributions of his seminal work *Totality and Infinity*. His argument is founded upon Husserl's insight into the intentionality of consciousness: that consciousness is always consciousness *of* something. Therefore, consciousness is first and foremost the opening to exteriority, the immediate sense of difference, of the specificity of the other, inexhaustible, irreducible, real. 'It is attention to speech or welcome of the face, hospitality and not thematization.'[5] By contrast, the tendency to thematize, to conceptualize, to seize and reduce others and otherness to a common concept is central to the programme of Greek thought. The further reduction of ideas to progressively more common and inclusive concepts ultimately results in, and is driven from the start by, 'the concept of totality which dominates Western philosophy'.[6] This programme, proceeding from Parmenides (even from Thales) through Plato, Aristotle, and on to Hegel and Heidegger, is a process of domination: to subsume all that is other, all difference, under a totality that represents the tyranny of the Same. Summarizing Levinas's formulation, Jacques Derrida observes that '"the Eleatic notion of Being" ... would demand that multiplicity be included in, subjected to, the domination of unity'.[7]

This Hellenistic programme anointed ontology as the sovereign field of Western philosophy, pursued as an attempt to articulate Being as the common ground or region for all beings.[8] Levinas sees here the primal violent act of

---

[5] Emmanuel Levinas, *Totality and Infinity*, trans. A. Lingis (Pittsburgh, 1969), 299.

[6] Ibid. 21.   [7] Jacques Derrida, *Writing and Difference*, trans. A. Bass (Chicago, 1978), 89.

[8] Martin Heidegger reduces Being itself to the most noncommittal abstraction: 'the regioning of that which regions' (*Discourse on Thinking* (New York, 1966), 66); see also Martin Heidegger, *Early Greek Thinking: The Dawn of Western Philosophy*, trans. David Farrell Krell and Frank A. Capuzzi (San Francisco, 1984), 57.

Hellenistic thought as an appropriation and reduction of specific others to the
One and the Same, in terms of the neutral:

Possession is preeminently the form in which the other becomes the same, by
becoming mine . . . Ontology becomes ontology of nature, impersonal fecundity,
faceless generous mother, matrix of particular beings, inexhaustible matter for
things. A philosophy of power, ontology is, as first philosophy which does not call
into question the same, a philosophy of injustice . . . Heideggerian ontology, which
subordinates the relationship with the Other to the relation with Being in general,
remains under obedience to the anonymous, and leads inevitably to another power,
to imperialist domination, to tyranny.[9]

Levinas here tracks the shift from the articulation of the sameness underlying
all difference, which is characteristic of Hellenistic thought, to the designation
of neutrality as the privileged position from which to view all beings, the
reductive region into which to subsume and resolve all differences, as an
expression of an imperialist and ultimately materialist mindset.[10] He sums up
this process in his conclusion to *Totality and Infinity*:

We have thus the conviction of having broken with the philosophy of the Neuter
. . . The exaltation of the Neuter may present itself as the anteriority of the We with
respect to the I, of the situation with respect to the beings in situation . . . To place
the Neuter dimension of Being above the existent which unbeknowst to it this Being
would determine in some way, to make the essential events unbeknown to the
existents, is to profess materialism. Heidegger's late philosophy becomes this faint
materialism.[11]

Under this materialist agenda, history is also conscripted into the service of
the reduction of all individuality to relative, neutral sameness: when every
person and every action is explained, accounted for, put in place by a temporal
causality, the effect is that individuality and specificity are dissolved into the
neutral sameness of the whole, the historical process as totality. In the words
of Derrida: 'Levinas will describe *history* as a blinding to the other, and as the
laborious procession of the same.'[12] This is not a weakness of historical
method per se, but rather of certain approaches to history: linear, dialectical,
reductive. It is possible to pursue history more deconstructively.

In the materialist meat-grinder of Western thought, its ontology and its
history, the neutral historical vantage point is used to grind down all individuality, as a means of dominating reality, such that respect for otherness and difference, the very ability to perceive and welcome otherness and difference as
such, which is the first movement of consciousness, is overlooked, and, as over-

---

[9] Levinas, *Totality and Infinity*, 46–7.
[10] Ibid. 127; see also Derrida, *Writing and Difference*, 85.
[11] Levinas, *Totality and Infinity*, 298–9.   [12] Derrida, *Writing and Difference*, 94.

looked, endangered, and often lost. Derrida calls us to 'the only possible ethical imperative, the only incarnated nonviolence in that it is respect for the other. An immediate respect for the other himself . . . because it does not pass through the neutral element of the universal.'[13]

The impact of this pervasive, neutralizing habit of thought is not restricted to the Academy, and its repercussions condition and poison fundamental Western attitudes in all realms of life. Derrida describes Levinas's metaphysics as an attempt 'to liberate itself from the Greek domination of the Same and the One . . . as if from oppression itself—an oppression certainly comparable to none other in the world, an ontological or transcendental oppression, but also the origin or alibi of all oppression in the world'.[14] The totalitarianism of the Same and the Neutral as a habit of thought is at the root of political totalitarianism and violence. It conditions social relations, politics, economics, mass culture, and war. It is also at the root of those attitudes Charles Taylor identifies as characteristic of contemporary Western liberal thought. What Taylor refers to as the 'naturalistic fallacy' that gives rise to moral and cultural relativism is based on a conception of the self as an anonymous individual, an isolated point in a neutral nature, and society as a neutral collective of faceless points each of which is equal to the other, degrading our very sense of justice to the merely distributive and egalitarian.[15]

This neutralism also endangers any chance for honest interfaith encounter. First, it obscures the irreducible Otherness of the Other, tempting us to conceptualize the Other in terms that render him or her more familiar, the same as us, thus neutralizing the differences. There is another, concomitant danger, rooted in the way the Neutral emerges out of the Same as its privileged vantage point. It was Nietzsche who identified this, who articulated the 'eternal return of the same' as the nature of reality, and yet gave us a provocative hint about how the will to control at the heart of the Same, the will to dominate the other, reverts upon itself to devalue itself. In *Thus Spoke Zarathustra*, Nietzsche labels the core strategy of the will in its relation to the past: 'revenge'.[16] In this

---

[13] Ibid. 96.   [14] Ibid. 83.

[15] Charles Taylor, *Sources of the Self* (Cambridge, Mass., 1989), 36–9, 53, 495–521.

[16] 'Powerless against what has been done, he is an angry spectator of all that is past . . . That time does not run backwards, that is his wrath; "that which was" is the name of the stone he cannot move . . . This, indeed this alone, is what revenge is: the will's ill will against time and its "it was" . . . The spirit of revenge, my friends, has so far been the subject of man's best reflection; and where there was suffering, one always wanted punishment too . . . Because there is suffering in those who will, inasmuch as they cannot will backwards, willing itself and all life were supposed to be—a punishment. And now cloud upon cloud rolled over the spirit, until eventually madness preached, "Everything passes away; therefore everything deserves to pass away. And this too is justice, this law of time that it must devour its children" ' (Friedrich Nietzsche, *Thus Spoke Zarathustra*, in *The Portable Nietzsche*, trans. W. Kaufmann (New York, 1968), second part, 'On Redemption', 251—2).

dynamic, the will is frustrated at its inability to dominate the ineluctable past and strips all temporal life of value. However, the will turns its revenge against itself by indicting the entire context of time in which it lives, devaluing all of life by regarding it as a punishment. This dynamic is not limited to the will's relation to the past. It is a fundamental strategy whenever the will comes up against a recalcitrant, intractable other. Unable to fully dominate, the will vitiates the meaning of the struggle: it neutralizes its relation to the other and attenuates the value of the relationship. The neutered value is a response of the frustrated will to dominate the other, turning its revenge against itself.

This archetypal inversion of the will, running up against intractable Otherness, is at the root of certain more extreme pathologies in human relations. In a syndrome found among abused spouses (most frequently, though not exclusively, women), the abused wife, suffering under the controlling strategies of her husband, regains some sense of control by an internalization of revenge. She blames herself, she reasons that if she were only a better wife, if she responded more promptly to her husband's demands, if she hadn't burned the dinner, if she could control herself in this interior space that is all that has been left to her, she would find favour in his eyes. In the Stockholm syndrome, the hostage comes to identify with the hostage-taker.

Jewish interfaith relations occasionally parallel these inversions of the will in the face of a dominant other. Some Jewish participants vitiate their own faith, ignoring or suppressing aspects that they fear would be off-putting to adherents of other faiths or keep discussions from going smoothly. They feel intimidated and uncomfortable about being forthright and disclosing the fullness of their tradition, particularly aspects that are critical of other religions or that are disparaged by adherents of other politically dominant religions. They may feel embarrassed by the particularistic aspects of their tradition. Jews have frequently been the abused spouse of world history, and some blame themselves for it: if only we could be more amenable, we would find favour in the eyes of others. Some scholarly participants read Jewish and non-Jewish traditions selectively, looking for a handful of precedents that facilitate smooth interfaith relations and dismissing those positions that do not. They attenuate and neutralize distinctions, assume commonality, or select materials that prove commonalities, trying to create a neutral, historically relative common ground that explains away differences. In dismissing the fullness of the Jewish attitude to the other, such approaches also miss the Otherness of other religious groups. Trapped in syncretism and relativism, some Jews in interfaith discussions have already fallen prey to the Hellenistic thought tendencies of which Levinas speaks, and the authenticity of both Judaism and non-Jewish religions is compromised from the start. Instead of an honest relationship with the religious other, instead of real hospitality, the result is a Procrustean bed or the beds of Sodom. In the Greek myth as well as in the rabbinic *aggadah*,[17] the host offers his guest a bed, and then fits him to the measure of the bed: if the guest is too tall, he cuts off his legs; if the guest is too short, he stretches him on the bed used as a rack. This is the essential transgression against true hospitality: a neutralizing, relativizing welcome, forcing the guest to fit the dimensions of the bed of the host.

Christianity in Jewish Terms offers some subtle and instructive examples of this syncretism, selectivity, and neutralization. Most of the contributors are acutely aware of these issues, and I only raise these few cases, in the spirit of 'open rebuke and hidden love',[18] because they offer contemporary, documented examples of problems that regularly occur in undocumented conversations between earnest individuals working to further interfaith understanding. In an article on the Eucharist, the Jewish author establishes a framework characterizing this central sacrament of Christianity in terms of sacrifice, remembrance, and thanksgiving. He claims these are terms in which Christians themselves conceptualize the Eucharist, though they have more to do with the liturgy and homiletics surrounding the Eucharist than with the act itself.[19] Despite several caveats about the distinctiveness of Judaism and Christianity, the purpose of the article is to render the Eucharist in categories familiar to Jews, who also think in terms of sacrifice, remembrance, and thanksgiving, and to minimize the strangeness of the ceremony to Jewish sensibilities. Structural parallels and historical influences are drawn from the sacrificial service of the Temple and the Passover Seder. Yet the article lacks an analysis of the essence of the Eucharist: in Catholic terms, the moment of transubstantiation; in Protestant terms, the moment of consubstantiation. It is here that the non-Jewish, in fact, the idolatrous pagan, aspect of the origin of the Eucharist is revealed, and it is in this that the real, irreducible, and inconvenient Otherness lies. The Christian respondent to the article senses and addresses this omission. He adds the category of sacrament to the characterization of the Eucharist, describing the reverential attitude of worshippers to the sacramental act itself and explaining that 'a spiritual grace is conveyed through sensible material', a formulation that, for all its polite abstraction, places the Eucharist outside the Jewish comfort zone.[20]

---

[17] BT *San.* 109*b*.

[18] Nahmanides, *Perush al hatorah*, proem (ed. H. D. Chavel (Jerusalem, 1969), i. 16); based on Prov. 27:5.

[19] Lawrence A. Hoffman, 'Jewish and Christian Liturgy', in Frymer-Kensky et al. (eds.), *Christianity in Jewish Terms*, 175–88.

[20] R. L. Wilken, 'Christian Worship: An Affair of Things as Well as Words', in Frymer-Kensky et al. (eds.), *Christianity in Jewish Terms*, 201–2. Personally, I think Wilken is just being polite, recognizing that the essence of a ritual that is sacred to him has not been fully understood and giving his Jewish audience as much as he thinks they can handle in terms of grasping the specific meaning it has for him and for Christians. See J. T. O'Connor, *The Hidden Manna: A Theology of*

It might be helpful to approach this more deconstructively. The principle of transubstantiation, from Justin Martyr through Aquinas and on to the Council of Trent, with all its subtle theological variants, asserts that the bread and wine of the Eucharist are transformed into the body and blood of the divine Christ, which is then ingested and assimilated by the recipient.[21] Luther's rejection of transubstantiation for consubstantiation still asserts the real, substantial presence of the body and blood of Christ in the sacrament.[22] In these terms, the Eucharist would have been familiar to early first-millennium Hellenistic pagans of the Mediterranean basin, Asia Minor, and the Middle East, from their understanding of the process of animation, in which a cosmic deity is believed to come to inhabit and transform a prepared statue or physical object, and from the ceremonies for the binding and loosing of a deity in a human medium, in which the human being becomes assimilated to the deity.[23] Justin Martyr himself was aware of the parallel of the Eucharist to contemporary pagan mystery rites: 'The wicked devils have handed on *the same thing* to be done in the mysteries of Mithras; for you either know or can learn that bread and a cup of water are set forth with certain incantations when one is being initiated in the rites.'[24] It is likely that the familiarity of the transformational moment at the heart of the central Christian sacrament and other Hellenistic aspects of Christian theology, together with powerful political and social conditions, contributed to some degree to the rapid acceptance of Christianity throughout the Roman empire. Early Christianity pursued an intentionally syncretistic programme, amalgamating elements of Judaic messianism, ethics, and theology with pagan Hellenistic theology and popular religious practice. Yet we can ask deconstructively: did Justin Martyr really think the Eucharist sacrament is 'the same thing' as the sacraments of pagan idolatry? Did Roman pagans understand the differences between the Eucharist and their own sacred animating rituals? It is probable that, even as they noted the similarities, they recognized the distinctions, such that the familiar context enabled what was new in the message of the Eucharist to emerge and be received.

Were the Jews who contributed to the authoritative formulation of rabbinic Judaism aware of the idolatry of the Eucharist in technical Hellenistic or halakhic terms? Most objections to Christianity focused on other issues: the perceived polytheism of the Trinity, the Incarnation, the symbol of the cross, the successionism, the messianic claims. Some Tosafists considered the censers

---

the Eucharist (San Francisco, 2005), 227. O'Connor notes that explanations of the Eucharist as sacrifice are always secondary to its essential understanding as sacrament.

[21] O'Connor, *The Hidden Manna*, 18–22, 207–26, 275–94.

[22] Ibid. 135–6.   [23] R. Majercik, *The Chaldean Oracles* (Leiden, 1989), 26–9.

[24] Justin Martyr, *The First Apology*, 66 (my italics), cited in O'Connor, *The Hidden Manna*, 19.

used in the Mass to be instruments used in connection with idolatry. They distinguish between bread used in the Eucharist and bread donated to the rectory as food for the priests: the former is prohibited in trade, the latter permitted. The Tosafists, using the appropriate halakhic methodology for identifying ritual elements of idolatry, compared the bread and wine of the Eucharist to the Jewish sacrificial service. Their question was whether they fitted into the categories of meal offerings and libations, that is, whether they were offerings to idolatry, not the idol themselves.[25] R. Ishmael ben Abraham Isaac Hakohen of Modena (1723–1811) addressing the question of Jewish trade in Christian wine, comprehensively summarized prior positions on this question, noting that there were major authorities who considered the Eucharist idolatrous and major authorities who did not. He himself, on the basis of his own acquaintance with contemporary Christian practice, maintained that the offering of wine during the Eucharist is an offering to idolatry, though he did not suggest that it became the idol itself.[26] There is one intriguing medieval text, attributed to R. Abraham ibn Ezra, that presents a theory and critique of idolatry in Neoplatonic terms based on pagan sources, which themselves employ a Neoplatonic framework. *Sefer ha'atsamim* describes the process by which a cosmic deity is thought to be drawn to inhabit a statue or a human medium. The text cites the Book of Nabatean Agriculture as its source, and refers to Chaldean practices. The symbol of the cross is explained using this theory, delicately, without overt mention of Christianity, but there is no application to the Eucharist.[27] The author of this book tries to understand pagan ritual from a pagan perspective. Though the book did not achieve authoritative legal status in itself, a similar approach can be found in Maimonides' account of Sabian ritual in his *Guide of the Perplexed*, though there is no evidence that this method was applied to Christian practice.[28] Nevertheless, even among jurists such as the Tosafists and R. Menahem Me'iri, who acknowledge that Christianity in their time should not be labelled idolatrous in a simplistic and literal sense, there is a general lingering perception that the sacrament of the Eucharist has something idolatrous about it, even if they are not specific as to what that is.[29] Generally speaking, Jews have struggled and continue to struggle seriously with the question of whether Christianity has idolatrous elements, a struggle which reflects not just the difficulty of categorizing Christianity in Jewish terms, but the syncretistic complexity of

[25] BT *AZ* 50a, 50b, 57b.

[26] Ishmael ben Abraham Isaac Hakohen, *Zera emet* [responsa] (Leghorn, 1796), vol. ii, fo. 34a.

[27] Abraham ibn Ezra, *Sefer ha'azamim*, in *Kitvei rabi avraham ibn ezra* [collected works] (Jerusalem, 2001), ii. 15–21.

[28] e.g. Maimonides, *Guide of the Perplexed*, trans. S. Pines (Chicago and London, 1969), iii. 29 (pp. 516–17).

[29] Jacob Katz, *Exclusiveness and Tolerance* (West Orange, NJ, 1961), 13–23, 126.

Christianity itself, and to paper over this divide does not serve either religion well.

A few articles in *Christianity in Jewish Terms* betray an over-eagerness to narrow the distance between Jewish and Christian theological views. This syncretistic relativization obscures important distinctions and short-circuits a more demanding process of understanding. For instance, two articles attempt to reveal commonalities between Christian and Jewish conceptions of divine presence. In one case, Christian use of concrete images is compared to Jewish approaches to feeling the real presence of God as *Shekhinah* (Divine Presence) in prayer, Torah study, or a court case.[30] In another article, the author collapses the distinction between incarnation and immanence, suggesting overly literal, reified readings of the delicate and even ironic uses of anthropomorphic imagery in classical and mystical rabbinic sources to make his point.[31] Biblical

[30] 'There is, I believe, an avenue to understanding this aspect of Christianity . . . The rabbinic concept of the Shekhinah as the indwelling presence of God, who joins Jews when they pray with a quorum, learn Torah (ideally with a study partner), or form a law court answers this same desire. We need to feel God's presence in our lives, and we seek for reliable ways to access it' (R. Langer, 'Liturgy and Sensory Experience', in Frymer-Kensky et al. (eds.), *Christianity in Jewish Terms*, 192).

[31] Elliot Wolfson, 'Judaism and Incarnation: the Imaginal Body of God', in Frymer-Kensky et al. (eds.), *Christianity in Jewish Terms*, 239–54. Wolfson claims that 'the evolution of the Christological doctrine of the incarnation of the Son is undoubtedly indebted to the scriptural tradition regarding the corporeality of God' (ibid. 240), whereas historically the more proximal, influential, and likely sources were the contemporaneous incarnation theologies of the demigod vegetation religions popular in the Roman empire. If anything, concern to accommodate the Jewish view of God may have constrained some early Christian thinkers to formulate more abstract conceptions of these pagan incarnation theologies. Following a recent line of Jewish scholarship that is enamoured of the late twentieth-century Continental phenomenology of embodiment, Wolfson asserts: 'I would argue that the possibility of God assuming the form of an angel is one of the ground myths that informs the liturgical imagination in rabbinic praxis' (ibid. 245). He claims that in certain biblical and rabbinic passages the ontological distinction between God, the glory, and certain angelic beings is 'blurred', 'obscured', 'ambiguous', 'obfuscated', and 'this obfuscation of the difference between God and the angel is related to the belief that God is incarnate in the form of the angel' (ibid. 244–5). In the most explicit example he cites, however, a complete reading leads to just the opposite conclusion: that in the very comparison between God and the angelic entity, clear ontological boundaries are carefully maintained. His example is the interpretation of Josh. 5: 14 in *Genesis Rabbah* 97: 3 by R. Yehoshua in the name of R. Haninah bar Isaac: 'I am the captain of what is on High, in every place that I am seen the Holy One, blessed be He, is seen.' This leads Wolfson to suggest that 'from a theophanic perspective, the highest angel and God are phenomenally interchangeable, for in every place that the former appears the latter appears'. However, the rabbinic source continues: 'The sign of this is that wherever Rabbi Yosi the Distinguished is seen Rabbi [Judah Hanasi] is seen.' As commentators such as R. David Luria and R. Naftali Katz make clear, the point is that R. Yosi (perhaps R. Joseph Hafni, mentioned as the attendant of Rabbi Judah Hanasi in BT *Ket.* 93*a*), as a student and attendant of Rabbi Judah Hanasi, received all his learning from his teacher, and expresses his teacher's traditions wherever he goes. The very point of the entire rabbinic statement is that the relationship between God and the angel is compared to the relationship between teacher and devoted student, in which the teachings of the master are faithfully conveyed by the disciple, while onto-

and rabbinic notions of divine immanence are notoriously difficult to pin down into a consistent theological system, and this is itself a distinctive and essential feature of Jewish religious thought. The author acknowledges the significant differences between Jewish and Christian ideas about the presence of the divine. Even so, in this article his chosen strategy of positing what he calls a 'docetist' formulation of incarnation as a bridge between Judaism and Christianity, a neutralizing common term from the start, tends to blur important distinctions between Jewish notions of immanence and Christian incarnation such that both traditions are at risk of distortion.[32] The respondents to this article are careful to emphasize these distinctions.[33]

Normative rabbinic authorities from the talmudic period on tend to navigate the correlation of divine transcendence and immanence, of divine hiddenness and the reality of divine presence, with nuance, complexity and delicacy. Following the destruction of the Temple, rabbinic thinkers were concerned to convey the necessarily elusive reality of God to Jews challenged by an overwhelmingly pagan, and later Christian world, while carefully distinguishing this reality from the concrete and accessible spiritualism of idolatry and incarnation. Christian incarnation theology, on the other hand, had more to do with accommodating contemporary religious beliefs of the pagan Roman empire than with Jewish theology. These differences in the provenance of ideas and the evolving consensus of their communal interpretation are important factors to consider in well-intentioned attempts at mutual understanding between different faith communities.

Projections based on incomplete information and understanding can lead to exaggerated alienation as well as exaggerated expectation of commonality in interfaith relations. In the long history of socio-economic relations between Jews and Christians, there is an exquisite complexity in the approaches to whether the halakhic ramifications of the charge of idolatry, in terms of trade and fraternization, are actually applied to the Christians of a given period.[34] This issue is only beginning to be researched and addressed in current Jewish relations with Hindus and Buddhists, as global trade, travel, and political

---

logical and phenomenological distinctions are all carefully maintained. I find Wolfson's other examples similarly unpersuasive (see Wolfson, 'Judaism and Incarnation', 244–5, 393 n. 34).

[32] Wolfson's formulation refers to Jacob Neusner's eccentric appropriation of traditionally Christian theological terminology to describe certain Jewish biblical and rabbinic anthropomorphic expressions in terms of incarnation. As such, Wolfson's approach is built upon a prior, highly syncretistic edifice (cf. J. Neusner, *The Incarnation of God: The Character of Divinity in Formative Judaism* (Philadelphia, 1988), 1–21; Wolfson, 'Judaism and Incarnation', 240 n. 6, 241).

[33] R. Rashkover, 'The Christian Doctrine of the Incarnation', in Frymer-Kensky et al. (eds.), *Christianity in Jewish Terms*, 254–61; S. A. Ross, 'Embodiment and Incarnation: A Response to Elliot Wolfson', in Frymer-Kensky et al. (eds.), *Christianity in Jewish Terms*, 262–8.

[34] Katz, *Exclusiveness and Tolerance*, 13–47.

dynamics and the wanderlust of Israeli youth bring these communities together with greater frequency and sociality. Hindu religious communities use
statues and images in ways Judaism deems unequivocally idolatrous, not veiled
in theological subtlety, but unapologetically overt. Even so, the varieties of
Hindu religious practice are often not understood with sufficient depth and
subtlety for Jews to make informed decisions on religious matters that affect
both communities. One recent example, from the spring of 2004, involved a
controversy in the Orthodox Jewish community over hair cut from Hindu
women which had been routinely gathered and sold to wig makers who sell to
Orthodox Jewish women. When Orthodox halakhic authorities learned that
the hair was cut in the context of a Hindu temple service in Tirupati, South
India, they needed to gather accurate information on the meaning of those
services and the intent of the participants to decide whether such hair would
be permitted or prohibited for Jewish use. As Daniel Sperber recounts, the
learning process was sloppy and incomplete, plagued by misinformation and
false assumptions, resulting in significant and perhaps unnecessary financial
loss to the Jewish community and needless antagonism between the two religious communities.[35]

In relations between Jews and Muslims, it is usually assumed that our understandings of monotheism and its corollaries are identical. Theoretically this
seems logical: one is one. Maimonides defends Muslims as pure monotheists.[36]
Yet we can ask whether the Jewish sense of divine oneness is really the same as
that of Islam. To what extent, for instance, in each religion and its communities, is oneness characterized by totality and exclusivity and to what extent by
infinity and openness? As Levinas shows, this makes a difference, socially and
politically.[37] Despite subtle theological formulations, how do Jews and
Muslims really understand oneness in practice? How do Jews and Muslims
draw moral and political implications from their core theological principles?
We could ask the same questions about any two Jewish groups with distinctive
theological approaches.

In terms of social ethos, which official exclusionary principles do religious
groups and their sects take seriously or exaggerate in importance? Which do
they tend to downplay or ignore and why? For instance, the talmudic imper-
atives *moridin velo ma'alin* ('push down and do not lift up') and *lo ma'alin velo
moridin* ('neither lift up nor push down'), referring to leaving or not leaving an
idolater in a pit to die, are still cited by contemporary Jewish halakhic decisors,

---

[35] D. Sperber, 'The Sheitel Memorandum', *JOFA Journal*, 8/2 (Fall 2009), 33–4; id., 'How
Not to Make Halakhic Rulings', *Conversations: The Journal of the Institute for Jewish Ideas and Ideals*,
5 (Sept. 2009), 1–11, available at <http://www.jewishideas.org/articles/how-not-make-halakhic-
rulings>. [36] Maimonides, *Teshuvot harambam*, ed. Joshua Blau (Jerusalem, 1960), ii. 725.
[37] E. Levinas, *Totality and Infinity* (Pittsburgh, 1962), 42–52.

but they have devolved into abstract organizing categories or as grounds for passive abdication of moral responsibility for those outside the religious group.[38] Until recently almost no one would think of acting on them literally.[39] Yet the existence of such laws promulgated in the talmudic period and the ways they are interpreted—even interpreted away—in later societies say something about the balance of exclusionary and inclusionary tendencies in Jewish culture and should be part of a complete diachronic assessment of Jewish interfaith attitudes. A clearer sense of this issue can also help us locate the genuine impulses within Judaism to appreciate the transcendent humanity of the religious Other. It may not be a question of a particular theological or legal content so much as the communal will and consensus that interprets and applies or responsibly ignores this traditional content. Historical understanding can and should be used to highlight details, provide context, and sharpen our sense of differences as well as similarities. That is, history can be pursued deconstructively, to help us understand how people really process the complexities of their world, how they make both comparisons and distinctions (often simultaneously), and therefore make decisions that are meaningful.

Does a more detailed sense of the Jewish tradition, with its central and peripheral elements, its principles and practices of exclusiveness as well as its tolerance and inclusiveness vis-à-vis other religions, and a corresponding effort at gaining a fuller sense of other religions in detail, make interfaith relations impossibly difficult? Or does this fullness of detailed understanding actually open the possibility of authentic relationship? When we release ourselves from the neutral vantage point, from the imposition of a forced theological and cultural sameness that employs truncated views of one's own religion and the religion of the other, from the Procrustean bed and from the perverse betrayal of hospitality at the heart of Western Hellenistic thinking, does some other approach open up?

JACQUES DERRIDA

Derrida repeatedly explored the nature of hospitality at length, employing it as a paradigm for the dynamics of interfaith relations. At the very heart of hospitality lies a paradox: 'If I welcome only what I welcome, what I am ready to welcome, and that I recognize in advance because I expect the coming of the *hôte* as invited, there is no hospitality.'[40] Hospitality is not achieved if it is

---

[38] BT *AZ* 13*b*, 26*a*, 26*b* (*inter alia*). R. Y. Y. Halberstam, *Divrei yatsiv* (Jerusalem, 1998), 'Yoreh de'ah', no. 50; R. E. Waldenberg, *Tsits eli'ezer*, vol. ix, no. 17; vol. xii, no. 66; vol. xvii, no. 48.

[39] The recent publication of *Torat hamelekh* has created considerable controversy and critical outcry in the Israeli religious and secular communities by seeming to suggest that these and related legal principles could be literally acted upon. See Y. Shapiro and Y. Elitzur, *Torat hamelekh* (Lev hashomron, 2010), 17–87.

[40] Jacques Derrida, 'Hospitality', in id., *Acts of Religion* (New York, 2002), 362.

extended only to the familiar, to the family, or even one welcomed as though they were family. In hospitality there must always be an element of surprise. 'One must not only not be ready nor prepared to welcome, nor well disposed to welcome—for if the welcome is the simple manifestation of a natural or acquired disposition, of a generous character or of a hospitable *habitus*, there is no merit in it, no welcome of the other as other.'[41] Real hospitality is a welcome that respects the other as himself, not because he can be rendered like oneself. The question Derrida poses is how far this can be pressed: on the one hand, 'hospitality—if there is any—must, would have to open itself to an other that is not mine, my *hôte*, my other, not even my neighbor or my brother'. While raising the possibility that the horizon of ultimate hospitality is not limited to the human, he acknowledges that when Levinas speaks of the transcendent act of welcoming the other, he whom we greet in his irreducible, endless otherness is '*my* neighbor, my universal brother in humanity'.[42] Levinas stresses, however, that he is transcendently welcomed, not on the basis of some cultural commonality, but precisely because I recognize in him his infinite otherness. His humanity is not a category, it is an endless mystery and opening. It is this otherness alone that we share in truth and reality, not any categories or concepts overlaid by culture.

Derrida contrasts this vision of unconditional hospitality with a more relative hospitality constrained by cultural practice. He identifies 'two regimes of a law of hospitality: the unconditional or hyperbolical on the one hand, and the conditional and juridico-political, even the ethical, on the other'.[43] Law, morality, and social custom place rules and mutual obligations on the way the stranger approaches the host and the way the host opens his home to the stranger, to the way the stranger behaves in the home of the host and the way the host cares for him. These constraints are not alien to the notion of hospitality, however. At the heart of hospitality, Derrida, following Levinas, discovers not just freely offered generosity and acceptance, but a binding responsibility. The host is also hostage to the guest, *hôte* to *hôte*. Derrida loves the playful wisdom encoded in language, here in French and Romance languages: host, guest (*hôte*), hostage, hostile, hospitality. 'The host thus becomes a retained hostage',[44] and 'the guest, the invited hostage, becomes the one who invites the one who invites, the master of the host . . . the guest becomes the host of the host'.[45] The encounter of host and stranger, host and foreigner, the transcendent horizon of human relations, is an opening and a responsibility, and the mutual obligations that come to attach themselves to this relation can do so because *hôte* and *hôte* are both hostage to each other from the start, an

---

[41] Derrida, 'Hospitality', 361.   [42] Ibid. 363.

[43] Jacques Derrida, *Of Hospitality: Anne Dufourmantelle Invites Jacques Derrida to Respond* (Stanford, 2000), 135.   [44] Ibid. 107.   [45] Ibid. 125.

initial hostility embracing otherness and difference that becomes authentic hospitality.

Derrida applies this paradigm of hospitality and its auto-deconstruction, as he calls it, the way it asserts and undercuts itself simultaneously, identity and difference at once, to the problem of interfaith relations, especially with regard to Islam. In 1997 he observed, with poignant prescience, that at issue is

hospitality according to Islam, a question that is intrinsically interesting and urgent today, when the gravest ethico-political stakes concern *both* the tradition of internal or external—if one may say so—hospitality, in the Arabo-Islamic countries, cultures, and nations *and* the hospitality extended or—most often—refused to Islam in non-Islamic lands, beginning here 'at home'.[46]

Moved by the work of the dedicated Catholic orientalist Louis Massignon, Derrida formulates a vision of sacred hospitality of the Abrahamic faiths, characterized not merely by acceptance of the other, but responsibility for the other. Massignon pursues this sense of responsibility in a specifically Catholic way, living among Muslims and perceiving himself as suffering for them; responsibility extended in compassion, sacrifice, and expiation. Derrida explores these themes as they are found, *mutatis mutandis*, in Judaism and Islam, stripping away patronizing paternalism and getting down to the bone of responsibility, called 'substitution', putting oneself in the place of the other, by Massignon and Levinas. Derrida sums it up: 'Substitution is not the indifferent replacement of an equal thing by an equal or identical thing ... No, the Abrahamic substitution implicates exceptional, elected existences that make themselves or expose themselves of themselves, in their absolute singularity and as absolutely responsible, the gift of the sacrifice of themselves.'[47] An acceptance and welcome of the other as other, not as oneself, and more, a giving of oneself in taking full responsibility for the other, not to convert him into oneself but just as he is, this stranger, this foreigner for whom one cares: this is the vision of Abrahamic interfaith hospitality towards which Derrida points.

The place of Judaism in the pursuit of interfaith hospitality is not incidental but pivotal. Derrida asks at the start of his response to Anne Dufourmantelle: 'Isn't the question of the foreigner a foreigner's question? Coming from the foreigner, from abroad?' The foreigner is the one who 'shakes up the threatening dogmatism of the paternal *logos*: the being that is, and the non-being that is not. As though the Foreigner had to begin by contesting the authority of the chief, the father, the master of the family ... the power of hospitality.'[48] The stranger, the foreigner, always initiates the challenge to the status quo, to the

---

[46] Derrida, 'Hospitality', 366.
[47] Ibid., 417.   [48] Derrida, *Of Hospitality*, 4–5.

stability of the same. That is the gift he brings: himself, the one who eludes and resists everything familiar, to remind us of the truly human, to refresh our sense of the transcendent otherness of the other.

It has been the destiny of the Jewish people, and still is, to be the stranger, the foreigner for others, and to find all others strange and foreign. In this sense, interfaith relations is a worthy field in which to discover true hospitality, not by treating non-Jews as though they were Jews, nor by treating Jews as though we were non-Jews, but precisely by treating non-Jews as not Jews, as not-our-selves, and yet, for that very reason, as simply and purely human, the other whom we welcome and care for as other. Here, accommodations of theology are not only unnecessary, they can encumber and endanger the real accommo-dation, the offer of sincere home hospitality to the really other.

Practically, this could mean that interfaith discussions of theology and custom are best pursued not as attempts to find common theological ground or make cultural accommodations, but in a spirit of authentic hospitality: lis-tening to the other in care and responsibility, speaking with honesty and without fear of offence, surprising each other with our differences, surprising each other with perceived commonalities that are really understood differently anyway. In this way we can help each other to clear away the antagonism and violence implicit in expecting the other to be like us, conceptual tendencies that are always in danger of leading to visceral emotional antagonism and even physical violence. In other words, interfaith discussions hold the promise of the discovery of our mutual humanity, caring for each other in just this humanity, and reminding each other of this humanity. This brings us close to how Rabbi Joseph B. Soloveitchik understood the value of interreligious discussions:

The discussion should concern itself not with theological but with secular matters of mutual concern. In the private religious realm, each faith has its own 'words' and forms which are uniquely intimate, reflecting its philosophical character, and are totally incomprehensible to people of other faiths. The chain of supernatural ex-periences on the part of each group differ, and an attempt to achieve dialogue on this level can cause more friction than amity, more confusion than clarity, and thereby prove harmful to the interrelationship. The areas of joint concern should be outer-directed, to combat the secularism, materialism and atheistic negation of religion and religious values which threaten the moral underpinnings of our society.[49]

PAUL RICOEUR

One more question: 'From where does the responsibility at the heart of hos-pitality issue?' Ricoeur gently rebalances the extreme asymmetry in Levinas's uncompromising concern for transcendence to the infinite other. Ricoeur

---

[49] Joseph B. Soloveitchik, *Reflections of the Rav*, ed. A. R. Besdin (Hoboken, NJ, 1993), 176–7.

suggests the self that receives the voice and face of the Other, that is responsible for the Other, hostage to the Other, must be kept in view. One can only offer hospitality when one is at home. He re-emphasizes the reciprocity of the relationship, tracking the way Otherness shapes our sense of our self. For Ricoeur, our sense of self is developed as a reflection of our experience of others and of the expectations of others, that others treat us as their Other and our experience of the passivity of the body, such that our self is actually a 'modality of otherness, namely *being enjoined as the structure of selfhood*'.[50] The modality thus constituted is, at core, the conscience. Paraphrasing Levinas's discussion of violence in *Difficult Freedom*, yet shifting its focus, Ricoeur says: 'Each face is a Sinai that prohibits murder. And me? It is in me that the movement coming from the other completes its trajectory: the other constitutes me as responsible, that is, as capable of responding.'[51] In the interfaith relation, which calls us to a radical awareness of the other, we should expect to find a reciprocity of impact. Along with being moved to pure responsibility for the other, we can expect to find ourselves moved by the other and his care to reconsiderations of our own-most selves. This is often so on personal and communal levels because every religious community sharpens its awareness of its own core principles, consciously or subconsciously, through its contact with other communities.[52]

Ricoeur's notion of the conscience, of the reciprocity of Otherness, of the response within responsibility, contributes an essential element to the groundwork for an authentic relationship outlined by Levinas and Derrida. We care for others while and as responding to others, and this response teaches us about ourselves as well. Respectful responsibility in this sense is an engagement that we are still trying to discover in pursuing interfaith relations in a manner that is authentic and appropriate: not violating others or ourselves, not paternalistic, not indulgent, not syncretistic, and not relativistic. It is not a neutral historical vantage point, not moral and cultural relativism, that provides the authentic framework for interfaith relations. It is rather a hospitality we offer from our home, in which we take responsibility for each other, calling each other to our own-most selves and challenging each other to find, within the best of our selves and the best of our religious communities, the true consciousness of our mutually transcendent humanity.

---

[50] Paul Ricoeur, *Oneself as Another*, trans. K. Blamey (Chicago, 1994), 336; see also Emmanuel Levinas, *Difficult Freedom*, trans. S. Hand (Baltimore, 1990), 354.

[51] Ricoeur, *Oneself as Another*, 6–10.

[52] In the words of Ralph Waldo Emerson, 'other men are lenses through which we read our own minds. Each man seeks those of different quality from his own, and such as are good of their kind; that is, he seeks other men, and the *otherest*' ('Uses of Great Men', in *The Complete Writings of Ralph Waldo Emerson* (New York, 1929), i. 328).

Jewish Liturgical Memory and the Non-Jew
Past Realities and Future Possibilities

RUTH LANGER

Liturgy and ritual serve not only as human vehicles for offering worship to the divine, but also as ways to transmit and shape a human community's understanding of its place in the world. For Jews, this community has historically been the 'people of Israel', a specific nation among nations in the world. This nation has a particular covenantal relationship with God, one that it understands to be different from other nations' relationships either with this God or with other (perhaps false) gods. Jewish rituals reflect on this boundary and reinforce it, constructing theological interpretations of history that shape Jews' self-understandings and their relationships to these religio-political Others. Jews today are heirs to this theology in their participation in received rituals; however, they also have opportunities to be shapers of this theology, particularly when they construct rituals that reflect on the traumas and transitions of the twentieth century. This essay addresses this opportunity within the parameters of the traditional, halakhic Jewish world; it does not consider the almost limitless possibilities offered within the liberal forms of Judaism.[1]

At the heart of this issue is the question of how Jews construct their ritual memory of the Other. My formulation of this question derives from a challenge encountered in the study of Christian liturgy, where *anamnesis* (remembering by re-experiencing; in this case, usually, the Last Supper) is a central element of ritual. If this is a characteristic of human ritual expression, it should also find expression in Judaism. If not, some alternative theoretical structure is needed. Having established a theoretical framework, we will turn to an analysis of how received Jewish liturgy 'remembers' the Other. This in turn will allow us to consider how new rituals do or ought to construct

[1] I have addressed these possibilities in a detailed analysis of American Jewish liturgies across the spectrum (see Ruth Langer, 'Theologies of Self and Other in American Jewish Liturgies', *CCAR Journal: A Reform Jewish Quarterly* (Winter 2005), 3–41, also available at <http://ccarnet. org/_kd/Items/actions.cfm?action=Show&item_id=465&destination=ShowItem>).

memories that concern the religious Other, most importantly with regard to the Holocaust.

MEMORY

Anthropological theories of ritual, developed mostly by scholars whose personal cultural origins lie in Christian society, and theories of liturgy, developed more explicitly with Christian liturgy at the centre, understand construction of memory to be a primary function of human ritual activity.[2] Leading Christian scholars theorize that the Christian concepts of liturgical memory derive from Christianity's Jewish rather than its Greek roots. However, these theoretical constructs apply rather poorly to rabbinic liturgy and are helpful neither for explaining most of what we have received nor as guidance for constructing new responses. Jewish liturgy rarely functions to make present for the living community a historically past event, though it does at times seek to bridge past and present. We therefore need to begin our discussion here by briefly exploring how memory does function within rabbinic liturgy.[3]

At the centre of the re-experienced memory encountered in rabbinic liturgical expression stands the historical narrative of the Torah, whether it be Creation (in sabbath rituals or the wedding ceremony), the Abrahamic covenant (of circumcision), the Exodus and Sinai experiences in the rabbinic foci of the biblical pilgrimage festivals, or the entire Torah narrative through ritual reading and study over the course of the year. The religious and national Other appears in these acts of memory primarily in the figures of the Egyptians and Amalek. Nor is the Torah the sole focus of such liturgical memories. Purim celebrates the events of the book of Esther, the Ninth of Av mourns those of Lamentations (and later tragedies), and Hanukah recalls the Maccabaean defeat of the Seleucids. Jewish rituals do engage a variety of points of biblical and post-biblical history and do recall their narratives in the midst of the contemporary community, a critical step in enabling memory. The religious or political Other is almost universally a negative.

As Yosef Hayim Yerushalmi points out, in their commemorations these rituals present history almost cyclically and certainly without a temporal dimension. They are not history in our modern scientific sense of recovered facts concerned with the specific details of the events, but are rather communal memories retrieved and transmitted for the occasion, expected to reappear at

[2] For the vast bibliography on this, see the materials cited in Michael Signer (ed.), *Memory and History in Christianity and Judaism* (Notre Dame, Ind., 2001); Bruce T. Morrill, *Anamnesis as Dangerous Memory: Political and Liturgical Theology in Dialogue* (Collegeville, Minn., 2000).

[3] For the sake of clarity, in what follows here I will not engage with the various theologically and ideologically based changes introduced into the synagogue by liberal Jewish movements over the past 200 years. Some of these changes deliberately reconstructed the memory recalled by these rituals (see e.g. Jakob J. Petuchowski, *Prayerbook Reform in Europe: The Liturgy of European Liberal and Reform Judaism* (New York, 1968); Eric Caplan, *From Ideology to Liturgy: Reconstructionist Worship and American Liberal Judaism* (Cincinnati, 2002)).

the next appropriate calendrical or life-cycle celebration, and highly selective in their content.[4] In this sense, then, the memory invoked in Jewish rituals is more mythical than historical. The rituals presume (or at least expect) an assent to the memories, a personalization of the memories to the point of identification with them, but they do not necessarily collapse the past into the present of the participants; if anything the community places itself back in the time of the event rather than giving the event an ongoing presence in the present.[5]

However, these observations pertain better to annual and life-cycle rituals than to day-to-day liturgical life. The most central liturgical elements, especially the recitation of the Shema and its blessings, include references to key historical moments, but these function as prooftexts for the prayers' central theological statements and are not their focus. For humans, history remains history in these cases, and God is the one who bridges past, present, and future. Creation, revelation, and redemption are ongoing characteristics of God's interaction with the world and with us. The historical event, and consequently its religio-political Other, does not become present to the community today.[6] The weekday Amidah contains essentially no overt references to the past; however, it functions within history as an elaborate prayer for a future redemption which will end Jewish subjugation to non-Jewish powers, more 'anticipation' than 'memory'.[7] Medieval alterations to the sabbath Amidah resulted in its middle section focusing over the course of the day on the historical events of creation, revelation, and redemption,[8] perhaps the closest this prayer gets to invoking memory.

[4] Yosef Hayim Yerushalmi, *Zakhor: Jewish History and Jewish Memory* (Seattle, 1982), 40–2, 95.

[5] In stark contrast to, for example, the act of memory in the Christian Eucharist (see Paul Bradshaw, 'Anamnesis in Modern Eucharistic Debate', in Signer (ed.), *Memory and History in Christianity and Judaism*, 73–84).

[6] It could be argued that Jews re-experience Sinai at every Torah reading, and indeed there are aspects of the ritual that suggest this (see Ruth Langer, 'Sinai, Zion, and God in the Synagogue: Celebrating Torah in Ashkenaz', in Ruth Langer and Steven Fine (eds.), *Liturgy in the Life of the Synagogue: Studies in the History of Jewish Prayer*, Duke Judaic Studies 2 (Winona Lake, Ind., 2005), 121–59). However, Judaism holds this in tension with the understanding that the Sinai revelation placed Torah in human hands in an absolute and irrevocable way. Therefore, Sinai was a one-time event (that we can remember and experience in the past, because, according to the midrash, we were all there) and does not re-occur in the present. Another counter-example might be customs, documented from the fifth century, of hanging Haman in effigy at Purim (see Elliott S. Horowitz, *Reckless Rites: Purim and the Legacy of Jewish Violence* (Princeton, NJ, 2006)). However, these are folk customs, not normative ritual.

[7] Reuven Kimelman argues convincingly that the Amidah is fundamentally a prayer for messianic redemption, as manifested most importantly in the restoration of the community to the land so that it can worship God in the restored Temple (see Reuven Kimelman, 'The Literary Structure of the Amidah and the Rhetoric of Redemption', in William G. Dever and J. Edward Wright (eds.), *The Echoes of Many Texts: Reflection on Jewish and Christian Traditions, Essays in Honor of Lou H. Silberman*, Brown Judaic Studies 313 (Atlanta, 1997), 171–218; id., 'The Messiah of the Amidah: A Study in Comparative Messianism', *Journal of Biblical Literature*, 116 (1997), 313–20.

[8] Naftali Wieder, ' "Yismaḥ mosheh": Opposition and Defence' (Heb.), in id. *The Formation of Jewish Liturgy in the East and the West* [Hitgabeshut nusaḥ hatefilah bemizraḥ uvema'arav] (Jerusalem, 1998), i. 295–322.

While certainly present in Jewish ritual life, historical memory does not form its core. The core is instead the covenantal relationship between God and Israel, a covenantal relationship that can be disrupted but not destroyed by human misbehaviour, whether the sins of Israel or even the sins of other peoples. For traditional Judaism the fundamental narrative transmitted daily by the liturgy is one of life in a state of disruption and in need of redemption. This is certainly a situation *within* history, but it is an existential statement, not an engagement with something remembered. Historical memory enters only consequent on this existential situation, creating opportunities to recall how covenantal life came to be and how the disruptions to its ideal form occurred, and then to pray for their messianic correction.[9] Non-Jews thus appear in traditional Jewish liturgy primarily as the sources of these disruptions. As a consequence, their portrayal is almost universally negative and the Jewish theology of the Other that these memories construct is almost entirely oppositional. From the perspective of those engaged in the bridge-building demanded by today's global society, this presents a serious challenge. To understand this challenge fully, we turn now to a more detailed examination of the theology of the other expressed in Jewish liturgy.

THE NON-JEW IN JEWISH LITURGY

With a few exceptions, non-Jews appear in three different modes in traditional Jewish liturgy: indirectly, by implication in positive statements about what constitutes Judaism's uniqueness; semi-directly, in statements about non-Jews in general; and directly, in references to particular historical encounters. This last, that which would build historical memory, has only minimal presence in the statutory prayers and hence could be considered the least important of the three. However, it plays an enormous role in liturgical poetry, especially for fast days and commemorations of particular events, often specific to a particular community's history. As these form the models for commemorations of more recent tragedies, they are important to our discussion. However, regular and obligatory references to non-Jews are almost completely non-specific, although they have not always been read that way. They do not present a theology of Christianity or Islam, let alone of Buddhism or Hinduism, or of Christians, Muslims, Buddhists, or Hindus. This reflects the rabbinic continuation of a biblical mode that simply casts everyone outside the Jewish community as undifferentiated gentiles and idolaters.

Indirect statements establish a positive Jewish identity in contrast to non-Jews

[9] The Jewish ritual that most obviously employs memory, the Passover Seder, operates in this situation of compensation for the loss of the Temple (see Baruch M. Bokser, *The Origins of the Seder: The Passover Rite and Early Rabbinic Judaism* (Berkeley, Calif., 1984), ch. 7: 'From Form to Meaning: The Significance of the Passover Rite and its Place in Early Rabbinic Judaism').

but rarely say anything about them. These include the morning blessing of identity ('who has not made me a gentile'[10]) and the similar acknowledgement at
the end of the sabbath that God's separations include 'between Israel and the
nations'. They also include positive mentions of God's choice of Israel from
among the nations, especially as the recipient of Torah and of the sabbath. This
theme appears in every home kiddush (the recitation over a cup of wine sancti-
fying the beginning of a sabbath or festival day), the most common form of the
Torah blessings, and in the intermediate blessing (*kedushat hayom*) of the festival
Amidah. The most explicit expressions and acknowledgement of the relatedness
of these themes of separation and chosenness appear in the sabbath morning
Amidah, where the prayer describes the unique relationship of Israel to the
sabbath, saying:

> For you, Eternal, our God, did not give it to the nations of the world,
> And did not give it as a heritage to idol worshipers.
> In addition, no uncircumcised shall dwell in its rest,
> For you gave it lovingly to Israel your people
> The seed of Jacob whom you chose.

Similarly, the theme of separation appears in the Kedushah Desidra, which
thanks God for 'separating us from the errant ones and giving us the Torah of
truth'. Related to this trope are various prayers whose horizons could be universal, but which instead were composed so as to apply only to Israel. These
include every single version of the many prayers for peace and for healing in
the traditional siddur.[11] Even where the prayers seem to be universal in their
scope, the 'world' still really means 'Israel'.

One eschatological consequence of this presentation of other nations is the
understanding that at the end of days all the nations will realize the error of
their ways and come to worship God. In other words, this separation will not
persist in its current form. However, the texts are ambiguous about whether
this means that all humanity will become Jewish or whether it means that all
the nations will come to worship God through their own individual paths. This
has practical consequences for our contemporary quest for interreligious
understanding and enters into contemporary discussions especially with the
Catholic Church over issues of mission and evangelization.

[10] At times this received the formulation 'who made me a Jew and not a gentile', or simply,
'who made me a Jew' (I translate *yisra'el* here as 'Jew') (see Joseph Tabory, 'The Benedictions of
Self-Identity and the Changing Status of Women and of Orthodoxy', *Kenishta*, 1 (2001), 114–15,
and especially Yoel H. Kahn, *The Three Blessings: Boundaries, Censorship and Identity in Jewish
Liturgy* (Oxford, 2011), 49–57.
[11] See also the kabbalistically influenced prayer, *Ribono shel olam*, prefaced to the bedtime
Shema, in which one forgives anyone—but literally 'any Jew'—whom one might forgive for any
wrong incurred.

This question arises particularly in three liturgical contexts: the Uvekhen inserts[12] into the *kedushat hashem* of Rosh Hashanah and Yom Kippur, the Aleinu prayer, and the Rosh Hashanah Zikhronot. All of these prayers, in their complexity, blend positive statements of Jewish identity with semi-direct statements about non-Jews and thus bring us to our second category. The Uvekhen inserts consist of three discrete sections, all elaborating on the theme of divine sovereignty expressed in the biblical verses with which the prayer ends. What is the nature and the fullest earthly expression of this sovereignty? The first section asks God to cause all creation to fear him, and as a consequence come to worship him in recognition of his divine might. As the conclusion of the section acknowledges that Israel recognizes God, 'all creation' here is clearly 'non-Jews'. The prayer thus anticipates universal human submission to God's will. Does this make space for other religions? Perhaps, as it does not explicitly anticipate that they will become Jews. On the other hand, it also anticipates that they will perform God's will wholeheartedly as an *agudah aḥat* (single society); consequently, the prayer does not really leave room for multiple forms of religious expression.[13]

This section also needs to be read in the context of the second and third sections, which focus narrowly on Jewish concerns. They call for the messianic establishment of the Jewish state, which will bring about the destruction of the 'evil ones' (censorship yielded the abstract 'evil') and of the 'empire of insolence', a standard term for the non-Jewish governing powers. What is the relationship between the destruction of the non-Jewish nations and the welcome of all humanity of the first section? If we read the three paragraphs together, only two possibilities emerge. In the first, all good non-Jews will have become Jews, living in Israel and rejoicing in its messianic restoration; the 'evil ones', subject to utter destruction, will be those who have not become Jews and who seek to prevent Israel's restoration. In the second reading, universality was never the first paragraph's intention, and all non-Jews and especially their governments are doomed. Both of these readings can be found in one place or another in biblical and rabbinic eschatological thinking, and it seems to matter little liturgically that the prayer combines them in a way that leaves its statement about the fate of non-Jews theologically incoherent.

In any of these readings, ultimately, the horizon of the praying community is really the boundary between Israel and the rest of the world. Most Jews historically have read these inserted sections as anticipations of the messianic restoration of an independent Israel no longer dominated by the 'empire of insolence', that is, the government under which they were suffering.[14] However, in our age

---

[12] In some rites, the third begins *ve'az*, not a significant change in meaning.

[13] In an imprecise echo of biblical chiastic structures, this line forms the centre point of this paragraph and hence arguably its most important statement.

[14] This reading resulted in the not infrequent censorship of this sentence from the early

of dialogue, this prayer is problematic. One possible solution is to focus exclusively on its first paragraph and to understand its 'single society' to encompass within it multiple expressions of submission to God. Another is to accept that messianic outcomes are in God's hands.

Similarly complicated is our second example, the Aleinu prayer, which entered public liturgy as an elaboration on the *malkhiyot* prayers preceding the shofar blasts in the Rosh Hashanah *musaf* service. Indeed, some of the similarities between the statements of these two prayers may arise from their Rosh Hashanah context. Aleinu became a much more influential prayer when, in the High Middle Ages, it came to conclude almost every service in most regional rites. While it is certainly possible that this composition originated in a world where the religious others were polytheist idolaters, there is no question that the prayer entered daily liturgy as a response to Christianity. The first paragraph, in its original wording, distinguishes Jewish worship of the true God, the Creator of heaven and earth, from the idolater's worship of 'nothingness and emptiness . . . that cannot save'. The second paragraph looks forward to messianic times when idolaters too will come to worship God. Medieval European commentators understood *varik* ('and emptiness') to indicate *Yeshu* (Jesus) because the numerical value of the letters of both words is equivalent. That this 'emptiness . . . cannot save' also found polemical meaning in the context of Christian conversionary pressures. Some twelfth-century liturgies contained extremely graphic anti-Christian expansions on this line. Consequently, there was significant Christian sensitivity to and censorship of it, but the line (sometimes accompanied by spitting because of the pun between *varik* and *rok*) seems to have disappeared from actual Jewish practice only rarely.[15] Thus, here too we have a prayer that functions to place Israel at the centre and to define non-Jews, sometimes even specific non-Jews, negatively.

Two contemporary issues arise from this prayer. One results from the near-universal retrieval of the censored line in contemporary Orthodox prayer books.[16] On the one hand, the prayer makes no sense with the line omitted: the line before it sets up a contrast between Israel and the nations, the omitted line expresses the reason for that contrast is the nations' mode of worship, and

modern period on in Christian Europe and the substitution, most commonly, of 'evil' and 'insolence' or 'insolent people' for 'evil doers' and the 'empire of insolence'. My reading of 'empire of insolence' (*memshelet zadon*) is consistent with its appearance in the medieval texts of the *birkat haminim* (as *malkhut zadon*), from which it was also widely censored.

[15] For a full exposition of these points and references to the literature, see Ruth Langer, 'The Censorship of *Aleinu* in Ashkenaz and its Aftermath', in Debra Reed Blank (ed.), *The Experience of Jewish Liturgy: Studies Dedicated to Menahem Schmelzer* (Leiden, 2011).

[16] The single exception of which I am aware is Rabbi Jonathan Sacks, *The Authorised Daily Prayer Book of the United Hebrew Congregations of the Commonwealth* (London, 2006). The line does appear in the *Koren–Sacks Siddur* (Jerusalem, 2009), though it receives no commentary.

the following line describes Jewish worship.[17] On the other hand, can we recite this line without applying it to contemporary practitioners of other religions? Some suggest that the 'others' of the prayer be understood figuratively and morally, but this fails to take into account the pairing of this line with its predecessor that clearly defines its 'they' as 'the nations of the world'. Many others today are unaware of the historical interpretation of the line and simply recite it without much thought. In any case, without a commentary accompanying each appearance of the prayer, it is difficult to presume that those reciting it will give it a meaning other than its obvious or received ones.[18]

The second issue is very similar to the problem with the Uvekhen inserts: does the second paragraph of the Aleinu prayer anticipate the conversion of all non-Jews to Judaism or just that they will come to worship God, each in their own way? The first was the substance of Jacob Neusner's public response to the controversies surrounding renewed Catholic attention to and revision of the Latin Tridentine-rite Good Friday 'Prayer for Conversion of the Jews'. He wrote that Jews should not object to Catholics praying for their baptism because Jews do the same thing in reverse.[19] But this is not a necessary reading of the text. The prayer anticipates the day when all will worship God, but it does not specify that this will be in a Jewish manner. This leaves ample room for other faiths to maintain their own integrity.

Most of these points apply as well to the Zikhronot prayer of the Rosh Hashanah *musaf* and the echo of its themes in the early *piyut* that introduces the Kedushah of that service, 'Unetaneh tokef'. The poetic introduction to the Zikhronot probably derives from the same world as the Aleinu prayer: it serves a parallel liturgical purpose and its stylistic characteristics are identical. Its topic is God's attention to and judgement of the behaviour of all humans. Its universalism derives from the Bible's first reference to divine memory: God remembers Noah, the father of all humanity, after the Flood (Gen. 8: 1).[20] However, once again, the rest of the prayer and the rest of its biblical verses turn the focus back to Israel. The rest of the verses as well as the paragraph that follows them pay no attention at all to non-Jews. In addition, read literally the

[17] 'Who has not made us like the nations of the earth or placed us like all their multitudes (*for they bow down to emptiness and nothingness and pray to a God who cannot save*) but we bow down and prostrate ourselves and give thanks to the King, the King of Kings, the Holy One Blessed Be He.'

[18] The ArtScroll commentary on this line (with the daily morning service, pages vary by edition) effectively perpetuates the anti-Christian interpretation by refuting it apologetically (and inaccurately).

[19] 'Catholics Have a Right to Pray for Us', *Forward* (28 Feb. 2008), <http://www.ccjr.us/dialogika-resources/themes-in-todays-dialogue/good-friday-prayer/465-neusner08feb28>.

[20] The halakhic sources do not dictate which verses to recite at this point, only their type. However, the earliest poetic elaboration preserved with its own set of verses, that of Yose ben Yose, also begins with this verse (see Aharon Mirsky, *The Hymns of Yose ben Yose* [Piyutei yose ben yose], 2nd edn. (Jerusalem, 1977), 106).

opening paragraph suggests a situation where God judges all humanity on Rosh Hashanah but only Israel has a covenantal relationship that helps them repent and avoid a negative judgement. The rest of the world is thus necessarily found guilty—a problematic theological presumption.

Indeed, it seems more appropriate to read these apparently universalistic themes within a pattern common to *piyut*. This literary genre often imitates the Bible's own narrative, prefacing its real discussion with a historical survey that begins with Creation (and all humanity) and wends its way to the point of the composition, which is always specific to Israel. We see this, for instance, in all versions of the Seder Ha'avodah on Yom Kippur, or in *piyutim* elaborating on the liturgical verses from the Song at the Sea ('Mi kamokha') for the seventh day of Passover. The point is not to reflect on the non-Jewish world, but to highlight Israel's uniqueness in contrast to it.

Bridging the boundary between semi-direct and direct reference to non-Jews are prayers like the *birkat haminim*, the 'malediction of the sectarians', which calls for the destruction of various categories of non-Jews and border-line Jews. Because this prayer is recited in every weekday Amidah including its repetitions, it arguably has a huge impact on the liturgical image of the non-Jew. We cannot reconstruct the original text of this prayer, which the Babylonian Talmud remembers as having been instituted under Rabban Gamliel at Yavneh (BT *Ber.* 28*b*–29*a*). Before the text was censored severely in the sixteenth century, it consisted of curses of two categories of people: Jews who crossed the communal boundary, either as apostates (most often to Christianity), informers, or other sorts of heretics; and non-Jews who maliciously harmed Jews, called the enemies of Israel and the empire of insolence. In this, Christians received explicit mention, in versions of the prayer discovered in the Cairo genizah, a repository of worn texts, as *notserim* and in medieval versions as *minim*.[21] These people impede the realization of the messianic scenario for which the Amidah petitions. Censorship eliminated all the prayer's nouns and hence its specificity; replacements resulted in a prayer for the removal of evil and for the elimination of *God's* enemies, making it no longer apply so obviously to non-Jews. However, one reciting today's text can still easily interpret it to apply to those non-Jews perpetrating evil in the world, and various communities have reintroduced or maintained some of the censored language. Note, though, that the prayer tells us nothing specific about these malefactors except that they are deserving of immediate and radical divine punishment for their treatment of Israel.

Non-Jews are a generalized source of fear for Jews. This finds expression

[21] See Ruth Langer and Uri Ehrlich, 'The Earliest Texts of the *Birkat Haminim*', *Hebrew Union College Annual*, 76 (2006), 63–112, as well as my forthcoming *Cursing the Christians? A History of the* Birkat HaMinim (Oxford, 2011).

most clearly in the Tahanun prayers. The compositions beginning 'Hateh elokai oznekha' and 'Hashem elokei yisra'el' both call on biblical tropes to remind God forcefully that when Jews are downtrodden, non-Jews perceive this, not as divine punishment for Jewish breaches of the covenant, but as a sign of God's weakness or lack of concern. God should therefore accept Israel's repentance, cease to be angry, and improve the situation.

More proactive are the many responses to unspecified persecutions that call on God to take vengeance on the nations. The most universally recited of these are the verses beginning 'Shefokh hamatekha' (Pour out your wrath) recited before continuing with the Hallel psalms of praise after the Passover Seder meal. But we also find this theme forcefully stated in the memorial prayer for martyrs, Av haraḥamim (Father of Mercy), recited after the sabbath Torah reading with varying frequency in different Ashkenazi communities.[22] Ashkenazi Jews expanded Avinu malkenu, asking God to act for the sake of the martyrs and then to 'avenge the poured out blood of your servants'. Universally censored, and therefore not known, is the original version of the blessing after the *haftarah* in all European rites that called on God to avenge fully (rather than the current text, to bring salvation to) the *aluvat/agumat nefesh* ('the deeply humiliated', that is, exiled Israel).[23] The theme is therefore deeply rooted and widespread in at least Ashkenazi liturgy.[24] While such sentiments do not precisely express a theology of the Other, they establish a negative context in which such a theology finds expression. At the same time, though, the non-specific nature of the memory established here is very important. Even where these prayers were composed in response to a specific interaction, they do not continue to inscribe specific historical events in liturgical memory.

Jewish liturgy does express a few more direct concerns about the theological boundary between Judaism and other religions and its transgression. The most popular and regularly recited are the medieval credal hymns, Adon Olam and Yigdal. These contain positive assertions of Jewish belief that are, in reality, specific refutations of Christian and Muslim theological tenets. In answer to

[22] This prayer was originally composed in response to the martyrdoms in the Rhineland during the First Crusade, but it does not need to be read with this particular tragedy in mind. Some communities recite it only twice a year, on the sabbaths before Shavuot and before the Ninth of Av, others almost every sabbath except during times of rejoicing.

[23] In manuscripts of all the rites (see e.g. E. D. Goldschmidt (ed.), *Seder rav amram ga'on* (Jerusalem, 1971), 77; Aryeh Goldschmidt (ed.), *Maḥzor vitry* (Jerusalem, 2004), i. 285).

[24] Israel Jacob Yuval, *Two Nations in Your Womb: Perceptions of Jews and Christians in Late Antiquity and the Middle Ages*, trans. Barbara Harshav and Jonathan Chipman (Berkeley, Calif. 2006), ch. 3, 'The Vengeance and the Curse'. This chapter gives some response to the very strong criticisms he received on his initial publication of this material in a dedicated issue of *Zion*, 59/2–3 (1994). There, leading scholars pointed out that these traditions of calling for divine vengeance are much more widespread than Yuval had posited.

Christian Christological claims, Adon Olam professes that 'he is one and has no second that can be compared or joined to him' and Yigdal states 'he has no bodily form and no body'. It continues, 'God will never change and will never change his teachings' in response to supersessionist claims about the Jewish covenant. In answer to Islam, Yigdal claims that 'no prophet will ever arise in Israel like Moses'.[25] More subtle is the Aramaic passage from the Zohar, 'Berikh shemei demarei alma', added to the liturgy for taking out the Torah in the early modern period, which claims, 'I do not trust in a human being, nor do I rely on a son of god [*bar elahin*], but in the God of heaven'. Even if worshippers living in Christian lands were fully aware of the Zohar's allusion to Daniel 3: 25 where 'son of god' is obviously an angel, they also knew its literal referent.[26]

Jewish liturgy also contains a series of discussions about non-Jews that are more direct comments on the historical relations between the two communities. This category ranges from purely historical references to the past interactions of Israel and other nations to presentations of these historical figures as archetypical enemies ever ready to persecute Jews. The Egyptians enslaved the Israelites, and the liturgy remembers their consequent punishment numerous times, ranging from the Ge'ulah benediction following the Shema, to the daily recitation of the Song at the Sea, to the Magid of the Passover Seder. In these instances, the Egyptians remain historical figures, and what is important to the living, experienced memory is God's redemption of Israel. However, in the Magid's retelling of the Passover story, the Egyptians also become prototypes, explicitly in 'Vehi she'amdah' ('For not only one enemy has risen against us, but rather in every generation, they rise against us to destroy us, and the Holy One Blessed Be He saves us from them') and more implicitly in the midrashic multiplications of the plagues, which can be readily interpreted as expressions of rabbinic anger against their current oppressor rather than as revisionist history. Similarly, Antiochus and his armies remain historical elements of the Hanukah story, as does Ahasuerus at Purim. But Haman and Amalek become at times living prototypes of persecuting enemies, to the point that this becomes a motivating factor for Jewish violence against non-Jews.[27]

Again, there is not a single positive image of the non-Jew on this list.[28] This

[25] It is of course in the nature of creeds to specify doctrines that are threatened by heretical alternatives (see Frances M. Young, *The Making of the Creeds* (London, 1991), 5–6). 'Yigdal', as is well known, is based on Maimonides' Thirteen Principles of Faith, itself a credal statement found in many prayer books.

[26] For a fuller discussion, see Langer, 'Theologies of Self and Other in American Jewish Liturgies', 9–10.

[27] For a critique of the implications of this identification, see Horowitz, *Reckless Rites*.

[28] Exceptions are very minor and generally found in poetic contexts, like the blessing of Harbona, the eunuch who suggests that King Ahasueras punish Haman by hanging him on his own gallows (Esther 7: 9). The early modern European blessing for the king, which seems positive, is actually quietly subversive. Its opening line, 'You who give victory to kings and dominion

situation becomes even grimmer when one considers those examples that apply to the existential situation in which rabbinic liturgy developed. The historical Babylonians, destroyers of the First Temple, almost totally disappear, subsumed in the situation of oppression by Rome. Pagan Rome, of course, became Christian Rome, which became the larger if fragmented Christian and especially European world. As the liturgy presents it, this world not only destroyed the Temple but continually seeks to destroy Jews and Judaism and certainly prevents any messianic restoration. Curiously, early medieval liturgy gave scant mention to the realm of Islam, to the point that Jews living under Islam seem to have applied the *birkat haminim* exclusively to converts to Christianity and to Christians.[29]

So far, we have considered almost exclusively what are termed 'statutory prayers', prayers whose recitation has been sanctioned by law and custom and which are considered obligatory. This liturgy was frequently enriched by *piyut*, liturgical poetry, which, particularly in certain genres, contains significant allusions to and/or specific discussions of non-Jews. As *piyut* first flowered in Byzantine Palestine and subsequently played a substantial role in European liturgies, it contains many references to Christianity, generally negative. Most of those in European rites were censored and never printed. A full discussion of the appearance of non-Jews in *piyut* is a desideratum but is not possible here.[30]

For an example, we turn to the Ninth of Av, a fast day observed as the anniversary of the destruction of both the First and Second Temples, as well as a long catalogue of subsequent tragedies inflicted by non-Jews on Jews up to the Holocaust. As we have seen, this 'lachrymose' focus is in general characteristic of the presence of the non-Jew in traditional Jewish liturgy, as is the consciousness of the unredeemed nature of life without a restored Jerusalem and its Temple. The day dedicated to this theme is thus an important focal point for understanding the portrayal of non-Jews in Jewish liturgy. The day also has a rich tradition of its own genre of *piyut*, called *kinot*, best translated as 'dirges' or 'lamentations'. These poems reflect individually on all the various tragedies

---

to princes', alludes to Psalm 144: 10. Psalm 144: 11 reads 'Rescue me, save me from the hands of foreigners, whose mouths speak lies and whose oaths are false.' This is only the first of a number of such loci in the prayer (see Barry Schwartz, '*Hanoten Teshua*': The Origin of the Traditional Jewish Prayer for the Government', *Hebrew Union College Annual*, 57 (1986), 119).

[29] The genizah versions of the blessing with one exception ubiquitously include explicit mention of Christians. They also understood *meshumad* (apostate), the opening word of the blessing, to refer to baptized Jews. Judaeo-Arabic texts employ a totally different term (from the root פשע) not included in the blessing, for converts to Islam. See chapter 2 of my forthcoming *Cursing the Christians? A History of the* Birkat HaMinim.

[30] For a discussion of Yannai's treatment of Byzantine Christianity, see Laura Lieber, *Yannai on Genesis: An Invitation to Piyyut* (Cincinnati, 2010), 270–85.

aggregated into this day and are its traditional acts of specific memory. The collections of *kinot* are enormous, and varied from town to town.[31]

In today's Ashkenazi rite, the vast majority of the *kinot* were composed by Elazar Kalir, the great classic poet of the Land of Israel. He lived around the time of the Arab conquest in the seventh century CE and composed over a hundred *kinot*, most of which are not preserved in today's collection. Some of his *kinot* demonstrate significant independence from the narrow themes of the book of Lamentations, elaborating on other related themes, such as the sins of the kings of Judah, or how foreign kings harmed Israel and received divine punishment.[32] Kalir's language and that of his imitators is also exceedingly difficult. Comprehending the poet's full meaning requires not only an ability to recognize allusive references to biblical verses and their larger contexts, but also knowing the midrashic traditions of commentary on that verse.[33] Therefore, detailed study of the *kinot* is necessary to penetrate their messages—and to understand the challenges that this genre presents to the formation of memory for those seeking interreligious understanding today.

Joseph B. Soloveitchik pointed to the end of Kalir's *kinah*, *Hateh elokai oznekha*, which makes explicit reference to the Christian claim that '[the Temple] is deserted, forgotten and forsaken, and it will be forever devastated'. Soloveitchik expanded on this, teaching that this is a perpetual and continuing Christian supersessionist denigration of Judaism. Now published by Jacob J. Schacter, Soloveitchik's comment perhaps pre-dated the Second Vatican Council and other similar Christian attempts to revise precisely this point. However, Schacter reproduced it without comment and, at least in 2004, included it in his own teaching of this *kinah* on the Ninth of Av.[34]

---

[31] On other penitential fast days, a similar sort of *piyutim*, called *seliḥot*, were originally inserted into the sixth benediction of the Amidah, which asks for God's forgiveness for sins (as *kinot* were initially inserted into the fourteenth benediction for the rebuilding of Jerusalem). This mode was also frequently employed to memorialize various local tragedies on their specific or symbolic anniversaries. A complete study of this topic would include this literature too, much of which is available only in manuscript. For an analysis of a collection of these *seliḥot* from medieval northern France, see Susan L. Einbinder, *Beautiful Death: Jewish Poetry and Martyrdom in Medieval France* (Princeton, NJ, 2002). A small fraction of this literature has been published in Daniel Goldschmidt, *A Collection of Seliḥot Hymns by German and French Poets* [Leket piyutei seliḥot me'et paytanei ashkenaz vetsarfat], ed. Avraham Fraenkel (Jerusalem, 1993).

[32] See Ezra Fleischer, *Hebrew Liturgical Poetry in the Middle Ages* [Shirat hakodesh ha'ivrit biyemei habeinayim] (Jerusalem, 1975), 71–2, 204–6.

[33] Einbinder describes this situation in the medieval synagogue (*Beautiful Death*, 19). See also the sources cited in Ruth Langer, *To Worship God Properly: Tensions Between Liturgical Custom and Halakhah in Judaism* (Cincinnati, 1998), 130–6; Shulamit Elizur, 'The Congregation in the Synagogue and the Ancient *Qedushta*' (Heb.), in S. Elizur et al. (eds.), *Knesset Ezra: Literature and Life in the Synagogue: Studies Presented to Ezra Fleischer* [Keneset ezra: sifrut veḥayim beveit hakeneset: asufat ma'amarim mugashim le'ezra fleischer] (Jerusalem, 1994), 171–90.

[34] Admittedly, in 2009, as I revise this paper for publication, there is more reason to question how deeply these revised teachings have taken root than there was when we celebrated the fortieth

Kalir's lament is a call for divine justice to respond appropriately to the abominable acts perpetrated in the course of the destruction of the Temple. This is, for the most part, all that one will find in the printed commentaries to this text too. However, closer study of the *kinah* shows that Soloveitchik was right in his historical interpretation. A significant number of the biblical verses to which Kalir alludes have midrashic interpretations that apply to Christians and Christianity. Kalir was therefore responding subtly to the Rome of his own day, the Byzantine empire and the Christians who maintained control of the Temple Mount but used it as a dung heap.[35] Kalir's portrayal of Christians is of those deriding the deepest hopes of Jews, arrogantly denying validity to Jewish beliefs and to Judaism itself as a religion and way of life pleasing to God. He barely engages with actual Christian beliefs beyond an allusion to the Trinity and he certainly grants Christianity no theological validity as a non-Jewish religion. That this was Kalir's understanding of history and of his own time is important. Entering into his grief can help deepen the contemporary experience of the Ninth of Av. However, his Christian Other is not identical with our Christian Other. Our Christian Other today struggles to confront its heritage of supersessionism and theological anti-Judaism. To presume that Christians today preserve Byzantine and medieval attitudes is the equivalent of the historical and damaging Christian presumption that Jews remain forever the people of the Bible.

Kalir shows no evidence in this *kinah* of personal negative interactions with Christians. Those enter the corpus of *kinot* only much later, with the introduction of laments for the martyrs of the First Crusade in 1096.[36] The standard Ashkenazi collection today contains four laments over the crusades and one for the burning of the Talmud in Paris in 1240.[37] Hundreds of other poems were

anniversary of *Nostra aetate* in 2005 (see Joseph B. Soloveitchik, *The Lord is Righteous in All His Ways: Reflections on the Tish'ah be-Av Kinot*, ed. Jacob J. Schacter, Selected Writings of Rabbi Joseph B. Soloveitchik [Meotzar harav], 7 (Jersey City, 2006), 181–4; *The Koren Mesorat Harav Kinot*, The Lookstein Edition, ed. Simon Posner (Jerusalem, 2010), 411–12). No date is given for the original discussion.

35 For my detailed commentary on this *kinah*, *Hateh elokai oznekha*, see Boston College, Center for Christian–Jewish Learning, 'Jewish Understandings of the Other: An Annotated Sourcebook', <http://www.bc.edu/dam/files/research_sites/cjl/texts/cjrelations/resources/sourcebook/kalir-hateh.htm>.

36 Substantial work on the development of traditions of *kinot* remains to be done. There have been no studies, to my knowledge, on the collections found in individual medieval rites. Work on the various medieval laments has mostly been from a literary rather than a liturgical perspective, with little attention paid even to the day on which a particular lament was recited. We therefore know essentially nothing about the development of the collections now standard among Ashkenazi Jews. Daniel Goldschmidt's critical edition *Order of Kinot for Tishah Be'av According to the Custom of Poland and the Ashkenazi Communities in the Land of Israel* [Seder hakinot letishah be'av keminhag polin ukehilot ha'ashkenazim be'erets yisra'el] (Jerusalem, 1976)) relies on several manuscripts to correct the printed editions, but does not trace or explain their development.

37 To my knowledge, no one has traced the evolution of this collection. I base this statement

composed in the High Middle Ages and beyond in response to other tragedies caused by Christian persecutions. These poems were recited locally with the intention of shaping memory. However, perhaps because many responded to local events and their communities ceased to exist, these poems no longer have a place in Jewish ritual life.[38] These five, thus, are the only ones which, if they are actually recited and recited with understanding,[39] continue to shape the Jewish communal memory of interactions with their Christian neighbours.

A detailed analysis of these *kinot* is beyond the scope of this chapter. Perhaps it suffices to say that a deep engagement with any of these texts is not a pleasant experience. The poets have succeeded in sharing their utter pain in witnessing these events. At the same time, the emphasis of these poems is on the act of sacrifice by the Jewish martyrs, not on the Christian aggressors. Indeed, their personalities and theologies hardly enter into the poetry, though their acts of desecration do. In a sense, then, these *kinot* continue the biblical tradition of the undifferentiated non-Jewish enemy; their concern lies within the boundaries of the Jewish community. However, the specificity of the memories leaves the identity of the aggressor unambiguous. To a Jew, even today, reciting these *kinot*, there is no question that the aggressors were Christians seeking the destruction of the Jewish communities in their midst through forced baptism or death. The continuation of Christian conversionary pressures, from some corners even today and within recent memory from all sectors of the Christian community, makes it difficult to distinguish between contemporary Christians and the Christians of the crusades. Indeed, when Jews of today identify with the Jews of that period, the crusaders and contemporary Christians become, in their eyes, part of the same historical continuum.

It is at this point, then, that the calls for divine vengeance that conclude these *kinot* become more problematic. For a witness to a disaster to call on God

on the collection found in Daniel Goldschmidt, *Order of Kinot for Tishah Be'av* and Abraham Rosenfeld's *The Authorised Kinot for the Ninth of Av*, 2nd edn. (Israel, 1970).

[38] Yerushalmi, *Zakhor*, 48–51, points to an exception: Rabbenu Tam called for universal observance of a fast on 20 Sivan to remember the martyrs of Blois (*c.*1171). This fast day was given a new lease of life when it was adopted to remember the Chmielnicki massacres in 1648 in Poland, a day observed in some communities until the Second World War. For a more detailed study of the Blois poetry (as well as several other themes pertinent to our topic here in the other chapters), see Einbinder, *Beautiful Death*, ch. 2. Elisabeth Hollender has examined particularly the *selihot* and *zulatot* written in response to medieval persecutions and suggests that most of these local commemorations were clustered, often on the sabbath, during the period of the *omer* or of the three weeks or on Yom Kippur (see Elisabeth Hollender, 'Zur Reaktion auf Gewalt in Hebräischen Liturgischen Dichtungen des Mittelalters', in M. Braun and C. Herberich (eds.), *Gewalt in Mittelalter: Realitäten—Imaginationen* (Munich, 2005), 203–23; ead., 'Single Zulatot in Ashkenaz', in Alessandro Guetta and Masha Izhaki (eds.), *Studies in Medieval Jewish Poetry: A Message Upon the Garden* (Leiden, 2009), 99–115).

[39] Rosenfeld, *The Authorised Kinot for the Ninth of Av*, published for the British Ashkenazi community, includes two additional laments for the Jews of York in 1190, which are relevant to the experience of Jews in England. He also includes an original composition in memory of the Holocaust.

to alleviate the situation, to do justice by punishing the perpetrators, is under-standable. But what do contemporary people hear when they recite heart-wrenching calls for divine vengeance, such as:

> How long will you just look, Seer of all secret things?
> Be zealous for your Torah that gentile rulers have despoiled.
> They have singed it, left it uncovered, torn it to shreds.
> Like tangled thorns, they enlarged the bonfires.
> 'At such things will you restrain yourself', Master of all Creation?
> Avenge the blood spilled like cascading water.[40]

Here, and in prayers like Av haraḥamim, such sentiments have the power to shape the way that the communities reciting them think about the world. The Jewish identity constituted by such texts is one that understands the non-Jew, and especially the Christian, as one to whom divine vengeance continues to be overdue.

HOLOCAUST LITURGIES

As I have demonstrated elsewhere,[41] there is a very strong correlation between disruptions of *minhag* (custom) and periods of halakhic inflexibility. When communities with differing traditions are thrown together and have to seek a new modus vivendi, received assumptions of correct practice tend to be resolved by attempts to establish an authoritative halakhic stance, often one that overrides the received customs of Jews' previous homes. We live today in one such period, perhaps the most extreme ever experienced. This is caused by the combination of the destruction of the European communities in the Holocaust with the decimation of the communities in Arab lands in the wake of the founding of the State of Israel. The only large Jewish communities not directly touched by these events are themselves the products of recent immi-grations. Thus, while we live in a period in which many local customs with their commemorations of local tragedies simply no longer exist, we also live in a period in which liturgical flexibility is at a minimum among traditional Jews. This can be attributed both to a positive need for halakhic 'authenticity' and to a sense that flexibility is characteristic of non-halakhic forms of Judaism and therefore to be avoided.[42] In addition, these communities attribute their loss

---

[40] From the concluding verses of the anonymous *kinah*, *Haḥarishu mimeni va'adaberah* (Goldschmidt, *Order of Kinot for Tishah Be'av*, no. 23, p. 88).

[41] Langer, *To Worship God Properly*, 248–51.

[42] Reform, Reconstructionist, and liberal Jews, in contrast, feel no comparable nostalgia for lost *minhag*, and have little accepted halakhic limitation on liturgical change. Indeed, their tra-ditions of liturgical change were historically driven by theological concerns. While Mordecai Kaplan was indeed very concerned about the theological implications of chosenness and issues affecting Jewish views of the non-Jew, this has not historically been a significant issue for Reform

of authentic *minhag* to their non-Jewish persecutors, whether Christian or Muslim, only complicating the process of making positive ritual space for non-Jews. The ongoing threats from the Palestinian and larger Muslim world do not open doors either. In the world of traditional Judaism, therefore, there are severe limits on the possible implementation of any constructive suggestions about liturgical theologies of the religious other. Received liturgical texts, because of the multiple challenges enumerated above, will not change; yet commentaries on the liturgy and how it is taught may influence which parts of these texts receive emphasis.

However, essentially all Jews create liturgy today to construct memory of the primary events of twentieth-century Jewish history: commemoration of the Holocaust and celebration of the founding of the State of Israel. In both cases, non-Jews play a negative role in the day's narrative. However, because the founding of the state is a cause for rejoicing, because Jewish tradition suggests that gloating over the downfall of an enemy is inappropriate,[43] and perhaps because Israel has only begun to struggle with how to understand the Palestinian narrative, the non-Jew is essentially absent from the day's observances in most places. The usual sabbath prayer for Israeli soldiers and even the prayer for the state pray for victory over faceless, nameless enemies, following (deliberately or not) in the traditions of the medieval *piyut*. More significantly, celebration of Yom Ha'atsma'ut (Israeli Independence Day) follows patterns of other non-biblical festivals, marked liturgically by Hallel and other psalms and in most cases not integrating a formal contemporary narrative account of the events commemorated. This may be because the holiday is not scriptural, but more likely because Israeli society still has not come to a consensus about how to tell that story. From the perspective of our discussion, the challenge is to find a way to celebrate the birth of the state without simultaneously creating a narrative (and a consequent identity) that makes true peace with Israel's neighbours impossible.

Yom Hasho'ah is an even more complicated issue, both in terms of its date and in terms of its ritual. The establishment of a new date on which to

Jews. Perhaps the involvement of several leading Reform rabbis in *Dabru emet* and in establishing interfaith relations in America is a sign of hope. The spring 2005 issue of the *CCAR Journal* is a symposium convened by David Sandmel on 'Towards a Reform Theology of Christianity', suggesting some continued interest there. However, the reality of intermarriage and the consequent presence of non-Jews in the synagogue shapes the liberal liturgical reality in ways that require their own discussion.

[43] For instance, the full Hallel is recited only on the first holy days of Passover. For the remainder of the festival, joy is reduced in recognition of the fact that Israel's redemption came only with the loss of Egyptian lives at the sea. Note, however, that this is not the explanation given in the Talmud itself (*Arakh.* 10*a*–10*b*), but it is that cited by Joseph Karo, *Beit Yosef*, 'Oraḥ ḥayim', 490; citing *Shibolei haleket*, no. 174. It is then commonly repeated by the supercommentators to *SA* 'Oraḥ ḥayim', 490: 4.

memorialize this complex tragedy is itself not unprecedented, as many communities commemorated local tragedies or deliverances, a local Purim, on the actual anniversary. But what is the anniversary of the Holocaust? Secular Jews in Israel did not want to associate it with Temple-oriented fast days. They also wanted to shape this memory to include not only mourning for the tragedy, but also celebration of acts of heroism and resistance. Finally, there was a theological statement to be made in the role that the Holocaust played in serving as a catalyst for the realization of Zionist dreams. Consequently, they formulated the day as Yom Hasho'ah Vehagevurah (Holocaust and Heroism Remembrance Day) and set it as close to the anniversary (during Passover) of the Warsaw ghetto uprising as possible, and a week before Yom Ha'atsma'ut, to build a communal identity through ritual that is markedly different from that of the diaspora past.[44] In contrast, there seems not to have been a serious attempt to think about appropriate liturgical ritual for the day, perhaps because of the strong secular hand in establishing the Israeli observance. Tragedies have usually been marked by fasting and other acts of mourning; communities generated *seliḥot* and/or *kinot* to transmit the memories associated with them. However, this precedent was difficult to apply here.

This creates a potentially dangerous situation. Typically, memorial liturgies focused on the martyrological elements: the victims' self-sacrifice, their virtuous piety—leaving the persecutors present mostly by allusion. This made it difficult to associate the perpetrators of a particular tragedy with subsequent generations of their community. However, the Yizkor (memorial prayer) recited for the victims of the Holocaust often elaborates on the normal text with numerous details, specifically and elaborately calling the Germans, not just the Nazis, murderers. The text in the *Rinat yisra'el* prayer book is more than twice as long as any other version of this prayer, including an explicit call for divine vengeance. If this becomes enshrined in liturgical usage, constructing the memory of the Holocaust, how does one honour the work of contemporary Germans to confront and critique their Nazi past?

There are many challenges to constructing an appropriate liturgical memory of the Holocaust. The questions relevant to this chapter address the sort of memory such a liturgy will nurture and how this memory will shape Jewish thinking about the religious traditions in whose cradle genocide was nurtured. As has been demonstrated, precedents would encourage expressions of pain, outrage, and anger, accompanied by calls for divine vengeance, likely in a context of fasting and acts of ritual mourning. Such expressions honour the memory of the victims and the unspeakable horrors they endured while

[44] For a summation of this history, see James E. Young, *The Texture of Memory: Holocaust Memorials and Meaning* (New Haven, 1993), ch. 10, 'When a Day Remembers: A Performative History of Yom Hashoah'.

personalizing an emotional response on the part of the participants in the ritual. But there is little here to guide us in presenting anything other than an oppositional relationship with those who co-operated with Hitler and their descendants.

Non-oppositional models are not numerous.[45] In May 2005, shortly after Yom Hasho'ah, I raised the question of constructing Holocaust liturgies with a group of American Reform rabbis. Every single person in the group had participated only in a community Yom Hasho'ah observance, with the Christians outnumbering the Jews in attendance. A liturgy for an interfaith setting must have a different purpose than one designed with the Jewish community at its centre. It can seek neither to narrate a story that will construct a memory that identifies with the victims nor to memorialize the community's own deceased. Instead, it necessarily seeks the broader and depersonalized goal of preventing future participation as a perpetrator or as a bystander, of raising moral consciousness and activism—a very different ritual. However, there are real benefits in terms of interreligious relations if such a ritual is consciously constructed so that the Jewish memories and the Christian memories are in discussion with one another. This would prevent Jewish demonization of their contemporary religious Other and allow for recognition of contemporary Christian repentance.

Such a context will not meet the needs of the traditional Jewish world, though, or even of Israeli secular society. I initiated an identical conversation that summer with a group of Orthodox rabbinical students. Their response was that Holocaust commemorations were ceremonies for schoolchildren, and liturgy was not a viable route to memory. For them, perhaps, as for other Jews for whom the traditional ritual calendar is meaningful, mourning for the victims of the Holocaust is gradually being assimilated into Tishah Be'av, for which new *kinot* have indeed been composed, and into the Tenth of Tevet, a fast day gaining new meaning as a day on which the Kaddish prayer is recited in memory of all those who have no one left to memorialize them properly. In other words, they distanced themselves from the integration of the Holocaust into the modern Zionist narrative of memory, integrating it liturgically into existing points of the Jewish year. Yom Hasho'ah itself they reserved for a primarily educational task. By minimizing the distinctiveness of the Holocaust, however, they place its memory entirely within the precedents set by other

[45] I am aware of two Holocaust liturgies arising in recent years from the Orthodox world: Avigdor Shinan (ed.), *The Shoah Scroll: A Holocaust Liturgy* [Megilat hasho'ah] (Jerusalem, 2003) which echoes Lamentations but narrates the story of the Holocaust in various literary modes, containing both new compositions and other's narratives; Avi Weiss published a Holocaust Seder that constructs memory in modes influenced by the Passover Seder, including various experiential elements (like collecting food, separating parents and children) to aid in the construction of memory beyond the intellectual levels.

disasters and do not respond to the opportunity and challenge to construct memory differently.

They are correct in pointing to other sources for the construction of Holocaust memory in our world. The controversies over the portrayal of Pope Pius XII at Yad Vashem raised prior to Pope Benedict XVI's 2009 visit there point to the relevance of our question to the portrayal of non-Jews in museums, film, and drama as well. However, the question of construction of memory goes beyond matters of getting the facts straight; it involves a more holistic kind of memory, one that involves emotional responses as well as ethical and theological ones. A world which perpetuates only oppositional understandings of the Other is one in which tragedies will continue to occur.

Many Jews today see Hitler as Amalek. Concerning Amalek, Deuteronomy says: 'Therefore, when the Eternal your God grants you safety from all your enemies around you, in the land that the Eternal your God is giving you as a hereditary portion, you shall blot out the memory of Amalek from under the heaven. Do not forget!' (Deut. 25: 19). This passage itself is part of Jewish liturgy, chosen to be read specifically on the sabbath before Purim. On the one hand, the command is 'Do not forget!' Hold on to the memory! On the other hand, the command is to block out Amalek's memory, to give Amalek no continuing hold over the lives of Israel. This is the tension of liturgical memory about the persecuting Other: on the one hand not to remake history and to make history a part of our identity, but on the other hand to allow that history to continue to unfold and evolve, to move beyond the specific tragedy. And if there is any need of vengeance, it is best left to God.

PART III

JUDAISM AND WORLD RELIGIONS

EIGHT

Rethinking Christianity
Rabbinic Positions and Possibilities

EUGENE KORN

INTRODUCTION

ONE OF THE most pervasive conditions of modern life is empirical pluralism. Social, cultural, and religious diversities pursue us relentlessly today.
The Emancipation of the eighteenth and nineteenth centuries moved most
Western Jews out of their insulated ghettoes, granted them citizenship, and
welcomed their participation in their mainstream national cultures, thus
inevitably increasing their contact with their non-Jewish neighbours. In
Europe and America, this meant closer, more harmonious, and more frequent
interaction with Christians and Christianity. Even Jewish statehood, born out
of the deep desire to free the Jewish people from subordination to non-Jews,
willy-nilly has brought about unprecedented requirements for Jewish interaction with Christians and Christianity. Israel now assumes sovereign responsibility for the welfare and rights of more than 140,000 individual Christian
citizens as well as numerous churches. And as the visits to Israel of Popes John
Paul II in 2000 and Benedict XVI in 2009 have demonstrated, Israelis now
must interact with Church officials to find respectful relations and common
ground. This is true not only in the realm of realpolitik, but also in the religious
domain, as the Chief Rabbinate meets regularly with high-level Vatican and
Protestant clergy from abroad to discuss issues of mutual spiritual and practical
concern.

Of course Jews and Christians met in medieval times also, but modernity
saturates us with pluralistic interaction of a frequency, intensity, and quality
not experienced in the past. The contemporary forces for social diversity are
inescapable, and avoiding the religious other is impossible for a modern Jew—
of any stripe.

The European Enlightenment created a vast secular space for the citizens
of the new world. Since the French Revolution Jews and Christians have been
meeting, speaking, and co-operating with each other in the offices of their pro-
fessions, the corridors of government, the lecture halls of universities, and the

public areas of their cities primarily as fraternal secularists. They have been pluralists who all too often were willing to trade their religious identities for the dream of social equality and mutual dignity. 'Be a Jew in the home and a man on the street' became the watchword for many Enlightenment Jews. From then until today, even when they met qua Jews and Christians, religion was often left behind. There is more than a little truth to the quip that the founding American members of the National Conference of Christians and Jews were Christians who did not believe in Christianity and Jews who did not believe in Judaism. Needless to say, they agreed on much.

None of this bargain with modern secular life can work for Jewish theology or religious Jews who seek to fashion their life experience into a holistic and coherent world-view. Here there is no secular space or naked public square, no experience devoid of religious meaning or human relationship unshaped by their Jewish values and halakhic world-views. In the words of the pre-eminent twentieth-century Orthodox philosopher Joseph B. Soloveitchik, 'God claims the whole, not a part of man, and whatever He established as an order within the scheme of creation is sacred.'[1] If so, a contemporary Jewish theology needs to formulate a coherent and sober understanding of Christianity and Christian belief today. What do Jewish thought or theologically oriented Jews make of their Christian neighbours and colleagues, particularly the pious among them who no longer seek to undermine Judaism or the Jewish people? Can Jews see the image of God in the face of a believing Christian? And can Jewish theology understand contemporary Christianity as a positive religious and spiritual phenomenon? Are there halakhic and religious grounds for appreciating contemporary Christianity and its current teachings?

Since religion has surged back to the forefront of contemporary culture and politics, investigating the possibility of relating to non-Jews *on religious grounds* assumes added significance for Jews who are unapologetic about appreciating

---

[1] Joseph B. Soloveitchik, 'Confrontation', *Tradition*, 6/2 (1964), 24 n. 8. Soloveitchik also emphasized this in 1971 in a conversation with Cardinal Johannes Willebrands: 'All dialogue between Jews and Christians cannot but be religious and theological . . . Can we speak otherwise than on the level of religion? Our culture is certainly a religious one' (*International Catholic–Jewish Liaison Committee: Fifteen Years of Catholic–Jewish Dialogue 1970–1985* (Vatican City, 1988), 273). Yet even Soloveitchik may have briefly fallen into the cultural trap of advocating meeting others on secular grounds. In 'Confrontation', which explored the correct parameters of Jewish–Christian dialogue, he initially advocated interfaith co-operation in 'secular orders'. Realizing this language was problematic, he qualified it as 'popular semantics' (ibid.) and soon thereafter in the Rabbinical Council of America Record for February 1966 he formulated the following statement: 'Rabbis and Christian clergymen cannot discuss socio-cultural and moral problems as sociologists, historians or cultural ethicists in agnostic or secularist categories. As men of God, our thoughts, feelings, perceptions and terminology bear the imprint of a religious world outlook.' For an analysis of 'Confrontation' and Soloveitchik's arguments relating to interfaith activity, see Eugene Korn, 'The Man of Faith and Religious Dialogue: Revisiting "Confrontation" ', *Modern Judaism*, 25 (2005), 290–315.

the pluralism and blessings of modern life, and who look to Jewish tradition, thought, and halakhah to shape their attitudes and experiences. A mature Jewish theology need not feel defensive about such an enquiry. Moreover, many Christians are now actively seeking to enhance their own identity through deepening their understanding of Judaism and theological reconciliation with the Jewish people and their faith. Thus for a variety of spiritual and empirical reasons, developing an understanding of contemporary Christians and Christianity remains a compelling post-Emancipation challenge, for both contemporary Judaism as well as for Jews who search for God in every corner of their experience and are committed to an integrated spiritual *Weltanschauung*.

PRELIMINARY OBSERVATIONS

We should bear in mind a number of points regarding a contemporary analysis of Christians and Christianity. First, Jewish consideration of Christianity today is theologically and halakhically different from the issues that faced Jewish authorities at the time of Jesus and the first century of the Common Era. This is due to the fundamental theological break that occurred among Jewish Christians sometime after the death of Jesus. During this period a new belief arose that the teachings of Jesus no longer fitted into mainstream Judaism as then practised. Instead, the later thinking claimed that belief in Jesus *replaced* obedience to the commandments of the Torah (*mitsvot*) as the way to reach God, thus rendering the Jewish covenant (*berit*) no longer valid.[2] Belief in Jesus was alleged to reflect a new, more mature covenant and constituted a different religious testimony pointing to a different revelation and path to salvation. With this development, Christian belief ceased being a tolerable deviance within the Jewish community and became an intolerable heresy for Judaism and its rabbinical authorities. Bitter feuds broke out, and Jewish Christians became *minim*, sectarian apostates to be excluded from the Jewish community.[3] At that point the two communities began to part ways and develop independent calendars, *sancta*, traditions, and theologies.

Yet something else occurred that simultaneously mitigated the strains. When Saul of Tarsus exported Christianity to the non-Jews of the Roman

[2] This teaching later became known as 'supersessionism'. While traditional scholarship and teachings maintained that Paul introduced this nullification of the Jewish law for Jews, much recent scholarship claims that Paul advocated that Jews continue to observe the *mitsvot* and only non-Jews did not need the commandments for salvation (see Alan Segal, *Paul the Convert* (New Haven, 1992); E. P. Sanders, *Paul and Palestinian Judaism* (London, 1977); James D. J. Dunn, *Paul and the Mosaic Law* (Grand Rapids, Mich., 2001); Krister Stendahl, *Paul among Jews and Gentiles* (Philadelphia, 1976)).

[3] See James Parkes, *The Conflict of the Church and the Synagogue* (London, 1934), chs. 1–3; Lawrence Shiffman, *Who Was a Jew? Rabbinic and Halakhic Perspectives on the Jewish Christian Schism* (Hoboken, NJ, 1985), ch. 7.

empire, he transformed the disagreement from an internal Jewish argument into an external one. Christianity then ceased being primarily a heretical strain of Judaism and became an independent non-Jewish religion. Later, the conversion of Constantine and the Council of Nicaea in the fourth century formally established Christianity and its doctrines as a different religion from Judaism, one predominantly for non-Jews. Theoretically, this made it easier for Jews to reconsider Christianity, since according to the Jewish law confronting Jewish heresy is different from evaluating non-Jewish religions. After the separation, the crucial Jewish question changed from 'How shall we deal with heresy?' to 'How should Judaism regard non-Jewish Christians and their religion?'

Second, in our time most Christian churches have changed their official teachings about Jews and Judaism. Since the Second Vatican Council convened in 1962, Catholic and Protestant thinkers have generated a robust literature of new Christian theology towards Judaism and the Jewish people. The genesis of this transformation was the Holocaust and its near-successful Final Solution for the Jews in Europe. For Jews, the Holocaust was a searing physical tragedy from which the Jewish people is still recovering; for Christians, the Holocaust caused a deep theological and moral trauma. Something in Christendom had gone undeniably wrong and Christian thinkers recoiled from what had been wrought. Reflection on this unimaginable evil that took root so easily in the heart of Christian culture was the impetus for Christians to reappraise their tortured history and theology regarding Jews. Over the past forty-five years this reassessment process has spawned a discussion no less remarkable for its content than for its quantity. One Catholic theologian succinctly dubbed the transformation of contemporary Christian thinking as 'the six Rs': (1) the repudiation of antisemitism, (2) the rejection of the charge of deicide, (3) repentance for the Holocaust, (4) recognition of the State of Israel, (5), the review of teaching about Jews and Judaism, and (6) rethinking the proselytization of Jews.[4] Judged in the light of traditional Christian teachings, most Christian theologies have undergone a revolution with respect to their spiritual and historical Jewish patrimony. The Second Vatican Council's proclamation, *Nostra aetate*,[5] in 1965 proved to be a point of departure for a Christian journey from which there has been no return.[6]

---

[4] Mary Boys, *Has God Only One Blessing?* (New York, 2000), 248; see also pp. 247–66. A more detailed description of the major changes in Christian theology related to Jews and Judaism is provided in the final section of this chapter.

[5] The text of *Nostra aetate* can be found at <http://www.jcrelations.net/en/?item=2552>.

[6] Two contrasting events dramatically indicate this change in Christian attitude to Jews and Judaism. Before the First Zionist Congress in 1897, an article appeared in the official Vatican periodical *Civiltà cattolica* explaining that Jews are required to live as servants in exile until the end of days, a fate which can be avoided only by conversion to Christianity. So when Theodor

This profound transformation in Christianity opens up new possibilities for a fresh contemporary Jewish theological approach to Christianity and has had a dramatic salutary effect in the last forty-five years on how Jews can relate on an experiential level to religious Christians. This is possible because neither normative Jewish law nor Jewish theology nor Jewish attitudes to Christians and their faith are wholly dogmatic or theoretical. Throughout history they have been influenced by what Christian doctrine says about Judaism and Jews and, perhaps more significantly, how Christians related to Jews in the economic, social, and political conditions of different eras. In short, Jewish theology about Christianity is partially rooted in the different experiences of the Jewish people with the Church.

Third, while the Written Torah generally paints a negative picture of non-Jewish nations,[7] it portrays the non-native stranger in Jewish society (the *ger*) as a positive but isolated figure. The talmudic rabbis expanded on the idea of the stranger and conceptualized it into a broad legal and moral category, demanding that Jews protect people in this category and relate to them with moral responsibility.[8] It came to include all non-Jews who accept the basic values of morality, known as the seven Noahide commandments: the six prohibitions on murder, theft, sexual immorality, idolatry, eating the limb of a live animal (a paradigm for cruelty and devaluation of life), and blasphemy against the single God of the universe, as well as the one positive injunction to set up courts of law that justly enforce these six prohibitions. All non-Jews who follow these basic laws of civilization are considered to be worthy *benei no'aḥ*.[9] Thus the talmudic tradition split the non-Jewish world into two sub-categories: the immoral heathen, practising an illicit and intolerable religion, and the positively regarded Noahide,[10] whom Jews are obligated to protect and sustain.

Herzl approached Pius X in 1904 to enlist his support for Jewish return to Zion, the pope declined: 'It is not in our power to prevent you from going to to Jerusalem, but we will never give our support. As the head of the Church, I cannot give you any other answer. The Jews do not recognize our Lord, hence we cannot recognize the Jewish people. When you come to Palestine, we will be there to baptize all of you' (*The Diaries of Theodor Herzl*, ed. Marvin Lowenthal (London, 1956), 429–30). In March 2000 Pope John Paul II made an official visit to Israel, met the president and chief rabbis, and prayed at Jerusalem's Western Wall for the welfare of the Jewish people as his elder brothers who remained the people of God's covenant.

[7] In Genesis, the non-Jews are immoral pagans with whom the partriarchs interact. In Exodus, they are the brutal Egyptians and Amalekites. In Leviticus, those who engage in abominable practices. In Deuteronomy, the seven idolatrous Canaanite nations. On this point see Ruth Langer in Chapter 7, above.

[8] Tosefta *AZ* 8: 4; Maimonides, *Mishneh torah*, 'Laws of Kings', 9: 1.

[9] Maimonides, *Mishneh torah*, 'Laws of Kings', 8: 10.

[10] The term *benei no'aḥ* or 'Noahide' is used in rabbinic literature in two different senses. Technically, all non-Jews are Noahides and stand under the seven Noahide commandments,

This revolutionized the biblical view of humanity from a largely binary one of Jews and evil non-Jews into a tripartite conceptualization of Jews, worthy non-Jews, and heathens.

Thus Judaism has long subscribed to what is now called a double covenant theology: Jews stand obligated as partners with God in one divine covenant containing 613 commandments, while non-Jews stand under the divine covenant of the seven Noahide commandments. Importantly, each covenant is valid for its respective adherents and there is no compelling theological or moral need for Noahides to convert and enter into the Jewish covenant. Noahides participate in an independently authentic covenant that prescribes a separate, valid, and religiously valuable way of life. In rabbinic tradition, they are accorded positive status—even to the extent that non-Jews who faithfully keep the Noahide commandments are regarded by God as more beloved than Jews who violate the fundamentals of their covenant of 613 commandments.[11] Rabbinic tradition paid some of these non-Jews the ultimate theological compliment by teaching that 'righteous non-Jews have a share in the world to come'.[12]

The last point is significant and presents a critically important theological asymmetry with traditional Christian teaching. As indicated, rabbinic Judaism taught that the Jewish covenant was not the sole valid religion or path to salvation. Judaism possesses a natural theological openness that flows from this double covenant theory. A non-Jew need not believe in Jewish theology or practise what Jews practise to be in a holy relation with God. By contrast, until recently Christianity never accepted any double covenant theory. The normative teaching was *extra ecclesiam nulla salus*, that Christianity is the exclusive path to salvation and those not subscribing to Christian belief lacked a valid relationship with God.[13] Hence Christianity has been historically keen on conversion, for without conversion those outside the Church are lost theologically—both in this world and in the world to come.

---

whether they observe them or not. However, the term is frequently applied only to those who observe the Noahide commandments and who are contrasted with those who violate them, such as an idolater or an *oved avodah zarah*.

[11] Jacob Emden, *Seder olam rabah vezuta*, cited in Oscar Z. Fasman, 'An Epistle on Tolerance by a "Rabbinic Zealot" ', in Leo Jung (ed.), *Judaism in a Changing World* (New York, 1939), 121–39.

[12] BT *San*. 105*a*; Maimonides, *Mishneh torah*, 'Laws of Repentence', 3: 5; 'Laws of Kings', 8: 11. For an extended discussion of the topic of salvation for righteous non-Jews, see Eugene Korn, 'Gentiles, the World to Come, and Judaism: The Odyssey of a Rabbinic Text', *Modern Judaism*, 14 (1994), 265–87.

[13] Whereas the early interpretation of this principle was that those not subscribing to Catholic belief were disqualified from eternal salvation, the more recent normative interpretation allows for some non-Christians to be saved, as 'anonymous Christians' (see *Catechism of Catholic Church*, 2nd edn. (Vatican City, 1997), pt. 1, §§846–8).

JEWISH LAW AND CHRISTIANITY

According to halakhah, is Christianity an invalid form of non-Jewish worship or is it an authentic, licit religion that conforms to the seven Noahide commandments? Interestingly, the talmudic rabbis do not discuss this question.[14] There is only one explicit reference to the theological status of non-Jewish Christians in the Talmud, and rabbinic opinions differ as to whether the text refers to Christianity or to a separate Persian cult.[15]

Yet the theological status of Christianity was discussed at length in the Middle Ages, when two well-known and fundamentally opposing views arose. One is that of Maimonides in twelfth-century Muslim Spain and North Africa. He maintained that Christianity constituted *avodah zarah*—foreign and illicit worship, often connoting idolatry.[16] To many moderns this may sound strange, but it was quite logical to Jews in the Middle Ages who were grounded in biblical and talmudic theology. Christianity violated the second commandment of the Decalogue: the prohibition against making graven images of God. Moreover, Christians venerated saints and prayed to intermediaries such as Mary, religious characteristics foreign to Jewish theology and practice. Yet for Maimonides the deepest problems of Christianity were the doctrines of the Trinity and the Incarnation.[17] Maimonides insisted that monotheism must be pure, and that any understanding of God that denied the absolute unity of God violated God's essence.[18] As a student of Aristotle's metaphysics, Maimonides maintained that to predicate any division of God is to imply that God is physical, limited, and imperfect, that is, that it is not God at all.[19] For Maimonides, to proclaim 'Hear O Israel, the Lord our God, the Lord is One' is to understand that God is not only one, but an absolutely unique, indivisible, and simple being—and this understanding is incumbent on Jew and non-Jew alike. Hence the Trinitarian object of Christian worship could never be identical with the single Creator of the universe, and was necessarily some foreign concept. Since one of the seven Noahide commandments is the prohibition of *avodah zarah*, Maimonides ruled that Christians were sinful Noahides, and that their religion was illicit.

The other rabbinic opinion was that of Rabbi Menahem Me'iri, in thirteenth- and fourteenth-century Provence. In his commentary on the tractate *Avodah zarah* and elsewhere, Me'iri taught that *avodah zarah* was not primarily

---

[14] See Louis Jacobs, 'Attitudes towards Christianity in the Halakhah', in Z. Falk (ed.), *Gevuroth Haromah: Jewish Studies Offered at the Eightieth Birthday of Rabbi Moses Cyrus Weiler* (Jerusalem, 1987), p. xix.   [15] BT *AZ* 7*b*; Me'iri, *Beit habehirah*, ad loc.

[16] Maimonides on Mishnah, *AZ* 1: 3–4; *Mishneh torah*, 'Laws of Idolatry', 9: 4 (ed. Yosef Kafih (Jerusalem, 1968)).

[17] For further elaboration on this, see Alon Goshen-Gottstein in Chapter 11, below.

[18] Maimonides, *Guide of the Perplexed*, i. 50.

[19] Maimonides, *Mishneh torah*, 'Laws of the Foundations of the Torah', 1: 7.

theological or philosophical, and the negation of God's absolute unity does not *ipso facto* represent a God foreign to Judaism or constitute idolatry.[20] If seen from the perspective of the Bible rather than from that of Aristotelian philosophy, *avodah zarah* is cultic worship whose primary characteristic is the absence of moral demands upon its worshippers. Illicit religion is represented by those religions that do not impose the prohibitions on murder, theft, sexual immorality, and cruelty upon their adherents, that is, they neither insist upon the Noahide commandments nor satisfy the Noahide covenant.[21] Me'iri claimed that while Trinitarian Christianity may violate pure monotheism, it is not *avodah zarah* because it worships the single Creator of heaven and earth and requires Christians to subscribe to the basic moral norms of civilization. Hence Christians fulfil the Noahide covenant, and Christianity is an autonomously valid religious form.

It is crucial to note the impact of experience on these opinions of Jewish law and theology.[22] Maimonides never had any positive first-hand experience of Christians to counteract his philosophical conclusions. Except for his brief stay in crusader Palestine, he did not live with Christians and his understanding of Christianity came exclusively from books. Unlike Maimonides, Me'iri lived in Christian society in an era of relatively good Jewish–Christian relations in the latter part of his life. Me'iri encountered believing Christians as living human beings, discussed religion with Christian priests, and understood that Christians could be moral and religiously sophisticated people.[23] It made no sense to him to categorize them as idolaters, identical to the pagans to which the Bible and the Talmud refer. Also crucial were the demographic and political realities of the medieval Jewish communities in Christian Europe. Historians agree that the pressing communal, economic, and social conditions throughout Germany and France of that period influenced Me'iri's legal opinion—and those of most rabbinic authorities in Ashkenaz—towards Christianity, effecting a more permissive halakhic attitude regarding Jewish contacts with Christians of that period.[24]

Life gave Me'iri what it never gave Maimonides, namely the incentive to

[20] See the recent scholarship of Jacob Katz, *Exclusiveness and Tolerance* (New York, 1962), ch. 10; Moshe Halbertal, *Between Torah and Wisdom* [Bein torah leḥokhmah] (Jerusalem, 2000), ch. 3; id., 'Ones Possessed of Religion: Religious Tolerance in the Teachings of Me'iri', *Edah Journal*, 1/1 (2000), <www.edah.org>.

[21] Me'iri, *Beit habeḥirah* on BT *San.* 57*a*; *AZ* 20*a*.

[22] On this point, see also Adin Steinsaltz, 'Peace without Conciliation: The Irrelevance of "Toleration" in Judaism', *Common Knowledge*, 11/1 (2005), 41–7. The article is discussed at length by Goshen-Gottstein in Chapter 11, below.

[23] Me'iri, *Ḥibur hateshuvah*, ed. A. Schreiber (New York, 1950), 2. I would like to thank Greg Stern for calling my attention to this reference. See also Katz, *Exclusiveness and Tolerance*, 119, 124; Salo Baron, *A Social and Religious History of the Jews* (Philadelphia, 1952–73), ix. 5–11; *Encyclopedia Judaica* (Jerusalem, 1971–72), xiii. 1260–1.

[24] Katz, *Exclusiveness and Tolerance*, 116–17.

rule as a point of Jewish law that Christians did not practise idolatry or 'foreign worship'. Me'iri understood the deep implications of his thesis, going as far as to include Christians in the biblical category of 'brother'.[25] In doing so Me'iri achieved a conceptual transformation of *avodah zarah* within Jewish law, one rich in implications for contemporary Jewish rethinking about Christians and their faith.

In fact, however, neither the ruling of Maimonides regarding Christianity nor the exact view of Me'iri represents normative halakhah. Among other things, Maimonides ruled that a Jew is forbidden to go to, reside in, or even traverse a city where a church is located[26]—a prohibition that no Jew, however scrupulous about adhering to halakhah, honours today. And we will soon see that no other authority accepts Me'iri's opinion regarding the status of a Jewish convert to Christianity. In point of fact, these two authorities represent end points of the spectrum of rabbinic positions, while the majority of halakhic opinions lie within two intermediate categories. The opinions in the first intermediate category maintain that the traditional legal prohibitions regarding Jewish contact with worshippers of *avodah zarah* and the economic halakhic discriminations against those who practise *avodah zarah* do not apply to contact with Christians. This position—that Jewish law does not consider Christians to be worshippers of *avodah zarah*—is held by R. Yosef Karo (sixteenth century, Turkey and Safed)[27] and virtually all the great rabbinic authorities living in European Christian societies (*ḥakhmei ashkenaz*) including Rashi (eleventh century, France),[28] R. Asher Ben Yehiel (Rosh, thirteenth century, Germany),[29] and early modern authorities (Aharonim).[30] These authorities left open the possibility, however, that Christianity might still be *avodah zarah* and forbidden for non-Jews.[31] And they certainly believed that Christianity was wrong for Jews, such that it is incumbent upon a Jew to die rather than to convert to Christianity.

The opinions in the second intermediate category claim that Christians do not practise *avodah zarah* precisely *because* Christianity as a system of belief and worship does not constitute *avodah zarah* for non-Jews. While Christianity is

---

[25] Me'iri, *Beit habeḥirah* on BT *BM* 59*a*.   [26] Maimonides on Mishnah, *AZ* 1: 1–3.

[27] *SA* 'Yoreh de'ah', 148: 2; *Beit yosef*, 'Ḥoshen hamishpat', 266.

[28] Rashi, *Responsa*, ed. Israel Elfenbein (New York, 1943), nos. 55, 155, 327.

[29] Asher ben Yehiel on BT *AZ* 4: 7.

[30] See later authorities, Peri Megadim, Mahatsit Hashekel, and Hatam Sofer, on 'Oraḥ ḥayim', 156; *Minḥat eli'ezer*, i. 53: 3; Samuel Landau, *Noda biyehudah*, no. 148, all of whom rule that non-Jews are obligated to be pure monotheists. On Samuel Landau and *Noda biyehudah*, see n. 41, below.

[31] The legal possibility that Christianity is *avodah zarah*, yet Christians would not be considered practitioners of *avodah zarah*, is based on the opinion of R. Yohanan: 'Gentiles outside the land of Israel are not practitioners of *avodah zarah*, but only follow the traditions of their ancestors' (BT *Ḥul.* 13*b*). Although the precise meaning of this statement is unclear, its legal import is not: non-Jews in the talmudic and post-talmudic eras are not subject to the halakhic restrictions applicable to those practising *avodah zarah*.

not pure monotheism, in fact it represents a valid positive belief in the same one Creator of heaven and earth that Judaism requires Jews to worship. The distinction between one standard of *avodah zarah* for Jews and another for non-Jews is exegetically based on the second commandment of the Decalogue addressed specifically to Jews at Sinai: 'There shall not be *for you* other gods before me' (Exod. 20: 3). According to rabbinic tradition, idolatry had already been prohibited to non-Jews and Noahides in Genesis 2: 16, hence the commandment in Exodus requiring pure monotheism must address Jews uniquely ('for you') and not apply to non-Jews.[32] In addition to Me'iri, this was the halakhic position of medieval authorities (Rishonim) such as R. Ya'akov Ben Meir (Rabbenu Tam, twelfth century, France),[33] R. Me'ir ben Shimon Hame'ili (thirteenth to fourteenth century, France),[34] R. Shimon bar Tsemah Duran (Tashbats, fourteenth century, North Africa),[35] and later rabbinic authorities such as R. Moses Isserles (Rema, sixteenth century, Poland),[36] R. Shabetai Hakohen (Shakh, seventeenth century, Bohemia),[37] R. Moses Rivkis

[32] See R. Joseph Saul Nathanson, *Sho'el umeshiv*, i. 26, 51; Dov Baer ben Judah Treves, *Sefer ravid hazahav*, on Exod. 20: 3. See also Obadiah Yosef, *Yehaveh da'at* 4: 45 (note), who finds textual warrant for this position in the book of Ruth and BT *Yev.* 47b.

[33] A number of scholars believe that this position is more correctly attributed to R. Isaac (Ri), Rabbenu Tam's nephew (see Katz, *Exclusiveness and Tolerance*, 35). Whether it is Rabbenu Tam's or R. Isaac's, it is based on the majority interpretation of BT *San.* 63b, *asur.* See David Novak, *Jewish–Christian Dialogue: A Jewish Justification* (New York, 1989), 42–53. For a comprehensive list of later authoritative rabbinic opinions on this issue, see Moshe Yehudah Miller, 'Regarding the Law that Noahides are not Admonished Against Associationism' (Heb.), in *The Torah of Life* [Torat hayim] (Queens, NY, 2000). For other interpretations that maintain that Rabbenu Tam believed that Christianity remained in the category of *avodah zarah*, see David Berger, *The Rebbe, the Messiah and the Scandal of Orthodox Indifference* (London, 2001), app. 3; J. David Bleich, 'Divine Unity in Maimonides, the Tosafists and Me'iri', in Lenn E. Goodman (ed.), *Neoplatonism and Jewish Thought* (Albany, NY, 1992), 239, who concedes that this variant reading is a minority opinion among later rabbinic authorities. It is important to note that even according to these minority interpretations of the Tosafot (whether Rabbenu Tam or R. Isaac), Christianity differs from the *avodah zarah* of antiquity, since it recognizes as God the one Creator of heaven and earth, whereas classical *avodah zarah* recognized as gods entities wholly different from the Creator. (Berger has termed the former '*avodah zarah* in a monotheistic mode'.) We thus arrive at a paradox: it is precisely these restrictive minority interpretations acknowledging the difference between classical and Christian forms of *avodah zarah* that create the logical opening for not applying to Christianity the halakhic requirement of intolerance towards (classical) *avodah zarah* and its worshippers in the Land of Israel under Jewish sovereignty. Berger correctly sees this logical implication and suggests such a policy (see David Berger, 'Jews, Gentiles, and the Modern Egalitarian Ethos: Some Tentative Thoughts', in Marc Stern (ed.), *Formulating Responses in an Egalitarian Age*, The Orthodox Forum (Lanham, Md., 2005), 101. This also appears to be the position of Isaac Herzog (see 'Minority Rights According to Halakhah' (Heb.), *Tehumin*, 2 (1981), 174 n. 9).

[34] Hame'ili considers Christians to be *gerei toshav* (resident aliens) who observe the prohibitions against *avodah zarah* (*Milhemet mitsvah*, fo. 225a).

[35] Shimon bar Tsemah Duran, *Responsa*, i. 139.

[36] Moses Isserles, *Darkhei mosheh* on *Tur*, 'Orah hayim', 151; id., gloss on *SA* 'Orah hayim' 156: 1. [37] Shabetai Hakohen, gloss on *SA* 'Yoreh de'ah', 151: 4.

(Be'er Hagolah, seventeenth century, Lithuania),[38] R. Ya'ir Baharakh (seventeenth century, Germany),[39] R. Jacob Emden (Ya'avets, eighteenth century, Germany),[40] R. Yehezkel Landau (Noda Biyehudah, eighteenth century, Prague),[41] R. Zvi Hirsch Hayes (nineteenth century, Galicia),[42] R. Avraham Borenstein (Avnei Nezer, nineteenth century, Poland),[43] R. Samson Raphael Hirsch (nineteenth century, Germany),[44] R. David Zvi Hoffman (nineteenth century Germany),[45] and others.[46]

Importantly, many of these later authorities go well beyond asserting that Christianity is not *avodah zarah* and accord positive theological status to Christian belief. Here are the words of R. Rivkis:

The gentiles in whose shadow Jews live and among whom Jews are disbursed are not idolaters. Rather they believe in *creatio ex nihilo* and the Exodus from Egypt and the main principles of faith. Their intention is to the Creator of Heaven and Earth and we are obligated to pray for their welfare.[47]

And R. Emden:

The Nazarene brought a double goodness to the world . . . The Christian eradicated *avodah zarah*, removed idols (from the nations) and obligated them [to follow] the seven *mitsvot* of Noah so that they would not behave like animals of the field, and instilled them firmly with moral traits . . . Christians and Muslims are congregations that (work) for the sake of heaven—(people) who are destined to endure, whose intent is for the sake of heaven and whose reward will not be denied.[48]

[38] Moses Rivkis, gloss on *SA* 'Hoshen hamishpat', 425: 5.

[39] Ya'ir Baharakh, *Havot ya'ir*, nos. 1, 185.

[40] Jacob Emden, *Seder olam rabah vezuta*, 35–7; id., *Sefer hashimush*, 15–17.

[41] Some scholars mistakenly identify Yehezkel Landau with his son, Samuel. The latter explicitly claimed that Christianity is *avodah zarah* for Christians because of its doctrine of the Trinity (*Noda biyehudah*, 'Yoreh de'ah', no. 148). R. Samuel signs his name to this responsum, hence its authorship is certain. I thank Marc Shapiro for pointing this out to me. The father, Yehezkel, had a positive evaluation of Christian belief for Christians: 'Regarding the nations of our day in whose midst we live, they believe in the fundamentals of faith, in creation and in the prophecy of the prophets and all the miracles and wonders that are written in the Torah and the books of the prophets' (Introduction to *Noda biyehudah*, ed. Mehadurah Tinyama (New York, 1960)).

[42] Zvi Hirsch Hayes, *The Works of Maharats Hayet* [He'elot veteshuvot maharats] (Jerusalem, 1948), 66, 489–90.   [43] Avraham Borenstein, *Avnei nezer*, no. 123: 9.

[44] Samson Raphael Hirsch, 'Talmudic Judaism and Society', in *Principles of Education*, Collected Writings of Samson Raphel Hirsch 1 (New York, 1996), 225–7; id., *Nineteen Letters on Judaism*, ed. and annotated Joseph Elias (Jerusalem, 1995).

[45] David Zvi Hoffman, *Der Shulchan-Aruch* (Berlin, 1885); id., *Melamed leho'il*, 'Yoreh de'ah', no. 55.

[46] This is also the explicit or implicit position of Me'ir Leib ben Mikha'el (Malbim), commentary on 2 Kgs 17: 7–9; 41: 32–4; Zvi Hirsch Shapira, *Darkhei teshuvah*, gloss on *SA* 'Yoreh de'ah', 151: 1; Jacob Ettinger, *Binyan tsiyon*, no. 63; Barukh Halevi Epstein, *Torah temimah*, on Exod. 21: 35 and Deut. 22: 3.   [47] Moses Rivkis, gloss on *SA* 'Hoshen hamishpat', 425: 5.

[48] Jacob Emden, *Seder olam rabah vezuta*, 35–7. For a fuller explanation of R. Emden's position, see Harvey Falk, 'Rabbi Jacob Emden's Views on Christianity', *Journal of Ecumenical Studies*, 19/1

The goal of [Christians and Muslims] is to promote Godliness among the nations . . . to make known that there is a ruler in heaven and earth, who governs and monitors and rewards and punishes . . . We should consider Christians and Muslims as instruments for the fulfilment of the prophecy that the knowledge of God will one day spread throughout the earth. Whereas the nations before them worshipped idols, denied God's existence, and thus did not recognize God's power or retribution, the rise of Christianity and Islam served to spread among the nations, to the furthest ends of the earth, the knowledge that there is one God who rules the world, who rewards and punishes and reveals himself to man. Indeed, Christian scholars have not only won acceptance among the nations for the revelation of the Written Torah but have also defended God's Oral Law. For when, in their hostility to the Torah, ruthless persons in their own midst sought to abrogate and uproot the Talmud, others from among them arose to defend it and to repulse the attempts.[49]

And R. Hirsch:

Judaism does not say, 'There is no salvation outside of me.' Although disparaged because of its alleged particularism, the Jewish religion actually teaches that the upright of all peoples are headed towards the highest goal. In particular, they have been at pains to stress that, while in other respects their views and ways of life may differ from those of Judaism, the peoples in whose midst the Jews are now living [i.e. Christians] have accepted the Jewish Bible of the Old Testament as a book of divine revelation. They profess their belief in the God of heaven and earth as proclaimed in the Bible and they acknowledge the sovereignty of divine Providence in both this life and the next. Their acceptance of the practical duties incumbent upon all men by the will of God distinguishes these nations from the heathen and idolatrous nations of the talmudic era.[50]

Before Israel set out on its long journey through the ages and the nations . . . it produced an offshoot [Christianity] that had to become estranged from it in great measure, in order to bring to the world—sunk in idol worship, violence, immorality and the degradation of man—at least the tidings of the One Alone, of the brotherhood of all men, and of man's superiority over the beast. It was to teach the renunciation of the worship of wealth and pleasures, albeit not their use in the service of the One Alone. Together with a later offshoot [Islam] it represented a major step in bringing the world closer to the goal of all history.[51]

In the twentieth century a number of rabbinic authorities did not rule officially on the halakhic status of Christianity for non-Jews or whether

---

(1982), 105–11; Moshe Miller, 'Rabbi Jacob Emden's Attitude Toward Christianity', in M. Shmidman (ed.), *Turim: Studies in Jewish History and Literature* (New York, 2008), ii. 105–136.

[49] Jacob Emden on *Avot* 4: 11.
[50] Samson Raphael Hirsch, *Principles of Education*, 'Talmudic Judaism and Society', 225–7.
[51] Samson Raphael Hirsch, *Nineteen Letters on Judaism*.

Christianity was a positive religious phenomenon.[52] Yet there were other great rabbinic authorities in this century such as Rabbis Yehiel Halevi Epstein (*Arukh hashulḥan*),[53] Abraham Isaac Hakohen Kook,[54] R. Yehiel Jacob Weinberg (*Seridei esh*),[55] Isaac Herzog,[56] Hayim David Halevi,[57] Joseph Messas,[58] and Joseph Eliyahu Henkin[59] who regarded Christianity positively and concluded that it does not constitute *avodah zarah* for non-Jews. Others ruled so implicitly.[60]

Thus an accurate logical map of Jewish legal opinions indicates that nearly all rabbinic authorities living in Christian societies ruled that Christians cannot be identified with the idolaters of antiquity and that the legal prohibitions attaching to biblical and talmudic non-Jews do not apply to contemporary

[52] It appears that the American Orthodox leader Joseph B. Soloveitchik is in this category. I have argued elsewhere ('The Man of Faith and Religious Dialogue') that Soloveitchik's essay 'Confrontation' is a statement of Jewish policy and because it is devoid of any halakhic language and argumentation it lacks halakhic status. Soloveitchik wrote 'Confrontation' before *Nostra aetate* and before the dramatic changes in Christian teachings about Judaism and Jews. In the essay he argued on prudential grounds against Jewish participation in theological debate or dialogue with Christian theologians, but advocated co-operation with Christians in moral, social, and political areas. To my knowledge, he never issued a formal halakhic ruling on the status of Christianity for Christians. From his behaviour, however, he could not have followed Maimonides, who outlawed residing in a city with a church (see Maimonides on Mishnah, *AZ* 1: 3–4). Living in the largely Catholic metropolis of Boston, Soloveitchik delivered his spiritual confession, 'The Lonely Man of Faith', at St John's Catholic seminary in Brighton. There is also anecdotal evidence that while recuperating in a hospital he tried to persuade his secular doctor to return to his Christian faith, something that Maimonides could not have done given his view of Christianity as *avodah zarah* for everyone.

[53] Yehiel Halevi Epstein, *Arukh hashulḥan*, 'Oraḥ ḥayim', 156: 4.

[54] Abraham Isaac Kook accepts Me'iri's position and considers Christians (and Muslims) in the category of resident aliens, who do not practise *avodah zarah* (Abraham Isaac Kook, *Letters of the Ra'ayah* [Igerot hara'ayah] (Jerusalem, 1985), vol. i, no. 89).

[55] Weinberg, who advocated unqualified acceptance of Me'iri's position, considers pious Christians who follow the precepts of Christianity 'to be blessed' (letter to S. Atlas (26 Oct. 1964), cited in Marc B. Shapiro, *Between the Yeshiva World and Modern Orthodoxy: The Life and Works of Rabbi Jehiel Jacob Weinberg, 1884–1966* (London, 1999), 182).

[56] Herzog, 'Rights of Minorities According to Halakhah', 174–5.

[57] Hayim David Halevi, *Make a Teacher for Yourself* [Aseh lekhah rav] (Tel Aviv, 1989), pt. 5, pp. 65–7. For a fuller analysis of Halevi's position on Christianity, see David Ellenson, 'Rabbi Hayim David Halevi on Christianity and Christians', in Franklin T. Harkins (ed.), *Transforming Relations: Essays on Jews and Christians throughout History in Honor of Michael Signer* (Notre Dame, Ind., 2010).

[58] Joseph Messas, *Shemesh umagen*, vol. iii (Jerusalem, 2000); id., *Sefer mayim ḥayim*, vol. ii, §66.

[59] See Berger, 'Jews and Gentiles and the Modern Egalitarian Ethos', 100.

[60] Marc Shapiro also noted that the following permit Jews to contribute to the building of a church, on the assumption that Christian worship is not sinful for gentiles: R. Marcus Horowitz, *Mateh levi*, vol. ii (Frankfurt, 1933), 'Yoreh de'ah', no. 28. See also David Ellenson, 'A Disputed Precedent: The Prague Organ in Nineteenth-Century Central European Legal Literature and Polemics', *Leo Baeck Institute Year Book*, 40 (London, 1995), 251–64; R. Isaac Unna, *Sho'alin vedorshin* (Tel Aviv, 1964), no. 35; R. Yehudah Herzl Henkin, *Benei vanim* (Jerusalem, 1997), vol. iii, no. 36 (Marc Shapiro: 'Of Books and Bans', *Edah Journal*, 3/2 (2003), <http://edah.org>).

Christians. Some Rishonim, namely Me'iri and Rabbenu Tam, and the majority of Aharonim had a more positive view of Christianity itself, ruling that it was a valid religion for non-Jews, but not for Jews. Hence there exists normative halakhic precedent for ruling that Christianity, qua religion, is a valid faith for non-Jews, one that is beneficial to the world and that Jews can appreciate and encourage non-Jews to practise. Given this spectrum of halakhic opinion, the decision to adopt the rabbinic position that regards Christianity negatively or the one that regards it as a positive theological phenomenon will most likely depend on sociological, historical, and ideological considerations that lie outside the domain of formal halakhah. The religious orientation of contemporary Jews towards Christianity is most often dispositional (based on history or memory) or prudential (based on expectation of future consequences).

There is a significant philosophical implication of the second position that demands absolute monotheism of Jews but permits non-absolute monotheism for non-Jews. Because it asserts one definition of 'foreign worship' for Jews that includes associationism, that is, the addition of another thing to the single Creator of heaven and earth, and yet another definition of *avodah zarah* for non-Jews (worship of entities that exclude the one Creator of the universe), the halakhic concept of *avodah zarah* is better understood as a legal standard of unacceptable belief and behaviour rather than as a concept implying a theological truth claim. Logically, ascribing a given property to a specific object is either correct or incorrect; it cannot be different for different people. This is also true for what one predicates of God. Were the legal concept of *avodah zarah* to imply a philosophical truth claim (that is, *avodah zarah* constitutes an ontological error because it misidentifies something that is in fact not divine with God), the criterion for *avodah zarah* would of necessity be universal and undifferentiated for both Jews and non-Jews. But according to most Aharonim, Jewish law *does* rule that the same belief may be 'foreign worship' for Jews when it is not so for non-Jews. Hence *avodah zarah* should be more properly understood as representing that which is beyond the limit of the legally tolerable—a standard that can vary for Jews and non-Jews without entailing any conceptual incoherence.

A simple analogy can help clarify this point: according to Jewish law, eating pork is an act that is forbidden to Jews but permitted to non-Jews. This is possible because the laws of *kashrut* do not refer to any inherent characteristic of pork. They merely lay down behavioural norms. So too, the laws relating to *avodah zarah* relate to norms and do not assert any inherent characteristic of God. This conceptualization of *avodah zarah* is true to the literal meaning of the term, for something can be 'foreign' (i.e. unacceptable) for one person or community, while not so to another. This conclusion has a crucial implication for theological pluralism: if the halakhic category of *avodah zarah* is a legal standard rather than a claim about theological (in)accuracy, then Jewish law does not take an ultimate metaphysical position regarding the nature of God and should be able to coexist with a limited number of contrasting theologies.

Finally, it is important to recognize that although Me'iri is often used as a basis for this second intermediary position, he went beyond it, ruling that Christianity was not *avodah zarah* even for Jews.[61] This aspect of his position is accepted by no other rabbinic authority and therefore plays no role in normative Jewish legal opinion.

Except for Maimonides and Messas, the aforementioned rabbinic authorities encountered Christians within their experience as real human beings, not as stereotypes or abstract legal categories. It is hardly credible that their social, moral, and interpersonal experiences with living Christians did not influence their halakhic and theological opinions. As cited earlier, there is no doubt that economic factors and Jewish commercial interaction with—and dependency on—their Christian neighbours in Ashkenaz also played a significant role in permissive rabbinic judgements towards Christians and Christianity.[62]

If one looks at this map temporally, one can plot four stages in the evolution of Jewish religious thinking about Christianity under different historical circumstances:

1. In the first and second centuries, Jewish Christians came to be regarded as heretics (*minim*) or apostates from Judaism. For Jews to believe in Jesus and the 'new covenant' was considered *avodah zarah*.

2. In the Middle Ages, when Jews lived in small communities in Christian Europe and were dependent on economic interaction with Christians, most Rishonim in Ashkenaz ruled (in accordance with the talmudic opinion of R. Yohanan previously cited) that Christians were not idolaters, but they still considered belief in Christian doctrine to be illegitimate *avodah zarah*.

3. In the late Middle Ages and early modernity, the majority of Aharonim did not consider Christianity to be *avodah zarah* for non-Jews.

4. From the seventeenth century to the twentieth, when Christian toleration of Jews grew,[63] a number of rabbinic authorities began to appreciate Christianity as a positive historical and theological phenomenon for non-Jews that helped spread fundamental beliefs of Judaism (for example, God, revelation, and the Noahide commandments) and thus advanced the Jewish religious purpose.

[61] Me'iri, *Beit habeḥirah* on BT *Hor.* 2 19.   [62] See Katz, *Exclusiveness and Tolerance*, ch. 3.
[63] Katz advances the causal thesis that budding Christian tolerance significantly influenced the development of a positive halakhic attitude towards them by traditionalist Orthodox rabbis of the time: 'The first signs of tolerance towards Jews . . . gave rise to a corresponding attitudes on the part of Jews to Christians' (*Exclusiveness and Tolerance*, 166). It is evident from the statements of Rivkis, Emden, and Ya'ir Baharakh (to which Katz is referring) that this positive attitude referred not only to Christians, but also to Christianity qua religious belief system.

Two points are critical: first, Jewish law regarding Christians and Christianity has undergone an evolution with changing historical circumstances. Second, halakhah and traditional Jewish theology contain the seeds for a limited theological openness by recognizing the possibility of other valid religions and forms of worship. In principle, halakhah allows for a positive view of Christianity (for non-Jews).

Jewish historical experience with Christians cuts both ways, however. In spite of the open halakhic and theological possibilities towards Christianity, many historically oriented Jews have been reluctant to accord Christianity positive value because of the traditional Christian supersessionist teachings about Judaism that spawned virulent *adversus Judaeos* Christian teachings. These teachings (later called the 'Doctrine of Contempt' by Jules Isaacs) denied any continuing theological validity to Judaism and promoted demonic understandings of Jews that were the basis for hateful antisemitic behaviour throughout much of the Middle Ages. Contemporary scholars have uncovered the substantive influence that the *adversus Judaeos* teachings have played in shaping antisemitic attitudes and antisemitic persecution throughout Jewish–Christian history, into modernity and including the Holocaust.[64] And for many Jews up to today—both rabbis and laity alike—the wounds of that suffering are still too fresh to allow for any religious re-evaluation of Christianity and its believers.

CHRISTIANITY AND JUDAISM TODAY

Jews who wish to preserve—or perhaps recreate—pre-Emancipation social conditions and isolate themselves from positive relations with Christians will find refuge in the halakhic attitude of Maimonides and his disciples.[65] Yet after the thicket of legal obstacles is cleared, Jews who have been touched by modernity and who value openness to Western culture, dignified relations with Christians, and appreciation of Christianity's moral and spiritual values can also find ample halakhic justification for their aspirations.

Of course, safeguarding Jewish identity demands limits on interaction with Christians and Christian culture. Without such limits in an open pluralistic society, assimilation is unavoidable and both Jews and Judaism are likely to be absorbed totally by the dominant Christian population and culture. Assuming such limits can be maintained, the salient question today for Jews regarding

[64] Boys, *Has God Only One Blessing?*, ch. 4; James Carroll, *Constantine's Sword* (New York, 2001); Edward Flannery, *The Anguish of the Jews* (New York, 1985); Malcolm Hay, *Europe and the Jews* (Boston, 1960); Jules Isaac, *Jesus and Israel* (New York, 1971); id., *The Teaching of Contempt: Christian Roots of Anti-Semitism* (New York, 1965); Joshua Trachtenberg, *The Devil and the Jews* (New Haven, 1943); Robert Wilken, *John Chrysostom and the Jews* (Portland, Oreg., 2004).

[65] As indicated above, this is a practical impossibility on a consistent basis for one who lives in a city or a culture containing Christians.

Christianity is: 'Is Christianity in the twenty-first century still a physical and theological threat to Jews and Judaism as in the past, or is it now a potential spiritual and political ally?' If the former, attempts at developing a positive appreciation of Christianity may well imperil distinctive Jewish survival; if the latter, then a more open Jewish theology of Christianity is possible—nay, desirable.

In considering this question, we must examine contemporary Christianity in more detail. With the Second Vatican Council's proclamation of *Nostra aetate* in 1965, the Catholic Church formally repudiated antisemitism, first 'deploring' it categorically, and subsequently 'condemning' it in official documents.[66] Later still, Pope John Paul II repeatedly called antisemitism 'a sin against God and humanity'.[67] Moreover, the condemnation of antisemitism is a tenet of every large Protestant church today, whether liberal or conservative.[68] At a time when antisemitism is widespread in the Islamic world and no longer an embarrassment in many secularist radical leftist circles of Europe, official Christian rejection of antisemitism functions as a strong positive force throughout the world.

Nostra aetate also formally rejected the ancient charge of deicide, which was the primary theological basis for so much violence against, and contempt for, the Jewish people. It is important to understand that the document did not 'forgive' the Jews for deicide—it rejected any basis for the charge. Once again, nearly every Protestant denomination has followed suit. Nor did these churches stop at repudiating this noxious doctrine: many have issued profound statements of repentance for their role in antisemitism and the Holocaust.[69]

---

[66] See Commission for Religious Relations with the Jews, *Guidelines and Suggestions for Implementing the Conciliar Declaration, 'Nostra Aetate' (n. 4)* (Vatican City, 1975), preamble; Commission for Religious Relations with the Jews, *Notes on the Correct Way to Present the Jews and Judaism in Preaching and Teaching in the Roman Catholic Church* (Vatican City, 1985), §6.

[67] Papal statements in Fall 1990 and Winter 1991, cited in *Vatican City Pontifical Council on Christian Unity: Information Service*, 75/4 (1994), 172–8; papal address, Hungary (16 Aug. 1991), cited in *Origins*, 21/13 (5 Sept. 1991), 203.

[68] See for instance the denunciation of antisemitism by the World Council of Churches in its first assembly (Amsterdam, 1948) and its third assembly (New Delhi, 1961) or the 1994 statement by the Evangelical Lutheran Church in America which repudiated Martin Luther's antisemitic statements (all statements available at <www.jcrelations.net>; see also Boys, *Has God Only One Blessing?*, 253–5).

[69] See Commission for Religious Relations with the Jews, *We Remember: A Reflection on the Shoah* (Vatican City, 1998); statement of the German Catholic bishops on the fiftieth anniversary of the liberation of Auschwitz (27 Jan. 1995); *Declaration of Repentance by the Roman Catholic Bishops of France* (30 Sept. 1997) (all available at <http://www.jcrelations.net>). During his visit to the Yad Vashem Museum in Jerusalem in March 2000 Pope John Paul II stated: 'God of our fathers, you chose Abraham and his descendants to bring your name to the nations. We are deeply saddened by the behavior of those who in the course of history have caused these children of yours to suffer. Asking forgiveness, we wish to commit ourselves to genuine brotherhood with the people of the covenant.' For Protestant documents, see Boys, *Has God Only One Blessing?*, 256.

The Vatican established diplomatic relations with the State of Israel in 1994, and today virtually every major Protestant church officially recognizes the right of Israel to live in safety and security. After the Holocaust, many Jews today consider Israel and its blessings of sovereignty and effective self-defence capacities to be the best security that Jews have for a future that is more hopeful than the past. Thus widespread Christian recognition of Israel increases the prospects for Jewish safety and security.

Yet part of the Christian picture regarding Israel remains troubling. Mainline Protestant criticism of Israel and hostile liberal church actions such as divestment from companies doing business with Israel are sources of deep concern. Although no government policy anywhere should be immune from moral critique—particularly from religious leaders—Jews of all political orientations cannot ignore the possibility that the vehement and unbalanced Protestant criticisms of Israel are rooted in traditional Christian biases against Jews and Judaism. Because Israel is the public face of the Jewish people today—indeed the 'body' of the Jewish people—unjust attitudes to Israel often indicate a continuing underlying animus to Jews and the Jewish people.

These attitudes are most obvious when Jews possess power and lay claim to national equality. A prime offender is the politically driven school of Palestinian Liberation Theology,[70] which has found its way to the sympathetic ears of many liberal Protestant churches in Europe and America. This thinking leads quickly to replacement theology that substitutes oppressed people (read: Palestinians) for the Jewish people as God's partners in the biblical covenant. Their theology assaults the Jewish covenant, the Bible, and the very legitimacy of Israel and Jewish peoplehood. Jews rightly understand this as a rejection of the recent salutary changes in Christian theology and a reversion to the traditional Christian denial of Judaism that is antisemitic at its core.[71] It is important to note that the Catholic Church has no connection to Palestinian Liberation Theology and little enthusiasm for liberation theology of any kind.

More common are some American national Protestant church positions on the Middle East conflict. While recognizing the right of Israel to exist, they identify nearly exclusively with Palestinian arguments and are so critical of Israeli defensive actions that it is difficult to see any serious concern for the welfare of Israel or individual Israelis. Such unjust criticisms undermine the security of Israel and raise the historical spectre of Christians again striving to render Jews defenceless and celebrating Jewish victimization. Given the violent past, Jews today are particularly vigilant about this possibility. Unlike

[70] See Naim Ateek, *Justice and Only Justice* (Maryknoll, NY, 1989); Mitri Raheb, *I Am a Palestinian Christian* (Minneapolis, 1995).
[71] See Adam Gregerman, 'Old Wine in New Bottles: Liberation Theology and the Israeli–Palestinian Conflict', *Journal of Ecumenical Studies*, 41 (2004), 313–40.

national church leadership, the majority of Christians in America and many in Europe are strongly sympathetic to Israel and reject this hostile view.[72] Yet all Christians need to better understand that national independence is constitutive of Judaism, that it is essential to the Jewish understanding of the Jewish people's biblical covenant with God, that for most Jews Israel is an existential issue rather than a mere political interest, and that serious Christian support for Israeli security is a *sine qua non* for good faith relations with the Jewish people.

Notwithstanding the liberal Christian criticism of Israel, the transformations achieved by official Catholic and Protestant renunciations of antisemitism and anti-Judaism have a significance beyond politics. The Second Vatican Council radically changed the theological posture of the Catholic Church towards the Jewish people, and helped stimulate the change in Protestant theology.[73] Later the Church rejected the old doctrine of hard supersessionism—in which Christianity entirely *replaced* Judaism—by acknowledging the living and autonomous validity of Judaism. (Hence some Christians no longer speak of the 'Old Testament' but of the 'First Testament', 'Hebrew Scriptures', or 'Shared Scriptures' to ensure there is no linguistic implication that the Jewish covenant has fallen into obsolescence and is no longer valid.) Church recognition of Israel also has theological implications: it willy-nilly vitiates the doctrines of the early Church Fathers that the Jewish people lost all rights to their biblical homeland because they rejected Jesus as the messiah and that God decreed that Jews wander throughout Christendom in abject humiliation because Jews bear the curse of Cain as collective punishment for deicide.[74] These early teachings not only provided the basis for historical discrimination against Jews in Christian societies, they also fuelled the polemic against the continuing spiritual integrity of Judaism. They are now both implicitly and explicitly repudiated by most churches. Although it is sometimes stated in nuanced or implicit fashion, some Christian theologians now appear to accept their own double covenant theory, affirming the concurrent validity of the ancient Jewish *berit* alongside the Christian covenant.[75]

[72] See Eugene Korn, *Divestment from Israel, the Liberal Churches, and Jewish Responses: A Strategic Analysis*, Jerusalem Center for Public Affairs, <http://www.JCPA.org/jcpa/JCPA/Templates/ShowPage.asp?DBID=1&LNGID=1&TMID=111&FID=254&PID=0&IID=1421>.

[73] For overviews of the changes in Christian doctrine, see Boys, *Has God Only One Blessing?*; Eugene Fisher and Leon Klenicki (eds.), *In Our Time: The Flowering of Jewish–Catholic Dialogue* (New York, 1990); Eugene Korn, 'The Man of Faith and Theological Dialogue'.

[74] This was understood early by Joseph B. Soloveitchik (see 'Kol Dodi Dofek', in Bernhard H. Rosenberg (ed.), *Theological and Halakhic Responses to the Holocaust* (New York, 1992), 70–1; Korn, 'The Man of Faith and Theological Dialogue', 301).

[75] e.g. Franz Mussner, *Tractate on the Jews: The Significance of Judaism for Christian Faith* (Philadelphia, 1984), 226; Marcus Braybrooke, *Christian–Jewish Dialogue: The Next Steps* (London, 2000); John Pawlikowski, 'Toward a Theology of Religious Diversity', *Journal of*

In 2002 delegates of the United States Conference of Catholic Bishops' Committee on Ecumenical and Interreligious Affairs seemed to acknowledge this explicitly. Basing themselves on earlier papal and Vatican statements, they proclaimed 'a Catholic appreciation of the eternal covenant between God and the Jewish people' and that 'campaigns that target Jews for conversion to Christianity are no longer theologically acceptable in the Catholic Church'.[76]

It is important to note that traditional supersessionist and 'mission to the Jews' doctrines still hold theoretical sway among some influential Christian ecclesiastic officials, causing justified consternation among the Jewish people. *Reflections on Covenant and Mission* caused alarm in some traditional Catholic circles[77] and some conservative Catholics and Evangelicals at the time promptly proclaimed the Catholic authors heretics for their limited theological pluralism. Witness also the 1999 mission statement of the Southern Baptist Board that denied the efficacy of Jewish prayer, and the debate over the proper interpretation of the 2000 Vatican document, *Dominus Iesus*,[78] written by Cardinal Joseph Ratzinger, now Pope Benedict XVI.

The discomfort regarding *Reflections on Covenant and Mission* has apparently continued, for in the summer of 2009 the United States Conference of Bishops felt constrained to issue a formal clarification of some of the document's ambiguities and insist on the continuing obligation of Christians to evangelize to Jews (as well as to all non-Christians), to which a number of prominent Jews representing Jewish organizations responded with serious concern.[79] Despite

Ecumenical Studies, 11 (Winter 1989), 138–53; see also Pawlikowski's excellent overview of these trends in 'Reflections on Covenant and Mission: Forty Years after *Nostra Aetate*', *Crosscurrents*, 56/4 (2007), 70–94.

[76] Consultation of the National Council of Synagogues and the Bishops Committee for Ecumenical and Interreligious Affairs, *Reflections on Covenant and Mission* (12 Aug. 2002), available at <http://www.jcrelations.net/en/?id=966>.

[77] See Avery Dulles, 'Covenant and Mission', *America Magazine*, 187/12 (Oct. 2002), <http://www.americamagazine.org/content/article.cfm?article_id=2550>; see also Korn, 'The Man of Faith and Religious Dialogue', 302–3.

[78] See David Berger, 'On *Dominus Iesus* and the Jews', and the response of Cardinal Walter Kasper, 'The Good Olive Tree', both originally delivered at the seventeenth meeting of the International Catholic–Jewish Liaison Committee, New York (1 May 2001), both printed in *America Magazine*, 195/7 (Sept. 2001) and available at <http://www.americamagazine.org/content/article.cfm?article_id=1034>.

[79] See Committee on Doctrine and Committee on Ecumenical and Interreligious Affairs, 'A Note on Ambiguities Contained in "Reflections on Covenant and Mission" ' (United States Conference of Catholic Bishops, 18 June 2009), available at <http://www.ccjr.us/index.php/dialogika-resources/themes-in-todays-dialogue/conversion/559–usccb-09june18.html>; Committee on Doctrine and Committee on Ecumenical and Interreligious Affairs, 'National Jewish Interfaith Leadership Letter on USCCB "Note on Ambiguities"' available at <http://www.jcrelations.net/en/pdf/covenant09.pdf>. The American bishops later agreed to rescind the statements relating the evangelization of Jews, at least in the context of Jewish–Catholic dialogue.

these dissenting reactions to *Reflections on Covenant and Mission*, it is important to note that today there is no office in the Catholic Church, nor any resources spent, dedicated to converting Jews specifically, nor have efforts towards conversion actually appeared in contemporary Jewish–Catholic dialogue. This is also the case in liberal Protestant churches, but not Evangelical ones.

Notwithstanding these points, it is hard to overestimate the difficulty—and the impressive character—of the changes represented by 'the six Rs'. Every religion with a rich tradition is necessarily conservative, and anyone familiar with orthodox religious systems knows how difficult it is to effect a change in theology and policy. If fundamental principles change at all, it is most often in an evolutionary fashion. However, in slightly more than forty years a revolution has occurred in Christian theology. The transformation is incomplete and its process is continuing, yet it is undeniable that a majority of ecclesiastical authorities have now adopted the 'new teaching' about Judaism and the Jewish people, and that the groundwork has been laid for an end to the spiritual and physical enmity between Christianity and the Jewish people.

A NEW THEOLOGY AND A DIFFERENT FUTURE?

Perhaps more important than the challenge of finding a path for neutral Jewish–Christian theological coexistence is the bolder enquiry of whether there are grounds for a new *theological* relationship and mutual appreciation between the faiths. If an important religious question for Jews before modernity was whether Christians gained legitimacy by fulfilling the obligations of the Noahide covenant, the bolder and more important contemporary Jewish theological challenge is whether Jews can understand Christians and Christianity in a new way. Are there grounds for a new *theological* relationship in which Jews understand Christians as participating in a common covenant with them? And can this new theological relationship function as the foundation for Jews and Christians for forging an active partnership in building a future based on a common religious mission?

On practical grounds, there should be no religious objection to such partnership, for even Maimonides—the harshest rabbinic critic of Christian theology—accorded Christianity a positive instrumental role in history:

There is no human power to comprehend the designs of the Creator of the universe . . . Thus the words of Jesus and of the Ishmaelite [i.e. Mohammed] who came after him were only to prepare the way for the messiah and to repair the whole world [*letaken et ha'olam*] to serve the Lord in unison, for it is written, 'I shall make all the peoples pure of speech, so that they all call upon the name of the Lord and serve him with one heart' [Zeph. 3: 9].[80]

[80] Maimonides, *Mishneh torah*, 'Laws of Kings', 11: 4 (ed. Kafih).

Note that Maimonides' statement claims that Christianity as a historical phenomenon helps fulfil *the Jewish covenantal mission* (however imperfectly) by preparing the world to serve the Lord.[81] The passage implies that Christians and Jews have different roles in the same divine mission in history, rather than being members of totally independent faiths. How Christianity as *avodah zarah* can do this is surely a divine mystery for Maimonides—hence his opening explanatory confession.

On the theological level, closer to our time rabbis Rivkis, Emden, Hirsch, and others were explicit in interpreting Christianity as going well beyond the Noahide requirements since Christianity commits Christians to believe in the Creator of the universe, the veracity of the Sinaitic revelation, and messianic history. In other words, there is an important theological affinity between Christian belief and mission and the Jewish covenantal role in history. To quote once again the clear words of Emden: 'Their goal is to promote Godliness among the nations . . . and to make known that there is a ruler in heaven and earth who governs and monitors and punishes'; and those of Hirsch: 'Israel produced an offshoot [Christianity] to bring to the world . . . the tidings of the One Alone . . . It represented a major step in bringing the world closer to the goal of all history.' Although Christianity and Judaism have critical—and seemingly permanent—differences in their eyes, Christianity has promoted fundamental aspects of Jewish theology and belief.

Catholic and Protestant doctrines have always insisted that Christianity is the extension of the Jewish covenant at Sinai, but this would constitute a radical thesis for Jewish theology. Indeed, it is difficult to see how Jews (or Christians) could logically understand Christians standing at Sinai while not being obligated to observe all the Sinaitic *mitsvot*, without at least part of the Sinai covenant being invalidated or superseded. As obvious illustrations, the Sinaitic Decalogue prohibits making images of God and requires sabbath observance on the seventh day of the week—two commandments that Christianity does not observe.

Yet Christians and Christianity are closer to Judaism in history, mission, and theological content than, for example, any Asian religion that might fulfil the Noahide commandments. It is clear that Christian covenant stands theologically somewhere between Noah and Sinai. According to the traditionalists

---

[81] Nahmanides (13th-century, Spain) concurs with Maimonides on this point. Quoting Maimonides at length, he emphasizes the moral and theological progress that Christianity brought to the nations of the world and distinguishes Christians and Muslims from pre-Christian practitioners of *avodah zarah*. This historical progress is a direct result of Christianity inheriting the religious and moral principles of Torah. In Nahmanides' words, Christians are 'inheritors of Torah' (*Writings of Ramban* [Kitvei haramban], ed. Charles Chavel (Jerusalem, 1969), i. 143–4). Simon Federbush maintains that Nahmanides agrees with those rabbinic authorities who deny that Christianity is *avodah zarah* (*Studies in Judaism* [Ḥikrei yahadut] (Jerusalem, 1965).

Emden and Hirsch, who claim that Christianity helped spread the knowledge of the Creator throughout the world, there are solid grounds for probing the possibility that Christianity has entered into the Jewish covenantal mission that began with Abraham. For numerous Jewish thinkers in medieval and modern times, it is teaching the world about God and his moral law that is precisely the purpose of the Jewish covenant. Maimonides too stressed that teaching the world the knowledge of the one God of heaven and earth was the primary vocation of Abraham,[82] and both Rabbi Obadiah Seforno in fifteenth- and six- teenth-century Renaissance Italy and Rabbi Hirsch in nineteenth-century Germany interpreted the covenantal charge to the Jewish people at Sinai: 'You shall be a nation of priests' (Exod. 19: 6) as an imperative to teach the nations of the world the reality of God.[83] And at the end of the nineteenth century, R. Naftali Zvi Yehudah Berlin (Netsiv) claimed that teaching the truth of God to all the nations of the earth is the ultimate purpose of the Sinaitic revelation. Hence for him, God's covenant at Sinai with the Jewish people is the culmina- tion of God's creation of the world, and the book of Exodus is but a continua- tion of the book of Genesis.[84]

Recent history gives credence to this theological direction. From the second half of the twentieth century until today, the Holocaust has cast an enormous shadow over Western history and philosophy—and it carries sub- stantive theological implications for Jewish theology and covenantal history. It has affected nearly all Jewish religious thinking since 1945 and has stimu- lated some contemporary Jewish thinkers to develop a positive attitude to Christianity. The two foremost post-Holocaust thinkers who argue for accepting Christianity as a positive spiritual force are Abraham Joshua Heschel and Irving Greenberg. In light of the Nazi experience, they contend that it is not merely possible for Judaism and Christianity to co-operate with each other, it is *essential* that they do so. In his ground-breaking essay 'No Religion is an Island',[85] Heschel taught that Judaism and Christianity must now be spiritual bulwarks against a godless world that produced the Final Solution and the abandonment of morality. In the context of secularist and postmodern values, the Judaic and Christian spiritual world-views have more commonality than difference, and it would seem that faithful Jews and

---

[82] Maimonides, *Mishneh torah*, 'Laws of Idolaters', 1: 3; id., *Sefer hamitsvot*, pos. no. 3; id., *Guide of the Perplexed*, iii. 51.

[83] Obadiah Seforno on Exod. 19: 6; Samson Raphael Hirsch on Exod. 19: 6. Because Hirsch believed that the fulfilment of God's covenant by spreading the reality of God throughout the world constituted the *telos* of sacred history, he could claim that Christianity (and Islam) 'repre- sented a major step in bringing the world closer to the goal of all history'.

[84] Naftali Zvi Berlin, *Ha'emek davar*, Introduction to Exodus.

[85] Reprinted in Abraham Joshua Heschel, *Moral Grandeur and Spiritual Audacity*, ed. Susannah Heschel (New York, 1996), 235–50.

Christians are natural partners.[86] Greenberg has gone further still, maintaining that Judaism and Christianity are different dimensions of the same covenant to work for messianic fulfilment and the sanctification of life in human history and culture.[87]

It must be emphasized that although both Heschel and Greenberg accept theological pluralism, each insists that Judaism is true absolutely for Jews and that it is contrary to God's will for Jews to cross the line to Christianity. Conflating their theological pluralism with any philosophical relativism that mocks religious truth or permanent difference is a logical confusion that both distorts and demeans their thought. Heschel even travelled to the Vatican in September 1965 when Church officials were drafting the initial versions of *Nostra aetate* to insist that there be no hint of Jewish conversion in the document. He emotionally professed to Vatican authorities: 'If faced with the choice of baptism or the crematoria of Auschwitz, I would choose Auschwitz.'[88]

Heschel and Greenberg are frequently seen as visionaries who are far ahead of their communities—a polite yet unmistakably dismissive description. Yet it is not difficult to understand why they see common spiritual ground between Judaism and Christianity, possibly intimating a differentiated role in the same covenantal mission, and why there are compelling reasons for Jews and Christians to rethink their theologies regarding the other and move beyond tolerance to become allies at this point in history. Whereas fifty years ago interfaith co-operation was championed primarily by liberals of tepid religious commitment and minimalist theological conviction, today it is theologically oriented people seeking a coherent conception of God in their lives and transcendent meaning in their ethics who stand to benefit most from this new relationship. This is undoubtedly why a significant number of Orthodox Jewish leaders participate in Jewish–Christian dialogue.[89] Despite their profound the-

---

[86] Even the modern Orthodox rabbinic opinion that officially shuns interfaith theological dialogue understands the importance of co-operation with Christians on social, political, and ethical matters: 'Communication among various faith communities is desirable and even essential. We are ready to enter into dialogue on such topics as War and Peace, Poverty, Freedom, Man's Moral Values, The Threat of Secularism, Technology and Human Values, Civil Rights, etc.' (Joseph B. Soloveitchik, Rabbinical Council of America Record for February 1966).

[87] Irving Greenberg, *For the Sake of Heaven and Earth* (Philadelphia, 2004).

[88] Judith Hershcopf, *American Jewish Year Book* (New York, 1965), 128; Reuven Kimelman, 'Rabbis Joseph B. Soloveitchik and Abraham Joshua Heschel on Jewish–Christian Relations', *Modern Judaism*, 24 (2004), 255. Greenberg also rejected relativism and sharply distinguished between them logically (*For the Sake of Heaven and Earth*, 196, 201–3, cited by Jospe in Chapter 3, above, pp. 99–100).

[89] It is noteworthy that individual Orthodox Jews in Israel, Europe, and America comprise a large percentage of those Jews engaged in formal interfaith relations. The Israeli rabbinate has official delegations appointed to hold regular dialogue with the Vatican on political, ethical, scriptural, and religious topics. Also in Israel, the Elijah Institute, headed by the Orthodox academic,

ological differences, traditional Jews and faithful Christians are nearly alone today in Western culture when they assert traditional core moral values.

The 1998 Vatican document *We Remember: A Reflection on the Shoah* indicates this commonality of moral values. The paper asserts that Nazism was a 'neo-pagan' phenomenon, suggesting that neither faithful Christians nor the Catholic faith ('the Church as such') bore direct responsibility for Nazi evil. This is simply wrong. Though Hitler, Himmler, Hess, and other high Nazi officials were baptized Catholics, they were not Christians in any meaningful sense. Yet most of the people who operated the crematoria of Birkenau and implemented the grisly Final Solution were believing Christians. Moreover, the scholarship referred to earlier has demonstrated that traditional Christian anti-Judaic teachings were a substantive factor in the popular Christian acceptance of the Nazi extermination of Jews.

We Remember was correct, however, in stating that Nazism is fundamentally anti-Christian. Nazism violated in the most heinous way the sanctity of human life and rejected the fundamental biblical axiom accepted by Judaism and Christianity alike—that there exists a transcendent God who has authority over human beings. Proclaiming that human power was the ultimate value, Nazism substituted the imperative, 'Murder', for the biblical commandment, 'Thou shall not murder.' This philosophy is the absolute antithesis of both Jewish and Christian ethics and an axiomatic denial of the world-views of both those spiritual traditions. Had Hitler succeeded in completing the destruction of the Jewish people, he would have gone after Christianity and its leadership.[90] This must be so, because just as there was no way for Nazism to triumph while Jews existed to give testimony to the authority of God and his covenantal ethics, there was no way for Nazism to coexist for any length of time with the deepest spiritual teachings of Christianity.

This common moral axiom of Judaism and Christianity is crucial today

Alon Goshen-Gottstein, and the Hartman Institute, headed by Orthodox rabbis David Hartman and Donniel Hartman, have active programmes in interfaith dialogue. Most recently, R. Shlomo Riskin, chief rabbi of Efrat, has launched the Center for Jewish–Christian Understanding and Co-operation, which is designed to promote Judaeo-Christian values and interfaith theological enquiry. In Europe, the United Kingdom's chief rabbi, Jonathan Sacks, has spoken often to the Church of England, and France's former chief (Orthodox) rabbi, René Sirat, has long been a significant participant in Jewish–Christian dialogue. R. David Rosen is past chairman of the International Jewish Commission on Interreligious Consultations (IJCIC) and Director of Interfaith Affairs, American Jewish Committee. In America, the Orthodox academic Alan Brill has a chair in Jewish–Christian relations at Seton Hall University and I am the American Director of the previously mentioned Center for Jewish–Christian Understanding and Cooperation as well as the director of its Institute for Theological Inquiry.

[90] Recent scholarship has confirmed this theoretical conclusion (see 'The Nuremberg Project', *Rutgers Journal of Law and Religion* (2002), which reports that documents from Nuremberg trials indicate Nazi plans to destroy Christianity, available at <http://www.unexplained-mysteries. com/forum/index.php?showtopic=181116>).

because postmodern secularism has given birth to a pervasive liberal value-orientation whose foundations contain seeds from which destructive forces can again grow. Hedonism drives much of the contemporary ethos. Violence saturates our media and popular culture, sometimes appearing as merely another justified form of pleasure. This contributes to the evisceration of moral concern and the numbing of individual conscience, both essential to securing the values of human welfare and dignity. Moral utilitarianism has also made a comeback in contemporary academia and the high culture of today. In this ethic human life no longer has intrinsic value and individual human life often becomes a mere commodity to be traded and sometimes discarded. This moral philosophy shares the Nazi denial of the Judaeo-Christian ethics that insists that all persons are created in God's image, and hence that each human life possesses infinite sacred value.

Relativism has become one of the most accepted moral theories in our time. Objectivity and moral absolutes are under ferocious attack and are now on the cultural defensive. This implies that there is no objective bar by which to measure human actions, and this easily slips into the belief that there is no bar at all for valid moral judgement. It is but a small step from this conclusion to the denial of ethics entirely. In the political theatre, an aggressive and imperial Islamist monism has emerged as a common threat to Judaism and Christianity. It denies Jewish and Christian legitimacy in the Middle East and by implication tolerance of all religious diversity—even within Islam itself. Finally, irrational religious extremism has become a potent force in both world politics and religious identity. Although the twenty-first century is but quite young, it has already seen too much violence and mass slaughter committed in the name of faith. All these phenomena constitute frightening dangers and are a call to joint action by Christians and Jews, for the Holocaust has taught us that when ethical values do not assume primary importance in human culture, radical evil results.

Can the future between Jews and Christians be better than their painful past? Does Judaism contain the seeds of a theology sympathetic to Christianity, where Christians play a complementary role to the Jewish people as part of God's covenant with Abraham? Will Jews have the courage to nurture, teach, and live this theology? Critical theological differences exist between Judaism and Christianity, yet both faiths demand belief in messianic history, obligating Jews and Christians to trust in the ultimate moral progress of humanity. Each of those religions teaches that their faithful have a common divine task to make the world a better place, where each person possesses sacred value because every person is created in the image of God, where moral values are real, where there is a spiritual centre to the universe, and where every human life is endowed with meaning.

This ideal of moral perfection and religious tolerance is the stunning vision of the prophet Micah:

Come, let us go up to the mountain of the Lord, to the temple of the God of Jacob. He will teach us his ways, so that we may walk in his paths. The law will go out from Zion, the word of the Lord from Jerusalem. He will judge between many peoples and will settle disputes for strong nations far and wide. They will beat their swords into plowshares and their spears into pruning hooks. Nation will not take up sword against nation, nor will they train for war anymore. Everyone will sit under their own vine and under their own fig tree, and no one will make them afraid, for the Lord Almighty has spoken. All the nations may walk in the name of their gods, but we will walk in the name of the Lord our God for ever and ever. (Mic. 4: 2–5)

This is the fulfilment of the Jewish covenantal mission and the messianic goal of sacred human history, the repaired world to which Maimonides refers when speaking about Christianity and Islam. For Micah it was indeed possible—perhaps desirable—for different peoples to call God by different names and worship the same Creator of heaven and earth in different modes.

Maimonides offers a fuller messianic vision at the end of his magisterial code of Jewish law, *Mishneh torah*:

At that time, there will be neither hunger, nor war; neither will there be jealousy, nor strife. Blessings will be abundant and comfort within the reach of all. The single pre-occupation of the entire world will be to know the Lord. Therefore there will be wise persons who know mysterious and profound things and will attain an understanding of the Creator to the utmost capacity of the human mind, as it is written, 'The earth will be filled with the knowledge of God, as the waters cover the sea' [Isa. 11: 9].[91]

Dare Jews and Christians believe that they can overcome the historical enmity in favour of mutual theological appreciation and religious harmony? If Jews and Christians can become spiritual and physical partners after nearly 2,000 years of religious enmity and physical violence, then peace is possible between any two peoples. That distant possibility is the very stuff of which the messianic dream is made.

---

[91] Maimonides, *Mishneh torah*, 'Laws of Kings', 12: 5 (according to the Yemenite manuscript). Most printed texts include the word 'Israel' to qualify those who will attain ultimate knowledge of the divine. This qualification is inconsistent with earlier manuscripts (see *Mishneh Torah*, ed. Shabse Frankel (New York, 1998)). It is also inconsistent with the earlier emphasis on the universal nature of messianic blessing: 'The single preoccupation of the entire world' (Menachem Kellner, '*Farteitsht un Farbessert*: Comments on Tendentious "Corrections" to Maimonidean Texts', in B. Ish-Shalom (ed.), *In the Paths of Peace: Topics in Jewish Thought in Honor of Shalom Rosenberg* [Bedarkhei shalom: iyunim behagut yehudit mugashim leshalom rosenberg] (Jerusalem, 2006), 255–63; Eng trans.: Joel Linsider and Menachem Kellner, '*Farteicht un Farbeserrert* (On Correcting Maimonides)', *Meorot*, 6/2 (2007), <www.yctorah.org/content/view/330/10/>).

NINE

Maimonides' Treatment of Christianity and its Normative Implications

DAVID NOVAK

THE QUESTION OF OTHER RELIGIONS

SINCE JEWS inevitably interact with adherents of other religions, it is inevitable that halakhists (experts in Jewish law) have had to judge what Jews are required to do in their various dealings with those adherents of other religions. Halakhists have also had to judge whether or not the adherents of these other religions are practising what Judaism teaches ought or ought not to be practised by all human beings. In fact, whether other religions teach their adherents to live up to these standards largely determines the way halakhists judge how Jews should treat adherents of those religions. In this essay I examine how Maimonides advocates that Jews should treat Christians. Since Maimonides is the most theological of all the halakhists and the one most interested in the ideas that underlie religious praxis, I will also examine how informed he is about the ideas underlying the non-Jewish practices he approves or disapproves of.[1]

To understand how Maimonides judges Christianity and the normative implications of that judgement, we need to ask some basic questions. These initial questions, though, must be asked about any religion other than Judaism, since Christianity is neither the only other religion Jews have had to deal with, nor is it even the first of those other religions. Thus Maimonides' rulings about Christianity always deal with it in comparison to Islam and to 'paganism' (which Maimonides seems to think is all of a piece). Islam and Christianity are, for Maimonides, the two other rival religions his contemporary Jews must still take seriously, just as paganism was the rival religion Jews had to take seriously before the rise of either Christianity or Islam, even if paganism per se is no longer encountered by Jews. And we shall see in due course that the question

---

[1] Earlier discussions of Maimonides on Christianity are found in David Novak, *Jewish–Christian Dialogue* (New York, 1989), 57–72; id., 'Maimonides on Judaism and Other Religions', Samuel H. Goldenson Lecture at the Hebrew Union College–Jewish Institute of Religion in Cincinnati, Ohio (23 Feb. 1997).

of whether paganism is still present in Christianity or Islam is of great concern to Maimonides when differentiating between these two other religions and their adherents. It makes all the difference in the world to Jews whether another religion is 'pagan' or not. All paganism, whether involving the worship of a plurality of gods (polytheism) or the use of images in worship (idolatry), is to be combated in every way.[2] But are all non-Jewish religions polytheistic and are all their adherents idolaters?

Let us now ask these most general questions to guide our reading of Maimonides on Christianity as a praxis and its normative implications for Jewish praxis, even for Jewish praxis today. For Maimonides, the correlation of praxis and theory, of law and theology, is of greater import than it is for nearly every other Jewish thinker.

How are other religions different from Judaism? Although it seems obvious that different theologies will entail different religious practices, does a different theology necessarily lead not only to religious practices that are different from those of Judaism, but also to practices that Jewish law teaches are prohibited to all human beings? If the practices of another religion are only different from those of Judaism, then there is no reason why Jewish law should have any objections to non-Jews practising them and to Jews having dealings with the non-Jews who practise them. If so, Jewish law should only prohibit Jews from engaging in explicitly non-Jewish practices (even if virtually identical with normative Jewish practices), because for Jews to do so would compromise the univocal covenantal relationship that they have with God. That relationship would still be compromised even if the adherents of a merely different religion in fact worship the same God the Jews worship, even though they are not doing anything Judaism prohibits either Jews or non-Jews to do. Of course, that univocal covenantal relationship of the Jews with God would be compromised even more if the adherents of another religion in fact worship a different God from the God the Jews worship, the God whom Judaism insists must be universally worshipped, or at least not be replaced by something less divine, by some 'other god'.

Indeed, recognizing this difference in non-Jewish religions might explain the ambiguity of the rabbinic term *avodah zarah*, which literally means 'strange worship'. What is *strange* about it, and for whom is it *strange*, that is, to be avoided? Thus in what might be considered the strong sense of *avodah zarah*, the strangeness of the worship is because of the strangeness of its object: it is worship of a 'strange god' (*el zar*).[3] But in the weaker sense of *avodah zarah*, the

---

[2] See Maimonides, *Mishneh torah*, 'Laws of Idolatry', 2: 2–3 (re: BT *Hor.* 8*a* (re: Num. 15: 22)); *Sifrei* on Num. 15: 31; Maimonides, *Guide of the Perplexed*, i. 36, iii. 37, iii. 41 (re: Num. 15: 30); iii. 49; see also BT *Git.* 88*b*; *Mekhilta* on Exod. 21: 1; Maimonides, *Mishneh torah*, 'Laws of the Courts', 26: 7.   [3] See e.g. Ps. 81: 10.

strangeness of the worship is not because of its object; it is because of its method.[4] It might well be worship of the same God as the Jews worship, but that worship is still proscribed to Jews. Now all the adherents of any non-Jewish religion are 'practising strange worship' (*ovdei avodah zarah*) in the weak sense, which rules out any Jewish practice of their religious rites. But the question is whether some of these religious non-Jews are also worshippers of a 'strange god' even when they claim otherwise—that is, when they claim to worship the universal God first proclaimed by Judaism, the God who is still, minimally, worshipped by the Jews. Needless to say, weak *avodah zarah* poses fewer and easier problems to Jews who encounter it than does strong *avodah zarah*.[5] Finally, if an adherent of a non-Jewish religion wants to practise some aspect of Jewish religious praxis, should Jewish religious authorities prohibit it, permit it, or encourage it? Is that *avodah zarah* or not?[6]

Let us now direct these questions to Maimonides, as we encounter his halakhic rulings in the writings he has bequeathed to us.

[4] For this difference, see Mishnah *San.* 5: 1.

[5] The rabbinic term *avodah zarah* might have come from the scriptural description of the sin of Nadav and Avihu, the two sons of Aaron the high priest who, on the day of the dedication of the wilderness sanctuary, 'brought before the Lord strange fire [*esh zarah*] which he had not commanded them' (Lev. 10: 1). The *esh* here refers to *what* they did and *how* they did it that brought about their immediate death (Lev. 10: 2), even though we are not sure exactly *what* they did wrong or *how* they did it (see *Sifra* on Lev. 10: 1); see also BT *San.* 84*a* (re: Num. 18: 7) (the opinion of R. Yishma'el); Tosefta *Zev.* 12: 17; Rashi on Num. 1: 51. Thus, one who is not a *kohen* (priest), who performs a priestly rite, is called a *zar* (see BT *Shab.* 31*a* (re: Num. 1: 51); also BT *Arakh.* 11*b* (re: Num. 3: 38)); and a non-Jew who performs a sacrificial rite prescribed for Jews alone is called a 'stranger' (*ben nekhar*—see BT *Pes.* 3*b* (re: Exod. 12: 43)). Both of these imposters are subject to the death penalty (whether at the hands of God or man), because of *who* they are, not because of *what* they did. Furthermore, a Jew who worships the one God in a (non-idolatrous) non-Jewish manner is only guilty of violating the negative commandment, 'in their statutes you shall not go' (Lev. 18: 3; see *Sifra*, ad loc.; BT *San.* 52*b*; Tosafot, ad. loc., *ela*). Hence such a person is not liable for the death penalty (see Maimonides, *Sefer hamitsvot*, neg. no. 30). All of the above could be considered *avodah zarah* in the weaker sense, viz. the subject of the act is inappropriate, but not the act per se or the object of the act. This kind of *avodah zarah* is like that mentioned in the Talmud's discussion of the traditional admonition: 'One should always rent oneself out to *avodah zarah* rather than become economically dependent on human beings' (BT *BB* 110*a*), where the Talmud assumes that this cannot be taken to mean literal (*mamash*) idolatry, but rather that one should do work (*avodah*) that is foreign to oneself (*shezarah lo*), that is, beneath one's dignity, and not have to become dependent on others. Here, the work or 'service' is not alien (*zarah*) per se, but is only alien in relation to the 'foreigner' doing it.

[6] Maimonides generalizes from the prohibition of a non-Jew keeping the sabbath and prohibits any non-Jewish practice of commandments prescribed to Jews if this is his own 'religious innovation' (*Mishneh torah*, 'Laws of Kings', 10: 9). However, there are commandments prescribed to Jews that non-Jews may practise for the sake of the reward they think Jews get for practising them (see *Mishneh torah*, 'Laws of Kings', 10: 10; for the difficulty in making this distinction, though see the note of David ibn Zimra (Radbaz) thereon).

POLITICAL AND ECONOMIC QUESTIONS

In his earliest halakhic work, his Commentary on the Mishnah tractate *Avodah zarah*, dealing with the restrictions on Jewish interaction with 'idolaters', Maimonides writes:

Know that this Christian nation, who advocate the messianic claim, in all their various sects, all of them are idolaters. On all their festivals it is forbidden to engage in commerce with them. All Torah proscriptions pertaining to idolaters pertain to them. Sunday is one of their religious festivals; therefore it is forbidden to deal with believers in 'the messiah' on Sunday at all in any manner whatsoever; rather we treat them as we would treat all other idolaters on their festival.[7]

Shortly thereafter, Maimonides extends the prohibition of dealings with Christians even further:

Therefore, one must know that any one of the cities of Christendom that has a place of worship [*bamah*], namely, a church, which is no doubt a house of idolatry: through that city one must not intentionally pass, let alone dwell there. But the Lord has turned us over into their hands so that we have to sojourn in their cities against our will in order to fulfil Scripture's prediction: 'You will serve other gods that are the work of human hands, wood and stone' [Deut. 4: 28]. If this is the law pertaining to the city, all the more so does it apply to the house of idolatry itself, which is minimally forbidden to be looked at, let alone to be approached, all the more so to actually enter it.[8]

These two passages clearly express Maimonides' early extremely negative view of Christianity. But is it so negative because Christians believe in a messiah Jews judge to have been a messianic pretender, or is it because Christians have made images of this messianic pretender and employ them in their worship, along with images of his mother and his disciples (the saints)? And even if Christians would argue that these images (whether three-dimensional as in the Western Church or two-dimensional as in the Eastern Church) are not the objects of worship themselves but merely aids to worship of the unseen Creator God, nonetheless Maimonides seems to rule that just as Jews may not have anything to do with images (even when not praying before these images) because of their idolatrous connotations, so must non-Jews not do so.[9] In other words, unlike most other halakhists, he is no more lenient with non-Jewish idolatry than he is with Jewish idolatry.

It seems, moreover, that Maimonides was aware of the fact that the images of Jesus in churches are not images of a purely human messiah, but that they

---

[7] Maimonides on Mishnah, *AZ* 1: 3.   [8] Ibid. 1: 4.

[9] See Maimonides, *Mishneh torah*, 'Laws of Idolatry', 2: 2 (re: BT *Shab.* 149*a*; cf. *AZ* 50*a*); 3: 10 (re: BT *RH* 24*a*).

are images of Jesus as the Christ, whom Christians believe is the bodily incarnation of the second person of the Trinity. Indeed, the second person of the Trinity is the only person of the Trinity who can be depicted inasmuch as he is the only person of the Trinity whom Christians believe has become incarnate or 'embodied'. (It is clear that neither the first person of the Trinity, whom Christians call 'the Father', nor the third person of the Trinity, whom Christians call 'the Holy Spirit', is incarnate. Hence neither of them could be depicted, in human or other form.) Thus for Maimonides, it is incarnationalism that underlies Christian idolatry, which suggests that he knew that the doctrine of the Incarnation is presupposed by the doctrine of the Trinity and that, in fact, it is the most basic of all Christian doctrines. (Thus the schism in 1000 CE of the Eastern and Western churches involved disputes over the nature of the Trinity rather than any dispute over the nature of the Incarnation.) Nevertheless, even if Christians do not literally worship an 'other god', their compromised monotheism is enough for Maimonides to designate it as *avodah zarah*. As such, it would seem that he would surely rule (he did not have to rule, himself, since he did not live or have authority in a Christian society) that if faced with the choice of converting to Christianity or death, one should chooses a martyr's death (*kidush hashem*).[10]

In his great encyclopaedic code of Jewish law, *Mishneh torah*, Maimonides reiterates his negative judgement of Christianity as idolatrous praxis, but without giving the reasons he gave in his earlier work. In a key passage in *Mishneh torah* (which contains the most sustained and systematic discussion of idolatry written by any halakhist ever), in dealing with the question of the use by Jews of wines made by non-Jews, Maimonides makes the following differentiation:

The resident alien, namely, one who has accepted the seven Noahide laws, as we have already explained: his wine is forbidden to drink, but it is permitted to derive monetary benefit from it . . . Such is the case with all the gentiles who are not idolaters,

---

[10] See Maimonides, *Mishneh torah*, 'Laws of the Foundations of the Torah', 5: 4; id., *Sefer hamitsvot*, neg. no. 5. In his Epistle on Apostasy, Maimonides rules that if one is presented with the choice of converting to Islam or death, one may convert to Islam, because that involves only a verbal affirmation (what the Muslims call *shahada*) of the supremacy of the prophecy/teaching of Muhammad (thus entailing the rejection of the supremacy of the Mosaic Torah) (see Maimonides, 'Epistle on Apostasy', in *Letters of Maimonides* [Igerot harambam], ed. I. Sheilat (Jerusalem, 1987), i. 53–5 (re: BT *San.* 74*a*–*b*)). Although Maimonides does not mention conversion to Christianity here, one could infer from this that forced conversion to Christianity is different, since it involves an *act*, baptism, as well as the fact that new converts to Christianity soon have to participate in the communion rituals like all other Christians. Furthermore, Maimonides' decision here may have also been influenced by his view that unlike Christianity, Islam is as monotheistic as Judaism: later Sephardi authorities were less lenient (see R. Yom Tov ben Abraham Ishbili, *Hidushei haritva*, on BT *Pes.* 25*b*; R. David ibn Zimra, *She'elot uteshuvot haradbaz*, vol. vi, no. 1163).

like these Muslims . . . so rule all the post-talmudic authorities. But even from the non-sacramental wine [*setam yeinam*] of idolaters, it is forbidden to derive monetary benefit.[11]

This judgement of Maimonides about the use of non-Jewish wine has considerable talmudic background. In the Talmud, Jewish use of non-Jewish wine involves two separate acts: (1) a Jew personally drinking the wine and (2) a Jew buying and selling the wine. Whereas no authority permits a Jew to drink any non-Jewish wine, it is an open question whether all non-Jewish wine is off limits for Jewish commercial dealings. That is because the Talmud presents two reasons for the general prohibition of non-Jewish wine.[12] The first is that it is assumed that when non-Jews handle wine, even wine belonging to Jews, they dedicate that wine to one of their gods (*yein nesekh*), and thus a Jew is not to benefit from it in any way.[13] As such, it falls into the category of those idolatrous accoutrements from which no Jew is to benefit, let alone personally use or imbibe.[14] However, when it is not known for sure that the wine has been so dedicated, it is 'just wine' (*setam yayin*) and a Jew may derive monetary benefit from it, while still being prohibited from actually drinking it.[15] The second talmudic reason is that drinking wine with non-Jews will break down social barriers and create a familiarity that could easily lead to intermarriage.[16] From this second reason, it would seem that Jews are permitted to be involved with non-Jews in the wine business, as they are permitted to be involved with non-Jews in other commercial ventures. Buying and selling wine does not necessarily lead to more intimate relations.

Whereas the first reason for prohibiting non-Jewish wine would apply to those non-Jews whose religion has been judged to be idolatrous, the second reason would not apply to those non-Jews whose religion has been judged to be a proper monotheism, that is, having no theology implying polytheism and no practices seen as idolatrous. This is the talmudic basis of Maimonides' stricter judgement of Jewish use of Christian wine than of Jewish use of Muslim wine.[17] (Of course, the irony here is that there is no official 'Muslim

---

[11] Maimonides, *Mishneh torah*, 'Laws of Forbidden Foods', 11: 7; see David Novak, 'The Treatment of Islam and Muslims in the Legal Writings of Maimonides', in W. M. Brinner and S. D. Ricks (eds.), *Studies in Islamic and Judaic Traditions* (Atlanta, 1986), 233–50.

[12] See David Novak, *Law and Theology in Judaism* (New York, 1976), ii. 174–83.

[13] Dan. 1: 8; Mishnah, *San.* 7: 6; JT *Git.* 52b–53a; BT *Ḥul.* 13a.   [14] Mishnah, *AZ* 2: 3–4.

[15] BT *AZ* 74a; Maimonides, *Mishneh torah*, 'Laws of Forbidden Foods', 16: 29; see BT *Ḥul.* 4b.

[16] BT *AZ* 36b; see BT *Shab.* 17b; Tosafot, ad loc., *al.*

[17] Maimonides' contemporary, Rabbenu Tam (d. 1171), the leading Ashkenazi halakhist of his time, was much more lenient regarding commerce with non-Jews, whether on their holy days (including every Sunday) or involving their wine. His reasons for such leniency were both theological and pragmatic. Theologically, he argued that Christianity is monotheistic and neither polytheistic nor idolatrous (see Tosafot on BT *San.* 63b, *asur*; on BT *AZ* 2a, *asur*). Pragmatically, he argued that such leniency was necessary for Jewish economic survival in a Christian society

wine', since the Quran prohibits Muslims from being involved with wine altogether. However, it is well known that individual Muslims have ignored this prohibition throughout history.[18])

Maimonides' invocation of rabbinic teaching about the resident alien (*ger toshav*) and the Noahide commandments (*mitsvot benei no'aḥ*) is very important in this context. These two ideas are interrelated in rabbinic teaching, according to which certain commandments are binding on all human beings. As such, these commandments were by no means abrogated when the Jews were given the Torah at Mount Sinai; instead, they were placed intact into the Mosaic Torah as its cornerstone.[19]

The first of these commandments is the prohibition of *avodah zarah*, proscribing the worship of anyone but the one God upon whom the existence of everyone and everything in the universe is contingent.[20] In addition, according to the rabbis in the Land of Israel during the First Temple (before 586 BCE), any non-Jew who wanted to become a permanent resident there with the definite rights and duties of a second-class citizen had to publicly abjure certain unacceptable non-Jewish practices.[21] While there is some debate among the rabbis as to how many of these practices are to be abjured, all agree that it at least involves abjuring *avodah zarah* in the strong sense. For Maimonides, the prohibition of *avodah zarah* is the first of what came to be known as the 'seven commandments (*sheva mitsvot*) of the descendants of Noah', who after the Flood comprise all humankind.[22] Thus any law-abiding Noahide has, minimally, abjured *avodah zarah*. Moreover, even though the political institution of the resident alien requires full Jewish sovereignty in the Land of Israel and has thus not been in actual force for many centuries, Maimonides applies the idea of the *ger toshav* as someone who has publicly accepted the Noahide prohibition of *avodah zarah* to the adherents of a religion that, to his mind, has fully

---

(northern France and the Rhineland) (see Tosafot on BT *Bekh. 2b, shema* (re: BT *AZ 6b*)). For the historical background of this general approach to Christianity, see Jacob Katz, *Exclusiveness and Tolerance* (Oxford, 1961), 24–36; and for a more detailed look at this approach to the question of non-Jewish wine, see H. Soloveitchik, *Their Wine: Trade in Non-Jewish Wine—On the Evolution of Halakhah in the Practical Realm* [Yeinam: saḥar beyeinam shel goyim—al gilgulah shel halakhah be'olam hama'aseh] (Tel Aviv, 2003).

[18] See Quran 2: 220, 5: 91.

[19] See David Novak, *The Image of the Non-Jew in Judaism: The Idea of Noahide Law*, 2nd edn. (Oxford, 2011), 153–75.

[20] See BT *San. 56b* (re: Gen. 2: 16) (the opinion of R. Yitshak); see also BT *Mak. 23b–24a* (re: Exod. 20: 2–3); Maimonides, *Sefer hamitsvot*, pos. no. 1; id., *Mishneh torah*, 'Laws of the Foundations of the Torah', 1: 1–6; id., *Guide of the Perplexed*, ii. 33 (re: Exod. 20: 2–3); cf. BT *San. 56b* (re: Gen. 2: 16) (the opinion of R. Yohanan).

[21] BT *AZ 64b; Arakh. 29a*; see Maimonides, *Mishneh torah*, 'Laws of Forbidden Relations', 14: 8; 'Laws of the Sabbatical Year', 10: 9; see also 'Laws of God's Chosen House', 7: 14.

[22] Maimonides, *Mishneh torah*, 'Laws of Kings', 9: 1.

renounced *avodah zarah* in public.[23] Thus the idea of the *ger toshav* became the criterion by which to judge whether a non-Jewish religion is sufficiently monotheistic or not, and then from which one can draw the appropriate normative conclusions. As we have just seen, that becomes the practical judgement on such matters as Jewish domicile in a particular non-Jewish society and Jewish use of wine in whose production and sale the adherents of a particular non-Jewish religion are involved. Moreover, as someone who thought that theory entails praxis rather than theory presupposing praxis, Maimonides' judgements regarding what Jews may and may not do with Christians in these areas of human interaction seem to reflect his theoretical understanding of what in any non-Jewish theology has led to any objectionable religious or moral practices.[24]

However, the normative implications today of the texts we have just examined from Maimonides' Commentary on the Mishnah and *Mishneh torah* are less far-reaching than they were in his own time. His insistence that whenever possible Jews should avoid living in cities dominated by churches is hardly a problem any more. Even contemporary diaspora societies where Jews live as a minority, including the United States where Christians comprise a majority of the population, are no longer officially Christian. They are decidedly secular both in principle and in fact. Surely, when Maimonides spoke of a city having a church, he meant more than the presence of the building of a particular religious community. (There must have been Coptic and maybe Ethiopic Christian churches where Maimonides lived in Muslim Egypt, but like the synagogues there they were the places of worship of tolerated minorities which, in fact, had to be far less conspicuous than the mosques, which represented the official Islam of that society.) Instead, Maimonides meant the presence there of the Church, a city that derives its very legitimacy from the Church, where the prominence of its edifices was a constant reminder of

[23] Maimonides writes: 'anyone who accepts them [the Noahide commandments] is called a *ger toshav* wherever [*bekhol makom*], and he must accept them for himself in the presence of three rabbinical judges [*ḥaverim*]' (*Mishneh torah*, 'Laws of Kings', 8: 10). Nevertheless, the fact that Maimonides applies this category to (universal) law-abiding non-Jews, even when there is no Jewish sovereignty and no legal authority in the Land of Israel to politically accept them on behalf of the Jewish people, thus designating them to be 'like a *ger toshav*' (e.g. *Mishneh torah*, 'Laws of Circumcision', 1: 6; 'Laws of the Sabbath', 20: 14), would seem to indicate that he saw some of the privileges afforded a *ger toshav* in ancient times to still be those of any law-abiding Noahide. Therefore, acceptance of the Noahide commandments before a Jewish court under conditions of full Jewish sovereignty in the Land of Israel is not a *conditio sine qua non* for a true Noahide getting at least some of the privileges of a real *ger toshav* (see R. Joseph Karo, *Kesef mishneh* on *Mishneh torah*, 'Laws of Idolatry', 10: 6; *Migdal oz* on *Mishneh torah*, 'Laws of Forbidden Relations', 14: 8—both of whom were answering the specific criticisms made by R. Abraham ben David (Ra'avad) against Maimonides' treatment of the institution of the *ger toshav*).

[24] See Maimonides on Mishnah *AZ* 4: 7; *Mishneh torah*, 'Laws of Idolatry', 1: 1–2; 12: 16; see M. Halbertal and A. Margalit, *Idolatry*, trans. N. Goldblum (Cambridge, Mass., 1992), 108–36.

that theological and political fact (think of the cathedrals of medieval Christendom).[25] Today, in contrast, in a very real sense faithful Christians are as much a marginalized minority as are faithful Jews. Hence rampant militant secularism is as much a problem for Christians as it is for Jews, making Jews and Christians common outsiders. They have much more in common politically than was the case when Jews were the most marginalized minority in an otherwise fully Christian Europe. As such, even if one agrees with Maimonides that Jews are forbidden to enter a church, even when there is no service being conducted—thus making it akin to a visit to a museum or art gallery—nonetheless entering a church building today is not the acceptance of political subordination that it was in medieval Christendom. Thus Maimonides' strictures have a different normative significance in our very different social and political context.

Furthermore, even if one shares Maimonides' strict views about the use of Christian wine, it hardly poses much of a problem today. If anything, the growing number and quality of kosher wines available today make life easier for Jewish oenophiles, who can easily get their non-Jewish friends and colleagues to drink their kosher wine with them. Even if a Jew wants to avoid social interaction with non-Jews, limiting him- or herself to minimal economic interaction, he or she will have a hard time basing that reluctance on Maimonides' strictures about Christian wine. Wine drinking has ceased being the pervasive social medium that it once was. Even in Maimonides' day, the Islamic regime under which he lived prohibited Muslim involvement with wine, although, as we have seen, the ban was no doubt violated by some Muslims. Accordingly, making and selling wine could hardly have been much of a commercial opportunity for anyone then, even Jews.

INTELLECTUAL INTERACTION WITH CHRISTIANS

Based on the texts we have just examined, most traditional students of Maimonides' writings conclude that he held a consistently negative view of Christianity, and, therefore, that Jews should have as little to do with Christians as possible. Yet that conclusion seems too simple, since it seems to ignore a responsum of Maimonides which makes matters more complex. It was apparently written late in his career, and we need to examine it carefully to decide whether it contradicts his earlier views of Christianity. In other words, did Maimonides change his mind about Christianity, or is the responsum talking about a very special state of affairs, thus proving to be an exception to an otherwise generally consistent approach to Christianity?

---

[25] Cf. Tosefta *Meg.* 3: 23 (re: Prov. 1: 21); BT *Shab.* 11a (re: Ezra. 9: 9); Maimonides, *Mishneh torah*, 'The Laws of Prayer and the Priestly Blessing', 11: 2.

The question posed to Maimonides is whether it is permitted for a Jew to teach Torah to a non-Jew. The Talmud had previously ruled that such instruction was to be limited to teaching the seven Noahide commandments.[26] Taken of itself, this means that a Jew may teach a non-Jew only that Torah that the non-Jew is already supposed to know. Thus the 'Torah' being taught is not the Torah as 'the inheritance of the congregation of Jacob' (Deut. 33: 4) but the 'Torah' that is the inheritance of all humankind.[27] In *Mishneh torah*, Maimonides codifies this view in a straightforward way. Perhaps in this ruling, the Talmud was influenced by another rabbinic opinion maintaining that non-Jews had rejected their own Noahide heritage.[28] That being the case, it is now the job of Jews to help non-Jews retrieve their Noahide heritage, if the initiative comes from a non-Jew seeking religious instruction from a Jewish teacher. Nevertheless, the Talmud is not clear whether Jews are obligated to go to non-Jews and instruct them in the Noahide Torah. Enter Maimonides:

It is permitted to teach the commandments to Christians and to draw them to our religion, but this is not permitted with Muslims, because of what is known to you about their belief that this Torah is not divine revelation . . . but the uncircumcised ones believe that the version of the Torah has not changed, only they interpret it with their faulty exegesis . . . Nevertheless, were the scriptural texts to be interpreted with correct exegesis, it is possible they would return to what is good [*lamutav*] . . . There is nothing they will find in their scriptures that differs from ours.[29]

It is clear that Maimonides meant that anything and everything in the Hebrew Bible may be taught by Jews to Christians. That seems to be more than just the Noahide commandments. For the original question posed to him was: 'Is every Jew obliged to refrain from teaching anything [*davar*] from the commandments [*min hamitsvot*] except the seven commandments or what is based on them, or not?' Moreover, 'correct exegesis' seems to encompass just about everything taught by post-biblical Judaism in one way or another. Therefore, Christian acceptance of the Hebrew Bible as the basis of their religion—as well as their recognition of it being the basis of Judaism—provides considerable commonality for what must be seen as Jewish–Christian dialogue or intellectual interaction. Indeed, the difference between Judaism and Christianity is not that each is the absolute negation of the other. Both Judaism and Christianity are 'biblical religions', but their interpretations of the Bible are different enough to make it impossible for them to be merely two sects within

---

[26] BT *San.* 59*a*.

[27] See BT *Ḥag.* 13*a* (re: Ps. 147: 19–20). Tosafot deals with the question of whether one non-Jew may teach Torah to another non-Jew—which seems to be an academic question, since what control would Jewish authorities have over that kind of inter-gentile intellectual exchange? (ad loc., *ein*).   [28] BT *AZ* 2*b*–3*a*; *BK* 38*a* (re: Hab. 3: 6).

[29] Maimonides, *Teshuvot harambam*, ed. Joshua Blau (Jerusalem, 1960), i. 284–5.

one people. Their respective interpretations of Scripture are not only different, but they often conflict with each other. However, if Jews are permitted to teach Christians anything and everything in the Bible, then unlike the ruling in the Talmud, they need not restrict their teaching to the 'universal' parts of the Torah, namely, the Noahide commandments that apply to any non-Jew. Certainly most of the Torah, both its narrative and its law, is addressed to 'Israel'. And Christians, unlike Muslims, consider themselves to be part of Israel; indeed, already from patristic times, many Christians regarded themselves to be 'the true Israel', having replaced or superseded the Jewish people as God's elect people. (There has always been a minority Christian view that the Church has not replaced the Jewish people as Israel, but that the Church as the Christian people has been added on to Israel along with the Jewish people.[30]) Thus the differences between Judaism and Christianity admit of possible resolution (however improbable in fact), because there is still enough commonality between Jews and Christians to have a conversation, one based on a common text.

Assuming Maimonides knew this, it is understandable why he assigns a proselytizing role to the Jewish teachers of Christians who come to them to study Torah. This can be seen in his emphasis of 'correct exegesis'. This clearly means the Oral Torah (*torah shebe'al peh*). Thus in the introduction to *Mishneh torah*, he states that the Oral Torah consists of the traditional interpretations of the Written Torah that have accompanied it since the time Moses received both Torahs.[31] But whereas the Written Torah has been translated into other languages, thus making it a universally accessible text, the Oral Torah has been the real 'inheritance' of the Jewish people, being something that can only be obtained from Jewish teachers transmitting the tradition to Jewish disciples.[32] That being the case, Christians have misinterpreted much of the Torah (for example, regarding the abrogation of many of its commandments by their messiah) because they have separated themselves from the Jewish people. Whereas the early Christians were almost all Jews, subsequent Christians have almost all been non-Jews and therefore, while in the first few generations of Christianity Jewish Christians would have only had to return (*teshuvah*) to normative (that is, Pharisaic) Judaism, by the time of Maimonides, Christians who

[30] This view, which has been a minority view in Christian theology since patristic times, has become the official teaching (*magisterium*) of the Roman Catholic Church since Vatican Council II in the 1960s (see *Nostre aetate*, in W. M. Abbott (ed.), *Documents of Vatican II* (Dublin, 1966), 664–6; see also Rom. 11: 13–33).

[31] Maimonides, *Mishneh torah*, Introduction; cf. *Mishneh torah*, 'Laws of Rebellious Elders', 1: 1, where Maimonides sees the Oral Torah as the construction of the Sanhedrin and its rabbinical successors. Nevertheless, either view still assumes that without the Oral Torah the Written Torah is unintelligible and normatively inapplicable.

[32] See BT *Git*. 60*b*; *Tem*. 14*b* (re: Exod. 34: 27); *Exodus Rabbah* 18: 4 (re: Hos. 8: 12).

could be persuaded to 'return' to Judaism would have to be literally converted to Judaism and the Jewish people. As such, whereas the early Christians would only have to return to their historic community, later Christians would have to return to their primordial community.[33]

There seem to be three possible approaches to non-Jews studying the Torah. First, as we have seen, non-Jews are not to be taught the full Torah. This seems to be based on the assumption that such non-Jewish interest could only be motivated by a desire to know enough about Judaism to be able to refute it. The Talmud and other rabbinic writings contain many cases where non-Jews take biblical verses and 'throw them in the face' of Jewish teachers (who were usually able to provide the 'correct exegesis' of these same verses, thus saving the intellectual respectability of the Jewish tradition).[34] Since the Written Torah is available, both in translation and in the synagogues, which are public places open to non-Jews also, there is no way of stopping malicious non-Jews from using it as ammunition against Judaism.[35] Yet Jewish teachers should not provide them with such ammunition. By Maimonides' time, that would be the case with any Muslim who wanted to learn the Torah, since Islam teaches that much of the Torah is a human fabrication that was totally superseded by the revelation of the Quran.[36]

Second is the case of non-Jews who of their own volition come to Jewish judges to be converted to Judaism, which is the only way a non-Jew can become a full member of the Jewish people. Here converting to Judaism would be an irrational act if the candidate did not know anything about the very Torah he or she is asking to accept. So the Talmud rules that candidates for conversion should be taught 'some of the easier commandments and some of the more difficult commandments' before accepting upon themselves the full authority of both the Written Torah and the Oral Torah.[37] In order to be

---

[33] In the uncensored editions of Maimonides, *Mishneh torah*, 'Laws of Kings', 11: 4 (re: Zeph. 3: 9), Maimonides speaks of both Christianity and Islam, despite the questionable characters of Jesus and Muhammad, to have been mysteriously useful nonetheless in the ultimate divine plan of spreading monotheism throughout the world (cf. Judah Halevi, *Kuzari*, 4: 23). However, when he discusses the errors of these religions, they seem to be more the errors of Christians than those of Muslims, involving as they do (in his view) assertions that the commandments of the Torah are not perpetually binding, plus assertions that their 'messiah' has given them the true esoteric meaning of the commandments. In conclusion, he speaks of them 'returning' (*ḥozerim*), which is the same term he uses when discussing the possible result of Jews teaching Torah to Christians. See, also, his offhand remarks about Christianity's Jewish roots and the subsequent distortion of the teachings of Jesus by non-Jews ('sons of Esau'), who invented Christianity as a new religion, in his Epistle to Yemen (*Letters of Maimonides* (ed. I. Sheilat), i. 120–1, 142). Importantly, he does not speak of Islam having any such Jewish roots. Moreover, in neither text does he assert that Christians literally worship an 'other god'.

[34] See e.g. JT *Ber.* 9: 1 / 12*d*–13*a*; BT *Shab.* 88*a*; BT *San.* 39*a*–*b*; *Numbers Rabbah* 18: 4 (re: Zech. 13: 2).   [35] See e.g. BT *BM* 24*a*.
[36] See Quran 2: 79.   [37] BT *Yev.* 47*a*; also Tosefta *Dem.* 2: 4; BT *Bekh.* 30*b*.

taught anything from the Torah that pertains to Jews, those non-Jews who are to be given instruction in the Torah must clearly demonstrate their sober decision to convert to Judaism under proper Jewish auspices.[38] That decision should be more than a 'leap of faith'.

The third option is for Jews themselves go out and try to interest non-Jews in converting to Judaism, the means thereto being instruction in the Torah. Although some rabbinic texts suggest that Jews did and even should engage in active proselytizing, the Talmud text dealing with the law of conversion is silent on this question.[39] Maimonides, though, seems to be of the mind that active proselytizing is not only permitted to Jews (which he states clearly in the responsum quoted above), but that it is in fact mandated. Thus in his enumeration of the 613 commandments of the Written Torah, which was his preamble to his codification of the Written Torah with the Oral Torah with subsequent rabbinic legislation, Maimonides explicitly states:

The ninth positive commandment is one which he commanded us to sanctify the divine Name. That is what He said: 'And I shall be sanctified in the midst of the people of Israel' [Lev. 22: 32]. The essence of this commandment, which we are commanded, is to publicize [*lefarsem*] this true religion in the world, and we should not fear any harm.[40]

Maimonides' basis for this statement is the Talmud's ruling that a Jew is required to die for Judaism, the true religion, rather than convert.[41] But the Talmud does not mention (much less mandate) that a Jew should risk death in publicizing Judaism. Instead, the Talmud seems to be dealing with a situation of Jewish passivity, one where non-Jews try to force Jews to convert, rather than Jewish missionary activism. By the time of Maimonides, when Jews were occasionally subjected to coerced conversions by the Christians or Muslims under whose rule they lived, Jews risked death or imprisonment if they tried to persuade any Christian or Muslim to convert to Judaism. So we see that Maimonides' mention of bringing Christians who come to learn Torah from Jews back to their primordial origins is based on his earlier designation of the commandment (*mitsvah*) to proselytize non-Jews, that is, to teach the Torah to the world. Maimonides' responsum is indeed radical and it is based on his even more radical designation of proselytizing as a positive commandment. Moreover, it is perpetually binding, which is the criterion for being one of the 613 commandments.[42] Unlike some commandments, such as those pertaining

---

[38] See BT *Yev.* 24*b*; Maimonides, *Mishneh torah*, 'Laws of Forbidden Relations', 13: 14–18.

[39] See B. J. Bamberger, *Proselytism in the Talmudic Period* (Cincinnati, 1939); Martin Goodman, *Mission and Conversion* (Oxford, 1994); cf. BT *Yev.* 109*b* (re: Prov. 11: 15); Tosafot, ad loc., *ra'ah*.

[40] Maimonides, *Sefer hamitsvot*, pos. no. 9 (ed. C. Heller (Piotrków, 1914)).

[41] BT *San.* 74*a*; Maimonides, *Mishneh torah*, 'Laws of the Foundations of the Torah', 5.4.

[42] See Maimonides, *Sefer hamitsvot*, Introduction, *shoresh* 3.

to the Jerusalem Temple, circumstances have not rendered it impossible for Jews to observe it today. It can and should be practised here and now, although it is questionable whether Maimonides thought Jews must risk their lives to proselytize non-Jews as they must risk their lives when they are presented with the choice of apostasy or death at the hands of non-Jews for the sake of their religion. Finally, of all the non-Jews in the world, Christians seem to be the most likely objects of Jewish proselytizing because they already accept the full Written Torah, which is the basis of Judaism. In other words, they are already partially there, and that makes them unique among non-Jews; indeed, they have the most potential for conversion to Judaism.

In the responsum, Maimonides assigned Christians to a different halakhic category from the one to which he had assigned them earlier. According to the Talmud, a non-Jew is either an idolater (*oved avodah zarah*), a slave owned by a Jew (*eved kena'ani*) or a resident alien (*ger toshav*).[43]

Regarding the observance of Torah commandments, an idolater seems to be someone who in fact observes none of the commandments of the Torah, not even the Noahide commandments, the first of which for Maimonides is the universal prohibition of idolatry.[44] As we have already seen, it is obvious why he or she should not be taught Torah. A slave, on the other hand, is required to observe all those commandments which a Jewish woman is obligated to observe.[45] Nevertheless, since a woman is exempt from the obligation to learn Torah, it follows that a slave is also exempt from that obligation.[46] Whereas it is questionable whether a woman's exemption from the obligation of learning Torah actually prohibits her from doing so, the Talmud is explicit that a slave must not be taught Torah by his Jewish master, although the possibility of him learning Torah by himself is recognized.[47] From this legal fact, one could well infer that if a slave who is obligated for many more than the seven Noahide commandments is not to be taught Torah, a fortiori this is so for a non-Jew who, as a law-abiding Noahide, is only obligated to obey seven commandments.

However, the category of resident alien gives Maimonides the opening he needs for permitting, and perhaps even mandating, teaching Torah to Christians. Maimonides has turned this category from being a strictly political

---

[43] See D. Novak, 'Gentiles in Rabbinic Thought', in S. T. Katz (ed.), *The Cambridge History of Judaism*, iv: *The Late Roman–Rabbinic Period* (Cambridge, 2006), 647–62.

[44] Maimonides, *Mishneh torah*, 'Laws of Kings', 9: 1.

[45] BT *Ḥag.* 4a (re: Deut. 24: 1; Lev. 19: 20); Mishnah *Kid.* 1: 7; Maimonides, *Mishneh torah*, 'Laws of the Festival Offering', 2: 1.

[46] BT *Kid.* 29a (re: Deut. 11: 19); Maimonides, *Mishneh torah*, 'Laws of Torah Study', 1: 1; Joseph Karo, *Kesef mishneh*, ad loc.; cf. Mishnah *Sot.* 3: 4.

[47] See BT *Ket.* 28b; JT *Ket.* 2: 10 / 26d; JT *Meg.* 2: 3 / 75a; Maimonides, *Mishneh torah*, 'Laws of Slaves', 8: 17–18; see Abraham de Boten, *Leḥem mishneh*, ad loc.

one (thus only applying when Jews have full sovereignty in their own land) into a theological one that can be applied to the religious status of those non-Jews who have publicly renounced idolatry.

As we saw earlier, Maimonides places Muslims in this category and then draws a halakhic inference. (In the talmudic era, while the existence of non-Jewish monotheists or non-idolaters was recognized, there does not seem to have been any recognition of actual communities of non-Jewish monotheists in the way later Jewish thinkers debated about whether the Christian Church or the Muslim *ummah* were such communities.[48]) Maimonides' recognition of Islamic monotheism is consistent throughout his writings, and it seems to be based on his recognition of the philosophical basis of their monotheism. Like Judaism, Islam for Maimonides affirms that the existence of the one God is rationally evident (*muskalot*) to any intelligent person.[49] Moreover, he rejects the charge that Muslims have preserved in some clandestine way the idolatry practised in Mecca before the conquest of Muhammad.[50] Following this line of thought, it seems clear that Maimonides would have no objection to Jews engaging in the study of Aristotelian or Neoplatonic metaphysics with Muslims, as he himself no doubt did. Jews have much more philosophical commonality with Islam than with Christianity.

Although Christianity possesses little or no metaphysical commonality with Judaism, there is non-metaphysical theological commonality based on the Christian acceptance of the basic Jewish dogma that the Torah is divine revelation. To be sure, Maimonides thinks Christians are confused regarding what God is because of their Trinitarianism. Yet since they believe that the Mosaic Torah is the revelation of the one God, Creator of heaven and earth, how could they be considered idolaters, to whom Jews are forbidden to teach Torah?[51] Furthermore, in our age, when metaphysics has been excluded from most philosophical discussion (even philosophical discussion of religion, whether of the phenomenological or analytic variety), and even those philosophers who engage in metaphysics usually avoid the ontological question of God altogether. Today there is much less 'God-talk' that is possible between Jews and Muslims than there was in Maimonides' day. Conversely, biblical theology is alive and well in both the Jewish and Christian communities, and it provides a

---

[48] For the notion of individual non-Jews monotheists as virtual Jews, see BT *Meg.* 13*a* (Dan. 3: 12). [49] See Maimonides, *Guide of the Perplexed*, ii. 33.

[50] See Maimonides, *Teshuvot harambam*, ii, 726; see also Novak, *The Image of the Non-Jew in Judaism*.

[51] Along these lines, see D. Novak 'Les Juifs et les Chrétiens révèrent-ils le même Dieu?', in S. Trigano (ed.), *Le Christianisme au miroir du Judaïsme* (Paris, 2003), 95–132; T. Frymer-Kensky, D. Novak, P. Ochs, D. F. Sandmel, and M. A. Signer, '*Dabru Emet*: A Jewish Statement on Christians and Christianity' (of which I was one of the authors), in eid. (eds.), *Christianity in Jewish Terms* (Boulder, Colo.: Westview Press, 2000), pp. xvii–xviii, 49–84.

perennially significant forum for Jewish–Christian dialogue even now. The implications of Maimonides' responsum are important for Jews who wish to engage in theological discussions with Christians in good faith. Nevertheless, those Jewish scholars who engage in theological dialogue with Christians and yet continue to think of them as idolaters are guilty of deception. The Talmud teaches that deception of any human being is prohibited,[52] and since I do not think Maimonides thought that Christians wanting to learn Torah from Jews were idolaters, I believe that he would not have been engaging in deception had he been approached by Christians to learn Torah from him. (Whether Maimonides himself ever taught Torah to any Christian is, to my knowledge, not known.)

CURRENT NORMATIVE IMPLICATIONS

We know that there were times, especially during the Renaissance, when Jewish scholars had intellectual discussions with Christian scholars about biblical texts. Moreover, it seems that the motive of the Christian scholars in seeking Jewish scholars was not to proselytize them any more than it was of the Jewish scholars. Yet if we want to see the argument in Maimonides' responsum as underlying a continuation of this enterprise, we must ask the question: 'Does the use of Maimonides' responsum require us to use our contact with Christians on scriptural matters for proselytizing?' If so, would that not pose a problem for Jewish–Christian dialogue today, since most Jews have been willing to enter into dialogue only when their Christian interlocutors have assured them that they have no proselytizing agenda? (Of course, other Jewish scholars do not trust that disclaimer, and hence refuse to engage in this dialogue—an honest if myopic view.) How could Jews enter a dialogue claiming privileges for themselves that they require their non-Jewish interlocutors to abjure?[53]

My answer is that one can claim that Maimonides distinguishes between non-Jews who want to learn Torah for the sake of conversion to Judaism—or who are at least open to that possibility—and non-Jews who want to learn how some of the Torah provides a foundation for their praxis. This latter option is what the Talmud meant by teaching non-Jews what the Torah itself teaches non-Jews. Moreover, if the Torah itself is the source of that knowledge for non-Jews, then perhaps they need to study all of it to be able to distinguish what pertains to them and what does not. In fact, whereas Maimonides teaches that Jews should force non-Jews to accept the Noahide law (when they have the political power to do so), they should not force anyone to convert to Judaism.[54] One can therefore claim that if non-Jews come to learn what the

---

[52] BT *Hul.* 94*a*. [53] See BT *BM* 59*b*; BT *San.* 18*a* (re: Zeph. 2: 1).
[54] Maimonides, *Mishneh torah*, 'Laws of Kings', 8: 10.

Torah requires of them, Jewish teachers should emphasize the theological–moral necessity of that learning for the sake of praxis. However, when non-Jews come to learn Torah to be converted to Judaism, Jewish teachers should also teach them that their conversion is a theological option—indeed, the optimal theological option—but that they need feel no theological–moral necessity to do so. In other words, even though the Noahide laws apply to all non-Jews, a good case could be made that only Christians accept them as such.[55] Finally, since for Maimonides the Noahide laws are learned from the Oral Torah, then showing Christians how these laws are derived would seem to require teaching them the methods whereby the Oral Torah is rationally formulated.

Of course, these normative conclusions are inferences from what Maimonides taught in this responsum. He did not state them explicitly, nor are they strict deductions from what he said explicitly. The most we can say is that these normative conclusions do not contradict what he said explicitly. Yet is this not what Maimonides himself did with his talmudic sources, especially in this responsum? In fact, he was neither the first nor the last to so reinterpret a normative source; and neither am I the first nor the last scholar to do the same with Maimonides as my normative source on the question of the nature of Christianity and how Judaism and Jews should judge it when we engage Christians.

[55] The usual interpretation of the famous passage in Maimonides, *Mishneh torah*, 'Laws of Kings', 8: 11, is that the only non-Jews who will attain the World to Come are those who have accepted the Noahide laws 'because of what God commanded them in the Torah and made known to them through Moses'. If so, then one could say that only Christians, out of any non-Jewish people, are eligible, since they alone totally accept Mosaic revelation. Yet if the Noahide laws are really known through Moses' Oral Torah, which Christians do not accept, then they too, like Muslims who do not totally accept the Written Torah as divine revelation, would not qualify for the World to Come, in Maimonides' view. However, one could interpret the above passage to mean that it refers to non-Jews who accept the Noahide commandments (or their equivalents) *as* Moses taught is the case with the law-abiding Noahides, whether exposed to Jewish revelation or not (see Maimonides, *Guide of the Perplexed*, ii. 40).

TEN

The Banished Brother
Islam in Jewish Thought and Faith

PAUL B. FENTON

Menahem Mendel, the Silent Tsadiq of Warka,
thus explained the verse:
'God heard the voice of the child' [Gen. 21: 17]:
'Yet the Torah records neither a sound nor even a word of Ishmael.
Therefore he must have made a silent and mute cry.'
This indeed was his own mode of worship.

MORDECAI LEVI, *Gedulat mordekhai*

No CULTURAL encounter can be said to have contributed as much to the shaping of Judaism over the past millennium as that of Israel and Islam. Indeed, the rise of the Crescent began a crucial period in the development of Jewish civilization that has left an abiding mark on all subsequent generations in the areas of literary, legal, and intellectual activity. Historically the religion of the Quran was initially inspired by its biblical forerunner, but it gradually outgrew its parent faith. Although it was tacitly accepted, Islam's ensuing cultural ascendancy was never openly recognized by the Sages of Israel, who continued to oscillate between attitudes of refusal and receptivity towards the new religion.

In a certain sense this dialectic movement was dictated by the midrashic portrayal of the biblical Ishmael, who was later to become the traditional eponym of the Arabs in medieval Jewish literature. Ishmael is one of the few biblical figures of whom no spoken word is reported, while his name means 'hearing' (Heb.: *yishma*, 'shall hear', *el*, 'God'). In the Midrash he is given as an example of 'one whose name was fair but whose deeds were foul . . . his name implies "he hearkens to God" but he does not hearken'.[1] This statement set the tone for subsequent Jewish perceptions of Muslim otherness: outwardly Islam has nothing to say, its religious discourse is devoid of any authenticity; yet inwardly the Islamic message is full of eloquence for one who knows how to listen.

---

[1] *Genesis Rabbah* 71: 4 (trans. H. Freedman (London, 1951), 654).

It is perhaps because the Ishmaelites were nomads that they came to be identified in rabbinic literature with the ancestors of the Arabs,[2] although there is no historical basis for this association. So strong was this identification by the time of Muhammad that the Muslim prophet designates Ishmael as the founder of the Arab sanctuary at Mecca and calls Jesus 'Isa'; that is, Esau, the traditional ancestor of Christendom. Furthermore, later biographies of Muhammad take pains to trace his own pedigree back to Ishmael, much as the New Testament seeks to connect Jesus' ancestry to David.[3] Midrashic sources that underwent their final redaction after the rise of Islam, such as the *Pirkei derabi eli'ezer*, regard Esau and Ishmael respectively as the historical archetypes of the Christian and Islamic traditions. They show no hesitation in relating Islam's triumph to the biblical prophecies concerning the future greatness of Ishmael's offspring. Whereas Muslims saw in their descent from Abraham through his firstborn Ishmael a token of their role as restorers of a supposed primordial monotheism, the Jews discerned therein an explanation for certain moral qualities that were to be found among the Ishmaelites, whose progenitor personified the virtue of kindness. Thus the late midrash ascribed to Rabbi Shimon bar Yohai states that if the Almighty had brought upon Israel the yoke of yet another exile, that of Ishmael (that is Muslim rule), it was a merciful act in order to alleviate the burden of the yoke of Esau (Christianity).[4] Notwithstanding the harsh treatment meted out by Muhammad to the Jews of Medina, there is something of a messianic fervour in the welcome Jews gave the Muslim victors in the initial stages of their conquests. Arabic chronicles claim that Jews actively collaborated with the Arab invaders who liberated them from the rod of their former Christian persecutors. However, the ensuing short-lived era of tolerance was less an expression of gratitude towards Jews than one of incapacity to engage them in theological polemics.

REFUSAL

It was only once Islam had learned to wield the casuistic and dogmatic arms borrowed from the arsenals of Christianity and Karaism that polemical battles began to be waged. It is in response to attacks on the Mosaic faith by Muslim theologians that the first reactions are voiced in the Jewish camp, some 300 years after the rise of Islam.

[2] See Targum Onkelos, Gen. 37: 25.

[3] A. Guillaume, *The Life of Muhammad: A Translation of Ibn Ishaq's Sirat Rasul Allah* (Oxford, 1955), 3.

[4] Shimon bar Yohai, *Mysteries of Rabbi Shimon bar Yohai* [Nistarot derabi shimon bar yohai] in *Midreshei ge'ulah*, ed. Y. Even Shemuel (Tel Aviv, 1953), 162–98; see also B. Lewis (trans.), 'On That Day: A Jewish Apocalyptic Poem on the Arab Conquests', in P. Salmon (ed.), *Mélanges d'islamologie: Volume dédié à la mémoire d'Armand Abel par ses collègues, ses élèves et ses amis* (Leiden, 1974), 197–200.

The Muslims claimed that Muhammad was the last of the prophets and that Islam embodied the pristine truth of the original monotheistic message, which had been adulterated by Jews and Christians. Thus his predecessors, the biblical prophets, had all expounded in reality the principles of Islam. Not only had the 'People of the Book' falsified the divine message, but they had also removed all mention of the advent of the ultimate prophet, Muhammad. For the sake of simplicity, it is possible to divide the pattern of Jewish retaliations to these allegations into three main trends: offensive, defensive, and abusive.

Offensive

The first of these tendencies probably reflects the earliest reaction to Islam, when its Jewish origins were still effectively recognizable. By virtue of its primacy, Judaism claimed pre-eminence in relation to Islam and perceived it less as a threat than as a confirmation of the falsehood of Christianity and its universalistic pretensions. Representative of this category is the remarkable Judaeo-Arabic tale preserved in a manuscript originating from the genizah, a hoard of medieval writings which came to light in Cairo in the late nineteenth century, 'The Account of Muhammad's Companions', which relates that the Quran was really written by a group of rabbis from Medina who intimated their names in the 'mysterious letters' of the Muslim scripture 'in order to save the people of Israel from the evil devices of the wicked one [Muhammad]'.[5]

Other later polemical works, such as the *Ma'amar yishma'el*, ascribed to Solomon ibn Adret (thirteenth century), and the *Keshet umagen* by the fifteenth-century scholar Simon Duran of Algiers, emphasized the Jewish origins of Islam, 'whose precepts were stolen from among us'.[6] Moreover, they point out the contradictions that exist between the quranic and biblical narrative. Perhaps on account of its biblical content, some Jewish thinkers were prepared to accord a certain legitimacy to the Islamic tradition. Such an opinion is imputed to a group of eighth-century sectarians who were willing to accept that Muhammad was a real prophet but that his mission was only intended for the Arabs, since each nation received a divine revelation in accordance with its specific language and requirements.[7] This view is also reflected in the work of the twelfth-century Yemenite mystic Nethanael ibn al-Fayyumi, who quotes profusely from the Quran in support of his arguments.[8]

[5] Jacob Mann, 'A Polemical Work against Karaites', *Jewish Quarterly Review*, 12 (1922), 146–7.
[6] J. Perles, *R. Salomo ben Abraham ben Adereth: Sein Leben und seine Schriften* (Breslau, 1863), 1–24 (Heb. section).
[7] L. Nemoy, 'Al-Qirqisani's Account of the Jewish Sects', *Hebrew Union College Annual*, 7 (1930), 317–97.
[8] Nethanael ibn al-Fayyumi, *Bustan al-Ukul*, Judaeo-Arabic text and English translation, ed. D. Levine (New York, 1908), 108.

Defensive

On the whole a relatively small fraction of medieval Muslim literature is devoted to anti-Judaic polemic, and the same is true of anti-Islamic texts in Jewish literature. The reason for this on the Muslim side is that, both theologically and politically, the Jews represented less of a threat to Islam than did Christians. Consequently, they were not worth the bother of refuting except in countries where they were the only religious minority, such as in the Maghreb, where indeed anti-Jewish tracts are more numerous. From the Jewish side, it was forbidden to polemicize against Islam, an offence incurring capital punishment, or at least the annulment of the *dhimma*, or 'the pact of tolerance'. Unlike the Jews of Christendom who would often engage in public disputations on religious issues, the Jews of Arab lands were, as Maimonides puts, it 'sufferers in silence'. Open criticism of Islam was unthinkable as it was inconsistent with the Jews' obligation to remain in a state of subordination and would have provoked severe reprimands. It is no wonder that one of the rare polemical tracts written by a Jew criticizing the Quran, that composed by Joseph Hanagid (eleventh century, Spain) has wholly disappeared. In his refutation of it, which has survived, the eleventh-century Andalusian Muslim theologian Ibn Hazm remarks: 'Lo the infidels have become arrogant and unbelievers wag their tongue ... a man filled with hatred towards our prophet, a Jew of that most contemptible of religions, the vilest of faiths ... loosened his tongue and became conceited.'[9]

The few Jewish polemical works mainly attempt to refute the arguments of the more noteworthy Islamic treatises, such as Ibn Hazm's *Kitāb al-fisal*. Stress was placed on the eternal character of the Mosaic revelation and the infallibility of its transmission as a retort to Muslim allegations that the Jews had falsified their scriptures and removed from them the announcement of the coming of Muhammad. Symptomatically, on account of these accusations, Maimonides (1135–1204) issued a responsum prohibiting the teaching of the Jewish scriptures to Muslims but not to Christians, since the latter accept the basic truth of the Bible whereas the former deny its authenticity outright.[10]

A further stigma with which the Jews had to contend was their downtrodden state, which Muslim theologians contrasted with the political triumph of their own religion and claimed as proof of its truthfulness. It did not occur to them that the discriminatory laws that Islam imposed upon *dhimmi*s (non-Muslims) were responsible for the Jews' abject state. In his *Kuzari*, Judah Halevi (d. *c.*1140) refutes the argument from abasement by pointing out that the harsh realities of the diaspora prophesied in the Bible are, on the contrary, proof of Judaism's authenticity. Moreover, he insists, greatness resides not in quantity

---

[9] Ibn Hazm, *Ar-Radd 'ala Ibn Naghrila al-Yahudi*, ed. I. Abbas (Beirut, 1981), 41–2.

[10] Maimonides, *Teshuvot harambam*, ed. J. Blau (Jerusalem 1960), i. 84–5.

but in quality. Despite their lowliness, the Jews had tenaciously upheld universally recognized sublime principles.[11]

Muslim polemics drew on information provided by Christians, Karaites, and Jewish renegades. Among the latter the most infamous was undoubtedly the twelfth-century Maghrebi apostate Samuel ibn 'Abbās, who, after his conversion to Islam, composed *Ifḥām al-yahūd* (The Silencing of the Jews).[12] Although history has recorded the names of several Jewish converts to Islam, among them some prominent personalities, apostasy seems to have been a rare occurrence, except under duress. This fact is emphasized by the thirteenth-century Baghdadi Jewish polemicist Ibn Kammūna, who only during the interruption of Muslim rule subsequent to the Mongol conquest of Iraq dared to compose a critical appraisal of Islam in his *Examination of the Three Faiths*, in which we read:

To this day we never see anyone converting to Islam unless in terror, or in quest of power, or to avoid heavy taxation, or to escape humiliation, or if taken prisoner, or because of infatuation with a Muslim woman, or for some similar reason. Nor do we see a respected, wealthy, and pious non-Muslim, well versed in both his faith and that of Islam, going over to the Islamic faith without some of the aforementioned or similar motives.[13]

Although forced conversion is forbidden by the Quran (2: 256), several instances have been recorded. The cruellest of these was certainly that under Almohad rule, an account of which has been left by Joseph ibn Aknin. Forced to profess Islam, he construes the ensuing persecutions as a punishment, since the Jews had outwardly embraced Islam instead of suffering martyrdom. He perceives in the discriminatory measures imposed by the Almohads the curses foreseen by the prophets, considering these hardships as the very worst to have befallen the Jewish people in the whole of their history. However, he perceives the fact that the second- and third-generation converts to Islam are still the object of derision and harassment as a divine mercy 'without which we would surely have perished', that is, been assimilated.[14]

As Muslim polemics grew more subtle, Jewish attitudes to Islam took on a decidedly more defensive stance. Confronted with the terror of forced conversions in Andalusia, North Africa, and Yemen, Jewish theologians were obliged to determine more radically their position in relation to the Muslim creed and to define Islam in regard to idolatry. This fundamental issue had

[11] Judah Halevi, *Kuzari*, 1: 113 (trans. H. Hirschfeld (London, 1905)).

[12] Samuel al-Maghribi, *Ifḥām al-yahūd* [The Silencing of the Jews], ed. M. Perlmann (New York, 1964).

[13] M. Perlmann, *Ibn Kammuna's Examination of the Three Faiths* (Los Angeles, 1971), 149.

[14] A. S. Halkin, 'Forced Conversions in the Time of the Almohads' (Heb.), in *Joshua Starr Memorial Volume* (New York, 1953), 110.

been avoided in geonic times when the matter was touched upon in connection with certain foods, such as wine, which would become unfit for consumption if handled by idol-worshippers. It was unclear whether the Muslims were to be considered idolatrous, for they did not themselves consume these foods, but an old tradition held that the Arabs worshipped idols. According to a rabbinical injunction, Jews are obliged to accept death rather than commit idolatry, one of the three cardinal sins. It seems that, prior to Maimonides, the religious authorities had stated categorically that martyrdom was the only option for a Jew threatened with conversion to Islam. This was the opinion of Maimonides' teacher, Judah ibn Shushan, who suffered death in 1165 for refusing to relinquish his ancestral faith during the Almohad persecutions. However, by Maimonides' time the problem had reached such proportions as to become one of existential purport. In a now celebrated responsum Maimonides states that although certain practices adopted by Islam had originally been idolatrous in nature (such as the worship at the Kaaba, which had formerly been a pagan shrine), they could no longer be regarded as such, for Muslims were now committed to a purely monotheistic cult. Consequently, he absolved Jews who converted to Islam under the threat of death from the sin of idol-worship, since although it is meritorious to forfeit one's life in such circumstances for the 'sanctification of the Name' it is not imperative to do so, according to the spirit of the law. However, Maimonides emphasizes in his *Epistle on Apostasy* that since an outward apostate is unable to perform certain precepts he is in a state of sin and is consequently duty bound to make every effort to quit his place of residence for a more tolerant one, where he could return to his true faith.[15]

Nonetheless, Maimonides considers Islam to be a derivative monotheism, of which Judaism, superior to all other forms of revealed religion, is the ultimate source. In a passage of the *Mishneh torah* that had long been suppressed by Christian censorship, he dealt with the messianic era and the role of Christianity and Islam in the divine economy:

Thus these words of Jesus of Nazareth and this Arab who succeeded him were only to make way for the King Messiah and to prepare [*letaken*] the whole world to serve the Lord altogether, as its says in Scripture: 'for I will unite all the peoples into pure speech, all of them to call upon the name of the Lord and to serve Him with one shoulder' [Zeph. 3: 9].[16]

A sixteenth-century Yemenite poet, Zekharyah al-Dāhiri, was inspired by Maimonides' position in a chapter of his entertaining *Sefer hamusar* devoted to an imaginary disputation between a Muslim and a Jew. The latter explains that, in his wisdom, God first sent Jesus to non-Jews in order to extract them

---

[15] Maimonides, *Teshuvot harambam*, ii. 725–8; id. *Igerot harambam*, ed. A. Lichtenberg (Leipzig, 1859), fos. 12–15; Eng. trans.: L. D. Stitskin, *Letters of Maimonides* (New York, 1977), 34–69.
[16] Maimonides, *Mishneh torah*, 'Laws of Kings', 11.

from the darkness of ignorance. Having apprised humanity of his existence, God subsequently sent Muhammad to uproot idolatry from their minds. However, the Muslim prophet added false notions to his mission and gave his flock 'a few confused precepts'. Yet since his religion also had positive aspects, it was allowed to endure in order to form a preparatory stage in the redemptive process. Indeed, the spiritual development of humanity is analogous to that of an infant who is introduced to solids only after having been weaned from its mother's milk.

The sage [Maimonides] stated that Muhammad's appearance was only to prepare the path of the Messiah. Indeed when Israel's saviour will come you will say to our ears 'our forefathers have inherited naught but falsehood' [Jer. 16: 19]. Do not then imagine that your creed is perfect and your religion complete, nor that your worldly triumph is a proof . . . for truth will triumph with the return of prophecy to Zion. He who says otherwise speaks falsehood, for prophecy is the exclusive prerogative of the Land of Israel and is not to be found amongst Se'ir and Ishmael [i.e. Christianity and Islam]. Indeed, a prerequisite of prophecy is to be endowed with wondrous knowledge, unlike the raving prophet [Muhammad] who, moreover, each day would deflower a different maiden. Only when man is sanctified and possessed of a 'new heart' can the Divine Presence rest upon him.[17]

Later theologians were by no means unanimous on the monotheistic nature of Islamic practices. Indeed Maimonides' ruling was to receive serious criticism from subsequent scholars. Even a Maimonidean such as Yom Tov ben Abraham al-Ishbili (*c.* 1250–1330), known more familiarly as the Ritba, has this to say of the Muslim form of monotheism:

Although the Muslims profess monotheism, their faith is utterly idolatrous. Consequently, a Jew [compelled to convert to Islam] should suffer martyrdom rather than apostatize. Indeed, whosoever admits their creed, denies by the same token the truthfulness of the Law of Moses in its present state and such a denial is tantamount to idolatry. It is permitted to transgress the precepts in order to escape death, except where the demand is made in order to show that the Torah is untruthful (such as in the case of apostasy) or to desecrate the sabbath (for example) in order to show that the Holy One Blessed Be He did not command us to observe it.[18]

The great sixteenth-century Egyptian halakhist David ibn Zimra challenged Maimonides' decision in a responsum concerned with forced conversion to Islam. Even where there is no collective coercive decree, in which case martyrdom would be the only option, isolated threats of conversion also require 'the sanctification of the divine Name', since, reverting to Ritba's definition, 'Islam is an idolatrous religion'.[19]

[17] Zekharyah al-Dāhiri, *Sefer hamusar*, ch. 7 (ed. Y. Ratzhaby (Jerusalem, 1965), 126–7).
[18] Quoted in David ibn Abi Zimra, *Responsa* (Leghorn, 1652), fos. 30–1, no. 92.
[19] Ibid. See also the opinions of Solomon ibn Adret (thirteenth century), *Responsa* (Jerusalem,

It would be erroneous to infer from Ibn Zimra's antithetic stand that Maimonides had adopted a lenient view of Islam in all respects, for in the polemical section of his *Epistle to Yemen*, written in 1198 as a consolation to the Jews there who were forcibly converted to Islam, his condemnation of Muslim tyranny is unequivocally harsh:

Remember, my co-religionists, that on account of our numerous sins God has hurled us in the midst of this nation, the Muslims, who have persecuted us severely and passed baneful and discriminatory legislation against us . . . Never did a nation molest, degrade, debase and hate us as much as they . . . Although we were dishonoured by them beyond endurance, we have borne fabrication and suffering in silence . . . despite this we do not escape this continued maltreatment which well nigh crushes us. No matter how much we suffer and choose to remain at peace with them, they stir up strife and sedition as David foretold in the Psalms: 'I am at peace but when I speak they are for war' [Ps. 120: 7].[20]

This passage constitutes one of the most eloquent condemnations of Muslim intolerance, voiced not by a Jew cowering with the wretched masses, but by one who moved in the highest circles of Muslim society. By no means unique in the history of the Jews in Muslim lands, this outcry painfully echoes the torments suffered by Israel in the shadow of Ishmael.

The protests that they provoked are of two types. Firstly, and still defensively, though this time not with the pride of superiority but rather with the pain of victimization, the Jews sought to find scriptural justification for the vexations and discriminatory measures to which they were subject. Secondly, in the abusive phase, they resorted to inveighing against Islam and reviling its practices in the face of their political impotence. In the first instance, they endeavoured, like Ibn Aknin, to explain their suffering in terms of the biblical accounts of exile. They interpreted Daniel's eschatology as referring to the exile of Ishmael, explaining their present woes in the light of past prophecies. Such a portrayal is unexpectedly found in the classic work of Jewish mysticism, the Zohar, which purports to describe events in second-century Palestine, but which really reflects thirteenth-century Spain, where the book was compiled:

1997), no. 345, and Nissim Gerondi (fourteenth century), on BT *San.* 61*b*, who considers that while Islam is not idolatrous, some Muslims in their worship may be. These positions were debated by countless generations of halakhic authorities, of whom the most significant are Simon b. Zemah Duran (Tashbez, fourteenth century), *Responsa* (Jerusalem, 2007), vol iii, no. 133; Isaac E. Spektor (nineteenth century), *Ein yitshak*, 'Orah hayim' (Vilna, 1889, repr. Jerusalem, 2004), vol. i, p. 45, no. 11; Abraham Isaac Kook (twentieth century), *Mishpat kohen* (Jerusalem, 1966), pp. 167–70, no. 89; Ovadiah Yosef (twentieth century), *Yabi'a omer*, pt. 4, 'Yoreh de'ah' (Jerusalem, 1993), pp. 226–8, no. 12; Yekutiel Y. Halberstamm (twentieth century), *Divrei yetsiv*, 'Orah hayim' (Jerusalem, 1996), vol. i, pp. 171–5, no. 90.

[20] Moses Maimonides, *Epistle to Yemen*, ed. and trans. A. S. Halkin and B. Cohen (New York, 1952), p. xviii.

For three things is the world disquieted, for a servant, when he reigneth and a hand-maid that is heir to her mistress, to Egypt and Ishmael [Islam]. There is no nation so despised of the Holy One as Egypt and yet he gave her dominion over Israel; while the handmaid, that is, Hagar, who bore Ishmael, who tormented Israel so cruelly in the past, still rules over her and persecutes her for her faith. In truth the exile under Ishmael is the hardest of all exiles. Once when going up to Jerusalem, Rabbi Joshua saw an Arab and his son meet a Jew. The Arab said to his son 'See there is a Jew whom God has rejected. Go and insult him. Spit in his face seven times for he is of the seed of the exalted ones and I know that the seventy nations shall be ruled by them.' So the boy went and took hold of the Jew's beard, whereupon Rabbi Joshua said 'Mighty one, mighty one, I call upon the supernal one to come down below.' And before he had finished, the earth opened her mouth and swallowed up the Arabs.[21]

This sentiment is echoed in a commentary by the great Moroccan kabbalist Rabbi Hayim ibn Attar, who left Morocco for Jerusalem, where he died in 1743:

Happy is he who has not suffered exile beneath the Muslims who have enslaved us and embittered our existence. Not only do they leave our labours unrewarded, but they order us to pay them. After having stripped us of our belongings, they demand of us that which we no longer possess and they make us drink of the cup of misery until death.[22]

The same yearning to be freed from the bondage of Ishmael is expressed in the poetry of Oriental Jewry. Their poems would often echo the idea that the ruthlessness of the Arabian exile was a sure harbinger of the approach of redemption. As Islamic tolerance waned, this theme became increasingly wide-spread and explains the proliferation of messianic movements among the Jews under Islam from earlier times right down to the seventeenth-century false messiah, Sabbatai Zevi. One of the most poignant of these poems is that com-posed by the seventeenth-century Persian Jewish poet, Mullah Hizkiyah, victim of the forced conversions under Shah 'Abbas II during whose reign several thou-sand Jews were compelled to forsake their ancestral faith in fear of their lives:

We, Moses' people, have become deranged and demented
As a result of our apostasy.
Devoid of glory and of the Torah,
Deprived of festivals, we weep as a willow.
Without peace of mind, nameless, we despair in the depths of the abyss.
Without houses of study and mullahs [rabbis],
We are indeed unworthy before God,

[21] Zohar iii. 16*b* (trans. H. Sperling, M. Simon, and P. Levertoff (London, 1949), iii. 5). Such tormenting of Jews by Muslim children was a common occurrence in Arab lands, widely docu-mented in accounts by European travellers.

[22] Hayim ibn Attar, *Or ḥaḥayim*, on Lev. 6: 3.

Having all become infidels as a result of our apostasy.
Outwardly Muslims, within our hearts we are Jews,
And verily we are totally dissimilar to the Muslims.
Outwardly we practise Islam, but we keep not the Ramadan fast,
All feigning to believe when we act as Muslims.
We are as soulless moulds,
Likened to helpless ants.
In unison we all lament on account of our apostasy.
Helpless and weak, we have fallen upon misfortune,
Through oppression we have delivered our souls to the Muslim creed.
O, Almighty, take pity on us.
The time has come to free us from the Muslim faith.[23]

Abusive

The third defence mechanism employed by the Jews of Islamic lands was derisive statements aimed at ridiculing and disparaging Islam and its tenets, and can be described as abusive. Such attacks were employed by all three monotheistic faiths during the medieval period to discourage apostasy.

I have already pointed out the scarcity of polemical writings against Islam by Jews in Muslim contexts. However, in Jewish theological writings intended for internal consumption and written in Arabic in Hebrew characters, if not in Hebrew itself, numerous polemical allusions are found that shower contempt on the most sacred concepts of Islam and in the most derogatory terms. The most characteristic of these are Hebrew puns on Arabic expressions which would not immediately be clear to a non-Jew. Thus the holy city of Mecca is referred to in the Hebrew as *makot* (plague). The holy book of Islam is dubbed *qalon* (shame) and Muhammad is referred to as *pasul Allah* (the unfit of Allah), a pun on the Arabic *rasul Allah* (the prophet of Allah). In addition, certain aspects of the Islamic cult were derisively targeted. A stinging satire on the pilgrimage to Mecca, one of the fundamental principles of Islam, is to be found in the *maqāmāt* (poems) of the sixteenth-century Karaite official Moses of Damascus, who, after having been forcibly converted to Islam, was obliged to undertake the pilgrimage. He subsequently composed a poetical account of his experiences in the holy city, in which he gives vent to his resentment in an ironic description of the Kaaba, deftly embroidered with biblical verses and concluding with his ardent desire to return to his ancestral faith:

> And when they went to Mecca, barefoot and naked,
> I went with them for twelve days full of desolation,
> and would have perished were it not that
> the Lord was of help to me.

[23] W. Bacher, 'Elégie d'un poète judéo-persan', *Revue des Études Juives*, 48 (1904), 94–105.

We reached the house of their worship
to which they turn their face in prayer,
And I observed the black stone
which leads them astray in their faith;
It looked to me as if it were a plague spot.
And they walked round it and reeled as if they were drunkards
For they said 'We are observing the custom of our prophet
And commemorating it.'
O God, mayest Thou sell these people into slavery for their sin,
And may the Divine King not account it a sin on my part.
I departed therefrom while they were yet engaged in great celebration,
And I said: 'O Lord avenge Thy profaned name and Thy neglected Law . . .
Turn Thine eyes to Thy devastated Temple
And restore Thy glory to it and raise its foundation.
Exalt Thine humbled people so that ye shall be holy unto me.
Behold this Muslim house and those that have come unto it,
While Thine own house is in ruins and we far from it.
Bring us back to dwell in its shade.'[24]

Often these outcries were in response to analogous Islamic criticism of Jewish tenets. Taking their cue from Christian polemics, Muslim theologians claimed, for example, that the numerous precepts imposed upon the children of Israel by Mosaic law were in fact a punishment for their disobedience. The disparaging references to the Islamic rules of cleanliness made, *inter alia*, by the sixteenth-century Karaite scholar Isaac of Troki are to be understood in the light of this polemic. 'In the verse "Those that sanctify themselves . . . and eat detestable things" [Isa. 66: 17], the prophet alludes to the Islamic nation, who outwardly show themselves to be holy and pure by repeating their ritual ablutions several times daily. What avails their outward cleanliness if inwardly they defile themselves with all manner of unclean foods?'[25]

Very often the accusation of irrationality was levelled against Muslim practices, and indeed the epithet with which Jewish sources most often refer to the Prophet of Islam is *meshuga*, 'the madman'. According to a popular legend related by a seventeenth-century Egyptian Jewish chronicler, Maimonides had been forced to flee from the Maghreb on account of a cynical reply he allegedly gave to a Muslim who mocked the Jewish use of a palm-branch during Sukkot (Feast of Tabernacles). Maimonides is said to have retorted, 'on the contrary, surely the throwing of pebbles at a stone pillar is the act of a madman', referring to the lapidation rite which Muslims perform at the pilgrimage to Mecca.[26]

[24] Moses of Damascus, 'An Account of his Conversion and Pilgrimage to Medina and Mecca', in L. Nemoy, *A Karaite Anthology* (New Haven, 1952), 165–6.

[25] Isaac of Troki, *Ḥizzuq ha'emunah*, ed. D. Deutsch (Sohrau, 1873), 54.

[26] *Sefer divrei yosef*, ed. S. Shtober (Jerusalem, 1981), 57–8; Adolf Neubauer, *Mediaeval Jewish Chronicles* (Oxford, 1887), i. 117–18.

Receptivity

In striking contrast to these derogatory attitudes, numerous instances are
encountered where Muslim practice is commended and even praised as worthy
of emulation. The fifteenth-century Provençal philosopher Profiat Duran
mentions, for example, in his discussion of education in the *Ma'aseh efod*:

According to legend, the Prophet of Ishmael enjoined his followers to recite contin-
uously his book so that he who has read it a thousand times will reap his reward in
the hereafter. If this nation believes and professes such a doctrine in respect of their
vain belief and discourses, how much more incumbent is it upon the Jew to follow
this in respect of our perfect Law and prophetic writings.[27]

Similarly, in the following poem by an anonymous author from the Muslim
East, the religious assiduity of the Jew is shown to fall lamentably short of that
of the Muslim, whose call to morning prayer from the minaret catches the Jew
still slumbering upon his couch.

> O, mortal, art thou not ashamed and abashed
> to sleep through the dawn and remain mute,
> Whilst thine ears perceive the noisy cry of the nations
> Entreating God with perfect heart?
> Arise, wherefore slumberest thou?
> Behold the strangers keeping watch while thou yet dreamest.
> If they that know Him not, serve Him thus,
> How can His very servants withhold their worship?[28]

The sixteenth-century Turkish mystic Menahem di Lonzano writes in the
same vein, upholding Muslim rules of ablution as a model of purity:

> Be sure to cleanse thyself of all impurity,
> So that the Muslim be not more pious than thou,
> Through his ablutions of hands, feet and face,
> Every morn, noon and eve.[29]

Such candid expressions are rare in both Judaism and Islam, but it is mainly
through this passive acknowledgement of Muslim virtue that a positive
approach to Islam can be detected

The most notable influence of Islam on Judaism is undoubtedly in the field
of linguistics, as for seven centuries, from the rise of the Muslim schools of
grammar and philosophy in the eighth century until the decline of the classical
idiom in the fifteenth, Arabic was the preferred medium of literary expression

---

[27] Profiat Duran, *Ma'aseh efod*, ed. J. Friedländer and J. Cohn (Vienna, 1865), 14.
[28] See Paul Fenton, 'Review of H. Zafrani, *Poésie juive en "Occident musulman"* (Paris, 1977)',
Revue des Études Juives, 139 (1980), 157.
[29] Menahem di Lonzano, *Shetei yadot* (Venice, 1618), fo. 93*b*.

for Oriental Jewry in both secular and religious matters. A remarkable indication of the depth of the penetration of Arabic language and culture is the adoption of Islamic terminology by Arabic-speaking Jews for even the most sacred
notions of the Jewish faith, something which has practically no parallel among
Ashkenazim prior to the modern era. For example, the Hebrew Bible would
be referred to as the Quran, halakhah as *sharia*, and Moses as *rasul Allah*, 'the
prophet of Allah'.[30]

The rise of Jewish lexicography, grammar, and exegesis was similarly
inspired by corresponding trends that first flourished in Karaite circles under
the impetus of the Islamic *'arabiyya*, or cult of Arabic, and the corollary study
of the Quran from a linguistic as well as a theological viewpoint. Even Jewish
poetry, the only form of expression to continue in Hebrew, was nonetheless
modelled on Arabic metrics and figures of speech and style. So closely were the
latter followed that certain reprehensible themes, such as bacchanalia and
homosexuality, were treated in poetry composed in imitation of Arabic prototypes. It is also well known that the logical structure of the legal codes, so
typical of Eastern authors, and the whole genre of responsa literature were
likewise based on Islamic models. Cultivated Jews seem to have had a fair
knowledge of the intricacies of Islamic law, a fact that is corroborated by the
extensive familiarity displayed by Jewish authors of the classical period with
the Quran and Hadith, which they sometimes quote in their exegetical works.

In later times, however, familiarity with Islamic institutions came to be
limited to the loopholes which could serve the Jews as expedients in an hour
of need. Thus the nineteenth-century Moroccan traveller Rabbi Mordechai
Abi Serur explains how he escaped from an awkward predicament, if not
certain death, by quoting to the Muslim assailants who waylaid him on his
journey to Timbuktu a *hadith* describing the punishment of those who murder
believers.[31] Even in recent times the Jews of Arab countries have found it wise
to memorize the opening chapter of the Quran as a means of concealing their
true identity in times of danger.

However, it is in the synagogue that receptivity is most obvious. Although
Jewish worship is markedly different from Muslim worship, the similarity
between the melodies intoned in the synagogue and the mosque is most striking. The resemblance is particularly manifest in the singing of para-liturgical
poems known as *bakashot*, during the spiritual concerts which the Jews of the
East were wont to practise before dawn on the sabbath, which were clearly
inspired by the nocturnal vigils kept by the Sufis in their *zāwiyyas*.[32]

[30] J. Blau, *The Emergence and Linguistic Background of Judaeo-Arabic* (Oxford, 1965), 159–60.

[31] See A. Beaumier, 'Premier établissement des Israélites a Timbouktou', *Bulletin de la Société
de Géographie*, 19 (1870), 345–70.

[32] Paul Fenton, 'Les Baqqashot d'Orient et d'Occident', *Revue des Études Juives*, 134 (1975),
101–21.

It is well known that medieval Jewish thought derived its framework from speculative trends prevalent in Islamic circles; it is less well known that Islamic esotericism in the form of Sufism provided Israel with a quite novel moral and ethical discipline known as the 'science of the hearts'. Commencing with the eleventh-century ethical theologian Bahya ibn Pakuda, whose Sufi-inspired *Duties of the Heart* has remained popular with countless Eastern and Western devotees down to modern times, the Jewish assimilation of Sufi doctrines undoubtedly reveals the most intimate influence of Islam on Jewish spirituality. This tendency culminated in the thirteenth-century Jewish pietist movement in Egypt, whose members, the most outstanding of whom were the descendants of Maimonides, endeavoured to reform the formalistic Judaism of their time by enacting certain modifications of the Jewish service in consonance with Muslim worship. These innovations included prostrations, weeping, protracted nightly vigils, and solitary meditation. The Jewish Sufis considered these innovations not so much a reform as a restoration of practices that had previously been in vogue in ancient Israel but which had since fallen into abeyance among the Jews as a result of the tribulations of the exile and had ultimately passed to the Sufis.[33]

The most eloquent testimony to this belief is given by Maimonides' son Abraham in his magnum opus the *Kifāya al-'abidīn* or the 'Complete Guide for the Servants of God', a comprehensive ethical manual along Sufi lines:

Do not regard as unseemly our reference to the practices of the Muslim Sufis, for the latter imitate the Ancient Prophets of Israel and follow their footsteps . . . the ways of the ancient Saints of Israel which have ceased to be practiced by our own coreligionists have now become the practice of the Muslim Sufis as a result of the iniquities of Israel. Observe, then, these wonderful traditions and sigh with regret over how they have been taken from us and bestowed upon other nations.[34]

However, the pietistic reforms of the Jewish Sufis met with considerable opposition in conservative circles, probably due to their markedly Islamic colouring. It is certain though that their mystical aspirations paved the way in the East for the spread of kabbalah, which was to absorb some of their pietistic practices. After the expulsion of the Jews from Spain, kabbalah became the dominant ideology amongst the Jews of the East. The influence of Islam on the nascent movement and its exponents, especially those of the Lurianic doctrine, which evolved in a Muslim environment, has been largely neglected by modern scholarship. The foremost sixteenth-century kabbalist Hayim Vital relates in his mystical diary his theological discussions with the Muslim clergy

[33] See the introduction to Obadiah Maimonides' *Treatise of the Pool*, ed. Paul Fenton (London, 1981), esp. 8–10.

[34] Abraham Maimonides, *The High Ways to Perfection*, ed. S. Rosenblatt (Baltimore, 1938), ii. 266, 320.

of Damascus, for which purpose he even had the serious intention of learning Arabic.[35] The most profound, not to say metaphysical, reflections concerning Islam are to be found in kabbalistic writings, and our subject would certainly be incomplete without a mention of their particular concepts.

ESOTERICISM

The esoteric traditions reflect the same dichotomy of receptivity and refusal found in exoteric writings, though this is obscured by the veiled language of kabbalah. Among the most prevalent themes is Ishmael as the prototype of a decisive cosmic force competing with Edom (Christendom) in an eschato-logical drama.

A lengthy passage of the Zohar endeavours to explain the Islamic empire's political success: Abraham's love for Ishmael, which preceded his love for Isaac, allowed Islam to gain sway over Israel. Furthermore, it is through the merit of circumcision that Muslims were entrusted with the guardianship of the Holy Land. Moreover, the Zohar states that a convert from Ishmael is superior to converts from other nations since, as the son of Abraham, he is the 'son of holiness'.[36]

A similar recognition of the superior status of Ishmael was expressed by the sixteenth-century Spanish kabbalist Shem Tov ibn Shem Tov:

The ancient kabbalists agreed that just as our forefathers Abraham and Isaac person-ified respectively the virtues of kindness and severity, so Ishmael and Edom have their roots in the respective spiritual residue [*kelipah*] of the Patriarchs. Ishmael is to the right and Edom to the left, each representing in turn the archetype of the nations of the world . . . Ishmael is however superior to his partner, in the same way as kindness is superior to severity. He is moreover the dividing line between light and darkness . . . and the closest to holiness. Just as Ishmael repented in his later years so the Muslims will repent at the end of days, for they are near and shall become proselytes.[37]

As both the Zohar and Shem Tov's *Sefer ha'emunah* were composed in Christian Spain, it is conceivable that their sympathy for Islam was a protest against the intolerance they encountered within Christendom. The case of the famous thirteenth-century kabbalist Isaac of Acco is the opposite. Residing in crusader Palestine he had an excellent command of Arabic, and traces of Sufi thought can be found in his works. However, when Acco fell to the Muslims in 1291, he fled to Christian Spain. The following passage might explain why he chose to live under the yoke of Edom rather than that of Ishmael:

---

[35] Hayim Vital, *Sefer hahezyonot* [Book of Visions], ed. A. Eshcoly (Jerusalem, 1954), 12, 37, 86; Eng. trans.: M. Faierstein, *Jewish Mystical Autobiographies* (New York, 1999), 51, 74, 113.
[36] Zohar ii. 32*a*, 87*a*.
[37] Shem Tov ibn Shem Tov, *Sefer ha'emunah* (Ferrara, 1556), fo. 54*a*.

The words of the psalmist 'the wild beasts of the field' [Ps. 90: 14] allude to Ishmael for he is a 'wild man' [Gen. 16: 12] since he dwells in the wilderness. Therefore he is also called 'beast of the field' [Ps. 104: 11] on account of his living in the desert and wilderness like an animal. Moreover, the word beast [*ziz*] is common in the Arabic tongue. For when they wish to say: 'Strike him a blow on the head' or 'strike him in the neck' they say *zazzhu*. Likewise, the Arabic word for robbery is *bazaz*. Indeed, on account of our numerous sins, the [Muslims] strike upon the head the Jews who dwell in their land and take their money by force,[38] since they are wont to say in their tongue *māl al-yahūdi mubāh*, 'the money of the Jew is lawful for us'. Just as a desert is open to all and sundry, so are the Jews open to the abuse of the Muslims. Even in their religious law they rule that the testimony of a Muslim is always to be believed against that of a Jew. It is for this reason that our rabbis of blessed memory have said: 'Rather beneath Edom than beneath Ishmael.' They begged for mercy saying 'Master of the World, either beneath Thy shadow or else that of the sons of Esau [the Christians]' [BT *Git.* 17a].[39]

Possibly excessive fraternizing between Jews and Muslims in Spain drew sharp criticism from the thirteenth-century Spanish kabbalist Moses de Leon, the supposed compiler of parts of the Zohar:

There are individuals who believe that the Muslims are not included in the category of gentiles, since they are monotheistic by faith, because they are circumcised and furthermore abstain from certain prohibited foods, in contrast to Christian practice. Know then that the Ishmaelites are most certainly to be included in the category of gentiles and indeed are as unclean as they ... for there is no nation so given to adultery as the Muslims. Moreover their circumcision being only partial is invalid, their monotheism is insincere and they are guilty of the very distortion of the Scriptures of which they accuse us. As such, they are to be regarded as worse than Christians. Indeed if we do not approve of the latter, who have partly accepted the truth of the written Law, how much more so the Muslims who deny the truth of the whole of Scripture?[40]

An analogous stance was taken in the following century by another kabbalist, Joseph Ashkenazi:

Consider closely the stupidity of our co-religionists who praise and exalt the Muslim religion thus transgressing the precept of the Law 'Find no grace in them' [Deut. 7: 2]. Not satisfied with that, when the Muslims profess their faith at the hour of their assembly in the mosques, these weak-minded Jews, who have no share in religion, associate themselves with them reciting for their part 'Hear O Israel' [Deut. 6: 4]. Then they actively praise the nation of that wretched individual [Muhammad]. The

---

[38] Probably an allusion to the humiliating ceremony which took place at the payment of the *jizya*, or capitation tax Jews paid to the Muslim authorities (see D. Littman and P. Fenton, *L'Exil au Maghreb* (Paris, 2010), 101).

[39] *Otsar hahayim*, Moscow State Library, MS Ginsburg 715, fos. 27b–28a.

[40] Moses de Leon, *Shekel hakodesh*, ed. A. Greenup (London 1911), 65–6.

result is that they and their children have become attached to the Muslims and thus vilify the holy faith of Israel, denying the divine Law pursuing emptiness and vanity. It is no surprise to observe simple folk of our nation allowing themselves to praise the Muslims. What grieves me is the fact that the very ones who claim to be versed in the religion of Israel—I allude to certain prominent persons in our community— proclaim the law of the Muslims and commend their unitarian faith.[41]

A similar opinion still prevailed in the *Kaf haketoret*, an anonymous kabbalistic commentary written most probably by a Spanish Jew who lived at the time of the expulsion from Spain:

'Deliver me out of the mire and let me not sink' [Ps. 69: 15] refers to those that esteem the religion of the Ishmaelites and sink into the mud . . . for the religion of Islam is likened unto an abyss into which one tumbles blindly. Thus many Jewish souls have fallen into this mire saying: 'They are not idolaters and they are circumcised.' But this is but the cleanliness of 'those that purify themselves . . . and consume detestable things'.[42]

Moreover, the anonymous author complains of Islamic oppression and condemns willing converts to Islam to reincarnation in the bodies of animals.

There are grounds for the claim that, in contrast to the earlier kabbalists, the exponents of the post-expulsion kabbalah exhibited a slightly more pronounced sympathy for Islam. The foremost kabbalist of Safed, Moses Cordovero (1522–70), wrote in his commentary on the Zohar:

'These are the generations of Ishmael' [Gen. 25: 12]. Behold Ishmael is virtuous [*kasher*] in one respect and defective in another. Per se he is virtuous, but on account of his descendants he is defective, that is the aspect which emanates from 'loving kindness' [*ḥesed*] through Hagar the maidservant, that is the outer husk [*kelipah*] that protects and serves holiness. Whenever 'loving kindness' irradiates it with a spark [of holiness], then [Ishmael] yearns to ascend and is holy, but whenever he turns to the outer side he descends. Thus one finds that Ishmael at times goes down and deals wickedly and at others, rises and repents . . . The name [Ishmael] indicates that he draws near to the supernal hearing and God hearkens to his cry, for externally he is nourished and subsists on loving kindness. Therefore the verse continues 'son of Abraham borne by Hagar' [Gen. 25: 12], that is he descends from Abraham, the branch of loving kindness. However, Hagar lowers him on account of her being an Egyptian, that is on the boundary of Israel, where she serves as a maidservant to Sarah, who embodies holiness. She bore these 'generations' to Abraham as an organic component of kindness. For this reason kindness is not valued in an individual who is naturally kind, only in a person who overcomes his inclination to act contrarily [to the dictates of kindness].[43]

[41] See L. Poliakov, 'Jews and Moslems', *Diogenes*, 32 (1960), 84.
[42] G. Vajda, 'Passages anti-chrétiens dans *Kaf ha-Qetōret*', *Revue d'Histoire des Religions*, 147 (1980), 57–8.   [43] Moses Cordovero, *Or yakar*, 'Ḥayei sarah' (Jerusalem, 1970), v. 110.

The great Polish kabbalist Nathan Nata Shapira (*c.* 1585–1633), commenting on the verse 'Abraham took all of these [*eleh*] and divided them in the midst'
(Gen. 15: 10), states the position of the two sister faiths in relation to Judaism:

This is an allusion to the parallelism of the princely thrones on high on each side of
[Jacob/Israel]. On the one hand, Rahab [Islam] to the right with his 36 princes, and
Samael [Christendom] to the left with his 36 princes, while Israel stands in the
centre. This conforms to Rabbi Bahya's comment on the verse: 'they sanctify and
purify themselves . . . behind one in the midst' [Isa. 66: 17] as referring to the
Muslims' observance of their day of rest on Friday, and the Christians on Sunday,
whereas Judaism is in between.[44]

There are three reasons for this more positive attitude. First, it may be conceived as a reaction to the terrible hardships suffered by the exiles in the wake
of their expulsion from Christian Spain. The kabbalists, the great majority of
whom were of Sephardi descent, saw in the lands of Islam a haven of tolerance.
In this they resembled the nineteenth-century orientalists and Zionists, whose
resentment of the impediments to emancipation in the Christian West led
them to idealize Muslim civilization. Secondly, mysticism transcends the
bounds of denominational religion and grasps the metaphysical truths that lie
beyond the limits of sectarian formalism. Whereas this tendency in early kabbalah had been impeded by intolerance, it was allowed to unfold under the
influence of a third element: the Lurianic doctrine of the 'ingathering of the
sparks of holiness' as a prerequisite for the final redemption. The kabbalistic
doctrine that Ishmael was basically close to holiness favoured the assimilation
of many elements of Islamic provenance, which brought about a partial
renewal of the Judaeo-Arabic cultural synthesis. Its impact on Jewish esotericism is yet to be determined by historians of kabbalah. To take but one significant example, the kabbalists made great efforts to adapt their esoteric poems
to Arabic melodies. In this connection, Menahem di Lonzano, whose admiration for the Muslim laws of purity has already been mentioned, states: 'Do not
be surprised at our having employed Muslim melodies, for I have found no
other tunes which are so heart-rending. Furthermore, I have done so on
account of the scale they employ, for that is what will be used in the messianic
era.'[45]

This attitude had far-reaching consequences for the literary creativity of
Oriental Jews and was an important factor in the composition of numerous
poems. Lurianic kabbalah devoted a large part of its speculative theology to
the role of the *kelipot*, or 'forces of evil' in the dynamics of the world of the

[44] Nathan Shapira, *Megaleh amuqot*, 'Lekh lekha' (Kraków, 1637), fo. 16*a*. The numerical value
of the Hebrew word *eleh* is 36.

[45] Menahem di Lonzano, *Shetei yadot*, fos. 65*d*, 141*b*; see Fenton, 'Review of H. Zafrani, *Poésie
juive en "Occident musulman"*'.

sefirot. Within these theories Ishmael personified the *kelipot* of the forces of *ḥesed*—compassion or leniency—and as such appeared in a more favourable light than Edom (Christendom), who embodied the forces of severity and harshness.

However, beneath this apparent benevolence towards Islam lay a hidden malignancy that emerged in all its vigour in the Sabbatian heresy. Notwithstanding their marginal character, the writings of the Sabbatian sectarians exhibit by far the most radical attitude towards Islam in which all previous tendencies crystallize. Following the example of Sabbatai Zevi, the mystical messiah (about whom it is related that in his cell he would study with the Zohar in one hand and the Quran in the other), a large number of his most extreme followers converted to Islam in 1683 in an organized apostasy.

The members of this sect, later known in Turkish as the Doenme, continued nonetheless to practise a secret and heretical form of Judaism while outwardly professing the religion of Muhammad. The early writings of the sect were devoted to the defence of Sabbatai Zevi's conversion to Islam. It was presented as a preliminary step in the process of salvation comparable to the primary stages of Moses' career when he is portrayed as an Egyptian (Exod. 2, 19), the prototype of Islam. Apostasy—which the Sabbatians called 'donning the turban', that is, Muslim headgear—was considered a sacred mystery accessible only to the select few.

The paradoxical situation in which the converts found themselves led them to develop a remarkable theory concerning the Godhead, parallels to which are only to be found in the dualism of the early Gnostics. In the first stage the exponents of the Sabbatian doctrine distinguished between the Torah of Israel and the Torah of Ishmael, called the Torah of Grace in keeping with Ishmael's traditional association with the virtue of kindness. Although the Torah of Ishmael, through which the messiah had to pass in order to realize his redemptive mission, was superior in some respects to the Torah of Israel, it was in general considered inferior to the latter, which remained the absolutely true Torah. In theological terms these two poles correspond to the dual aspect of the divinity, the God of Grace manifest in the creation and the God of Judgement, who had revealed himself in the Sinaitic theophany.

The frustration arising from their ambiguous situation as crypto-Jews found its most poignant expression in Israel Hazzan's commentary on the book of Psalms, written shortly after Sabbatai Zevi's conversion. The author interprets each psalm in terms of the messiah's yearning to escape from the prison of Grace (Islam) and return to the Torah of Moses.[46] Another aspect of

---

[46] Gershom Scholem, 'A Commentary on Some Psalms from the Circle of Sabbatai Zevi in Adrianople' (Heb.), in *Aley ayin, minhat debarim leshaz shoken* [S. Z. Schocken Jubilee Volume] (Jerusalem, 1952), 157–211.

this frustration is intimated by the Sabbatians' ambiguous attitude to their adopted faith. Mordecai Eisenstadt, writing in the 1680s, explained their conversion as salvific for Islam, whose imminent destruction was thus averted.[47]

On the other hand, there is a distinct longing for personal salvation that sees the downfall and destruction of Islam as its corollary. This attitude is particularly noticeable in one of the Eighteen Articles of the Doenme faith which declares: 'Be heedful to respect some of the Islamic prescriptions in order to deceive them. As for *Ramadan* and the *Bayram*, it is necessary to observe those precepts of which the non-observance would attract attention . . . the hour of vengeance is not yet ripe.'[48]

Indeed, the motto of the Doenme was 'To resemble, but not to be'. In their desire for liberation from an oppressive duplicity, it is known that the Doenme participated prominently in the reform and liberalization movements that arose in the Ottoman empire in the early twentieth century. An analogous aspiration may have prompted many Jews to join the Baha'i movement in its initial stages in Persia at a similar period.

I have tried to restrict myself to the writings of Oriental Jews for the sake of authenticity, but would like to end this brief survey with a selection of passages from the relatively recent hasidic masters of Poland. It would be wrong to assume that Ashkenazi Jews had no knowledge of Islam. Indeed, some of the most profound and illuminating Jewish attitudes to Islam are found in their writings. Ashkenazi Jews experienced direct contact with the Muslim populations of central Europe, such as the Muslim Tartar communities. Furthermore, the fate of their institutions in the Holy Land led them to pay close attention to social and political events in the East, such as the Napoleonic Wars, which aroused messianic expectations. They also had occasion to meet Muslims when part of Poland came under Ottoman rule. Hence it is not extraordinary that Muslims figure more than once in the stories of the Ba'al Shem Tov (1700–60), the founder of hasidism. Moreover, significant passages are devoted to Islam in the speculations of his followers.

My final examples are taken from the writings of some of the most profound thinkers of the hasidic movement. Rabbi Alexander Zushya Kahana of Plock (1795–1837), a disciple of Rabbi Simhah of Pryzyscha, understood the verb in 'Sarah saw the son of Hagar the Egyptian jesting [*metsaḥek*]' (Gen. 21: 9) to mean that Ishmael was 'Isaac-ing', that is, impersonating Isaac (*metsaḥek* and *yitsḥak* (Isaac) derive from the same Hebrew root). This in turn illuminates Sarah's observation 'the maidservant's son will not inherit my son Isaac' (Gen.

[47] Gershom Scholem, 'Apocalyptic and Messianic Chapters on Rabbi Mordekhai of Eisenstadt' (Heb.), in *Sefer Dinaburg* (Jerusalem, 1949), 249.

[48] Gershom Scholem, 'The Sprouting of the Horn of David', in Daniel Jeremy Silver (ed.), *In the Time of Harvest: Essays in Honor of Abba Hillel Silver* (New York, 1963), 368–86.

21: 10). Although the impersonation is counted as an imposture on Ishmael's part, the rabbi concluded that his aspiration towards elevation was nonetheless praiseworthy.[49]

Similarly, Rabbi Yehudah Aryeh Leib Alter of Gur (1847–1905), one of the great figures of Polish hasidism known, after his commentary on the Pentateuch, as the *Sefat emet*, perceives Ishmael in the positive role of intermediary between holiness and profaneness:

Abraham was the pillar of the universe and, as is stated in the Midrash, prior to his circumcision he sustained the whole world. However, after his circumcision his conduct conformed in every respect to the special way of the Children of Israel, that is, the way of the Torah, which transcends nature. Therefore God appeared unto Abraham [Gen. 18: 1] in a particular way in which others have no share. Now since he begot Ishmael before he was circumcised, Ishmael provides a possibility of drawing near for all nations. When they convert to [Judaism] they can become one people. Even before this conversion, subsistence necessarily extends to all nations through Israel, providing there be an intermediary between them. As is stated in the holy books [*Ets ḥayim*, 42: 1] in regard to the four levels of existence: mineral, vegetable, animal, and human. Between mineral and vegetable there is an intermediary which shares the characteristics of both, such as truffles and mushrooms. Likewise, between the vegetable and animal realms there are 'stones of the field', a well-known bird which grows like a tree. Likewise the intermediary between beast and rational man is the ape. We are of the opinion that beyond rational being 'true man' is to be found, referred to in the verse: 'You are man' [Ezek. 34: 31] 'for ye are called man and not the nations' [BT *Yev.* 61a]. Now Ishmael is the intermediary, therefore he is called *pere'adam* 'a semi-man' [Gen. 16: 12]. Thus he has a hand in *bakol* ['fullness'] and the hand of 'fullness' has a hold upon him [Gen. 16: 12]. For through him there is a connection between the level of rational being and that of 'perfect man'.[50]

Elsewhere, Rabbi Alter states:

'And Abraham again took [lit. 'added'] a wife, and her name was Keturah' [Gen. 25: 1], as if he had added from the profane to holiness . . . and this is why he begot the son of Hagar before Isaac's birth and the sons of Keturah after Isaac's birth.[51]

With great insight, Rabbi Elie Munk (1900–81) expatiates on the notion of 'added holiness' in this passage with the following commentary:

Of Abraham's children, Isaac was the one who most perfectly embodied the saintly ideal which was the inheritance of his father. But the patriarch wanted this core of saintliness to be surrounded by a sacred zone, just as shabbat, a day of holiness, overflows its own bounds and forms a zone around itself. Its heralding rays envelop both the hours which precede it and those which serve to prolong it at nightfall. So

---

[49] Rabbi Alexander Zushya Kahana, *Torat kohen* (Warsaw, 1939), fo. 36a.
[50] Judah Aryeh Leib Alter, *Sefat emet*, vol. i (Piotrków, 1904–8), fo. 73a.   [51] Ibid., fo. 45a.

too, the nucleus of holiness that Isaac represented availed itself of his brother Ishmael, born 13 years before him, to send out the heralding rays which began to illuminate the horizon of humanity. And it continued past its own limits through the children of Keturah, the younger brothers and sisters of Isaac as [explained] by the *Sefat emet*.[52]

In his *Peri tsadik*, a commentary on the weekly readings, Tsadok Hakohen (1823–1900) discusses too the difference between Esau and Ishmael in their relationship to Israel.

Esau embodies the attribute of 'anger', which has no redemption in the spiritual realm. By way of contrast, Ishmael inherited the dross of Abraham's attribute of 'love' but used it only to satisfy his selfish 'desires'. Nonetheless, the latter can be turned to goodly purpose and undergo purification [*berur*] with a view to their inclusion in the realm of holiness. 'Desire' can be 'taken to the House of Learning and the delights which attend it will be clothed in the words of Torah'. Esau is called a *goy*, 'a people', whereas Ishmael is, like Israel, known as a *le'um* 'a nation'.[53]

This is indeed is an explicit avowal of the basic admissibility of Islamic values within the Jewish fold on condition that they are given a Jewish appearance. A similar note is struck by the following passage, which is to be found in the *Beit ya'akov*, written by Rabbi Jacob Leiner (1814–78), of the hasidic Izbica-Radzyn dynasty:

Ishmael is the negative feeling [*kelipah*] of desire . . . now the feeling of desire is not as remote from [holiness as anger]. It is for this reason that they bear the name Yishma'el, which contains the words *shema eli*, 'hearken my God', for they have a [genuine] craving for the Holy One Blessed Be He, but he does not desire them in return. Nonetheless, Ishmael is the best and choicest of the nations, for he is less attached to sin than they.[54]

This passage shows that Judaism displayed a remarkable degree of permeability to Islam, despite the latter's tyranny and oppression. It was above all in certain esoteric spheres that the limitations of outward religious formalism were transcended and that, rising above the bigotry that separated Jew and Muslim during the medieval period, Israel would, in rare instances, heed the discourse of Ishmael.

An apt conclusion to this survey might be this extract from a letter written on 7 Iyar 5681 (1921) by one of the greatest hasidic rabbis of pre-war Poland,

---

[52] Elie Munk, *The Call of the Torah: An Anthology of Interpretation and Commentary on the Five Books of Moses*, vol. i: *Genesis* (Jerusalem, 1980), 257, quoting Alter, *Sefat emet*, vol. i, fo. 45*a*. According to the Midrash, Keturah was really Hagar whose further offspring from Abraham were then also Hagarites, a name synonymous with 'proselytes'.

[53] Tsadok Hakohen, *Peri tsadik* (Lublin, 1934; repr. Jerusalem, 1972), ii. 101; see also iv. 51; v. 271.   [54] Jacob Leiner, *Beit ya'akov* (Warsaw, 1890; repr. Jerusalem, 1969), 336.

Abraham Mordecai Alter of Gur (1866–1948), known as the Imrei Emet, describing his impressions of a visit to the Holy Land:

When I walked in the streets of Jerusalem in the places where the Arab inhabitants circulated with their camels, almost everywhere I passed they made way for me with extreme deference. If we could only merit even some of that amongst the inhabitants of other countries! I construed that we could establish relations with them and dwell there in tranquillity and security.[55]

FROM PAST TO FUTURE:
THE INVERSION OF THE POLES

This overview of the complex of Jewish attitudes to Islam through the centuries raises the question of what insights and assistance these texts and teachings might offer us in our endeavour to articulate Judaism's contemporary relationship with one of the world's great religions. It is my conviction that, on the whole, they are not very helpful in their traditional form, addressing as they do challenges that are diametrically opposite to the ones we face today. Many of the passages were written by Jews in Muslim lands who were in a position of subservience and dhimmitude. The concept of *dhimmi*, with its discriminatory theology, has now all but disappeared, simply because the number of Jews residing in Muslim countries is negligible. The exodus from almost all of the Arab countries and the establishment of a sovereign Jewish state in the heartland of Islam have created a new religious perspective. Changes in political circumstances have completely redefined the present-day agenda of Jewish–Muslim relations, making a large part of the past irrelevant. With the exception of Israel, the traditional societies of the Middle East where Jews once dwelt alongside Christians and Muslims have disappeared, making the former modes of thought and their models—even the mystical ones—seem less appropriate and productive for meeting the current challenges.

In circumstances in which the Jewish community struggles with a newly awakened militancy in parts of the Muslim world, it is hard to maintain the kabbalistic conception of Islam as an expression of compassion, in contrast to the idea of Christianity as one of severity. When we consider recent developments in Christianity's view of Judaism, which came about precisely as Jewish subservience in Muslim countries gave way to the political confrontation that increasingly defines Jewish–Muslim relations, the kabbalistic scale appears the reverse of how Jewish authors in the not too distant past saw it.

[55] Abraham Mordecai Alter, *Osef mikhtavim* (Warsaw, 1927), 65; (Jerusalem, 2008), 75.

CONVERTED DOGMAS

Just as there has been an apparent 'conversion' of the old socio-political situation, so too we need to convert our former models and develop new modes of interpretation. As the doors of interreligious dialogue open, all religious communities are called to examine fundamental aspects of their teachings with a view to advancing peaceful relations in the world. To those who believe in divine providence, Islam's confrontation with Judaism does not appear to be fortuitous. Is it not an invitation to try to forge a form of peaceful coexistence between communities of faith in the same territory and in the same pluralistic and multicultural society?

It is clear from the Quran and Hadith that at its inception the most significant Other to which Islam was doctrinally and practically opposed was Judaism. Could it be that its road to coming to terms with the Other passes through the resolution of its conflict with Israel? In the context of wider Jewish–Muslim relations there is also important work to be done, independently of easing the political tensions between the Jewish state and the Muslim world. Both Jews and Muslims are called upon to engage in such work. The principle in the light of which such a task should be carried out can be referred to as 'conversion' or 'reversal', a concept expressed in the Hebrew term *teshuvah*, meaning simultaneously 'response' and 'repentance'. The hermeneutics of centuries of mutual suspicion and exclusion, of competing exclusivist visions, can now serve as mirror images of what we must construct theologically together. We are called to develop new theologies of otherness. Our challenge is how to retrace our steps to the parting of our paths in order to discover our common origins, our common denominators in terms of ethical and spiritual values. This is a task that both Islam and Judaism must undertake.

'Convert', which is akin to 'converse' means to 'turn with', and also calls to mind the verb to 'converge'. Concentrating on the differences between religions is not constructive: we must concentrate on what unites us. Dialogue cannot proceed by affirming our 'truth' in opposition to their 'error', but compassionate 'matricial' truth—*raḥmān* in the Arabic of the Quran, *raḥmana* in the Aramaic of the Talmud, related to the Semitic word for 'womb'—allows for the existence of 'kindred truths', so that beyond the differences between religions, the most important fact is the unity of humanity, a unity of origin since God created all people and shows them equal compassion. Indeed, the biblical statement: 'The Lord is good to all: and his tender mercies [*raḥamav*] are over all his works' (Ps. 145: 9) is mirrored by the quranic verse: 'Our Lord, you embrace all things in mercy [*raḥmatan*] and knowledge' (Quran 40: 7).

This does not imply that all faiths are identical, for the very recognition of the place of Otherness implies the possibility of difference. Indeed, religious dialogue requires each participant's essential faithfulness to his own religion: the truth of another's faith provides an opportunity to deepen one's own— Leopold Sedar Senghor's 'authenticity and openness'.

Thus interreligious dialogue implies reciprocity, the conviction that the Other has a unique intuition of the truth, which can also be meaningful to me. One thereby avoids the double pitfall of syncretism and relativism, two concepts which suppress otherness.

Muslims also urgently need to retrace their theological, hermeneutical, and historical path in a movement of 'conversion', *teshuvah* (*tawba* in Arabic), aimed at restating Islam's relations with other religions. While the work must be done by Muslims, it is legitimate for a Jew to suggest some areas that require such an approach. Though not its original doctrine, later Muslim theology developed the dogma of the 'pre-existence' of the Quran, which embodied the ultimate and definitive truth. Indeed, Islam, chronologically the most recent of theistic religions, sees itself ontologically as the earliest: 'last come, first served', as it were. This crowning accomplishment of Muslim metaphysics has in turn brought about a closing of history at both ends. In contrast to Judaism's messianic hope which opens up human history to the future, Islam (at least in its Sunni form), as the expression of the definitive divine revelation, anticipates nothing beyond the repetition in the future of a present, which itself is the restoration of the absolute past of its origins.

This belief has led to Muslim claims to a monopoly on truth, while denying the historical possibility of other origins, particularly Jewish, to Muslim teachings. The metaphysical claim to the pre-existence of the Quran precludes any recognition of its historical affinity to Islam's sister faiths. Muslims must by themselves undertake a real return to the Quran involving a historical and philological analysis of its sources, just as Christians since the Renaissance have explored the roots of the Bible. They would then discover the 'Jewish element' in Islam. The often unconsidered Other would then be found to be a tangible component within the Quran, in which can be heard the echo of what was probably the very first sacred book rendered into Arabic—the Hebrew Bible.

Similarly, the history of Muslim exegesis reveals other fundamental departures from Islam's original tradition. One such key moment is the identity of the son whom Abraham attempted to sacrifice. Early interpreters understood him to be Isaac, as in Genesis 22; later interpreters understood him to be Ishmael. Revisiting the history of interpretation, in light of historical tradition on the one hand and contemporary needs on the other, can go a long way to redressing an imbalance in Muslim perceptions of the relationship of Ishmael and Israel. More broadly, we can think of an invitation to reconsider the nature of the Abrahamic covenant. At a minimum, we might acknowledge the equal love that Abraham bore towards both his sons. Such acknowledgement could pave the way to recognizing the great debt that Islam owes the Israelite descendants of Isaac.

An outside observer might wonder whether it is possible for classical Muslim theology to carry through a programme of reversal which could be considered theologically legitimate for Muslims, and whether such a programme could be usefully implemented by Sufi teaching. Perhaps schools that have held up the ideal of abolishment of Otherness and identification with the original truth are better suited to meeting some of the challenges of a theology of Otherness that we face today. Such a theology would have to take us beyond the difference and separation, beyond the parting of the ways, to a domain that is spiritually powerful enough to raise us above present-day political circumstances and the Othering they lead to—an Othering that is increasingly diabolical. Only by returning to their own historicity, through the prism of modernity, can Muslims retrieve their humanity.

Jews too must meet the requirements of 'conversion', must return to before the division, and must recognize the Other, but without losing sight of modernity and the problems that it poses to all believers. Indeed, those that engage in dialogue would do well to abandon all notion of chronology, which engenders the sentiments of 'precedence' for some and 'completion' for others.

As well as overcoming our fear of dialogue and our preconceptions, especially Jewish belief in Israel's exclusive chosenness, one of the fundamental prerequisites for exchange is knowing oneself while recognizing the Other. In other words, dialogue implies the establishing of a community. I would call this a conversion of *beḥirah* (chosenness) into *ḥebrah* (community) (both Hebrew words have the same letters). We have to relinquish that part of our heritage which is infused with the radical sterility of theological controversy, which only leads to the blind alley of religious complacency.

Symbolically, the key to the acceptance of Otherness lies in the reversal of Abraham's ninth and, until then, most difficult trial: the banishment of Ishmael and Hagar to the wilderness of Paran.[56] This is a potent story that may be read as foreshadowing key moments in Muslim–Jewish relations. Read differently, another possible attitude to Islam and its founder emerges. The 'flight' or *hijra* of Muhammad from Mecca marks the inception of Islam just as the 'flight from Egypt', the Exodus towards the Promised Land, ushers in the beginning of the Israelite religion. Could not Muhammad's 'flight' from Mecca to Medina, the Jewish city, be construed as an attempt to reverse the departure of Ishmael from Abraham's tent, in a return to the fold? Is it not significant that the word *hijra* derives from the same Semitic root as Hagar, Abraham's ultimate and repentant spouse, according to the midrashic interpretation of Gen. 25:1?[57]

---

[56] *Pirkei derabi eli'ezer*, 30.   [57] *Genesis Rabbah*, 61.

Yet the Arab prophet was met with derision and mockery—the archetype of the recurrent 'Arab humiliation'—and his hurt eventually turned into hate. It is up to modern-day rabbis and theologians to reinstate Paran as the doorstep to the Land of Israel. When the children of Israel set forth from Sinai, their first stop was Paran, the Arabian Desert (Num. 10: 12). The rabbis interpret another biblical verse referring to Paran (Deut. 33: 2) as an allusion to the offering of the Torah to the sons of Ishmael. In a 'conversion' of the rabbinic narrative that casts this offering as a moment of refusal (by the sons of Ishmael) and their consequent rejection by God, we ought to consider the positive dimensions of Paran, a 'station of the divine word', encompassing the sons of Ishmael (*atifat yishma'el*). In a modern midrash, one might contemplate something of the prophetic spirit Israel had experienced and that had been offered to the sons of Ishmael, as overflowing into the wilderness of Arabia, transforming it also into a future *dor hamidbar*, 'abode of the divine word', according to its alternative meaning.

In light of today's challenges we must renew ancient stories, create new midrashim, and articulate innovative theologies. We must make space in our own world-view for the other of Islam, not as the banished son, but as a member of the Abrahamic family. Our cherished wish would be that, in return, the *ummah*, too, would recognize Israel's *hijra* back to the Abrahamic cradle, of which they were the long-standing custodians, awaiting the return of their covenantal brother.

ELEVEN

Encountering Hinduism
Thinking Through *Avodah Zarah*

ALON GOSHEN-GOTTSTEIN

INTRODUCTION

PART of what makes a Jewish theology of world religions a vital contemporary concern is that in the past few decades Judaism has come into contact with religions with which it previously had no significant dealings. These religions pose new challenges. Judaism has only recently encountered Hinduism in an organized way and on a large scale. Tens of thousands of Jewish, particularly Israeli, youths have encountered it. Commercial and political relations have created many opportunities for the two faiths to meet, and a formal dialogue between Jewish and Hindu religious leadership now takes place. Despite all this, there has been little reflection on the meaning of the present encounter with Hinduism, the challenges and opportunities this encounter provides, and what it might have to teach us for a Jewish theology of religions. The issues are as broad as they are complex and will require the efforts of many thinkers over an extended period of time. I am currently working on a monograph devoted to these issues, tentatively titled *Beyond Idolatry: The Jewish Encounter with Hinduism*, but have no illusions that I will resolve or reach finality on any of the issues raised by Judaism's encounter with Hinduism. At this point, perhaps all we can achieve is raising the questions, developing a better grasp of their complexity, and moving from simplistic notions to more complex, even if more confusing, understandings of Hinduism. Even if some answers emerge already now, we are at an initial stage of learning within this encounter. It suffices for the time being to understand the challenges of the moment and the tasks that lie ahead.

I wish to share in this chapter some of the insights that are elaborated with greater detail and complexity in the forthcoming monograph. Limitations of space force me to concentrate primarily on one issue of the many raised by the encounter. It seems to me that Hindu worship, offered to many beings, all of whom are recognized as representing god and hence divine, is the most pressing issue for most Jewish observers of Hinduism. In other words, Hinduism is considered *avodah zarah*—illegitimate alien worship, equivalent to idolatry. Because this perception is so common, dealing with it seems both the most urgent, and the most appropriate, way to begin the engagement with Hinduism.[1] As the issue of Hindu worship cannot be divorced from other aspects of Hindu religious life, or from Jewish perceptions of those aspects, I will briefly touch upon several other dimensions of Hinduism that provide a spiritual and religious context for a discussion of *avodah zarah*.

ON JUDAISM(S) AND HINDUISM(S)

No religion is a monolith, but some are more so than others. This is probably a fair way to sum up the following discussion and it touches on the fundamental assumptions of this chapter. When we speak of Judaism's encounter with Hinduism, we assume a meeting of two entities that should be described and related to in roughly the same terms and categories, along the lines of a meeting between two individuals. The reality, however, is that religions are far more complex.[2] They include different religious, ideological, and practical ways of expressing a broad tradition. Under certain circumstances the different expressions of a religion may recognize one another and be recognized as belonging to the same religion; at other times, even this may be questioned. This issue is relevant both for Judaism and for Hinduism, but particularly for the latter. In the case of Judaism, the complexity of defining Judaism and recognizing its different manifestations as expressions of a single religious system have led Jacob Neusner and scholars who follow his lead to speak of 'Judaisms' in the plural, rather than the singular. Still, for purposes of the present discussion we may identify Judaism in a way that includes its diversity within a broader unifying framework: the rabbinic tradition encoded and expressed in the halakhic tradition that grows out of the Talmud and its commentaries. This tradition includes also the various superstructures that give meaning to the halakhic way of life, including Jewish philosophy, kabbalah, and their various offshoots. While this Judaism has much diversity, its various components have come to recognize themselves as part of a whole. From this sense of a whole one may explore what it means to engage another religious tradition like Hinduism.

Turning to Hinduism, we discover the term 'Hinduism' is problematic in far more complex ways than the term 'Judaism', leading some scholars of religion to speak of both religious traditions in the plural, 'Hinduisms' and 'Judaisms'. If we are to speak of Judaism's engagement with Hinduism, we

---

[1] A discussion of Hinduism in terms of *avodah zarah* provides an opportunity to re-examine how we think of *avodah zarah* in general and the theological assumptions that inform our religious views. Constructive thinking on *avodah zarah* in the light of Hinduism will be left for *Beyond Idolatry*.   [2] On this issue, see Stanisław Krajewski in Chapter 5, above.

must know what this Hinduism is, who speaks for it, and who represents it. These remain debated issues within Hindu scholarly and religious communities. The difficulties in providing unequivocal answers to these questions touch the heart of the concerns of this chapter, making its conclusions and suggestions in some way tentative, dependent on the resolution of what 'Hinduism' is and how we represent it.

There are several difficulties with defining 'Hinduism'. We lack a historical tradition that conceptualized the religion or religions of India in these terms. Hence 'Hinduism' is a very young category and is in part indebted to the emergence of the modern study of religion. While the category did draw on earlier forms of constructing the identity of a religious community, specifically in contrast with the religious identity of the Muslim community, we do not have any classical Hindu category that corresponds to the Western religious '-ism' of 'Hinduism'. Properly speaking, Hinduism could be described as a loose federation of religious traditions. These religious traditions can be quite disparate or they can share features making them recognizable to each other as species of the same genus. The variety pertains not only to the deities worshipped (an obvious consequence of polytheistic practice, as distinguished from belief), but also to the philosophical understanding of the religion, the chain of tradition and authority, the form of ritual practice and observance, the understanding of the goals of the religion, and more. Both theologically and ritually the range of legitimate divergence is great. In terms of practice it exceeds the range of legitimate divergence of practice within Judaism, probably even if Jewish heterodox groups and sects are included. Philosophically and theologically the divergence is at least as large as that characterizing the differences between Jewish philosophy and kabbalah. For thousands of years, complementary and partially overlapping Hindu religious traditions have been living alongside one another in a basic mode of tolerance and acceptance, notwithstanding intergroup tensions that might erupt from time to time.

Like all religions, Hinduism has been changing for centuries in response to its encounter with external forces. Under colonial rule, changes took place in Indian religious life, either through legislation or through the challenges and opportunities presented by British culture and Christianity. Internal reform has led to various religious movements and new forms of Hindu identity. Various religious teachers over the past 150 years have helped shape the religious imagination of what Hinduism is both in India itself and in the West, creating greater convergence between different understandings of Hinduism. Other external forces have also greatly influenced a growing sense of a unified religious identity. Communications and media have played a great role in spreading religious knowledge and creating a common sense of ownership of many Hindu traditions and practices. This movement has been greatly aided also by migration and the emergence of a powerful Hindu diaspora. Increasingly, when we think of 'Hinduism', we no longer think exclusively of the Indian subcontinent, but of the global context and the presence of Hindus in most parts of the world. The Hindu diaspora plays an important role in the shaping of Hindu identity and will continue to do. Hindus from different localities, practising different forms of Hinduism, believing in different deities, following different customs, and having diverse understandings of Hinduism itself are forced to share one common temple, one community, limited resources, and common challenges in a new environment. Diaspora Hinduism is not simply a replica of Hinduism as practised on the subcontinent. It functions, rather, as a means of synthesizing multiple traditions, preferring some over others and constructing some sense of a common Hindu identity. This new identity is then projected back to the homeland through the ongoing two-way communication of ideas and practices. Diaspora Hinduism, one of the loci of Judaism's encounter with Hinduism, is thus a force in shaping Hindu identity and the concomitant understanding of what Hinduism is, how it functions, and what challenges it presents to Judaism. To take one example relevant to the present discussion, Vasudha Narayanan points to the fact that in the diaspora Hindus are challenged to explain what the idols they worship are and how they are understood. She notes that temple literature in the United States of America presents Hindu deities in ways that conflict with traditional practice but that make Hinduism more palatable to the Western audience. Idols are, accordingly, presented as merely symbolic.[3] We are facing new articulations of core issues that have a profound bearing on Judaism's encounter with Hinduism. It is not enough to dismiss certain voices as apologetic, for today's apologetics are tomorrow's faith, especially when it comes to a religious tradition that is as pliable and changes as easily as Hinduism does. Diaspora thus presents us with new possibilities and opportunities for understanding Hinduism, even as it continues to serve a unifying function for Hinduism's self-understanding.

One of the realities associated with the emergence of a unified Hindu understanding of religion is the rise of a view of Hinduism from the perspective of a particular philosophical vantage point, sometimes called 'New Hinduism'. The coming of Hindu teachers to the West (specifically America) since the visit of Swami Vivekananda in the late nineteenth century has done much to shape what 'Hinduism' is for both Hindus and non-Hindus. The voice of this movement is primarily the voice of one school of Indian philosophy, the non-dualistic philosophical school known as Advaita Vedanta. Followers of this school see it as the ultimate form of Hindu philosophy, incorporating all others. It is a

[3] See Vasudha Narayanan, 'Diglossic Hinduism: Liberation and Lentils', *Journal of the American Academy of Religion*, 68 (2000), 767.

monistic world-view that recognizes the unity of all being and sees all diversity, in life as well as in the divine and its worship, as secondary phenomena and removed from the ultimate reality, to be accounted for philosophically. The figurehead of this line of teaching is the eighth-century teacher Sankara, who for many now functions as the authoritative and ultimate voice of Hinduism. It seems fair to suggest that the present-day representation of Sankara's philosophy and how it has come to speak for increasingly larger portions of Hinduism is a new phenomenon that would not have been witnessed several hundred years ago. Nevertheless, it is an important part of what Hinduism has become, particularly because it is increasingly presented as the proper understanding of Hinduism.

Vedantins are in a doubly advantageous position. Their world-view is all-inclusive and accounts for all forms of religious practice, including the lower, less philosophically informed practices of Hinduism such as the various smaller, local manifestations. Vedanta need not consider Hinduism as we see it as the final or perfect form of Hinduism. It considers Hinduism in the ideal, accommodates lower and imperfect forms of its religious life, and offers a narrative to bridge the two—the continuing chain of teachers who seek to elevate humanity to greater spiritual heights through correct teaching. It is thus a total world-view that integrates various expressions of Hinduism. Vedantins enjoy the additional advantage of having a voice, representation, and recognition. Most of the major religious teachers of India are indebted to a vedantic understanding and appeal to it, even if they are not philosophically inclined themselves. Thus, Advaita Vedanta has more of a voice in contemporary Hinduism than any other stream. While a Jewish view of Hinduism and an attempt to understand whether Hindu worship is indeed *avodah zarah* cannot rely completely on a vedantic viewpoint, we must recognize that this is a dominant and to a large extent representative voice within Hinduism, and for this reason it informs the few Jewish attempts to engage with Hinduism. The complexity of Hinduism is captured by the recognition that Vedanta provides a representative voice that nevertheless cannot speak for all Hindu traditions.

ENCOUNTERING HINDUISM: HISTORICAL PRECEDENTS

Several early modern rabbinic tracts offer the following apologetic as a foreword: 'all references to *avodah zarah* in the following treatise do not refer to the people among whom we live (Christians), but to people of distant lands, such as India'. The need to both neutralize references to Christians as *avodah zarah* and to maintain the relevance of the category has on occasion led to the identification of Indian religion with *avodah zarah*. Such an identification was

possible precisely because India is a distant land, known from tales and imagination, rather than from the reality of day-to-day encounter and living in
proximity. India has been the subject of hearsay, projection, and imagination
for centuries, even millennia. Attitudes to Hinduism have thus taken shape and
continue to be informed by the unique circumstances of reference to a religion
that is decidedly other, strange, and distant, foreign in the most basic sense of
the foreign worship that constitutes *avodah zarah*, and we must reckon with
this fundamental fact when we consider Jewish attitudes to Hinduism. All previous instances of dealing with the religion of the other and the consequent
proclamation of the worship of that religion as *avodah zarah* have been the
result of life experience in cultures with which Jews have come into close
contact. Hinduism and other Eastern religions are different in that they have
not been part of the Jewish historical encounter. Jewish understanding of
Hinduism is consequently subject to rash judgements and the application
of criteria that are important for Jews, but that are understood differently and
in various ways in Hindu writings and by Hindus themselves. The concern for
the worship of images and the facile declaration of Hinduism as *avodah zarah*
are natural consequences of the sudden exposure to new and strange forms of
religious life.

It is important to remember that despite the seeming novelty of the contemporary Jewish encounter with Hinduism, the two religions actually have
a history that may be two millennia old.[4] In light of this, what would be more
natural than to turn to that history in search of precedents for a Jewish view of
Hinduism, and in particular of how Jews living among Hindus viewed Hindu
gods and their worship? I have been unable to establish any references in literature written by Indian Jews to Hinduism as *avodah zarah*. In part this may
be due to the fact that Indian Jewry was not a centre of rabbinic literary activity. Nevertheless, such silence is still striking. Moreover it is heightened by
indications of a different attitude, one that either does not consider the religion of India to be *avodah zarah* or at least does not consider it to be a major
concern in defining attitudes and relations with Hindus. Walter Fischel posed
the question to twentieth-century Indian Jews and reported that the prevailing
attitude was recognition of multiple spiritual paths, which allowed for the religious and spiritual validity of Hinduism.[5] Contemporary Indian Jews offer
similar answers, even though their replies reflect a secularized cosmopolitan

---

[4] See Nathan Katz, 'The State of the Art of Hindu-Jewish Dialogue', in R. Chakravarti, B.
Sinha, and S. Weil (eds.), *Indo-Judaic Studies in the Twenty-First Century: A View from the Margin*
(New York, 2007), 113–26.

[5] Walter Fischel, 'The Contribution of the Cochin Jews to South Indian and Jewish
Civilization', in S. S. Koder et al. (eds.), *Commemoration Volume: Chochin Synagogue Quarter-
Centenary Celebrations* (Cochin, 1971), 60; see also Nathan Katz and Ellen Goldberg, *The Last
Jews of Cochin: Jewish Identity in Hindu India* (Columbia, SC, 1993), 249.

understanding that already bears the imprint of such Indian spiritual giants as Ramana Maharshi and others.[6] Still, the impression is consistent: rather than highlighting the idolatry, strangeness, and otherness of the religion of their Hindu neighbours, Indian Jews seem to have reciprocated the acceptance and tolerance they enjoyed. If correct, this is very significant. It suggests that different cultures and different historical contexts tend to highlight different aspects of the encounter between religions. What seems to us to be of vital concern is only one of several options of how the relationship may be constructed. As such, it is both culturally and historically contingent. This relativizing perspective also emerges from an examination of medieval perceptions of India.

Indian Jewry did not live in complete isolation, and throughout the centuries various travellers visited India. Perhaps the earliest relevant records come from the Cairo genizah, where we find notes of Jewish merchants who wrote from India or who had visited India. S. D. Goitein, who published these records, comments on their silence regarding the religion of the people of India. The tone of the writers is warm and they refer to the Hindus as brothers, but say nothing of their different religion. Surely the Jews must have realized how different the religious landscape was. Why, then, is this difference not expressed in their writings?[7] One answer might be that we simply do not have all the relevant materials in our possession. But there may be another answer. The lack of interest of these Jewish merchants may reflect the lack of interest of the Indian Jewish community in these issues. It may, in theory, also reflect their successful resolution. If Jews viewed Hinduism similarly to how Hindus understood their own faith, then they would have viewed Hindus as monotheists who worship different representations of one God. The level of tension in relation to Hindus would obviously be lower than if they were concerned about polytheism as forbidden idolatrous worship.

CONTEMPORARY HINDU–JEWISH ENCOUNTERS: THE QUEST FOR SPIRITUALITY

Commerce and day-to-day coexistence defined the earlier stages of historical encounter. While also served by commercial and diplomatic concerns, our present-day encounter is also driven by a particular contemporary concern—the quest for spirituality. Jews from all over the world turn to India, its teachers, and its traditions as part of their ongoing quest for spiritual meaning and lifestyles. American Jewry's turn to India from the 1960s onwards has become

---

[6] See Joan Roland, 'Religious Observances of Bene Israel: Persistence and Refashioning of Tradition', *Journal of Indo-Judaic Studies*, 3 (2000), 41–2.

[7] See S. D. Goitein, *A Mediterranean Society* (Berkeley, Calif., 1971), ii. 277.

a flood of travellers from Israel.[8] This is true not only for secular Jews and Israelis, but also for an increasing number of religious youth and their educators, who seek to complement and deepen their religious experience of Judaism by drawing on practices and teachings found in Hinduism.[9] There are various models for reconciling the turn to India with faithfulness to Jewish identity and practice. One model plays with questions and answers. Questions are posed from a Hindu context and answers are provided from within Judaism.[10] In some sense such a model and the turn to Indian spirituality generally may be taken as a sign of crisis. Of course, crisis contains opportunity and holds within it the promise of growth. While this type of spiritual encounter may be driven by the desire for growth, this desire is nevertheless fed by crisis in Jewish spiritual reality. Talk of 'spirituality' veils what can be considered the greatest aspect of Jewish spiritual crisis: that most of Judaism is unable to talk of God or to provide a conscious relationship with him. Different people would see Judaism's present crisis differently. While some see it in terms of identity and others in terms of continuity, still others conceive of it in terms of either learning or practice. In the present context, I would like to argue that Judaism's deepest crisis concerns God. Judaism is a religion that centres around God, but that to a large extent has lost touch with the living God.[11] God has not lost touch with Judaism, nor have the people of Israel lost their faith in God. But Judaism has lost, to a significant extent, the awareness of God at its centre and the ability to structure the entire life of the religious community, let alone the people of Israel, around access to divine presence and its grounding in the community's life. This loss has deep historical roots, and may itself be an expression of the destruction of the Temple, the loss of prophecy, and a long history of exile. This loss is, to my mind, included in what kabbalists speak of when they refer to the exile of the Shekhinah.

Jews are both a faithful people and a people of faith. But their religious life is presently constructed so that other religious values occupy places of primary importance, often eclipsing God's centrality within the religious system. One commonly attributes to Zoharic literature the maxim that the Torah, Israel, and God are one.[12] In one way this could express the unity of all values within

---

[8] See Daria Maoz, 'Every Age and its Backpack: On the Different Groups Traveling to India' (Heb.), in Elhanan Nir and Rubin Mass (eds.), *From India to Here* [Mehodu ve'ad kan] (Jerusalem, 2006), 107–25.

[9] A representative collection of essays that reflect this trend is *From India to Here*.

[10] Elhanan Nir, 'Where is the Time of Non-Movement? On Hasidism, East and West, and Something about the Israeli Present' (Heb.), in Nir and Mass (eds.), *From India to Here*, 12.

[11] Some of these ideas are articulated in Alon Goshen-Gottstein, 'When Will I See the Face of God?' (Heb.), *Akdamot*, 9 (2000), 119–30.

[12] The maxim itself seems to have been coined by Moses Hayim Luzzatto (1707–46) (see Isaiah Tishby, 'God, the Torah and Israel are One: The Source of the Saying in Ramhal's Commentary on the Idra Rabba' (Heb.), *Kiryat Sefer*, 50 (1975), 480–92).

the divine beautifully. Yet the union of these values with the divine may also lead to their becoming the primary foci of religious attention and devotion at the expense of God as the ultimate point of the spiritual quest. To a large extent this is precisely what has happened.

The exile of God, his hiding, the difficulty in finding or accessing him—however we conceptualize it—seems to me to be the heart of the Jewish spiritual crisis. And it is only when we are able to confront the fact that we are in crisis that we may consider what the turn to Indian spirituality seeks to heal. It is not only that Jews find a spirituality in India that addresses a deep hunger in their souls; rather, India makes available a directness of approach to God that is often lacking in Judaism. This direct approach to God may be the hallmark of India's spiritual life and why it is so attractive to Jews.

When Jews conceive of the goals of the religious life, few of us think of communion or relationship with God, let alone consider it the only thing worth desiring. We seek happiness, family life, the well-being of our group, a life of values, learning, and overall flourishing. God plays a meaningful part in this package of ideals, but for very few is God actually the central focus of their quest. Here India provides so many opportunities for an alternative testimony that it has come to represent for many that very alternative. Indeed, the goal of the spiritual life as stated by so many spiritual teachers of the Hindu tradition says it all: 'God realization'. Perhaps not all know what God realization means. Perhaps very few attain it. But it is a central governing ideal that informs the lives of thousands, if not millions, of spiritual seekers. Hinduism, as encountered through various teachers and religious groups, presents God at the centre and a systematic path to reach knowledge and awareness of God.

One of the most common practices of Hindus of different traditions is *japa*, the repetition of God's name. The quest to keep God's name a constant reality keeps God very much at the centre of one's awareness. Even more significantly, the theological structure of Hinduism makes God more readily available than do the Abrahamic faiths. Fundamental to the Hindu approach is the recognition that God is omnipresent and all-pervading. This view allows one to recognize God in all and to find him everywhere. Most forms of Judaism think of God in transcendent terms, even if they employ a religious language that speaks of God in personal terms. Even those Jewish traditions that portray God in pantheistic or panentheistic terms do not turn that insight into the governing approach to divinity, readily available for worship and contact. Thinking of God in terms of his omnipresence, as all-pervading in all forms of life, orients religious thought and practice in such a way that highlights God's accessibility. In terms of spirituality, this more than any other may be the one element that defines Hindu spirituality compared with Jewish spirituality. I contend that the centrality of God and God realization is what draws Jewish seekers to Hinduism. Thus God realization lies at the heart of the Jewish encounter with Hinduism.

I conclude this section by sharing the testimony of an Israeli writer speaking of the impressions of her first visit to India. Rivka Miriam is observant and active in Torah study and various literary and religious forums. Her knowledge of Torah allows her to relate to her experience in India in terms taken from classical Jewish texts. Her testimony confirms the suggestion I have just made and points to what might be the source of India and Hinduism's appeal for Israelis and Jews:

And now to divinity. Meeting its expressions in India brought about a transformation in me. We Jews employ the common expression 'there is no place that is devoid of Him'. In India I discovered a world where indeed so it is. I discovered a world in which there is no one who does not believe. I discovered a world where one sees divinity in every tree and in every stone. But also in every deed and in every matter. The entire world is full of his glory.

Seeing divinity in India brought about a transformation in me. Indeed, there I saw a place full of faith. Another, different, way to believe, a path that may have been uprooted from us when, as the Talmud tells, the evil inclination for idol worship was uprooted. And perhaps together with that uprooting a part of faith as such was also uprooted.[13]

Faith is the all-pervading reality, a faith in the all-pervading Divinity. One sees God everywhere. This gives life to what are otherwise mere texts, words, and ideas found in Jewish sources. Miriam paraphrases Isaiah 6: 3 in light of the *musaf* Kedushah text that proclaims the entire world is full of divine glory.[14] Significantly, she appeals to a kabbalistic source to affirm that there is no place devoid of the divine presence.[15] The religious reality of India makes sense in light of kabbalistic language and insight. Miriam experiences India as a place full of faith and that faith is transformative. She struggles with the relationship between this faith and idolatry, and our own complex loss/gain upon removal of the inclination to worship idols based upon a story narrated in the Talmud.[16] Idolatry enters the overall assessment of the Indian religious reality; indeed, it is the flip side of the all-pervasiveness of faith in India. Faith draws; idolatry repels.

---

[13] Rivka Miriam, 'I Was a Prism for Light' (Heb.), in Nir and Mass (eds.), *From India to Here*, 41–2, 45.

[14] Not only the earth, as in Isaiah. Christian liturgy achieves the same by adding the heaven to the earth, filled by God's glory.

[15] *Tikunei zohar*, Tikun 57 (91*b*); Tikun 70 (122*b*). This statement is often juxtaposed with the previous paraphrase of Isaiah in hasidic literature (see Elimelekh of Lyzhansk, *No'am elimelekh*, 'Terumah', s.v. *vezehu dirshu*; Moses Hayim Ephraim of Sudylkow, *Degel maḥaneh efrayim*, 'Beshalaḥ', s.v. *vayomeru*).

[16] Rivka Miriam, 'I Was a Prism for Light' (Heb.), 45, alluding to BT *San.* 64*a*.

HINDU SAINTS — TESTIMONY AND CHALLENGE

Hindu spirituality is not encountered in the abstract. To a large extent, Jewish seekers encounter it through the teachings and person of Hindu teachers and saints: gurus.[17] One of the first challenges that faces serious and open-minded Jews who engage with Hinduism is the fact that some people, even if only a few, have attained extraordinary spiritual heights through Hinduism, or, more broadly, within the spiritual context of Indian religious life. How we view Hinduism will vary greatly depending on whether one is or is not able to acknowledge this. My own thoughts have been formed by my impressions of some Hindu religious figures. For me, their sanctity and spiritual achievement are beyond question, and hence an important point of departure for theological reflection upon other religions generally, and Hinduism in particular. The challenge of accounting for another religious tradition changes radically the moment one admits that great spiritual heights, perhaps even greater than those seen in one's immediate vicinity or even within Judaism as practised today, have been or are realized in the lives of individuals of another tradition. It may take only one such person to transform one's theological views or change one's spiritual horizons to include others. Even granting that for every true teacher there are a hundred others who fail to reach such heights and that for every guru who is a model there are many fallen, this does not change the fundamental theological challenge. It only makes the question of discernment more urgent and calls us to cultivate spiritual tools for recognizing true from false spirituality. Those tools would have to be applied in relation to our own great teachers and would not be a means of distinguishing one religion from another, but distinguishing the higher from the lower and the authentic from the inauthentic forms of spiritual life as these are manifest in all religions. The same kind of intellectual honesty that calls us to apply criteria to help us discern and recognize true spiritual teachers also calls us (certainly it has led me) to recognize the authentic spiritual lives of saints outside Judaism and, in the present context, within the spiritual framework of the religious life of India.

Saints are appreciated in the broader religious world-view within which they operate. In the case of Hinduism this has implications for the recognition of the divinity manifest in the spiritual teacher. Nuances vary, but the core issue— and herein lies the challenge from a Jewish perspective—is the Hindu view of the teacher as divine. There are different ways of understanding this approach.

[17] See the reflections on the consequences of meeting Indian gurus in Nir, 'Where is the Time of Non-Movement?' Significantly, Nir uses classical rabbinic terminology, referring to them as *tsadikim*. The choice of terminology will determine the attitude to the spiritual phenomenon under discussion. Referring to aspects of Hindu religious life in the same terms in which Jewish spiritual virtuosi are considered assumes they are of a kind, can be compared, and that one can learn from the Hindu species of the same genus.

On one level, it is a matter of respect, etiquette, and propriety. The guru is approached *as if* he were God. The 'as if' approach is, of course, reminiscent of various midrashic statements that inculcate a religious attitude by means of 'as if' statements, which narrow the divide between the human and the divine.[18] However, in the Indian context the recognition of the divinity of the teacher is more far-reaching than a rhetorical device or the inculcation of a respectful attitude. In many senses, the teacher is, or can be, seen as divinity proper. While being absolute and transcendent, divinity is also understood as capable of incarnating itself. The teacher, as mediator of divine life and teaching and as model of spiritual perfection, is often considered as an incarnation of the divine. Needless to say, this attitude is at odds with classical Judaism's fundamental objection to the idea of the divinization of humans. Whether this fundamental difference can be bridged will be discussed below, but for now it is enough to recognize that Hindu saints are an important site for a Hindu–Jewish conversation about the divine and how it is approached.

THE WISDOM OF INDIA: ANCIENT IMAGES AND CONTEMPORARY CHALLENGES

Encounters of cultures happen in rich and complex ways. They can also be conceived of in various and changing ways. Encounters of cultures can never be reduced to a single dimension. Any attempt to frame the encounter, to highlight what another culture is or represents, to focus upon the challenges and problems of the encounter of cultures, already reflects a conceptual agenda. The choice of how cultures are juxtaposed and how their point of encounter and ensuing challenges are presented already betrays a certain understanding of what is important to a given culture. The changes in how one culture imagines another, how it portrays it, and what it deems important in the meeting provide an important lens through which the two cultures and their interactions can be studied. Because cultures are complex, we may expect different and changing conceptions of what they mean to each other to emerge over time. This has important consequences for Judaism's encounter with Hinduism. If, for many contemporary Jewish observers, the Hindu worship of idols is the defining feature of Hindu religion and is considered to be the most interesting and significant dimension of a Jewish appreciation of Hinduism, this has not always been the case. Earlier periods captured India through another lens, almost completely ignoring the worship of images. That lens was the lens of wisdom.

Recognition of India and its religious tradition as a repository of wisdom is the most persistent view of India in Jewish literature, and it is about as old as

---

[18] The rabbinic terms are *ke'ilu* and *kiveyakhol*. On the latter, see Michael Fishbane, *Biblical Myth and Rabbinic Mythmaking* (Oxford, 2003), app. 2.

rabbinic Judaism itself. Regardless of how well previous generations knew the religion of India and whether that knowledge was direct or mediated, wisdom was a recognized way to engage with Hinduism. Many Hindus will feel comfortable with a description of their tradition in terms of wisdom, and they would probably even consent to distinguish it from the concept of revelation as used by the Abrahamic faiths. Wisdom is thus an important dimension for mutual understanding that is by now a fundamental aspect of the Jewish tradition's view of India and its religion. Even within contemporary discourse, which often makes the worship of idols a primary dimension of a Jewish view of Hinduism, wisdom remains an important aspect of the encounter. It provides a way for both partners to understand themselves, their uniqueness, and the meaning of their encounter. Recognizing this dimension allows us to balance other perspectives, and to reflect upon the enduring challenges of the Hindu–Jewish encounter for Judaism's growth and development.

One example of a positive evaluation of India and its sages is found in the writings of Menasseh ben Israel. He recognized the value of Indian wisdom and saw it as part of the Abrahamic heritage. He relied on the narrative in Genesis 25: 6, which describes Abraham giving gifts to the children of his concubines and then sending them to the East.[19] Menasseh ben Israel provided the theoretical foundations for one of the most interesting attempts to relate Hinduism and Judaism, that of Matityahu Glazerson, who authored a book entitled *From Hinduism to Judaism*.[20] Glazerson approached Hinduism in an open and positive way. In fact, his is probably the most favourable treatment of Hinduism by any Jewish author. This is made possible through the twofold strategy of concentrating on Hinduism as wisdom, rather than worship or religion, and approaching that wisdom as our own in the inclusivist mode developed by Menasseh ben Israel. The book's logic runs as follows: Hinduism teaches . . . ; we also find this in Judaism. The basic premise is that Hindu teaching is valid. Glazerson wants to demonstrate that there is no need to turn to Hinduism in order to obtain that wisdom because it is fully available in Judaism as well. Hinduism emerges as valid and meaningful for non-Jews. In Glazerson's scheme, Jews are endowed with a special soul and therefore can only find their spiritual fulfilment through the observance of the *mitsvot* and by following Judaism. Hinduism is thus a valid path of wisdom, but an inadequate one for Jews. Glazerson never uses the word religion in this context, nor does he address the problems associated with *avodah zarah*, and his work is proof of the possibility of appreciating Hinduism as a wisdom tradition while putting aside all issues related to *avodah zarah*.

[19] *Nishmat ḥayim*, pt. 4, ch. 21; see Richard Marks, 'Abraham, the Easterners and India: Jewish Interpretations of Genesis 25: 6', *Journal of Indo-Judaic Studies*, 3 (2000), 49–71.
[20] Matityahu Glazerson, *From Hinduism to Judaism* (Jerusalem, 1984).

The problem with Glazerson's logic becomes obvious when presented in this way. What makes Judaism appropriate for Jews is that it is more than a set of wisdom teachings and practices; it is religion in the full sense. Hinduism is never acknowledged as such. The comparison is made in a partial way and ends up working in Judaism's favour. That Glazerson's argument is partial should not lead us to minimize his achievements. Glazerson was able to highlight what is positive in Hinduism while bracketing all that most rabbinic figures find problematic, namely *avodah zarah*. Constructing this argument and developing it as extensively as he did is thus an important strategy that must be respected.

CONFRONTING THE WORSHIP OF IDOLS: DEFINING THE CHALLENGE

It should by now be apparent that there are multiple perspectives from which to conceptualize the Jewish–Hindu encounter. In different ages we note different paradigms that govern either the image of India and its religion or the actual contact of Jews with Hinduism. Each of these captured a different facet of the complex web of possible and actual relationships between the two religions. The present discussion focuses on what is considered today by some the most crucial aspect of dealing with Hinduism and certainly the thorniest and most complex issue from the perspective of traditional Judaism. Highlighting this dimension implicitly establishes what is important in the Hindu religion in Jewish eyes, how the encounter is envisioned, and how Hinduism is judged. For reasons that we may no longer be able to trace, the issue of worshipping idols has become the defining issue, and for many Jews that is all that they see in Hinduism and is the sole basis for assessing Hinduism.

The Jewish view of other religions as *avodah zarah* was not formed as a response to Hinduism. Contemporary approaches to Hinduism that make this the primary lens are carrying over attitudes that are thousands of years old and that were formed in relation to other religions. Objection to foreign worship helped establish Jewish identity in the biblical and rabbinic periods, in relation to the various gods of surrounding cultures, and for the past two millennia has been an important element in Jewish consideration of Christianity and even of Islam. The battle against *avodah zarah* is a fundamental feature of Jewish identity and thus an important safeguard for its protection.

Avodah zarah's ready application to Hinduism stems from several considerations. The first, as suggested, is simply the carryover of age-old attitudes to the encounter with a new religious phenomenon. A second is the predominance of the worship of idols, images, *murtis*, in the Indian religious context.[21]

---

[21] Images are problematic in and of themselves. But they also suggest the multiple divinities worshipped through the various images, thereby making the view of God wholly incompatible

To the extent that *avodah zarah* is really a struggle against the worship of idols, it seems that India is a good case in point. This leads to the third point, namely that there has been little serious study of Hinduism as a religious system. Almost no effort has been made to understand it on its own terms, as a counterpoint to the application of the ready-made categories through which Jews assess other religions. This may or may not change the halakhic consequences associated with the claim that another religion is *avodah zarah*, but at the very least it contextualizes and nuances such claims. Hinduism provides a wonderful opportunity to re-engage with the subject of *avodah zarah* and to examine how we apply it. Precisely the fact that this is a new encounter unencumbered by attitudes that are thousands of years old, and by the painful history that did much to reinforce such attitudes, allows us to make the encounter with Hinduism more than an occasion to assess that religion and its potential meaning to Judaism. It provides an opportunity to think through in fresh ways the categories that have furnished our attitudes to other religions and that are consequently applied, at times carelessly, to a Jewish view of Hinduism.[22]

Avodah zarah involves interrelated aspects, the identity of the god under discussion as another god, and the inappropriate worship of God, through idols and images. That these two distinct issues can be used indiscriminately within one conceptual rubric tells us something important about the category of *avodah zarah* and how it has been defined and sustained. Applications of *avodah zarah* for thousands of years make the implicit assumption that wrong worship—in particular worship through forms and images—suggests another, different god. Because historically these two issues have been closely related, their conflation persists, even in face of the theoretical possibility that the same God is worshipped through other means. The challenge at hand is to examine the facile leap from foreign worship to foreign god. The religion of India confronts us precisely with the challenge of separating ritual from philosophy and theology and posing the question of how one knows, other than by means of ritual, that the God worshipped by two religions is the same God. If we can advance in our thinking on this issue, we may not only help deepen our understanding of Hinduism, but also deepen our reflection upon the fundamental category of *avodah zarah*.

But raising the question of the relationship between worship and philosophy leads us to an even more complicated fundamental consideration: 'Who speaks

with that of Judaism. The issues overlap, at times to the point of confusion. The present discussion collapses both issues into the problem of the image. A fuller exposition of *avodah zarah* must deal with each of the issues on its own terms, as well as with their interrelatedness.

[22] The discussion in *Beyond Idolatry* examines many of our assumptions concerning how *avodah zarah* functions as a category and how the encounter with Hinduism invites us to reconsider our application of the category.

for the religion?' Who holds the key to the proper interpretation of Hinduism, and whose voice should we take into account as we seek to understand Hinduism in relation to the Jewish concern with *avodah zarah*? This is a fundamental question of any Jewish theology of other religions, one completely ignored by the leap from the use of images in worship to the declaration of another religion as *avodah zarah*. If we reflect upon the relationship between ritual and philosophy, then we might consider the philosophers, the teachers of religion, as those who hold the key to the meaning and correct interpretation of the religion. The other extreme would be to consider the 'man in the temple', the common person who worships or on whose behalf worship is performed, as the authoritative voice inasmuch as he or she holds the key to the intention and hence to the theological understanding that drives a particular action. A median position might be the local authority, perhaps the local temple priest, who would offer the appropriate explanation of the ritual performed and the correct understanding of the deity worshipped. Finally, perhaps the meaning of the religion is best found in the writings of great figures of the past, regardless of contemporary understanding?

The multiplicity of interpretative perspectives is confusing and highlights a serious problem with understanding Hinduism. Conflicting evidence can be brought in an attempt to assess the religious understanding of the 'man in the temple', evidence that moreover changes from one form of Hinduism to another, both in terms of schools of thought and practice and in terms of the geographical presence of Hinduism in different countries. We are thus left with the question: 'Who speaks for Hinduism?'

Upon further reflection, we might be led to the conclusion that it is impossible to pass judgement on an entire religion, let alone one so diffusely defined and constructed as Hinduism. It may be that in the final analysis we must resort to answering the question on a person-by-person basis, in terms of the individual believer, or at least in terms of an individual school of thought and practice. In that case, one man's idolatry would be another's true religion. While this seems paradoxical, it highlights the difficult choices we are forced to make as we undertake an understanding of Hindu faith and worship from a Jewish perspective. The present discussion continues to explore 'Hinduism' constructed broadly from a Jewish perspective, along lines developed by rabbinic authorities in relation to other religions, primarily Christianity. The possibility of abandoning such a broad and generalizing viewpoint in favour of more particular assessment of individual and group forms of Hinduism is examined in my *Beyond Idolatry*.

Following these introductory considerations concerning how Hinduism may be understood, I turn to the most public and widely advertised instance of Jewish encounter with Hinduism, which occurred during the twenty-first century and had a global impact, making international headlines. This encounter illustrates just how much present-day engagement with Hinduism is a major contemporary reality that cannot be sidestepped. It also illustrates the problems associated with learning about another religion and calls us to examine how we go about doing so.

In 2004 the court of Jerusalem's Rabbi Yosef Elyashiv issued a halakhic ruling concerning the permissibility of wearing wigs (*sheitels*) made of human hair offered in Hindu temples as part of the devotions of Hindu believers. The halakhic background of the discussion is that a Jew may not benefit in any way from an offering of *avodah zarah*. He (or she) must burn it. Accordingly, if female devotees offer their hair in Hindu temples, the hair may not be used by Jewish women. The question that arose in 2004 was 'Was the offering of hair by Hindu devotees an offering of *avodah zarah* that should be forbidden to Jewish women?' The natural thing was to study the matter first hand, and so a prominent London rabbi, Aaron Dunner, was sent to India as Rabbi Elyashiv's emissary to study the matter personally. The emissary did not go to the School of Oriental and African Studies of London University for a course on Hinduism. He made his way to Tirupati, one of India's most celebrated temples, and returned home after 48 hours, so we are told, with his mission accomplished. He was able to provide the needed information based upon which Rabbi Elyashiv could rule that wigs that originated in Hindu temples could not be worn by Jewish Orthodox women. According to reports that followed the visit, Rabbi Dunner engaged locals in an enquiry about the nature of their ritual act. When they responded that they were offering their hair to the deity, he concluded that this was an offering to an idol, and hence should be forbidden for use. Rabbi Elyashiv's ruling followed suit.

Let us begin by noting the unexamined assumption of the entire rabbinic discussion. No one ever stopped to ask the question of whether this worship was indeed *avodah zarah*, what the status of Hinduism in this respect is, and how the worship in the Tirupati temple under examination conforms or does not conform with a broader view of Judaism on Hinduism as a religion.[23] There did not seem to be a need, even for those who sought to permit the wigs, to ask that most fundamental question.[24] At the time, I went through the voluminous

[23] The methodological flaws, even from the viewpoint of halakhic discourse, in how rabbis went about, or rather did not go about, discerning the nature of Hindu religion are explored in Daniel Sperber, 'How Not to Make Halakhic Rulings', *Conversations: The Journal of the Institute for Jewish Ideas and Ideals*, 5 (Sept. 2009), 1–11, available at <http://www.jewishideas.org/articles/how-not-make-halakhic-rulings>.

[24] Joshua Flug's conclusion is telling. He speaks of the value of this controversy as an opportunity to explore issues that are rarely of practical relevance, such as offering to an idol and the statistical principle of *kavua*. Nothing is said of the opportunity to explore what *avodah zarah* is ('A Review of the Recent *Sheitel* Controversy', *Journal of Halacha and Contemporary Society*, 49 (2005), 5–33, esp. 33).

responsa literature that the situation generated. I was struck by the fact that not a single halakhic decisor felt the need to raise the question of whether Hinduism, or the worship in Hindu temples, should be considered *avodah zarah*. There seems to me only one possible explanation for this. The power of images and their worship is so great and their impact upon Jewish memory and imagination so complete, that it leaves no room for querying this fundamental assumption of the discussion. The power of the immediate vision is so great as to determine unequivocally that the specific form of Hindu worship under discussion ought to be considered *avodah zarah*.

The challenge of distinguishing between the visible form of worship and the theological superstructure can only be articulated on the basis of a more thorough knowledge of a religion. One must be aware of the deep Jewish antagonism to *avodah zarah* and of how easily this resorts to the power of the visual as a first step in applying a more critical methodology to the Jewish study of Hinduism. The exclusive appeal to worship while ignoring philosophical understandings of the religion is the root problem. It points to a weakness in the classical Jewish approach and reminds us of how difficult it is to achieve a balanced understanding of Hindu religious life. Even if we concede there is value in sending a rabbinic emissary, who should he have spoken to? The priests who receive gifts for the deity?[25] The heads of various spiritual schools and dynasties who honour the site and frequent it on regular pilgrimages? If the latter, the meaning of Hinduism might be found outside the temple, among a narrow section of its users. One further relevant possibility is that the temple at Tirupati was dedicated, actually rededicated, by one of India's greatest philosophers, Ramanuja in the eleventh century, who is said to have consecrated the temple and established its ritual practices. In a situation in which the meaning of an action is unclear, it would make sense to turn to the institution's founder and learn his intentions. Ramanuja was a proponent of a school of Vedanta called modified non-dualism. At stake in the differences between the different

[25] The question of who holds the key to interpreting a religion is actually one of the issues that arose in the context of the *sheitel* controversy. Whether one relied on priests, worshippers, or barbers would have different halakhic consequences and even accounts for the reversal of earlier rulings, resulting in the 2004 prohibition of *sheitel*s (see Flug, 'A Review of the Recent *Sheitel* Controversy', 19, 22). Note, however, that Hindus were only asked about the meaning of their action, not their view of God, which is the focus of my own discussion. Benjamin Fleming exposes the problematic nature of the responses offered by Hindus questioned by rabbinic emissaries. Their answers contradict Hindu self-understanding, creating a gap that Fleming seeks to fill by pointing to the complexities of traditional understandings of hair and the meaning of its cutting in Hindu sources (see Benjamin Fleming and Annette Yoshiko Reed, 'From Tirupati to Brooklyn: Interpreting Hindu Votive Hair-Offerings', *Studies in Religion / Sciences Religieuses*, 40 (2011), 1–36). This complexity, typical of so much of Hindu religious thought, alerts us to the care that must be taken when posing questions to practitioners, based on the concerns and categories of another religious system.

schools is just how extreme the monistic vision of reality is and consequently, the relationships of deity and devotee, and of God and the world. While this school is not identical with the brand of Vedanta that has increasingly come to represent Hinduism associated with the eighth-century teacher Sankara, it still enjoys great prominence and remains one of the major philosophical and religious schools in India. Thus, in turning to Ramanuja we are not simply turning to a founding figure. Rather, we are turning to a figure whose teachings continue to have broad, even if not universal, impact and whose legacy is mediated also through this specific temple. It would thus seem appropriate to consider how Ramanuja himself would have viewed the worship of idols and how his own religious teaching could provide a frame of reference for assessing what goes on in Tirupati today.

Introducing so many factors into the discussion increases its complexity. First-hand testimony of contemporary image worship provides clear and unequivocal answers. The method I propose raises more questions than I can answer. Indeed, I myself am unable to make an unequivocal pronouncement one way or another on an issue as weighty as *avodah zarah*. For many, the ability to uphold clear-cut and unequivocal positions seems desirable. My own approach is characterized by attempting to arrive at the root of things and recognizing their complexity, even at the cost of not resolving fundamental questions, at least today. To me, this seems preferable because it paves the way for a fuller understanding that can emerge tomorrow at a time when conditions have ripened and understanding has deepened. The alternative leads nowhere.[26]

---

[26] After reading Sperber's 'How Not to Make Halakhic Rulings', I recalled a conversation with him over a decade ago. During a discussion of Christian art, he suggested Christianity was not *avodah zarah*, whereas Hinduism obviously was. I expressed doubts at the time concerning how unequivocal we should be about Hinduism. I was therefore struck to see that Sperber's discussion includes quotes from the recent dialogue of the chief rabbinate and Hindu leaders as the kind of resource that should inform halakhic thinking. I queried him as to whether his opinion had changed and also noted that his comment was methodological, but stopped short of viewing Hinduism in the same light as he had viewed Christianity more than a decade earlier. Sperber conceded his viewpoint had indeed changed and ascribed it to his ongoing involvement in dialogue with Hindus. The more he got to know Hinduism, the more complex it seemed, and the harder it was for him to take an unequivocal position on its status as *avodah zarah*. Clearly, his earlier views had been informed by the appearance of Hinduism, while his later views were informed by greater exposure to its philosophy, as expounded by some of its leading contemporary exponents. Growing complexity thus often comes at the expense of clear-cut perspectives. This, however, is not a loss, but a gain, and one whose significance may only become obvious in the long run.

In Sperber's case their significance has emerged even in the 'short run'. In a forthcoming study of Hinduism and *avodah zarah*, he argues that the halakhah can completely accept Hindu self-understanding, thereby exonerating it from the charge of *avodah zarah*. Sperber's forthcoming study reaches the same conclusions as those reached by Steinsaltz, below.

HINDU IDOL WORSHIP IN LIGHT OF JEWISH VIEWS
OF CHRISTIANITY: THE *SHITUF* PARADIGM

The exclusive appeal to what we see when we observe Hindu worship, namely the worship of images, followed by the declaration of Hinduism as *avodah zarah* is to a large extent a carryover of biblical and rabbinical attitudes to other religions. In this approach, the otherness of the god is confirmed by the otherness of the image and the worship offered it. However, Jewish tradition also developed alternative models that can be applied to Hinduism. These come from the Jewish Middle Ages and grow out of Judaism's encounter with Christianity. Rabbinic authorities articulated various positions about Christianity, declaring it either to be not idolatrous or to be a form of *avodah zarah* permissible to its non-Jewish practitioners. These views of Christianity are important resources for considering Hinduism and its worship of images.

The two strategies that have been used by Jewish legalists and theoreticians to deal with Christianity are mapped out elsewhere in this volume.[27] The first perspective, associated with the Tosafists, became the default position of much of Ashkenazi Jewry over the past several hundred years. According to this position, non-Jews are not obligated to have exclusive allegiance to God and they may worship another being alongside or as part of their view of God, provided they maintain awareness that the object of worship is God the Creator of heaven and earth that Judaism acknowledges.[28] This is called *shituf*—the association or worship of another being alongside God. Different standards apply to Jews and non-Jews. Since non-Jews are permitted to worship through *shituf*, Trinitarian Christianity is a valid religion for non-Jews. One of the pioneering discussions of the status of other religions in the soon-to-be-born State of Israel was that of Chief Rabbi Isaac Herzog. He devoted a detailed discussion to other religions, focusing for the most part on the permissibility of maintaining Christian worship within the future Jewish state. Towards the end of his discussion, Herzog goes beyond Christianity and Islam and poses the question of the status of other religions.[29] While acknowledging his limited knowledge of Hinduism, he raises the possibility that Hindu worship can also be considered a form of *shituf*. Herzog does not enter into a detailed discussion of the substance of Hindu faith, but when we review his understanding of *shituf* and

[27] See my discussion in the Introduction and Eugene Korn's in Chapter 8, above.

[28] Note that the emphasis here is on the multiple recipients of worship and not on the problem of image worship. Solving one issue does not necessarily solve the other. However, because the two are related within the conceptual framework of *avodah zarah*, one issue does have an impact upon the other. If image worship implies that another being is worshipped and is therefore problematic, we can understand how the theological response might address the problem created by image worship.

[29] Isaac Herzog, 'Minority Rights According to the Halakhah' (Heb.), *Tehumin*, 2 (1981), 178–9.

how he applied it to Christianity, his suggestion becomes plausible. If Hinduism recognizes a formless God as the source of creation beyond the myriad manifestations of divinity worshipped in a variety of ways, we may apply to Hinduism the same logic that applied to Christianity. Of course, the actual relationship between the absolute Brahman and the various manifestations of God, Ishwara, is understood differently than the relationship of the three persons of the Trinity. But the *shituf* construct is not based on a particular understanding of the relationship of the object worshipped with God in the absolute, as much as on the affirmation that in some sense one continues to worship God the Creator, or the Absolute, beyond the worship offered to the creature alongside or as part of the Creator. Our concern here would accordingly be less to appreciate Hinduism in its own terms than to identify a mechanism for viewing Hinduism broadly in a way that takes it out of the bounds of *avodah zarah* for its non-Jewish practitioners. Extending the concept of *shituf* to Hinduism achieves this goal.[30]

This leads me to a discussion of the only rabbinic author to have discussed Hinduism with some degree of familiarity. While the discussion is not extensive, at least it attempts to portray Hinduism in its own terms. The following passages by Rabbi Adin Steinsaltz show us how a contemporary halakhic perspective on world religions can be constructed. The sum total of his discussion is, as a respondent to his piece correctly observed, extraordinary, if not absolutely exceptional.[31] As the respondent continues, while making no concessions to modern liberalism or even ecumenism and while characteristically identifying his position with that of the Talmud, Steinsaltz reassesses the current world religions, including Hinduism and Buddhism, as adequately monotheist, adequately non-idolatrous, and at least adequately ethical to qualify as compliant with the Noahide laws. Steinsaltz's article represents an approach so open-minded that it would not be followed by more than a few contemporary Orthodox rabbis. With this introduction, let us consider the teachings of Steinsaltz, and how they relate to the discussion of *avodah zarah*, *shituf*, and a Jewish view of Hinduism.[32]

Steinsaltz begins by acknowledging the changed nature of contemporary reality. Interactions that are presently possible between Jews and non-Jews are

[30] In *Beyond Idolatry* I intend to look more specifically at different manifestations of the divine within Hindu culture in light of Rabbi Herzog's suggestion that they may be permissible in terms of *shituf*. While *shituf* is a broad category within which various forms of worship may be included, it is worth reflecting on what this might mean according to the different kinds of objects that are worshipped—gods, forces of nature, saints.

[31] Alick Isaacs, 'Benamozegh's Tone, A Response to Rabbi Steinsaltz', *Common Knowledge*, 11/1 (2005), 48.

[32] The following discussion is based on Adin Steinsaltz, 'Peace without Conciliation: The Irrelevance of "Toleration" in Judaism', *Common Knowledge*, 11/1 (2005), 41–7.

fundamentally different from those of any previous era in Jewish history. This poses the challenge of religious tolerance, a term that Steinsaltz is not enamoured of. His challenge is to find a way of accommodating other religions from a Jewish perspective. Accordingly, Steinsaltz seeks to create a model that would allow monotheistic Judaism to recognize other world religions. The language of 'recognizing' other religions is significant. It appeals implicitly to the language of diplomacy and to ways in which states recognize each other's legitimacy. Can Judaism recognize other religions and if so, how does recognition relate to Judaism's monotheistic faith and its attendant truth claims? To appreciate Steinsaltz's suggestion, recall that the standard view of Judaism's message to the world consists in the main of the seven Noahide commandments, a code of moral laws that includes the prohibition of idolatry. Steinsaltz's presentation takes as its point of departure the existence of two tracks to spiritual reality: the Jewish one that is more stringent consisting of 613 commandments, and the one for all other humans, the Noahide path. The Noahide commandments serve as the yardstick for assessing world religions and determining what is demanded of them to be acceptable to Judaism. This includes expectations regarding the knowledge of God and how it coheres with the demands on purity of approach to God, as these are made of Jews.

Steinsaltz establishes his argument on the broader recognition that law is not a universal phenomenon and that it applies to different groups in the community in different measures:

The idea that certain laws of Judaism do not apply to all is an essential feature of the *halakhah*. Special standards of religious practice apply to men, while women are exempted from all commandments that must be practiced at a fixed time. The people of Israel are not bound by the special obligations incumbent upon the priesthood: *kohanim*, the descendants of Aaron, must keep from contact with the dead outside their immediate families in order to preserve the ritual purity of the priesthood. And the priesthood is not bound by the same rules of purity that must be observed by the high priest, who cannot attend the funeral of even his own parents and children. The high priest would not think to censure his fellow priests for attending their parents' funerals; a common priest, a *kohen*, would not think to censure an ordinary Jew for attending the funeral of a friend, teacher, or cousin (indeed an ordinary Jew might be censured for not attending). Different standards apply to different groups even within the Jewish community. The Noahide laws operate on the same principle: differing standards apply to different groups.

To this must be added a deeper philosophical understanding that respects the multiplicity of religions. In addition to the appeal to the different paths for Jews and non-Jews, Steinsaltz makes a more radical claim that touches upon Judaism's future vision and ultimate hope. Judaism's ultimate vision does not, according to Steinsaltz, consist of all of humanity adopting Judaism:

Judaism, despite the absolute and exclusionary quality of its monotheism, has a side that tends towards openness and toleration. This side of Judaism has also an expression in the Jewish abstention from proselytizing. Even ultimately, Judaism does not view itself as the religion of all people. It is the religion of the Jews alone and is, for almost all its practitioners, inherited. The assumption that Judaism is the religion of one people (and a few unsought converts) is emphatically a normative principle and is important to our discussion because it suggests that within Jewish doctrine there is room for the religious beliefs of others.

This principle applies not only to the world as it is today, but also to the messianic projections that Judaism makes for the future. Although the messianic era represents an ultimate vindication of truth as Judaism understands it—a time when the God of Abraham, Isaac, and Jacob will assert his dominion over all the world—at that time the peoples of the world will not embrace Judaism and will not come to observe Jewish law. In the closing chapters of his monumental Code of Jewish Law, Maimonides gives an account of the end of days. In his portrayal, the messianic realm is one of peace, but not uniformity of faith. According to Maimonides, when Isaiah saw the wolf and the lamb lying down together, what he envisioned was not a change in the nature of creation. Wolves will still be wolves, and lambs will be lambs; what will change is the relationship between them. At the end of days, the different peoples of the world will not become less different. And because they will not embrace a single faith, the prohibition against gentiles undertaking distinctively Jewish practices will continue. However, each religion will come to share with all the others a small set of fundamental truths, and people everywhere will abandon violence, theft, and oppression.

This is a stunning statement. Abstention from proselytizing is not seen as a consequence of political circumstances but as a fundamental characteristic of Judaism, that is supported by its messianic vision. As Maimonides' description of the messianic era does not include a description of Judaism prevailing, Steinsaltz concludes that all religions will remain in the messianic era and that their relationships will be harmonious and characterized by mutual exchange and enrichment, or at least the sharing of a common core of moral and spiritual truths.

With these foundations in place, Steinsaltz moves on to develop the notion of different approaches to God that characterize the Jewish track and the Noahide track.

'Toleration' would not be an accurate name for this doctrine, and certainly the doctrine is not one of religious equivalence. However, the approach that Judaism takes towards righteous gentiles offers a partial solution to the problem of intolerance in monotheist religions. By establishing different sets of expectations for different groups, Judaism makes room for adherents of other faiths to perform their own religious obligations in a way that entitles them to salvation by the God of Israel. While Jews are enjoined to follow 613 commandments of the Torah, the demands that normative Judaism makes of gentiles comprise only seven laws. These six prohibitions and one positive commandment are together known as the Noahide laws because (according to chapter seven of Sanhedrin) they were the series of laws given to Noah after the flood (though they differ little from the basic laws given to Adam). The Noahide laws set a universal standard for gentile religions and embody the truths that, according to Maimonides, the peoples of the world will come to recognize and share at the end of days. Thus, the Noahide laws delineate the boundaries of Jewish religious toleration: failure to observe these laws would bar a person or a people from entering their own gate into heaven.

One of the highest principles of the Noahide laws is belief in the one God. Both Islam and Christianity (though Trinitarian doctrine presents a complication) satisfy this key demand and clear the way for Jewish recognition of these religions . . .

It is an entirely normative principle in Judaism that the monotheism expected of gentiles by the Noahide laws is of a less absolute kind than that expected of Jews. In the Middle Ages, many authorities indeed recognized Christian doctrine (even the doctrine of the Trinity) as basically monotheistic belief. One can readily understand how the doctrine of a triune Godhead could contaminate Christianity's claim to be monotheistic. However, Christianity was generally not considered polytheistic or idolatrous, though Maimonides—who did not live in Christendom—dissented from the widespread rabbinic agreement on this point. The concept of the Trinity was represented in the church as a mystery or paradox because it apparently contradicted a central component of their faith in the one God. Thus the Trinity, even though it is an essential feature of Christian theology and not merely one of folk religion, could be taken by Jewish scholars as a supplement to, rather than a replacement for, the idea of God as one. By Jewish standards as applied to Jews, Trinitarianism is not monotheism. But by the standards of the Noahide laws, the doctrine of the Trinity is not an idolatrous belief to which Judaism can express an objection.

Steinsaltz first establishes the rule that expectations differ for Jews and non-Jews. Not only is the number of commandments different, but what is actually expected of Jewish believers is different from what is expected of non-Jewish believers, even in relation to the very same commandment. Thus, the demand to worship one God alone may be interpreted and applied differently to Judaism and to other religions. I believe that this statement is unique. It grows out of a lengthy tradition of Ashkenazi dealing with Christianity and the development of a de facto lower standard for non-Jews, captured in the recognition that a Noahide is not commanded to avoid worship through *shituf*. However, I am not familiar with any earlier statement that grounds this view of the Noahide's theological obligations in a broader view of Judaism's relationship with world religions and its future hopes or in a theory of how the Noahide laws function as a code of law and their relationship to what is expected of Jews. The statement is novel not only in terms of the broader context that it offers, in trying to make sense of a tradition that existed in practice for hundreds of years, but also in terms of how Steinsaltz grounds it. He presents this view as the normative, indeed as a majoritarian, view. Thus he turns the principle permitting *shituf* for the non-Jew into Judaism's representative statement.

For all its thoroughness and its systematic approach, this statement rewrites the history of Jewish law for the sake of achieving a comprehensive view and system. Indeed, the view that *shituf* is permissible to non-Jews creates parallel tracks, while maintaining a hierarchy that affords Judaism the superior spiritual status. Yet this view is far from representative. The debate still rages today as to whether *shituf* is permissible for a non-Jew or not. More significantly, the Maimonidean position may well be the majority position in relation to Christianity.[33] Accordingly, the standards expected of Jews and of non-Jews would be identical, as would be the definition of what constitutes *avodah zarah*. Steinsaltz casts Maimonides into a minority position and even hints at historical factors that may have led to his not understanding Christianity sufficiently: he never lived among Christians.[34] This is an interesting argument that is rarely heard in halakhic circles. Even more interesting is the fact that Steinsaltz develops a view that is based on *shituf* without ever appealing to the term.[35] In any event, Steinsaltz has taken a disputed, possibly minority, view and constructed a broad theory from it. He presents it as Judaism's representative message that accommodates lower religious understanding within a hierarchical view. This is an inclusivist move allowing him to give legitimacy to lower forms of approaching God.

One of the arguments in Steinsaltz's presentation relates to the question of who speaks for the religions. As we already know with reference to Hinduism,

[33] The assessment of majority and minority views is hard to gauge and will remain impressionistic until further study has been conducted. While for Ashkenazi authorities, Steinsaltz's statement is clearly true, it is less clear that a majority would be found for this view when the entire corpus of halakhic literature is taken into account. My own impression is also that there has been a shift in this regard and that the Maimonidean position is gaining the upper hand among contemporary decisors, regardless of its prominence or otherwise throughout the centuries. While an assessment of majority and minority views can affect a halakhic discussion, developing a contemporary Jewish view of world religions should not be dependent on majority/minority considerations. Halakhic discussions reflect contemporary attitudes, and these were influenced by a variety of things. Most authorities repeat earlier views, without entering into a careful consideration of what the view of another religion ought to be. Therefore, when these issues are revisited within a contemporary re-evaluation of Jewish attitudes to world religions, the positions, their historical context, and their philosophical merit need to be weighed as seriously, if not more so, as issues of majority and minority views, as these may have found varying expressions in different periods and centres of learning.   [34] On this point, see also Korn in Chapter 8, above.

[35] In offering a justification for his theory, he quotes Me'iri (Steinsaltz, 'Peace without Conciliation', 45 n. 6) with whom we shall deal shortly. Me'iri is outside the common consensus and certainly cannot provide the basis for such a far-reaching view, even if one agrees with him. Me'iri does not build on *shituf*, but on another logic presented below. Apparently, Steinsaltz does rely on Me'iri, leading him to avoid reference to *shituf*, but the theological construct he presents is that of *shituf*.

religions are complex entities. Steinsaltz's discussion proceeds in terms of broad entities, such as 'Hinduism', upon which the halakhah pronounces judgement. This takes him into the question of what is essential to a religion and what is secondary. His decisions may not be shared by the scholar of religion or the theologian, yet they are important both in terms of raising these questions for the first time in the history of rabbinic literature and in terms of the positions he adopts. Steinsaltz's answer is clear. It is theologians who speak for the religions.[36]

Steinsaltz seems to assume that there is a core religious teaching that one can identify. This is the higher form of the religion, presumably as preached by theologians or the officials of the religion, and is distinct from what he terms folk religion. He thus recognizes that under the name of a given religion we may find a variety of phenomena. Critically, he insists that the halakhic judgement is made about the essence of the religion. There seems to be one pronouncement per religion, rather than multiple rulings, depending on the specific form or practice under discussion, and it is this single ruling that determines Judaism's attitude to that religion. It is this strategy that allows Steinsaltz to make his breakthrough statement in relation to Hinduism.

What about Indic religions and various kinds of Buddhism? Again, I do not believe that a definitive solution is possible, but a partial solution may be considered. It is important to introduce a distinction between theology and religious practice. In the ancient religions grouped under the name of Hinduism, there are many gods and local shrines, but the theological principles that guide belief and provide a uniformity of moral standards assume that all the deities revered in India or elsewhere are forms of, expressions of, or names for, one ultimate reality or God. Saivites propose Siva as the best name (among many names) for this ultimacy; Vaisnavites prefer Visnu or Krishna; *atman* is an Upanisadic word for the same principle—and *brahman* is perhaps the most common way among non-Muslim, non-Christian Indians of naming ultimacy . . .[37]

By the standards of Jewish law as applied to Jews, Hinduism (and Buddhism) do not count as monotheistic traditions. However, the essential point of the Noahide laws is that the standards of Jewish law do not apply to non-Jews. Radically pure monotheism is expected by Judaism only from Jews. The Noahide laws do not preclude gentile religions from developing softer, more complex, and compromised forms of monotheism. Under the Noahide laws, it is possible to assume that Hinduism and Buddhism are sufficiently monotheistic in principle for moral Hindus

---

[36] A panel on 'Who Speaks for Hinduism?' was featured in the pages of the *Journal of the American Academy of Religion*. Several of the speakers adopted the very same perspective as that recommended by Steinsaltz: theologians are the voice of religion (see *Journal of the American Academy of Religion*, 68 (2000), 705–835; note in particular the discussions by Brian Smith (p. 744) and John Thatamanil (pp. 791–803)).

[37] A paragraph on Buddhism follows, omitted from the present discussion.

and Buddhists to enter the gentile's gate into heaven. Jewish law regards the compromises made or tolerated by the world's major religions as ways of rendering essentially monotheistic theologies easier in practice for large populations of adherents. The fierceness of Islamic opposition to such compromises has no counterpart in Judaism. In Islam, it is seriously blasphemous for anyone of whatever faith to combine belief in the one God with popular ideas about other heavenly powers or with subtle theological doctrines such as the Trinity. Islam cannot tolerate such compromises because the truth that they violate is applicable universally and not simply to Muslims. The problem is that Islam is radically monotheistic (like Judaism), yet is also (unlike Judaism, which is the religion of one people) universalistic as well.[38]

Steinsaltz extends the paradigms established in relation to Christianity to Hinduism and Buddhism. But doing so requires him to focus on theology rather than worship. He offers us a corrective to the propensity that Jewish viewers have to focus on the action at the expense of the understanding of the action. He puts aside the ritual, which means putting aside the worship of images and the myriad gods of the Hindu pantheon, and focuses on the philosophy that underlies them.[39] The philosophy he offers us is fully vedantic. It seems no accident that someone who seeks to understand religion from the perspective of hierarchy and offers a hierarchical reading of Judaism's relations to world religions would appeal to a highly hierarchical view of Hinduism itself. The vedantic view is a hierarchical view that considers the vedantic teaching of the ultimate unity of Being as the highest form of Hindu teaching. For vedantins, lower forms of understanding and practice may be tolerated and accepted, while Vedanta holds the ultimate key to their proper understanding. It is thus a patient spiritual outlook. Hindu belief in reincarnation and in gradual evolution eliminates the pressure to resolve philosophical and theological differences immediately and creates a space for processes that are long-term, resulting in an attitude of tolerance. Steinsaltz develops a spirit of tolerance, while rejecting the term, without even awaiting final messianic resolution of differences. In Steinsaltz's view, religions may hold on to their imperfect views even in the eschaton. In Steinsaltz's construct, accommodation stems from the election of Israel and from the fact that different tracks have been established for Jews and non-Jews. As such, one can tolerate compromises to monotheism. Steinsaltz uses a striking phrase: 'softer, more complex, and

---

[38] Steinsaltz, 'Peace without Conciliation', 44–5.

[39] Steinsaltz extends a strategy first developed in relation to Christianity to Hinduism. One should note that in the case of Christianity, the ritual is transparent to the theology, that is, the theology comes through the ritual in a clear way. Accordingly, the possibility for error and misinterpretation is reduced, making the move from ritual to theology credible. By contrast, the vedantic position is often a superimposition on a ritual that is not transparent to this world-view. If so, making this theological move is literally a leap of faith, from the ritual, in faith that Vedanta offers a correct interpretation, to the realm of faith and understanding.

compromised forms of monotheism'. It is interesting that the kabbalistic tradition that informs his theological thinking may be described in the same words. To the outsider there appear to be structural similarities between kabbalistic, Trinitarian, and Hindu understandings of God. It is thus no accident that a kabbalistically minded rabbi entertains notions of softer and more complex monotheism. Hinduism is compromised monotheism, and as such is valid.

Something further is gained by this move. Religions with compromised monotheism are only valid for non-Jews. Such was the view of the early modern rabbis who upheld Christianity's value on the grounds of permissible *shituf*. In the contemporary context this provides a protective mechanism against Jewish attraction to Eastern religions. The argument echoes the teachings of Glazerson, but along more halakhic lines. What is permissible for non-Jews is considered idolatrous for Jews. Respect and protection of identity are achieved in one move.

Steinsaltz took his knowledge of Hinduism from a Hindu textbook, and in the process distorted a fact or two. Written from the perspective of Vedanta, the textbook allowed him to deal with the entire scope of Hinduism within a few lines. Perhaps it is advantageous to take a single perspective and develop a halakhic position from it, but one wonders whether more detailed study of the religion might make it harder to make broad pronouncements. Perhaps the context dictates the method. Steinsaltz wrote for a panel on religious tolerance, where he represented Judaism. Such situations seem to have their own dynamics, leading to results, even if positive in and of themselves, that are not always commensurate with the message that emerges from other contexts and genres. They bring out the best in a given presentation, but they are written in English and spoken academically. Would Steinsaltz also say these very things in Hebrew, in the framework of a *pesak*, a ruling of the halakhah?[40] Nevertheless, he has certainly taken us a long way into thinking about Hinduism and *avodah zarah* and offered us a way of thinking that is systematic and grounded in theological principles. Above all, it is an alternative to the impressions arising from the visual aspect of Hinduism and reminds us of the priority of theology over and against practice.

If we understand Hinduism as *shituf*, Hindu religious life offers us a variety of challenges. Steinsaltz's discussion focused on the worship of gods and deities, all of whom are understood to represent a single divine principle. But another challenge is more complex and problematic: the worship of human beings, saints, sages, and teachers. One might argue that this is not fundamentally different from the Christian worship of Jesus. If a theory of *shituf* can accommodate the worship of Jesus as part of the Christian understanding of God, it

[40] As an aside, Orthodox teachers at Steinsaltz's yeshiva have travelled to India. One wonders what the relationship between Steinsaltz's ruling and his students' practice is.

should also be able to accommodate the worship of gurus and holy men in the Indian religious landscape. There is, however, one major distinction. Even if Jesus was a human person, to the best of our knowledge he was not worshipped while alive. To this very day, devotional attitudes to Catholic saints are practised only posthumously. Thus, in Christianity no special devotion or worship is shown to a living person. While in the case of Jesus one could argue that one is worshipping a human person, in fact it is the idea or memory of the person that is worshipped. Even if for believers that person continues to be present, in terms of ordinary day-to-day social relationships he no longer is. Thus the worship of Jesus as an incarnate human being remains ideal and in some sense only theoretical. Even if Jesus' humanity is affirmed alongside his divinity, there are no social and political consequences to worship stemming from Jesus' earthly personality. The only operative factor is the faith of believers.

The situation in India is different. Saints are worshipped while alive and often treated as divinities even as they go about their daily business. The theoretical basis for this is a combination of the recognition of God's omnipresence and its realization in the life and consciousness of an individual. However, this is an individual of flesh and blood, with bodily needs and personality, who is being treated in some way as a god. The potential for abuse is obvious. The inevitable human propensity for error and sin is at odds with the view of a person as god, and even more with the offering of worship and adoration to such a person.

Recognizing the dangers, we are also called to appreciate the depth and beauty of devotion towards spiritual teachers and leaders, the profound reverence they receive, and the absolute centrality that is accorded to the spiritual life and its representatives in India. There is also something inspiring in the reverence shown to spiritual teachers. When, as does happen occasionally, those teachers are truly great spiritual beings, there is a coherence in the system between its interior logic and its outward manifestations.

Shituf theology is pluralistic in the sense of recognizing different spiritual paths. The Jewish path has no room for the worship of human beings, not even teachers and great spiritual figures.[41] But this does not mean that Hindus who practise the veneration of their teachers are engaged in *avodah zarah*. Their actions should be interpreted within the broader religious system in which they operate. The worship of teachers is part of the quest for God. Even if the teacher is seen as God and part of the object of worship, he or she is also an instrument, a means of attaining a goal surely beyond him- or herself. Thus, in the figure of the living teacher, the guru, means and ends are in some way collapsed and identified. This can be seen as an important expression of *shituf* theology. Non-Jews may approach God through the guru, the saint, the

---

[41] This is part of what has led to David Berger's critique of the Chabad movement (see *The Rebbe, the Messiah and the Scandal of Orthodox Indifference* (London, 2001)).

teacher. That is their path and it passes through a person, who is in some way incorporated into the believers' notion of God. God may be the same for Jews and Hindus, but the paths are different and they lead to significant differences along the way, including the worship of teachers.

If we think deeply about *shituf* and understand it in theological terms, we are open to a different attitude to other religions. One important consequence is that one can no longer accept the kind of dismissive *avodah zarah* discourse, so common in Jewish references to other religions and in what little Jewish discussion about Hinduism there has been. Another consequence is the possibility of opening up a dialogue between what would be considered two valid approaches to God, one incorporating *shituf* and the other Jewish path avoiding *shituf*. Judaism can develop a meaningful spiritual dialogue with other religions, within which it has something to say, but also has much to learn. If we recognize in India a great spiritual culture, a beacon of spirituality, and a source of saints, we cannot simply dismiss its forms of worship as *avodah zarah*. If we can see them as legitimate in light of a theory of *shituf*, we must take them seriously. This is an invitation to listen to the spiritual testimony they offer and to the understanding of God they convey. Within this dialogue Judaism too has a message. It is the message of what it means to worship the one God exclusively, to approach him without any intermediary, to look to him alone. A healthy dialogue on goals and means in approaching God may be a way of affirming the unique spiritual vision of Judaism as part of the spiritual heritage of humanity. At the same time, it is important for us to hear and to assimilate other religious visions, not because we should take up their methods of worship, but because they can remind us of spiritual truths we have lost. The dialogue has not yet begun and it is hard to anticipate where a serious dialogue about God and the spiritual life could take us when carried forth from the dual platform of covenantal exclusivity and a *shituf*-based pluralism. The fruits of such a dialogue hold the promise of being spiritually beneficial to both sides.

HINDUISM IN THE LIGHT OF THE TEACHINGS OF MENAHEM ME'IRI

The Middle Ages provide us with two primary strategies for dealing with Christianity. The first strategy is *shituf*. The second is based on the teachings of Rabbi Menahem Me'iri.[42] According to Me'iri, Christianity, like Islam, is not *avodah zarah*. The common understanding of Me'iri, grounded in some of his own formulae, explains his views as a consequence of the fact that both religions have an ethical code, enforcing morality, law, and order. Me'iri posits a

---

[42] I discuss Me'iri's views in the Introduction, above, and will spell them out in greater detail in *Beyond Idolatry*.

moral criterion in the light of which these religions should be viewed, and this criterion should be equally valid in relation to Eastern religions and all other religions that do not know Israel's God. This provides a basis for recognizing other religions by shifting the discussion from theological to moral consider-ations. A closer look at Me'iri's work reveals that underlying his recognition of other religions is more than simply recognition of their moral value. Moshe Halbertal has shown that Me'iri has a highly developed sense of what a religion is.[43] Rather than simply present Christianity and Islam as non-idolatrous, Me'iri describes them as 'religions'. His appeal to the category of religion assumes certain parameters, in the light of which a religion is recognized as a valid 'religion'. These parameters include the moral dimension. However, the argument from morality does not simply point to God directly, but appeals to the notion of 'religion' as common and recognized ground between religions. Recognizing the centrality of the category 'religion' and 'the ways of religion' in Me'iri's thought allows us to apply his views of other religions and their legitimacy to religions he never considered. The very appeal to 'religion' as a means of legitimating other religions assumes that other religions, once they are recognized and classified as such, have validity. True or valid religion does not stop with Judaism.

Let us now consider a possible approach to Hinduism in the light of Me'iri's views. Let us consider first the moral dimension, understood independently of specific theological claims. If Me'iri posits the legitimacy of a religion as a func-tion of its upholding moral living (as opposed to idolatry that encourages all forms of ugliness and sin), then surely Hinduism would also fall under the rubric of 'nations bound by the ways of religion'. Judging a religion by its fruits, be they moral or spiritual, places before us an interesting challenge. In the history of Hinduism (perhaps of all religions) we encounter the highest and the lowest of moral and spiritual values. On the one hand, it is clear that Hinduism upholds a highly disciplined life unlike the free pandering to desire and sinfulness that Me'iri associates with idolatry. Basic moral precepts govern Hindu life, and in that sense fulfil the requirements of the seven Noahide com-mandments. On the other hand, there are many expressions of Hindu religious life that could be construed as contrary to the sense of morality espoused by Judaism. Some of these are issues that are no longer relevant and some endure within Hinduism to this very day. Temple prostitution was part of Hindu reli-gious life, at various points in its history.[44] This is explicitly condemned by the

[43] Moshe Halbertal, 'Ones Possessed of Religion: Religious Tolerance in the Teachings of the Meiri', *Edah Journal*, 1/1 (2000), <www.edah.org>.

[44] See Frédérique Apffel Marglin, 'Hierodouleia', in Mircea Eliade (ed.), *The Encyclopaedia of Religion* (New York, 1987), vi. 309–13. Much has been written about the status of the *devadasi*s, temple dancers, and courtesans in the quarter of a century since the publication of this article. While a complex picture of their self-understanding and the realities of their lives emerges from

Torah and has close associations with idolatry among ancient Israel's immediate neighbours. Some customs that were common at various points in history may also be queried in relation to our sense of morality, for example *sati*, the burning of widows on their husbands' funeral pyres. More fundamentally, we may find fault with the social teachings and practices associated with the caste system and many of its oppressions.

This raises the difficult question of when disagreement concerning practices and moral teachings is just that, and constitutes an important dimension of the identity and teaching of Judaism in relation to other religions, and when such differences are so egregious as to force one to consider another religion as not 'bound by the ways of religion', according to the principles formulated by Me'iri. The question is not specific to Hinduism. David Berger recently queried the impact of suicide bombing on a view of Islam in the light of Me'iri's principles.[45] Does either wrong religious teaching, if it is indeed a teaching of the religion, or wrong practice, if it is the fruit of a misunderstanding or misinterpretation of the tradition, render an otherwise legitimate religion an expression of *avodah zarah*? Put differently, could the god who tolerates the bombing of women and children or the god who tolerates temple prostitution be the same God as we proclaim?

The problem is twofold. On the one hand, if we find moral fault in another religion and declare its god to be another god, we are assuming that any religion can attain a reasonable standard of moral living that would never be called into question. While in theory this is an attractive proposition and might in some way be implied by the ethos of the Noahide commandments, in reality it is a standard we may never achieve. Upon close scrutiny we are bound to find moral fault with every religion. Indeed, the other side of the problem is that Judaism too might not emerge blameless from such moral scrutiny. Whether it be slavery of old, present-day oppression of other peoples, or a host of other spiritual ailments with which we have been plagued over the millennia, it is impossible to imagine a Judaism above moral criticism. It therefore may be preferable to use the negative pole of the definition, as indeed Me'iri does. *Avodah zarah* is identified with wanton libertinism. Whatever jihadistic Islam is, and however strongly we may disagree with its practices, it is not *avodah zarah* in the moral sense portrayed by Me'iri. And the same will probably be

these studies, the fundamental issue, in terms of the present discussion, remains. For purposes of this discussion it would seem that limiting *devadasi* practice both historically and geographically, thereby making it either marginal or something of the past, and bearing in mind the efforts of reformers is more helpful than various attempts to understand the complexity of the phenomenon in sociological, psychological, or religious terms.

[45] David Berger, 'Jews, Gentiles, and the Modern Egalitarian Ethos: Some Tentative Thoughts', in Marc Stern (ed.), *Formulating Responses in an Egalitarian Age* (Lanham, Md., 2005), esp. 108 n. 54.

true of many Hindu practices that we may condemn on moral grounds. That immoral acts are committed within a religious framework does not mean the religion lacks morality. It only means that corruption has entered the religion or that somehow what we consider to be moral has been radically reconfigured within a different religious system.[46] But this need not affect the basic definition of the religion and its ability to point to God as its ultimate referent. Misapplication of moral, legal, or ritual principles is not wanton libertinism.

We might add that Hinduism itself has been steadily undergoing changes. It is part of the Hindu view of history that *dharma*, the teaching and practice of religious duty and obligation, steadily declines. Hinduism accommodates its own weaknesses and imperfections within a conceptual structure that accounts for how such imperfections come about. The flip side of this recognition is that such moral and spiritual decline is the occasion for the coming of great teachers, who come precisely in order to correct the balance and to restore the pristine teaching. One classical expression of this view is found in the most popular of all Hindu religious works, the Bhagavad Gita. The understanding that the present-day teacher has come to restore lost balance is common in relation to various teachers and groups.

The loss and re-establishment of teaching is not a purely internal matter for a tradition. It is also driven by encounters with other civilizations. For several hundred years India was part of the British empire, which had a profound impact on some of its practices. The British did much to uproot those dimensions of religion they considered immoral, such as the practice of *sati* or the temple dances of *devadasis*. It is commonly considered that Hinduism as encountered by early British and Portuguese colonialists was not the same as present-day Hinduism. In this discussion we should therefore consider Hinduism's contemporary expressions, rather than various practices belonging only to its past. Looking at a religion from the vantage point of the present is in fact an important dimension in Me'iri's own thinking. As Halbertal has argued, Me'iri was informed by a theory of religious progress. Religions progress and the standards for proper religious behaviour change over the ages. It is this sense of progress that led Me'iri to declare *avodah zarah* mainly a thing of the past. This theory allows Me'iri to draw practical and halakhic consequences for a contemporary view of *avodah zarah*. It is fully consistent with his thinking to recognize progress or evolution within another tradition as a basis for new reflection on its status in terms of *avodah zarah*. It is thus reasonable to conclude that in terms of the morality-based understanding of Me'iri, Hinduism should also be considered to be bound by the ways of religion.

---

[46] This formulation would allow us to consider phenomena such as *tantra*, where morality is inverted as part of a transcendental spiritual quest.

In the Introduction to this volume, I raised the possibility that Me'iri's principles could be expanded from a moral lifestyle to all aspects of the spiritual life that offer a testimony to the God who is known through personal experience. This would surely open up possibilities for recognizing God through Hinduism independently of the details of a theological view of God. Our earlier discussion of spirituality suggested that this is a major attraction of Hinduism. Indeed, Hinduism has produced and continues to produce holy men and women. Me'iri's wanton libertine should be placed at the opposite extreme of the spectrum because he stands in direct contrast with the Hindu saint. Of course, saints are few and they may be further between than popular Hindu imagination would like to admit, but the fact that Hinduism has produced great spiritual saints whose sanctity should be beyond dispute suggests that God can be known and recognized within Hinduism by the traces he leaves in the lives of those who have come close to him, who have known him, and who have reached union with him.

Thus far I have reflected upon Hinduism in the light of Me'iri's core notion of a 'nation bound by the ways of religion'. We can now move the discussion to the next level and tie explicit theological awareness to moral teaching. Me'iri sometimes stipulates 'knowledge of God' as part of his positive view of other religions. The formulations vary. In one instance, he speaks of serving 'divinity in some way, even though their faith is far removed from our own faith'.[47] That is, the other culture must have a notion of divinity, even if different from our own. According to Me'iri's broader view, that sense of divinity would be more encompassing than the worship of isolated trees, stones, stars, and idols could provide. It is a sense of divinity in its totality and that provides the ground for the moral life.

I cannot see how anyone could exclude Hinduism from such a formulation. Despite the fact that in theory everything is subject to worship, the governing notion is one of divinity in the broader sense posited by Me'iri. One could, of course, suggest that the distinction between a broader notion of divinity and the limiting of attention exclusively to some specific manifestations of power, trees, stars, and so on, would be the criterion that distinguishes legitimate from illegitimate religion. It may be that some forms of religious life, some practices of individual Hindus or communities, might be seen as the worship of isolated forces, removed from the broader notion of an all-encompassing divinity. In other words, it is conceivable that within Hinduism there may be expressions of *avodah zarah*, if this particular criterion is applied. However, it is fair to say that the governing understanding of the Hindu religious culture is that there is a broader notion of divinity, as opposed to viewing various powers in isolation. While this is the case for the theological schools, it also seems to be the

[47] Me'iri, *Beit habeḥirah* on BT *BK* 113*b*.

case for a large part of popular understanding of Hinduism. Thus, according to this basic definition of what is theologically required, Hinduism would again meet with Me'iri's approval. We have thus introduced into the discussion the second dimension of Me'iri's thought, the recognition of another religion as valid.

My own reading of Me'iri suggests that the question he asked of a religion is not whether it is idolatrous or even whether it is moral, but whether it is 'religion' in the full sense that he attaches to the term.[48] In relation to Hinduism as a family of religious beliefs with broad common traits and increasingly a common theological framework, it seems that it is very much a 'religion'. In fact, Me'iri might provide a way of helping us to identify what a religion is and to consider Hinduism in this light. If by 'religion' we refer to a particular combination of constitutive beliefs about the divine, a comprehensive world-view, fundamental moral teachings, and ritual expression, certainly all of these apply to the various forms of Hinduism. Yet more significant is the transformative power of religion. In Me'iri's view, what gives religion as such its weight is its power to transform human nature and to help guide a person in the ongoing battle against the weaknesses of human nature. Judged from this anthropocentric and spiritual perspective, not only is Hinduism as much a 'religion' as those with which Me'iri himself was familiar, but it can serve in many ways as a model that other religions should emulate. Much of its self-understanding focuses upon structuring life towards an ultimate *telos*. I refer here to the famous fourfold division of the life cycle (*varnasramadharma*) leading to the final goal of liberation, itself an expression of how religion intervenes in the battle against physical nature. This battle has produced expressions of asceticism, sacrifice, and religious ways of life that make India a model of how religion works, how its philosophy and institutions mediate the sacred, and the impact its transformative power has upon the life of individuals and society. Thus, if religion is measured by its transformative power and in accordance with the core components that make any belief system a 'religion', it is clear that Hinduism must be acknowledged as a full 'religion' and is immune to the classical Jewish charge that it is *avodah zarah*.

CONCLUSION

The conversation is at its very beginning. If this chapter has achieved anything at all, it is the recognition that a conversation must take place. The lack of historical contact and largely imagined Other have led to a default position that Hinduism is *avodah zarah*. This implies that Hinduism is forbidden and

---

[48] For a fuller discussion of the criteria of 'religion' in this reading of Me'iri, see my *Beyond Idolatry*.

irrelevant, because it has nothing to teach us and therefore requires neither study nor dialogue. Yet this point of view is untenable because it is belied by the spiritual riches of Hinduism, by the powerful testimonies of Jewish seekers concerning Hinduism, by the classical image of India as a land of wisdom, and by the continuing testimony of Hindu saints. All these facts require us to reconsider our approach to Hinduism and to seek ways to make sense of it, despite the fact that many Jews reject Hinduism because of Hindu worship of idols.

This chapter suggests how a conversation on these issues could proceed. Whether or not my suggestions are accepted, the challenge remains and cannot be ignored. It is deeper than pronouncing a ruling on wigs made of hair offered at Hindu temples or even ruling on the halakhic status of Hinduism. Ultimately, it is a challenge of understanding what *avodah zarah* is and consequently what Judaism stands for. If we take Judaism seriously we must take this challenge seriously. In engaging this challenge in earnestness, we will probably find no worthier partner for dialogue than Hinduism.

TWELVE

Judaism and Buddhism
A Jewish Approach to a Godless Religion

JEROME (YEHUDA) GELLMAN

I

IN THIS chapter I would like to propose how a traditional Jew such as myself could address the godlessness of Buddhism and yet not reject Buddhism because it knows not God. But more than that I want to show how a proper understanding of Buddhist godlessness can allow a traditional Jew to find insight and religious enhancement from Buddhist teachings.

There is a worrisome element of Buddhism for traditional Judaism that I will not address here, namely the worship of the Buddha and statues of the Buddha in many forms of Buddhism. This practice must strike a traditional Jew as idolatry, or something close to it. So I will restrict my conclusions to those forms of Buddhism that do not include worship of the Buddha. This includes much of the Buddhism of the first several hundred years after the Buddha's death (around 500 BCE), as well as some forms of later Buddhism, including at least some forms of Zen.

My approach to Buddhism comes from a traditional Jewish perspective and can be characterized as 'religious receptive exclusivism'. There are various categories of exclusivism, but here I am interested only in *truth-exclusivism*. An understanding of a religion is *truth-exclusivist* when it officially teaches or its devotees commonly maintain that the core teachings of the religion are all true, and that all other religions have at least one false core belief. (Note that there need not be unanimity on what any of the core teachings are.) It is *exclusivist* in the sense of *excluding* all other religions from having uniformly true core beliefs. (Exclusivism, in this sense, is compatible with recognizing falsity in one's own religion as long as it is deemed not to affect core beliefs.)

This exclusivism is 'receptive', because it accepts that religions other than Judaism might contain religiously significant truths or practices not found in Judaism, which it would be worthwhile for Jews to be familiar with, especially those that have the power to drive home shared truths in an especially poignant and impressive way. Religions other than Judaism might contain stories, allegories, teachings, and practices that give a cognitive or emotional vividness to things that Judaism itself teaches. In short, this exclusivism is open to the real possibility that the accumulated wisdom of other world religions can enhance and enrich my own Jewish spiritual life.

My exposure to Christianity and Islam, and to a lesser extent Hinduism, has enhanced my personal religious understanding and enriched my religious life. This might be understandable since the former two religions share the monotheistic outlook of Judaism, and because some of Hindu religiosity is or comes close to being really a monotheistic outlook, such as the belief in a supreme being such as Nirguna Brahman.

Thus, from the *Confessions* of Augustine I have learned of an individual's way to God and of God's ways of bringing people to God. Augustine relates how his Christian mother prayed with all her heart that God not let Augustine leave North Africa for Rome lest he befriend Manichaeans and be lost to Christianity. Augustine writes that God 'answered her prayers' and sent him off to Rome— where he converted to Christianity and ultimately became 'St Augustine'. I am profoundly moved and religiously enriched by this story, in spite of the fact that I do not believe Jesus was divine, nor do I believe in a divine Trinity.

The great thirteenth-century Sufi mystic Rumi told of a disciple who cried 'Allah' over and over again, but heard no reply from God saying, 'Here I am!' In a dream the disciple saw the master, who told him he was wrong to think that God had not answered him. 'Nay', said the master, 'God says, "That 'Allah' of thine is my 'Here I am', and that supplication and grief and ardor of thine is my messenger to thee . . . Beneath every 'O Lord' of thine is many a 'Here am I' from me." '[1] Thus I have learned that when I call to God again and again and hear no reply, I should not think that God has not answered my call. On the contrary, God's reply to me was in my very call. This teaches me a lesson of what it means for God to be close to me, despite the fact that I believe neither that the Quran is God's word nor that Muhammad is God's prophet.

Sri Ramakrishna, the 'Hindu', has brought home to me how to see God everywhere, even in the lowly cat and the charging elephant. That was why he fed the cat the offering that had been given to the Mother and why he taught that it is really God who is the charging elephant. And Ramakrishna also wisely taught me that although the elephant is God, I should run like hell out of the way of the charging animal! This I have internalized in spite of the fact that I do not believe in Krishna or 'The Mother'.

Yet the same is true for me with non-theistic Buddhism. My knowledge of Buddhist literature and my familiarity with Buddhist practices have added greatly to my religious sensibilities and understanding. From the Buddhist

---

[1] Cited in Annemarie Schimmel, *Mystical Dimensions of Islam* (Chapel Hill, NC, 1975), 165–6.

Prajnaparamita Heart Sutra and the *Prajnaparamita Diamond Sutra*, from Dogen Zenji's *Shobogenzo*, from the Sixth Patriarch's *Dharma Jewel Platform Sutra*, and from the writings of Thich Nhat Hanh, I have learned of ways of holiness that I would not have imagined as a Jew. Buddhism has deeply affected my spiritual inwardness even though I neither worship the Buddha nor believe in the cycle of rebirth. And of course many other Jews have been profoundly influenced by Buddhist teachings and practices, some becoming Buddhists and abandoning Judaism, others becoming 'Bujews', practising Buddhism while somehow holding on to their Jewish identity and elements of Jewish religiosity.[2]

I will try to outline an approach to Buddhism that can explain how all of this is possible for a traditional Jew. I will begin with Buddhist agnostic and atheistic attitudes and proceed to the grounds for these attitudes. I hope to find in these grounds reason for significant appreciation of Buddhism, while undercutting the negative attitudes towards belief in God that these grounds generated historically.

II

There is much in the early Pali canon that suggests that the Buddha did not teach for or against any metaphysical doctrines, but only gave guidance on how to be free from the anguish that fills one's life. I begin with a Pali Sutra[3] that has the Buddha categorize responses to questions. He lists four:

> First, the categorical answer,
> then the qualified,
> third, the type to be counter-questioned,
> and fourth, the one to be set aside.[4]

The categorical answer is a 'Yes' or a 'No'. The qualified answer makes distinctions in answering a question that the questioner failed to make. The counter-question attempts to go deeper into the mind of the questioner so as to be in a position to give a useful answer. My focus here is on the fourth category: the questions to be set aside. To these no answers are to be given.

[2] For an especially poignant depiction of a rabbi's fascination with Buddhism, see Alan Lew, 'Why Did Bodhidarma Come to the West? Eight Jewish Glimpses of Buddhism', <http://www.elijah-interfaith.org/materials/conference-proceedings/towards-a-contemporary-theology.html>.

[3] Technically speaking, a Pali text should not be called a 'sutra' because that word is Sanskrit and not Pali. The Pali term is 'sutta'. Nevertheless, since 'sutra' is the more familiar term I will use it throughout.

[4] *Panha Sutra, Anguttara Nikaya* 4: 42, trans. Thanissaro Bhikkhu, <www.accesstoinsight.org/tipitaka/an/ano4/ano4.042.than.html>; see also *Numerical Discourses of the Buddha: An Anthology of Suttas from the Anguttara Nikaya*, ed. and trans. Nyanaponika Thera and Bhikkhu Bodhi (Walnut Creek, Calif., 1999).

There are several Pali Sutras about the Buddha's attitude to metaphysical issues which raise 'questions to be set aside'. In the *Cula-Malunkyovada Sutra* the Buddha chastises his disciple Malunkyaputta for asking for guidance on metaphysical questions such as: 'Is the cosmos eternal?' 'Are the soul and the body the same?' 'Does a Tathagata [one liberated] exist after death?' Metaphysical truths do not aid, and even hinder, liberation, and hence questions concerning them should be set aside:

Malunkyaputta, if anyone were to say, 'I won't live the holy life under the Blessed One as long as he does not disclose to me that "The cosmos is eternal", or that "After death a Tathagata neither exists nor does not exist" ', the man would die and those things would still remain undisclosed by the Tathagata.[5]

In the *Sabbasava Sutra* the Buddha speaks of ideas not fit for attention. There he declares that one who holds either the view 'I have a self' or the view 'I have no self', 'is bound by a thicket of views and is not freed from distress and despair . . . He is not freed, I tell you, from suffering and stress.' The Buddha then generalizes to all views, that is, to all metaphysical beliefs.[6] We are to put all of them aside.

In the *Alagaddupama Sutra* the Buddha speaks of a right and a wrong way to catch a water snake. Catch it by the tail and it will turn around and bite you. You must catch it by the head. Then you can control it and benefit from having caught it. Just so, to take the Buddha's teachings as 'doctrines' to be defended is to grab those teachings by the tail. That attitude will end up with the teachings turning back on you to bite you. You will be pulled in to identifying yourself with the doctrines and fighting for them. It will lead to 'long-term harm and suffering'. You will miss liberation. Catch the Buddhist teachings by the head, not as doctrines, but as methods for liberation, and you will achieve 'long-term welfare and happiness'.[7]

In the *Ananda Sutra* the Buddha remains silent when a wanderer, Vacchagotta, asks him, 'Is there a self?' He again remains silent when Vacchagotta next asks him, 'Then is there no self?' When asked about his silence by his disciple Ananda, the Buddha replies,

'If I . . . were to answer that there is a self, that would be conforming with those . . . who are exponents of eternalism. If I . . . were to answer that there is no self. That

---

[5] *Cula-Malunkyovada Sutra*, trans. Thanissaro Bhikkhu, <www.accesstoinsight.org/tipitaka/mn/mn.063.than.html>.

[6] *Sabbasava Sutra*, §6, trans. Thanissaro Bhikkhu, <www.accesstoinsight.org/tipitaka/mn/mn.002.than.html>; see also F. Max Muller (ed.), *Buddhist Suttas*, trans. T. W. Rhys Davids (New York, 2007), 296–308.

[7] *Alagaddupama Sutra*, trans. Thanissaro Bhikkhu, <www.accesstoinsight.org/tipitaka/mn/mn.022.than.html>; see also Thich Nhat Hanh, *Thundering Silence: Sutra on the Better Way to Catch a Snake* (Berkeley, Calif., 1993).

would be conforming with those . . . who are exponents of annihilation.' The Buddha goes on to add that whatever answer he would have given to Vacchagotta, the latter would have become bewildered.[8]

And finally, in the *Brahmajala Sutra* the Buddha rejects all speculation about the origin of the world and whether it has always existed or not. Likewise, for the soul.

From these and other Pali Sutras we get a picture of the Buddha not as an anti-metaphysician, proclaiming the falsity of sweeping metaphysical declarations about the self, the cosmos, and, by implication, about God. Rather, the Buddha thought that metaphysical issues should be set aside because they were not relevant to liberation or salvation. It is non-productive, even counter-productive, to deal with them. Hence, the Buddha took no position on these issues.

Buddhist meditative practice can proceed in light of the attitude of setting aside metaphysical questions, including whether there exists a 'self' or not. I will refer to two classic sutras on meditative practice, the Pali *Satipatthana Sutra* (*Sutra on the Four Foundations of Mindfulness*) and the originally Sanskrit *Prajna Paramita Hrydaya Sutra* (*The Heart Sutra*). In the former, the Buddha calls upon the practitioner to remain:

established in the observation of the body in the body . . .
established in the observation of the feelings in the feelings . . .
established in the observation of the mind in the mind . . .
established in the observation of the objects of mind in the objects of mind.[9]

The *Heart Sutra* opens with these lines:

The Bodhisattva Avalokita, while moving in the deep course of Perfect Understanding, shed light on the five *skandha*s and found them equally empty. 'Listen, Shariputra, form is emptiness, form does not differ from emptiness, emptiness does not differ from form. The same is true with feelings, perceptions, mental formations, and consciousness.'[10]

Skandha is a Sanskrit term, and the above lines identify the five of them with form (body), feelings, perceptions, mental formations, and consciousness. There is no unanimity in Buddhism on how to interpret each *skandha*, but all agree that the five refer, roughly, to the entirety of experience. According to this sutra, they are all 'empty'.

According to the standard metaphysical interpretation of these sutras, the

---

[8] *Ananda Sutra*, trans. Thanissaro Bhikkhu, <www.accesstoinsight.org/tipitaka/sn/sn54/sn54.013.than.html>.

[9] *Transformation and Healing, Sutra on the Four Establishments of Mindfulness*, trans. Thich Nhat Hanh (Berkeley, Calif., 1990), 3–4.

[10] *The Heart of Understanding: Commentaries on the Prajnaparamita Heart Sutra*, trans. Thich Nhat Hanh (Berkeley, Calif., 1998), 1.

purpose of meditative practice is to come to know that there is no abiding self. There is only the transitory body and the ephemeral, ever-changing, mental goings-on. There is not and will never be an experience of an abiding self somehow behind these passing phenomena. One comes to know this by carefully attending to the buzzing, booming, ever-changing nature of the body and mental events. Conclusion: there exists no abiding self.

In keeping with the non-metaphysical approach of the Pali sutras I cited earlier, these two sutras receive a non-metaphysical interpretation. I focus only on those aspects of these meditative practices relevant here (although there are others, no less important). Ordinarily, when I am conscious and aware of the world I take my body and mental goings-on to be on 'this' side, 'my' side, of experience and the rest of the world to be on the other, outside, 'objective' side of experience. Because of this, the body and the mental goings-on come to be absorbed into 'me' or 'mine' since it is I who am doing the experiencing. To be sure, there are times when my body or some mental goings-on become objects of my awareness, but even then the rest of the subjective complex is enlisted on the subject side. And soon enough that part of the body or the mental life returns to this side, the inner side, of experience, to resume being that to which experience takes place.

On the non-metaphysical interpretation of these two sutras, the meditative practice neutralizes the tendency to identify one's 'self' with the body and/or mental events, without any conclusion about there not being a self at all. When in the meditative practice everything becomes an object of awareness, everything becomes transferred, relocated, exported over to the 'outside', objective side of experience. The entire body–mind complex becomes an object of experience. In that way the complex becomes dissociated from one's sense of 'I'. There is no longer a divide between the 'inside' and the 'outside'. In a sense, all is outside, since all is optimally always an object of awareness.

To be sure, there might remain on this side of experience the very bare awareness by which the body and mental events are detected. Yet that will not be the self. Bare awareness has no thoughts, no emotions, and no values. It is just awareness, pure and simple, awareness of thoughts, emotions, mental events, and body. It has no fear; it is only aware of fear. There is no distinguishing between one bare awareness and another, neither of which have personality or an individual quality. Thus no self is to be found there. In addition, in some Buddhist practices one attains 'empty mind', or a pure consciousness in which, in a sense, even awareness itself fades. In some Buddhist schools the non-personalistic nature of awareness may very well have given rise to the notion of a universal Mind in which all awareness adheres, which is a rather startling course for a teaching that began by rejecting the Hindu teaching that atman, the self, is Brahman, the supreme reality. (More on this below.)

The meditative practice on the non-metaphysical interpretation drives home the fragility of the body–mind complex and thus discourages identifying a 'self' with it. It is in constant change, constantly in flux between arising and passing away. The lesson to be learned is to refrain from identifying anything familiar with the self. On the non-metaphysical interpretation this leaves one bereft of conviction and devoid of speculation on the existence and nature of the self. There is no necessary inference from 'no self sighted' to 'there is no self'.[11]

So we have seen a non-ontologizing strand of early Buddhist thought and practice, in which God's existence would not be denied. However, there is little comfort in it for a traditional Jew. Although this strand does not reject the existence of God, it clearly believes that the path one should follow need not refer to God and can succeed without consciousness of God. More so, it believes that invoking metaphysical platforms is counter-productive to the work of redemption and salvation, and that includes the existence of God.

But matters get worse, because as Buddhism developed it became more explicitly atheistic. One of the greatest Buddhist thinkers, the founder of Madhyamika Buddhism, Nagarjuna (first to second centuries CE), argued extensively against the coherence of the concepts of God and divine creation. This followed from his analysis of causation and his doctrine of dependent co-arising. Not only was there no substantive self, there was no substantive anything. The conclusion from this is that 'God' is unintelligible. Moreover, Nagarjuna produced a battery of arguments not unfamiliar to Western atheists. These included the problem of evil, the problem of who created God, and the problem of God (allegedly) creating the world in stages when he should have been able to create it in one sweep. Notice how far this preoccupation with arguing against there being a God is from those early Pali sutras that insist on putting aside all metaphysical questions.[12] Although Nagarjuna insisted on 'emptiness' as excluding metaphysical beliefs, his discussion of God's non-existence had a profound effect on the development of overt Buddhist atheism.

Richard Hayes has documented the development of Buddhist thought into full-blown atheism, with Vasabandhu (*c*.400–*c*.480), Dharmakirti (*c*.600–*c*.660), Santaraksita (725–88), and Kamalasila (740–95).[13] These thinkers argued for various incoherencies in the God concept, from which it followed that there was no God. Hayes states that, 'of the issues concerning the existence of God

[11] For a contemporary, semi-popular presentation of a non-metaphysical approach to Buddhist meditative practice, see Stephen Batchelor, *Buddhism Without Beliefs* (New York, 1997).

[12] For an overview of Nagarjuna on God, see Hsueh-Li Cheng, 'Nāgārjuna's Approach to the Problem of the Existence of God', *Religious Studies*, 12 (1976), 207–16.

[13] Richard P. Hayes, 'Principled Atheism in the Buddhist Scholastic Tradition', *Journal of Indian Philosophy*, 16 (1988), 5–28.

... the one that received the greatest attention from the Indian Buddhist academic tradition was that of the possibility of God's unity, simplicity and permanence'. That is to say, they argued for the impossibility of there existing a being possessed of these attributes. So, there was no God.

In the light of this, Hayes asserts that 'atheism ... is a doctrine of fundamental importance within Buddhist religious philosophy rather than a mere accretion acquired through historical accident. As such it was a doctrine for which the Buddhist apologists during the academic period were strongly motivated to find good arguments.'[14] Thus has Buddhism come to be called an 'atheistic religion'.

Now it is clear that when these thinkers advanced their atheistic arguments they were not always the basis of their Buddhist atheism, just as arguments for God's existence were not the basis of the theism of Maimonides or Aquinas. Maimonides and Aquinas held a firm belief in God prior to and independently of their formulations of proofs for God's existence. Similarly, these Buddhist thinkers' atheism was driven by beliefs and attitudes prior to and independent of their arguments for atheism. It is to these prior beliefs and attitudes that we must look in order to find a proper attitude for traditional Judaism to take to Buddhism, including its atheism.

III

A traditional Jew could look deeper than the early non-theism that comes from the reticence towards metaphysical ontologizing, and a traditional Jew could look deeper than the metaphysical ontologizing of Buddhist atheism, so as to get to the ground of that ontologizing, to the attitude that drives the ontologizing in the first place. When that is done, a traditional Jew could find, as I have, a kinship with Buddhism, without agreeing with its non-theism.

I begin with a general enquiry into what properly grounds metaphysical ontologizing. In the past this general question was not often asked since people's metaphysical beliefs were thought to be obvious and not really in need of grounding, or their grounding was deemed obvious. The Enlightenment changed all that and spoke strongly in favour of the need to ground metaphysical claims 'rationally'. Rational grounding was to be limited to 'self-evident', necessary propositions and/or sense experience and scientific theorizing. And so in time it became fashionable to demand 'proof' for a metaphysical position on those grounds, and lacking that, to reject it.

Willard van Orman Quine, an American philosopher, carried this further when he decreed that objects of any sort could be posited only if needed for the purposes of science. And he saw the task of science to be 'predicting future

---

[14] Hayes, 'Principled Atheism', 16.

experience in the light of past experience'. On these grounds Quine was willing to posit the existence of abstract sets, but not of Homer's gods, because the former, but not the latter, made for good science:

For my part I do, qua lay physicist, believe in physical objects and not in Homer's gods; and I consider it a scientific error to believe otherwise. But in point of episte-mological footing the physical objects and the gods differ only in degree and not in kind. Both sorts of entities enter our conception only as cultural posits. The myth of physical objects is epistemologically superior to most in that it has proved more effi-cacious than other myths as a device for working a manageable structure into the flux of experience.[15]

So, we are told either that we can 'posit' metaphysical objects only if we have good 'evidence' for them or, qua Quine, only if they are needed for science. However, these stipulations are wholly unjustified. Sense experience and science represent only one part of human existence, all of which requires 'a manageable structure'. For example, the philosopher Nelson Goodman asked, in response to Quine's narrowness, why we could not posit entities needed, for example, for art theory. If art were important to us we could by all means posit, say, the existence of an abstract, metaphysical template of 'beauty' if that's what we needed to give a satisfactory theory of art. Justification by sense evidence and 'self-evidence' is only one kind of valid justification. Here I want to suggest a specific dimension of human existence that can ground metaphysical ontol-ogizing just as much as does 'evidence'. That dimension I will call 'attitudinal', and its epistemic power, 'grounding by attitude'. By 'attitude' I mean a value that a person or a group holds that guides their way of relating to the world.

When we have normal empirical experiences, we often find them com-pelling enough to want to call them true or real. The question we typically ask is: what would have to be the nature of reality for these experiences to be valid? To answer this question we engage in ontologizing, deciding what entities we need to posit in order for our experiences to be true to reality. Thus do these experiences form, and properly so, the initial ground for scientific theorizing and metaphysical ontologizing.

Similarly, we could have an *attitude* to the world and to ourselves that was no less compelling, or maybe even more compelling, than a sense experience. In that case, by analogy with compelling empirical experiences, the natural ques-tion to pose would be: what would have to be the case for this attitude to be correct, that is, for it to be appropriate to reality as it is? And the reply, positing a metaphysical ontology, could be as well grounded as ontologizing for empir-ical experiences. An attitude can be so basic, so pervasive, and so convincing that

---

[15] W. V. O. Quine, 'Two Dogmas of Empiricism', in id., *From a Logical Point of View* (Princeton, NJ, 1953; 2nd rev. edn., 1961).

it demands a correlative ontology to adequately account for it. Suppose, for example, a large group of people were perennial optimists. This attitude could be so profoundly basic to their relation to reality that it could justify an ontologizing answer to the question: what would reality have to be like to make this optimism justified?[16] A value can be so basic, so pervasive, and so convincing that it demands a correlative ontology to adequately account for it. To reject a convincing value as illusory can be as unacceptable, or even more so, than having to reject the authenticity of a convincing sense experience. This I call 'justification by attitude'. Of course, we are not to give a carte blanche to just any justification by attitude. The conclusion reached must cohere with other forms of justification, and be morally defensible as well.

The early Pali sutras that I have cited resisted the desire to ontologize, thinking that ontologizing was counter-productive. Yet some later Buddhist thinkers did pursue metaphysical ontologizing with great vigour. They forcefully denied the existence of God and of the self. And what I urge is for a traditional Jew to look beyond or beneath both the rejection of ontologizing, and thus doing without God, and the drive to ontologizing, that goes further and denies God, to examine the Buddhist attitudes that drive both moods. It is there that the traditional Jew can find an appreciation of Buddhist spirituality.

IV

The attitude driving Buddhist ontologizing is the desire to be released from the egocentric predicament which we humans are in. Release from that predicament brings release from the anguish and bitterness of clinging, demanding, grabbing, and all of the other consequences of egocentrism. The Buddha is said to have discovered that the egocentric predicament was the source of one's sorrows and to have discovered how to extricate oneself from it. Buddhism provides meditative practices to progress on the path of becoming free from the egocentric predicament. While these practices share with some Western methods their 'meditative' character, the central Buddhist meditative practices are unique and foreign to Western religions.

The attitudinal basis of the Buddha's insight into the way out of anguish was reported to be his coming to see the fragility and ephemeral nature of life. He saw that there was birth, sickness, old age, and death. The Buddha saw that our anguish came from not accepting, calmly and graciously, the facts of human existence and therefore running up against the bars of our cage over and over again only to fall back in pain and frustration. The source of the

---

[16] This is close to the pragmatist ontology that William James introduced in his 'The Will to Believe' and elsewhere, where belief in God is motivated by the conviction that reality is ultimately, and in the long run, good (see 'The Will to Believe', in William James, *The Will to Believe, and Other Writings*, ed. and introd. Trace Murphy (New York, 1995)).

Buddhist teaching was, therefore, an attitude to life, the world, and our place in it.

In the early Pali sutras that I have cited the Buddha advocates internalizing the flimsiness of life and thereby escaping the egocentric predicament without any metaphysical support. These sutras saw, quite rightly I believe, that the ascent to metaphysics can become a distraction from the business of extrication from egocentrism. This also applies to a religious doctrine of God. Theological reflection threatens to draw one's energies and interests away from extrication from egocentrism. In addition, belief in God, like other doctrines, can become, in the words of one sutra, a doctrine to fight for and to defend against others. If that happens, then belief in God will become a possession of the self, and to defend it will be to defend one's self against other selves, only strengthening our egocentric malaise. We will have grabbed belief in God by the tail.

Belief in God can feed one's ego, for God easily becomes a source of egocentric satisfaction, granting well-being for good deeds and answering fervent prayers for help. God can turn into nothing more than a protector who looks after us if we heed his word. For good reason, Jewish authorities have had to consistently warn against turning God into a source of egocentric satisfaction. The kabbalistic work *Tikunei zohar* (ch. 6) rebukes those who on the Day of Atonement, Yom Kippur, the holiest day of the Jewish calendar, pray to God for their own needs, calling them, 'Dogs who scream, "Give! Give!" They should be praying for God's sake, not their own welfare.' As Buddha would have put it, belief in God has turned about and bitten them.

If we are in the business of seeking freedom from self-centred craving, we must be very cautious about believing in God.

The later Buddhist material answered the drive to ontology and advanced metaphysical grounds for the sense of the contingency and fragility of life. For this purpose they declared that there was no self, only the ever-changing kaleidoscope of mental and physical goings-on, possessing no substantive duration or permanence. And they declared that there were no substantive existents at all. All was 'empty'. Since that was so, there was no sense in becoming attached to anything, because nothing possessed substantive and enduring reality. Nor was there a substantive God, for if there could be a permanent, substantive God, there might be a permanent, substantive self as well.

Buddhist atheism is thus profoundly different from Western atheism. Western atheism is grounded in the belief that humanity, through human 'reason', replaces God and takes its destiny into its own hands. Worship of God was to vanish in favour of firm dedication to human flourishing, and only human flourishing. Human beings were to exercise autonomy and accept responsibility for their fate. In the words of the American Humanist Association manifesto, 'Humanism considers the complete realization of human personality to be the end of man's life and seeks its development and fulfilment in the here and now'.[17] Hubris stands at the source of Western atheism. Once again in the words of the American Humanist Association, 'Humanism asserts that the nature of the universe depicted by modern science makes unacceptable any supernatural or cosmic guarantees of human values.'[18] The outspoken Jewish humanist Saul Tchernichovsky (1875–1943) put the Western humanist credo quite succinctly when he wrote: 'For yet I shall believe in Man / And in his spirit, a bold spirit.'[19]

Buddhist non-theists and atheists alike stand in stark contrast to all of this. They never depended on scientific success and tended not to make scientific proclamations, preferring to build 'the palace of Buddhism' above the scientific fray. In contemporary times, science has generated interest in Buddhism, and some Buddhists find congeniality in scientific advances.[20] Yet this congeniality serves only to reinforce the Buddhist recognition of the ephemeral and dedication to release from our egocentric predicament.

Buddhist atheism differs profoundly from Western atheism in endeavouring to provide a rationale for decentring the self while not placing anything else in the centre—and certainly not humanity. Nothing should be invested with ultimate value, and nothing is to become an object of craving for the sake of the self. In the most consistent forms of Buddhism this applies as well to the Buddha himself. There the Buddha is not an object of worship. So we have the saying, attributed to Lin-Chi (*Rinzai*), founder of a school of Zen, 'If you meet the Buddha, kill him', indicating that one is not to be fixated on the Buddha. The Buddhist aim is to get release from egocentrism and obsessive concern over the self by acknowledging and flowing with the utter insecurity of life.

Positing the existence of God can, if done wisely, serve the same end of internalizing the vulnerability of life and can further the same desire to find release from egocentrism. Recognition of God's existence need not necessarily exemplify the worries about believing in God that I mentioned earlier. Starting from the attitude that we must overcome our egocentric condition, ontologizing this attitude into the existence of God can be a most effective move. This happens when we project away from our selves to outside our world all the attributes we crave for ourselves, and that we pride ourselves on when we think

[17] This is not to imply that theistic religion cannot recognize human dignity and human rights. But it does so within a broader scheme in which our relationship to God is at the centre.

[18] See the manifesto at <www.americanhumanist.org/who_we_are/about_humanism/Humanist_Manifesto_I>.

[19] Cited and translated in Lea Shakdiel, 'Feminism as Tikkun Ha-olam', in Rachel Elior (ed.), *Men and Women: Gender, Judaism, and Democracy* (Jerusalem, 2004), 98.

[20] For a paradigm of contemporary discussion of Buddhism and science, see Alan Wallace (ed.), *Buddhism and Science: Breaking New Ground* (New York, 2003).

we are progressing towards them. When ontologizing from this motive, when we say 'God exists' we are declaring that within the world is only finiteness and severe limitation. And we further testify that the source of our achievements and our value is not from within us, but from outside of us. We may be in the image of God, but we are only an image. If we are able to be merciful as God is merciful, that is only because we receive from God the means with which to be merciful, and our mercy is but a pale copy of God's mercy.

To say 'God is entirely self-sufficient and independent' is to declare that we are not to strive for being such, because such is not obtainable within our world. Each of us is essentially enmeshed in networks of dependence and inter-active structures. To deem ourselves to be otherwise is pure illusion. Furthermore, whatever sustaining strength we have has its source in God. In our world, independence is not to be found.

'God creates from nothing' points to how our creative endeavours require materials, co-operation with others, education, and acculturation. Nothing we accomplish is our own possession, but instead is a product of untold numbers of people and the co-operation of nature. Moreover, ultimately our ability to create has its ground outside us, not within us. In our world, creation from nothing does not exist.

It is in this way that positing God's existence can be a path to existential freedom from an ego-driven life. Because there is God, I must divest myself of the illusion of my being the centre of the universe. God, not I, lives at the centre of reality. God is a warning to us, a warning against self-idolization. God's existence tells us that we are human, 'all too human'. 'Divinity' is beyond us. As Aldous Huxley once wrote, 'when we try to make ourselves more than human, we make ourselves less than human'.[21]

But in order to ontologize in this way we must be on guard for the dangers of belief in God. We must take to heart Maimonides' distinction between service of God from 'fear' and from 'love'. To serve God from fear is to serve God from egocentric motives. Such a person says to himself that he will fulfil the divine commandments in order to reap the benefits, including a share in the World to Come, and will not transgress in order to avoid punishment. 'It is not proper to serve God in this way', insists Maimonides.[22] On the other hand, the lover of God serves God not for any benefit he will derive, but simply 'acts on the truth because it is the truth'.[23] This, stresses Maimonides, is very

---

[21] This ontology of God goes half the way with the German philosopher, Ludwig Feuerbach (1804–72). In *The Essence of Christianity*, Feuerbach argued that we ascribe to God precisely those attributes we most cherish in ourselves. But Feuerbach interprets this ascription as a failure of nerve, an alienation of humans from their own great potential. Belief in God would disappear were humankind to be reconciled to its true self and accept the challenge of the greatness of humanity. While I begin with Feuerbach, we part ways quite soon after.

[22] Maimonides, *Mishneh torah*, 'Laws of Repentance', 10: 1.   [23] Ibid. 10: 2.

difficult to obtain and only a few wise people reach it. The ideal, then, is to divest oneself entirely from the egocentric predicament.

When properly directed and safeguarded, ontologizing to either the non-existence of God or to the existence of God share related attitudinal stances. Of course, while classical Buddhism may be said to be all about release from self-absorption, Judaism is not only about that. Judaism has a story about a chosen people, a God of history, and God's commands to be obeyed. Yet Judaism also contains a strong tradition of concern for freedom from egocentrism. Loving one's neighbour as oneself (Lev. 19: 18) is the central pillar of the obligation not to count yourself as more important than others. Rabbinical literature also lauds freedom from egocentrism: 'No person is free except one who occupies himself with Torah.'[24] I have already cited Maimonides' requirement of non-egocentric worship of God.

There is another vital movement in Judaism that tried to overcome the egocentric predicament, making that the centre of its endeavours: hasidism.[25] In doing so, hasidism embraced an acosmic ontology of God. According to this acosmism, the inner substance of the world is God, or better, the Ein Sof, the one, infinite reality: 'There is none other than it.' The world as it appears, as a finite, complex, limited reality, is illusion, a false appearance, taking place, as it were, upon the face of the Ein Sof. The religious life requires working towards seeing through the illusion in order to see oneself as devoid of independent, bounded existence. Roughly, one's substance is the Ein Sof, while one's individuality is an illusion. This kind of deflation of self-existence is called in Chabad hasidism *bitul hayesh*, literally 'annulling of the existent', an erasure of the self, into the Ayin, the 'nothingness' of the infinite. The result is a profound sense of existential humility and freedom from the egocentric predicament.

Nullification of the existent is a ubiquitous theme in the writings of Rabbi Shneur Zalman of Liadi (1745–1812), the founder of Chabad hasidism. He compares the sense of having a distinct self-identity to the illusory sense a tiny quantity of water deep in the ocean might have of being a distinct, bounded drop in isolation from the ocean, or he compares our existence in relation to the Ein Sof to a mere 'light' inside a giant torch. In a more modern image, we might compare our own reality to that of a spot of light on a wall, being but the beam of the lamp itself at a particular location. How absurd of the spot to think it had a self-being self-existence ontologically distinct from the being of the beam of light.

---

[24] BT *Avot* 6: 2.
[25] The late Slonimer Rebbe, Rabbi Shalom Noah Brezovski, summed up concisely the hasidic ethos of defeating egocentrism, with a play on words from Deut. 5: 4, where Moses tells the people, 'I stand between God and you'. He read this as follows: 'The "I" stands between God and you.'

Rabbi Shneur Zalman borrowed a kabbalistic theme to undergird the theme of *bitul hayesh*. Here is a greatly simplified version of it. In Lurianic kabbalah, in the process of the world coming into being there occurs a 'breaking of the vessels'. There were ten emanations of powers, *sefirot*, from the infinite Ein Sof, each of which had a vessel to contain the light of the Ein Sof. Had each *sefirah* functioned properly it would have taken into its vessel a weak light of the Ein Sof and would then have been part of a supernal harmony in which the light of the Ein Sof would fill the world in a perfect way. Instead, however, each *sefirah* said, 'I will rule! I will be king!' and so strove to internalize into its vessel a degree of divine light too powerful for its vessel to hold. The result was that the vessels shattered under the power of the light and fell, scattered in broken fragments, and 'died'. The supernal light ascended and darkness resulted. The world must therefore be laboriously reconstituted to its pre-broken state, to supernal harmony, and then to light flooding reality.

Rabbi Shneur Zalman applies metaphorically the concept of self-nullification to the breaking of the vessels and their subsequent reconstruction. Each *sefirah* suffered, as it were, from a sense of a distinct self-identity, and thus fell into the trap of a grasping egocentrism, reflected in each declaring 'I will rule!'—the secret desire of the self-absorbed. This led to cosmic catastrophe, and the return requires of each *sefirah* an ontological self-nullification in which it knows itself as but a manifestation, a mode, of the infinite, and nothing more. Ontological humility will repair the sin of ontological pride. Just so, personal egocentrism is to be overcome by recognizing an ontological nullification of the self into the Ein Sof, including a living awareness of our true substance as not 'ours'. Egocentrism brings a shattering of the world, and ontological self-nullification is the key to redemption.[26]

Interestingly, a similar ontology of the self surfaced in some schools of Buddhism. For example, the Buddhist scholar Walter Evans Wentz described both the *Tibetan Book of Liberation* and the Chinese *Treatise on Achieving Pure Consciousness* as maintaining that 'the only reality is mind or consciousness, and that no living thing has individualized existence, but is fundamentally in eternal and inseparable at-one-ment with the universal All-consciousness'.[27] As I have already noted, this is a turn back in the direction of the Hindu teaching that atman, the self, is Brahman, the supreme reality. This ontology matches hasidism in terms of its direction in overcoming self-absorption.

We have seen four different approaches to ontologizing that serve the aim

[26] The link between self-nullification and the breaking of the vessels occurs many times in the writings of R. Shneur Zalman (see *Torah or, likutei torah* (Brooklyn, 1986/7); *Ma'amarei ha'admor hazaken* (Brooklyn, 1983/4)).

[27] W. Y. Evans-Wentz, *The Tibetan Book of the Great Liberation: The Method of Realizing Nirvana through Knowing the Mind* (Oxford, 2000), 196. For an elaboration on this theme see the introduction especially.

of the decentring of the self: the non-theistic, non-ontologizing of Buddhism, the atheistic ontology of Buddhism, the theistic ontology of much of Judaism, and the acosmic theistic ontology found in early hasidism. All four serve a common attitudinal justification: the overcoming of our egocentric orientation towards reality; all four are profoundly different from standard Western atheism. When a traditional Jew looks deeper than the entrenched metaphysical expressions of Buddhism, he or she can come to appreciate a significant, if partial, communality of purpose between Judaism and Buddhism. Once again, I do not mean to imply that belief in God in Judaism is based solely on the aim of abolishing egocentrism. That is why I wrote of a 'partial' communality of purpose, since that aim does exist in Judaism prominently and finds an ally in Buddhism. Yet a shared ethos does exist.

Given this partial commonality, a traditional Jew such as myself can discover in Buddhism practices for self-decentring that do not exist in Judaism. But more than that is at issue. I have noted already the danger that belief in the God of theism could easily descend into an egocentric exercise, in which God serves our needs and protects us. When that happens, devotion to God is a screen for craving our own well-being. Engaging in Buddhist spiritual practices for self-nullification, which for the moment leaves God out of the picture, can be an effective, welcome corrective for a traditional Jew to the dangers inherent in theistic religions, and can reinforce the worship of God from love, all by weakening an egocentric pull to God.

Judaism compounds the dangers of reinforcing self-indulgence and self-importance by the potential dangers inherent in the traditional notion of the 'Chosen People'. This notion all too often feeds into the syndrome of 'I will rule', degenerating into 'nation-centrism' as a proxy for my personal craving for power or protection. My nation becomes the centre of my self-absorption. Søren Kierkegaard put it well:

Everyone who is in despair has clung to one or another of the dissimilarities of earthly life so that he centers his life in it, not in God, and also demands that everyone who belongs to the same dissimilarity must hold together with him . . . The one in despair calls it treason to want to have fellowship with others, with all people.[28]

Indeed, for many people 'Judaism' is little more than the self-identification as a Jew with a desire for concomitant imagined prerogatives that go with being the 'Chosen People'. Placed within an overwhelming reality of being a Jew and co-opted willy-nilly into what might be a spiritually (and otherwise) dangerous nation-centrism, Buddhist practices for personal self-decentring can be a breath of fresh air and an important mending of the broken vessels. By turning

---

[28] Søren Kierkegaard, *Works of Love*, ed., trans., and introd. Howard V. Hong and Edna H. Hong (Princeton, NJ, 1995), 73.

to Buddhist practices divorced from the theme of nation, a traditional Jew can acquire a refined sense of Jewish nationhood that avoids these tragic dangers. I suspect that this is one major attraction of Buddhism for contemporary Jews.

V

I admit that all of this is not enough. In the end, Buddhism remains godless and in contrast Judaism commands me to love God with all my heart, with all my soul, and with all my power. In the final analysis, how can I reconcile love of God with appreciation of a religion that, like Pharaoh, knows not God? Does not the essential disparity between a theistic religion and Buddhism far out-weigh the partial commonality of purpose between us?

On the surface, the problem is insoluble. But there is no reason to remain on the surface. One way to move below lies in the following declaration by one of the greatest rabbinical figures of the twentieth century, Rabbi Abraham Isaac Kook (1865–1935):

> There is denial that is like an affirmation of faith, and an affirmation of faith akin to denial. A person can affirm the doctrine of the Torah coming from 'heaven', but with the meaning of 'heaven' so strange that nothing of true faith remains . . . And a person can deny Torah coming from 'heaven' where the denial is based on what the person has absorbed of the meaning of 'heaven' from people full of ludicrous thoughts. Such a person believes that the Torah comes from a source higher than that! . . . Although that person may not have reached the point of truth, nonetheless this denial is to be considered akin to an affirmation of faith . . . 'Torah from Heaven' is but an example for all affirmations of faith, regarding the relationship between their expression in language and their inner essence, the latter being the main desideratum of faith.[29]

According to Rabbi Kook, we must make a distinction between the inner essence of faith and its linguistic expression. A person can embrace a linguistic expression of faith while missing its inner essence, and a person might be living the inner essence of faith while not only not employing its linguistic expres-sion, but also rejecting it as false. An affirmation of faith can take the content of that affirmation so crudely that it misses the truth of the inner essence as much as heresy would. On the other hand, a denial of faith might come from an inner point of great spiritual sensitivity, when what it is denying is the crude formulations it has known, and it rejects those because of a justified shrinking back from the crudeness. Such spiritual sensitivity is akin to true faith.

I recognize that Buddhists, given the holy motivations and purposes of their proclaimed atheism, might be touched by God in a way that traditional Jews might not be. To sincerely seek freedom from egocentrism is, to me as a

[29] Abraham Isaac Kook, *Lights of Faith* [Orot ha'emunah] (Jerusalem, 1985), 25, my loose translation, for easier understanding.

traditional Jew, to be touched by God, since my God is a warning. In order to be touched by God it is not necessary to call God by the name 'God' or to identify the call as God's. Indeed, naming God, attesting to God's existence, can be a deeply idolatrous act, if it goes little further than the linguistic formulation and fails to express an existential orientation that R. Kook calls the 'essence'. Idolatry to forms and declarations follows.

God's infinite nature may have many voices, including the sound of Buddhist emptiness, which speaks of release from attachment to oneself and to one's own world. If the Buddhist officially denies God's existence, that denial will be an affirmation of God if what the Buddhist knows about God transcends the God captured by linguistic formulations or the God of 'Give! Give!' This is not to say that a Buddhist is really an 'anonymous theist', since what the Buddhist knows about God might be profoundly different from what avowed theists know about God. In any case, the term 'theist' is a linguistic construction which itself shares in the discrepancy between expression and essence. We should acknowledge that a person can have a relationship with God without calling God by the name of 'God', without knowing God as God. My God does not require that those who truly know him give him a name.

I propose that we should look below the surface of Buddhist non-theism and atheism, to the original motivations driving those positions. Doing so will enable a traditional Jew to perceive a holy source in Buddhist godlessness. If traditional Jews can let go of the need to call God by name (and if for present purposes we limit ourselves to Buddhism that does not worship the Buddha), they could acknowledge that within Buddhism one can discern, at times, a denial that comes close to, or even constitutes, an affirmation.[30]

In the religious life there are times when denials are really affirmations, and indeed these denials can be more warming to the heart than affirmations that are in fact denials.

---

[30] I am indebted to Alon Goshen-Gottstein for his insightful comments on an earlier version of this paper, and for encouraging me to write on Judaism and Buddhism.

Concluding Reflections

ALON GOSHEN-GOTTSTEIN

AN IMPULSE to compose concluding reflections arose as I reviewed the chapters in their final form. After reading them, I felt a profound sense of gratitude for all the project's collaborators—the contributors and especially Eugene Korn, whose initiative and drive were the necessary condition for this volume to take shape. I also realized what a rich collection we have produced and how much we have accomplished intellectually, religiously, and spiritually by bringing the contributors together and completing this project. More precisely, it was the high quality of the essays that led me to reflect on whether we can articulate conclusions emerging from our project, beyond the individual contributions. It is not in the nature of this type of project to have conclusions, but I can point to where the discussion has moved forward, how it has been reframed, and how it has opened up new perspectives. I think it is best to offer such reflections personally—in the first person singular. Reflections and impressions are subjective, relating always to a previous point of reference associated with an individual. Identifying core themes and revisiting discussions as rich as ours are both intuitive and selective and rely on the reviewer's personal choices. While my colleagues may agree with some or most of what follows, each one would probably offer his or her concluding reflections and highlight different dimensions of the project. What follows is therefore my way of saying thank you to all my collaborators and of acknowledging where my thinking has moved forward, and how a synthetic view of our project allows me to continue thinking about the issues that initially drove this project.

WORLD RELIGIONS AND THE RELIGIOUS OTHER: TWO PROJECT FORMULATIONS

When the project was originally conceived, it was entitled 'Towards a Jewish Theology of the Religious Other', as Meir Sendor reminds us in his quote and subsequent challenge of a key sentence from the mission statement of the Scranton conference. The title of this volume refers not to the 'religious Other', but to 'world religions'. We have learned that there are two different discourses that flow from each of these conceptualizations. Reference to world religions leads us to reflect on specific religions then and now, and on Judaism's historical and theological attitudes to those religions. Reference to 'the religious Other' involves us in theories of otherness and in the philosophical background for reference to religions as other. The essays in our collection suggest that these in turn break down to refer to the other as an undifferentiated category (Ruth Langer), or to the other in his or their identity as a particular religious other (Stanisław Krajewski, Meir Sendor).

The theoretical considerations related to the religious Other are complemented by another set of theoretical discussions, those concerning pluralism. Alongside theoretical discussion of the respective value of pluralism and exclusivism offered by Avi Sagi, we have several attempts to refer to the history of Jewish tradition in these terms by Alan Brill, Raphael Jospe, and Jolene Kellner and Menachem Kellner.

Our project is rich precisely because it took shape in the space between these two definitions and through the dialogue between theoretical/philosophical discussion and historical/theological discussion of Jewish orientations to other religions. The reflections on pluralism translate the reference to Judaism into the philosophical language. Regarding theories of otherness, a good part of the discussion remains implicit, awaiting future explication of the relationship between the theoretical dimension and specific Jewish positions. It is clear nevertheless that even those authors who did not engage otherness explicitly are aware of those discussions and informed by them.

While all are aware of the range of philosophical, theological, and practical issues with which our project engaged, the emphasis on a given dimension of the problem varies according to the perspective adopted by the author. It was fascinating to see how the fourfold presentation of the issues that I offered in my opening essay played out differently according to the different methodological backgrounds, as well as the choices and preferences, of the authors. The discussion of pluralism tackles head-on the problem of religious truth, as though it was *the* crucial issue in relation to other religions. It is interesting to follow Jospe's dialogue with Kellner and Kellner, as well as Sagi's article, when considering the value of truth and the alternatives to it. Jospe's highlighting of revelation rather than truth points to one important move. Similarly, beginning with religious community or beginning with religious teaching yields different results when considering other religions, as Kellner and Kellner note in their response to Jospe. A whole other set of issues emerges when we consider theories of otherness as a basis for a view of the religious Other. Much of the discussion that is carried out in this light focuses on issues of identity rather than religious truth. Given the centrality of collective identity to the definition of Judaism as a people and a covenanted community, issues of identity and processes of othering are fundamental to exploring Jewish attitudes to other religions. Moreover, attitudes to other religions and to other religious communities become almost indistinguishable.

When we turn to classical religious discourse, another set of issues emerges. Here we encounter the concern for idolatry and the possibility of recognizing and legitimating other religions. Moving between our disciplines contributes to the richness of the project, and reminds us of its complexity and of how it is fed by multiple currents as it tackles multiple topics.

The tension between 'the religious Other' and 'world religions' leads to another important distinction. To talk of world religions leads us to taking a position regarding the legitimacy and possible recognition of other religions. To talk about the Other invites us into the domain of relationships, and leads us to reflect on how else we might conceive or rather relate to other religions other than through the classical discussions centring on recognizing other religions.

MODELS OF RELATING TO WORLD RELIGIONS

Looking at our collected essays, I note the wide range of models that our authors propose regarding how we can relate to other religions—and I recognize with satisfaction that the range is wider than I first imagined. I hope most readers share with me the sense of excitement at broadening the range of possible ways we might think of relations with other religions, thereby making Judaism's encounter with them much richer in theoretical and practical terms.

The classical model that governs most discussions in rabbinic literature regarding other religions and consequently figures heavily in our volume is the model of recognition. Doing theology of religions is thus an exercise in divine diplomacy—that is, we recognize another religion, in part or in full, in light of the criteria we consider most important. Many of the essays in our collection engage the issue of recognition of other religions even if they do not spell this out. This is true for my Introduction and my chapter on Hinduism, as well as for the chapters on Christianity by Korn and David Novak, and to a certain extent those of Jerome Gellman, Paul Fenton, and Raphael Jospe. Fenton takes us through a series of postures that Judaism developed towards Islam, including recognition, borrowing, acculturation, and most significantly spiritual inspiration. Future discussion might reflect on whether spiritual inspiration presupposes recognition of another religion. I consider it a model of relationship independent of recognition. Several chapters in the volume lend support to such a possibility. Gellman's discussion of Buddhism suggests that inspiration and spiritual support can be derived from Buddhism, without attempting to 'recognize' it, certainly not in its entirety. More importantly,

Sendor develops the notion of hospitality to the Other, a significant point of integrating the theoretical discourse towards the Other and concrete attitudes to other religions. It is precisely the Otherness of the Other that calls me to extend such hospitality without effacing the differences between the Other and myself. Following Sendor's logic, it would seem that there is no need to 'recognize' a religion or to proclaim it beyond the charge of *avodah zarah* in order to apply to its followers the hospitality and responsibilty called for by a theory of the Other. Gellman's exercise in relation to Buddhism seems to be a profound example of practising such an attitude. The logic of recognition seeks to highlight that which is common, as a basis of recognition. Note the voices cited by Korn in an attempt to 'recognize' Christianity and their appeal to commonalities. Note Novak's attempt to identify a 'same God' strategy in Maimonides' reference to teaching Torah to Christians. Perhaps even the appeal to a common moral code, whether in the form of the Noahide commandments or in the form of Menahem Me'iri's theory, is an attempt to recognize through what is common. The logic of hospitality, by contrast, tolerates differences without overlooking or minimizing them. What makes us Other is what invites hospitality; differences may be celebrated.

Theories of otherness open up new horizons of how we might conceive of other religions. Complementing the emphasis on 'recognition' has been the traditional emphasis on 'knowing' the other. Such knowledge has led to the study of other religions, both as a basis for determining their legitimacy and as the consequence of such recognition. It also informs much of the contemporary interfaith agenda, which seeks to increase knowledge of the Other. Yet knowing is not the only way of being in relationship. According to Levinas, knowledge is not the purpose of the relationship with the Other. As Krajewski points out, there is something prior to knowledge that is fundamental to relationships: attitudes. Krajewski's powerful metaphor of the two ways in which the priest can stand before the people (facing them or with his back to them) points to the importance as well as the nuance of 'attitude', as distinct from position, statement, or recognition.

One of the important lessons I learned from our project concerns the centrality of attitudes. From different quarters the message emerged that attitudes are prior to positions and that they depend on relationships and on situatedness in life, rather than on knowledge and theoretical analysis. From Sagi's discussion I learned of the attitudinal priority of faith, as well as of tolerance and openness to the Other. His citation of Plantinga's claim that faith is a primary tendency or disposition that requires no justification in other terms is matched by Sagi's recognition that the attitude to the datum of religious difference does not emerge from the datum itself. Thus, Adin Steinsaltz suggests (as quoted in my chapter on Hinduism) that tolerance is itself an attitude. Indeed, the history of the Jews in India confirms that attitude is primary, preceding and even replacing the position that hardens into recognition, or lack thereof, of another religion. Recognizing the centrality of attitudes is also a tool for critique. Sendor critiques the attitudes of certain practitioners of interfaith dialogue. I would add that if one considers certain Jewish positions as attitudes, especially *avodah zarah*, this could take discussion beyond the bipolar positions of affirming or rejecting other forms of religious life. In short, many of our chapters bring home the centrality of 'attitudes' as a primary dimension of relating to other religions—and thereby broaden the range of models available to us when we consider other religions.

THE QUESTION OF CONTEXT

There does seem to be one fact or recognition informing our entire project. It is that context matters. Historically, various readings are offered that highlight the context of former relationships as a way of understanding the formation of Jewish attitudes. Korn, Novak, and Steinsaltz mention the context in which various Jewish positions on other religions (with special reference to Maimonides) were formed. Historical context accounts for changes in Jewish–Muslim relations. As I explore various historical approaches to Hinduism, I claim that context also defines what we find relevant in another religion and how we define the challenges posed by it.

In fact, our entire project is founded on the recognition that context may determine theological views or at least provides an invitation to re-examine them. Korn is most explicit in exploring the impact of changed conditions on a Jewish view of Christianity. Because the reality of other religions has changed, we must reconsider our views. Langer engages in a similar exploration in terms of Jewish liturgy, arguing that changed context, particularly an interfaith context, will lead to novel liturgical expressions suitable for the context.

It may be that changed historical context does not provide sufficient grounds for carrying out our project in a neutral way, as Sendor claims. But then Sendor himself offers us another kind of context, that of contemporary philosophy, in the light of which he revisits attitudes to the religious Other. Our project's twofold emphasis on philosophical discussions contrasted with particular attitudes to other religions appeals implicitly to an understanding of context. With changes in philosophical understandings of pluralism and otherness, we are invited to revisit our sources and to restate our views of other religions. The philosophical discussion is thus highly conscious of context. I find the intellectual moves that Sagi makes particularly striking. Having highlighted the value of truth and its exclusivist potential (in light of which he criticizes David

Hartman and his own claim concerning how faith is related to history), he concludes by affirming pluralism mainly because of the modern context to which
he belongs with its dispositions and attitudes.

Attitude / Context

CHOOSING OUR CATEGORIES,
REFINING OUR CATEGORIES

My Introduction attempted to map the range of issues that we must confront
in dealing with other religions and developing contemporary theologies of
world religions. Yet there is a problem in tackling so many variables as we consider other religions. Some of the discussions concerning pluralism and exclusivism led me to wonder to what extent differences in positions taken in the
Sagi–Jospe–Kellner and Kellner debate were a function of 'attitudes', or
whether they were the result of different people talking about different things.
(In this context, perhaps, I might better use the metaphor of the different parts
of the Hindu elephant.) The discussion of theoretical models of pluralism,
exclusivism, and their various shades led to different conclusions because each
author appealed to different regions of the project's map. Whether one begins
with truth, revelation, or election leads one to different conclusions, as Kellner
and Kellner aptly note. So we are challenged to account for the categories we
use and why we privilege one starting point over another.

What you focus on will determine the conclusions you reach. If you seek to
prove that Christianity is not idolatrous, you can focus on the nature of the
Christian view of God, identifying commonalities with the Jewish view of God
and working out the boundaries of permissible variance in faith. Korn has done
this for us. If you start by focusing on the Eucharist, you may be led to another
view of the religion that allows you to speak of it as pagan and idolatrous, as
Sendor does. This has both halakhic consequences and attitudinal consequences. Yet it raises once again the problem of choosing our categories and
our proofs, and ensuring that we all talk of the same thing.

Choosing emerges as a conscious strategy of coming to terms with other
religions, especially in the context of recognition or tolerance. Witness how
Novak seeks to get around Maimonides' declaration of Christianity as *avodah
zarah* by highlighting another category, making it as important as Maimonides'
explicit discussion of Christianity's status. Witness also Steinsaltz's remarkable
choice of theology over worship as a means of coming to terms with most
religions.

I would like to make two points about choosing our categories and criteria.
Choose we must, and whoever is engaged in a project such as ours ends
up choosing his or her evidence, definitions, and categories. If so, the choices
should be conscious and visible. We may not agree on what the formative

categories are and which should take precedence, but let the discussion focus on the choices, let us make them explicit and the subject of further debate, rather than concealing them as an expression of the author's attitudes.

Second, the confusion we often face stems from the fact that our fundamental category, 'religion', is less self-evident than we often think. My discussion of what constitutes Hinduism is a case in point, but the problems associated with defining 'religion' are vast. Krajewski wonders whether we can even speak meaningfully about relations between religions and whether religions share common definitions. Interestingly, the earliest Jewish sources do not refer to 'religions', but to gods and to customs. While it is both convenient and necessary to speak of religion and 'world religions', as we become more specific and focus on details, particular components, and varying categories of religions, we may be forced to relinquish that generic category and move the discussion to a more particular level. That step, however, may still be far down the road.

One of the strategies our authors exhibit is nuancing categories. If thinking of other religions involves choosing our categories, how we view them and the positions we take are achieved by rethinking and nuancing those categories. One salient example is the transition from discussing other religions in terms of *avodah zarah* to viewing them through the lens of the 'same God' question. This proves to be a powerful strategy in moving the discussion forward by reframing the question and nuancing the categories. David Novak (who does not refer to the notion of 'same God', though it informs his chapter and figures in *Dabru emet*, which he co-authored), allows us to consider 'non-metaphysical theological commonality'. This is an important nuance, which introduces an alternative to metaphysical affirmations concerning the nature of God as expressed in the thought of Maimonides. Korn's history of Jewish appreciation of Christianity goes beyond recognition by introducing new categories into the discussion—a rabbinic historical and spiritual assessment of Christianity and its contribution to the world. And my own attempt to take a Jewish view of Hinduism beyond the blanket declaration of it as *avodah zarah* is achieved in part by nuancing the discussion by introducing multiple dimensions and categories through which Hinduism is viewed and in the light of which its ritual practices are differently contextualized.

Perhaps the most important nuancing in our project applies to the notion of the Other. One problem with Jewish attitudes to other religions is that they are informed by a blanket sense of otherness. As Langer demonstrates, the Other is not necessarily a particular religion but the (faceless) totality of all non-Jews. This indication, which emerges from Jewish liturgy, calls for nuancing the Other by making the other particular, individual, and giving him or her a face. This is a liturgical, educational, and theological challenge.

MYSTICISM AND MESSIANISM

Before I studied our chapters together, I could not estimate how present both mysticism and messianism would be. They are never the explicit subject of discussion, yet they appear unmistakably at major intersections. It seems that a Jewish view of other religions is incomplete if it does not explore these two dimensions. It may be that our discussion is so governed by the discourse of recognition that we fail to note the great potential that these two dimensions hold for our topic.

Mysticism provides an important dimension of Jewish pluralism. Brill identifies one type of Jewish pluralism as mystical pluralism, and Fenton illustrates how within the mystical sphere the Jewish acceptance and recognition of Islam was facilitated. Something in the mystical world-view or mystical reality seems to facilitate accommodation of the Other. Perhaps with mysticism comes a healthy kind of relativizing of one's own tradition that opens the gates to greater acceptance of all traditions, because they come to be seen as relative expressions of a greater view of reality. I consider this notion in my Introduction. That mystical literature also displays the opposite tendency does not detract from its pluralist potential. Fenton suggests that within mysticism there is the drive to rise above the boundaries of a given religion and seek the unity underlying the diversity of religions. Contemporary Hindu thinkers certainly agree with this view, and in the light of this view they construct Hinduism in ways that draw Jewish practitioners and make greater understanding between the religions possible.

Mysticism's significance to our project is not just its ability to lead to unity beyond diversity. We need not assume commonality of mystical experience for mysticism to play an important role in the encounter between religions. It is a historical fact that mystics of different traditions were drawn to learn from, share with, and emulate the other. This was as true of Abraham Maimonides' Jewish Sufism as it is for today's Jewish seekers of Hinduism and Buddhism. Gellman's chapter demonstrates this. In the same way that we have broadened our discussion from positions to attitudes, we may consider the importance of attitudes and dispositions as common ground in the sharing of mystical traditions, irrespective of the content and identity of experience. It may be that mysticism provides rich ground for encounter not because it is the same, but precisely because it allows us to revisit in new ways differences between the traditions. None of our chapters has sought to explore the relations between alterity and mysticism, although Sendor may do so in a future essay. Recognizing mysticism's centrality may point to new ways of both recognizing the other's sameness and recognizing alterity for what it is and providing the needed tools to accommodate it.

The theme of messianism emerges time and again, because the messianic perspective is the ultimate judge of the veracity of our tradition and that of others. We portray the messianic times as an expression of our fundamental attitude to other religions, and so Kellner and Kellner highlight the messianic period as the ultimate indication of Judaism's non-pluralistic nature. Jospe does not make an explicit messianic counter-argument, but Steinsaltz certainly does when he affirms the plurality of religious beliefs in the messianic era. Steinsaltz builds his entire pluralistic edifice on the foundation of his reading of Maimonides' messianic views. Messianism holds out the perspective of a broader vision, wide enough to include others within the scheme of history and its purpose, which is to be revealed only at the end of time. Thinking of the end of time allows us to live in a present with unresolved tensions and competitions with other religions. It allows us to subordinate present-day reality to the greater view of the future and thereby to partially accommodate the reality of another religion. This was famously done by Maimonides, who is quoted by several of our authors. Perhaps the messianic perspective also relativizes our own hold on the truth. If the fullness of knowledge will only become available in the messianic future, we can live with today's partial knowledge in an imperfect world because in the future another reality will prevail.

Ruth Langer teaches us that casting our eyes on the messianic future is religiously more significant than we might think. The messianic future provides the framework for understanding today, as indicated by Jewish liturgy. Liturgy is informed by the tension of Israel and its Other, and this tension is contained within a time-frame defined by the messianic future. Channelling these issues into prayer means that what cannot be resolved through life or through thinking gets resolved through prayer, hope, and a projection to the future. Prayer brings messianic hope alive. It channels the powers of expectation and frustration into the point of encounter with God and brings about the temporary relief afforded by a living faith and living hope that in the end God's kingdom will reign. Israel's relation with others is urgent because it is such a central theme in Jewish prayer. The messianic horizons of prayer offer the ultimate means of coming to terms with today's reality, governed by the distinction of Israel and others.

REVISITING ME'IRI

My final reflections indicate my personal interests even more than the previous topic. I am particularly fascinated by Me'iri's views on religions and consider them to be a major resource for contemporary religious thought. I believe the significance of Me'iri far exceeds his halakhic views in relation to Christianity as commonly understood. This is not the place to spell this out in all its detail, but I would like to draw attention to how useful many of our discussions have been to making sense of Me'iri and to how he can be brought into conversation with some of the theoretical discussions of our volume. Me'iri seems to me an excellent candidate for bringing the three parts of our volume closer together.

Let me begin by noting how comfortably Me'iri fits into the pluralist–exclusivist discussion. Because our horizons are usually framed by issues of *avodah zarah* and the question of recognizing other religions, we do not consider the philosophical import of his views, when seen against the background of broader philosophical currents. Reading Sagi's presentation of Hick, as well as Jospe's identification with elements of it, I am led to wonder to what extent we might have here a position that could describe Me'iri's views and contextualize them within contemporary philosophical discourse. Me'iri was a pluralist, and clearly his pluralism required criteria in the light of which boundaries for legitimate religious phenomena could be determined. This is precisely Hick's project, and his ultimate appeal to moral criteria to distinguish true from false religion (quoted by Jospe) sounds as though it were lifted out of Me'iri's commentary. Much of the discussion of pluralism is carried out in the abstract rather than in relation to individual figures. Looking at the thought of individual thinkers could be helpful for advancing a discussion on the issues of truth, pluralism, identity, and more. How has Me'iri reconfigured truth and what role does it play in his system, given his pluralist approach? What are the criteria for establishing true from false, if these exist at all, and how do these safeguard identity? Kellner and Kellner deem Jospe's position philosophically indefensible, but they are Maimonidean thinkers. Me'iri (another Maimonidean thinker) seems to make Jospe's position much more credible. In any event, bringing Me'iri into the conversation of contemporary theorists seems to me hugely promising. Both sides stand to be enriched by it.

Me'iri may be important not only for his views, but because he illustrates the very distinction between positions and attitudes, suggested above. Following earlier cited work on Me'iri by both Jacob Katz and Moshe Halbertal, it is appropriate to think of Me'iri's views as grounded in a broader disposition: the 'attitude', of which Krajewski speaks. Me'iri offers us a corpus detailed and extensive enough to allow us to revisit the question of position versus attitude. We might be able to trace how attitudes are formed and how they in turn give birth to positions, views, and halakhic rulings.

This does not exhaust the range of possible insights from Me'iri that emerge from our project. While Me'iri is usually thought of in terms of his contribution to the discussion of *avodah zarah*, considering his thought in the framework of our project leads us to reflect on his views that are related to other points in our discussion. What is the value of truth and how central is it to the construction of Judaism? What are the implications of a pluralist position to

Jewish identity? Kellner and Kellner are only willing to die for their religion if it involves absolute truths. Contrast this with Me'iri's position on a Jew practising other religions, alluded to in Korn's chapter. Because Me'iri speaks to almost every major issue that confronts us in our contemporary context, he provides an important testing ground for many of the theories propounded in this volume. To take one final example, Sendor develops a theory of hospitality to the otherness of other religions. How would such hospitality look when carried out from Me'iri's position? Even if we recognize that such hospitality does not presuppose recognition, do Me'iri's broader views pave the way more readily to such practices of interreligious hospitality? And in what way could they provide direction for us in dealing with increasingly complex problems associated with multiple religious belongings? Me'iri seems uniquely positioned as a guide for this generation when we deal with problems that are historically and theologically distinctive in their present configuration. Our chapters provide the discourse by means of which Me'iri's thought can be further interrogated.

Focusing on Me'iri allows me to emphasize what our volume has achieved and the work that lies ahead. As I suggested at the beginning of these reflections, our project takes place in the space between two kinds of discourse, the theoretical discourse of philosophers and the historical/theological discourse of the rabbis. It would take more than one volume to explore the potential conversations that emerge from bringing these two bodies of knowledge together. Me'iri is but one notable case study of how the dialogue of discourses shaping this volume can yield new understandings for formulating responses to the challenges Judaism faces in relation to world religions. Other readers will surely identify other insights that can emerge from continuing the conversation between our authors and the disciplines they represent. So I conclude with the hope and prayer that beyond the riches contained in our volume, these chapters will continue to frame, define, and inspire ongoing conversation on these issues.

Notes on the Contributors

ALAN BRILL is the Cooperman/Ross Endowed Professor in Honor of Sister Rose Thering, Seton Hall University, South Orange, New Jersey.

PAUL B. FENTON is co-director of the Department of Arabic and Hebrew Studies at the University of Paris-Sorbonne, where he is Professor of Hebrew Language and Literature, and a Fellow of the Centre de recherche français de Jérusalem (CNRS).

JEROME (YEHUDA) GELLMAN is Professor Emeritus, Department of Philosophy, Ben-Gurion University of the Negev.

ALON GOSHEN-GOTTSTEIN is the founder and director of the Elijah Interfaith Institute and director of the Center for the Study of Rabbinic Thought at Bet Morasha, Jerusalem.

RAPHAEL JOSPE teaches in the Departments of Jewish Philosophy at Bar Ilan University and at the Hebrew University of Jerusalem.

JOLENE S. KELLNER is a reference and periodicals librarian at the University of Haifa.

MENACHEM KELLNER is Professor of Jewish Thought at the University of Haifa and a Senior Fellow at the Shalem Center, Jerusalem.

EUGENE KORN is American Director of the Center for Jewish–Christian Understanding and Cooperation in Efrat, where he is co-director of the Institute for Theological Inquiry. He is editor of *Meorot—A Forum for Modern Orthodox Discourse*.

STANISŁAW KRAJEWSKI is Professor of Philosophy at the University of Warsaw and Jewish co-chairman of the Polish Council of Christians and Jews.

RUTH LANGER is Associate Professor of Jewish Studies in the Theology Department at Boston College and associate director of its Center for Christian-Jewish Learning.

RORI PICKER NEISS is the co-editor of *Interactive Faith: The Essential Interreligious Community Building Handbook*.

DAVID NOVAK holds the J. Richard and Dorothy Shiff Chair of Jewish Studies as Professor of Religion and Philosophy at the University of

Toronto. He is vice president of the Institute on Religion and Public Life (New York).

AVI SAGI is Professor of Philosophy at Bar Ilan University, director of Bar Ilan's Graduate Program for Hermaneutics and Cultural Studies, and a faculty member at the Shalom Hartman Institute of Jerusalem.

MEIR SENDOR is rabbi of Young Israel of Sharon, Massachusetts, teaches for the Me'ah Program of Boston Hebrew College, and is a member of the Elijah Interfaith Institute's Think Tank.

Index